W9-CPG-979

THE SPECTACLE

of the

RACES

THE SPECTACLE

RACES

Scientists, Institutions,

and the Race Question in Brazil

1870–1930

LILIA MORITZ SCHWARCZ

TRANSLATED BY LELAND GUYER

A division of Farrar, Straus and Giroux / New York

Hill and Wang
A division of Farrar, Straus and Giroux
19 Union Square West, New York 10003

Distributed in Canada by Douglas & McIntyre Ltd.
Printed in the United States of America
Designed by Abby Kagan
First published in 1993 by Companhia das Letras, Brazil, as O Espetáculo das Raças: Cientistas, Instituições e Questão Racial no Brasil 1870–1930
First English-language edition published in 1999 by Hill and Wang

Library of Congress Cataloging-in-Publication Data
Schwarcz, Lilia Moritz.
[Espetáculo das raças. English]
The spectacle of the races : scientists, institutions, and the race question in Brazil, 1870–1930 / by Lilia Moritz Schwarcz ; translated by Leland Guyer.
p. cm.
Includes bibliographical references and index.
ISBN (invalid) 0-8090-8789-9 (alk. paper)
1. Brazil—Race relations. 2. Miscegenation—Brazil—History. 3. Associations, institutions, etc—Brazil—Sociological aspects. 4. Decision-making, Group—Brazil—History. 5. Race discrimination—Brazil—History. I. Title.
F2699.A1S3313 1999
305.8′00981—dc21 *98-42234*
CIP

CONTENTS

ACKNOWLEDGMENTS vii

MAP OF BRAZIL x

INTRODUCTION: THE SPECTACLE OF MISCEGENATION 3

1. AMONG "MEN OF SCIENCE" 21
2. RACIAL DOCTRINES IN THE NINETEENTH CENTURY: A HISTORY OF "DIFFERENCES AND DISCRIMINATION" 44
3. ETHNOGRAPHIC MUSEUMS IN BRAZIL: "CLAMS ARE CLANS, AND MOLLUSKS ARE MEN AS WELL" 71
4. HISTORICAL AND GEOGRAPHICAL INSTITUTES: "GUARDIANS OF THE OFFICIAL STORY" 111
5. SCHOOLS OF LAW, OR THE NATION'S CHOSEN 168
6. SCHOOLS OF MEDICINE, OR HOW TO HEAL AN AILING NATION 234

7. BETWEEN THE POISON AND THE ANTIDOTE: SOME FINAL THOUGHTS 297

NOTES 311

GLOSSARY 335

BIBLIOGRAPHY 337

INDEX 351

ACKNOWLEDGMENTS

To finish a book is not the simple act of placing a period at the end of the last sentence, nor does it even mean the end of a research project. It is also the end of one stage in life and the beginning of another. The conclusion of a work such as this one seems more like a test of endurance, at the end of which the last word signifies not a happy ending, with all loose ends tied up, but merely time to stop.

In a book's final form, its organization, sequence of chapters, and introduction, which portentously unveils the conclusion, tend to conceal inevitably tortuous routes—the forever elusive document, the unconfirmed hypothesis, the clues that send us afar.

This circuitous journey is made in the company of others, who are not spared its fatiguing tasks. The first version of this book was a doctoral dissertation at the University of São Paulo, and what formerly seemed such a solitary effort now seems much less so. It is to all the people who contributed that I dedicate this book.

To Manuela, my guide in the truest sense of the word, I give thanks for her care, for her multiple readings of the numerous versions, and for her exacting demands.

I am immensely grateful for the support of my friends from IDESP [the São Paulo Institute of Economic, Social, and Political Research]: Cecília Forjaz, Fernanda Massi, Fernando Novaes, Fernando Limongi, Maria da Glória Boneli Santos, Maria Arminda do Nascimento Arruda, Maria Hermínia Tavares de Almeida, Silvana Rubino, and especially Heloísa André Pontes. I owe Professor Sergio Miceli, who also formed part of the examining committee, a question that remained in the back of my mind throughout the course of my research, and whose answer I am not certain I have clarified yet: "What's your point?"

Of my colleagues from the University of São Paulo Department of Anthropology I have fond memories of solidarity. Maria Lúcia Montes was, in this sense, a constant source of warmth and wisdom. She played a role not only in the early moments of the organization of my research but also in the "ritual defense of the thesis." Paula Montero took an important part toward the end, and she put in an enormous effort to achieve, together with colleagues from the Laboratory of Social Anthropology, her dream: the photographic exhibition "Men of Science and the Race of Man," held at the University of São Paulo in October 1993.

Without excellent editorial assistance, the preparation of this book would have been immeasurably more difficult. I thank Fátima Augusto for help in organizing the graphic materials, and Maria Emília Bender, who taught me "how to cross every *t* and dot every *i*."

The suggestions of Roberto Schwarz and Roberto Ventura were helpful at several stages in the process, and the kind and judicious readings of Mariza Corrêa and Francisco Iglésias were invaluable in the final version.

Library personnel also made countless kind efforts on behalf of my research. The joy with which Marita Causin of the IEB sought odd documents long believed lost was particularly inspirational.

And of the involvement of personal friends there was no shortage. Any Weisbich, Gabi Borger, Guita Debert, Heloísa Prieto, Maria Tereza Sadek, Marta Gronstein, and Omar Ribeiro Thomaz offered great understanding in my moments of doubt.

My family—Lelé, Noni, Beto, Sergio, Omi, Vovô, Ginho, Ciu, Many, Sílvia, Baba, Vova. Who else could listen to endless tellings and retellings that make sense only to those who love you?

And I can't forget Ju and Pê, for whose patience and belief that "one day I'll really finish that thesis," I give thanks.

But most of all, I thank Luiz. Without him it could only have been more difficult. He deserves the acknowledgment usually reserved for a coauthor, although I take full credit for the book's shortcomings.

Finally, it seems time to say that, although these words come first in order, they have been the last, and the hardest, to write as I conclude a work that has seemed to begin again eternally.

Nineteenth-Century Brazil

THE SPECTACLE

of the

RACES

INTRODUCTION

The Spectacle of Miscegenation

The color of race gives off a scent and a savor.
—*Samba lyrics, Acadêmicos do Salgueiro, 1992*

Toward the end of the nineteenth century, the world looked on Brazil as a unique specimen: a country with a remarkably high degree of miscegenation. It was a "festival of colors" (Aimard, 1888), a "society of mingled races" (Romero, 1895). Some of the strongest voices in this chorus were those of Brazilian intellectuals. Silvio Romero,[1] a prominent literary critic, declared, "We are a country of mixed blood. . . . We are mestizos if not in our blood at least in our soul" (Romero, 1888/1949). João Batista Lacerda, director of the Rio de Janeiro National Museum, was invited to represent his "typical 'inbred' country" in the First Universal Races Congress, held in London in July 1911. The conclusion of his paper was clear and direct: "The hope for Brazil within this century looks to the whitening of the mestizo as its escape and its solution" (Lacerda, 1911). The essay itself provoked a scandal and included in its introduction the reproduction of a painting by M. Broccos, an artist from the School of Fine Arts in Rio, with the following caption: *"Le nègre passant au blanc, à la troisième génération, par l'effet*

This painting by M. Broccos summarizes the process of branqueamento, *or whitening, whereby the offspring of mixed-race unions would lose the most pronounced physical characteristics of the Afro-Brazilian. It was believed that through this process and over the course of a century the country would become white, like the child in the photograph*
(MUSEU DE BELAS ARTES [MUSEUM OF FINE ARTS], RIO DE JANEIRO)

du croisement des races" [The black becoming white, in the third generation, because of the mixing of the races].

It was not only Brazilians who held this extraordinary "mestizo vision" of the country, however. Foreigners, too, clung to this image. It was especially evident throughout the nineteenth century in the work of various naturalists who came to Brazil in search of rare specimens of flora and fauna and encountered in addition the spectacle of humans: *"J'ai remarqué un fait singulier que je n'ai observé qu'au Brésil: c'est le changement qui s'est opéré dans la population par les croisement des races, ils sont les fils du soleil"* [I have noticed a singular fact that I have observed only in Brazil: it is the transformation of the people caused by the blending of races.

They are the children of the sun], concluded Gustave Aimard, a French traveller to Brazil in 1887 (1888: 255).

From the brush of W. Adams and other artists who accompanied these scientific expeditions emerged a mulatto Brazil, always in the same image, regardless of the sex, race, or social status of the person represented.

It was also a mestizo image that Louis Agassiz took away from the country when he returned to the United States in 1865, carrying fresh notes on the land that had become a naturalist's paradise. In 1868 the renowned Swiss researcher described the country thus:

> Let any one who doubts the evil of the mixture of races, and is inclined, from a mistaken philanthropy, to break down all barriers between them, come to Brazil. He cannot deny the deterioration consequent upon an amalgamation of races, more widespread here than in any other country in the world, and which is rapidly effacing the best qualities of the white man, the Negro, and the Indian, leaving a mongrel nondescript type, deficient in physical and mental energy. (1868: 71)

"We're dealing with a totally mulatto population, corrupt of flesh, empty of spirit, and frightfully ugly," disapproved Count Arthur de Gobineau, who spent fifteen months in Rio de Janeiro as France's envoy (Raeders, 1988: 96).

In this instance, as elsewhere, the miscegenation found in Brazil was not only portrayed but offered as a clue to the underdevelopment of the nation, perhaps even as a reason why the country might perish. But how did Brazil achieve this unique status? Why was Brazil's racial makeup so different from that of other countries in the New World? And, rhetoric aside, once the country gained its independence, what impact *did* that racial makeup have on Brazil's state-building efforts, and on its political, cultural, and intellectual institutions?

No single book can answer all of these important questions, but I hope at least to touch on some of them. But the context for these questions will not be clear without a little background in Brazilian history. The Brazilian monarchy was relatively stable, if not particularly popular, after the country gained political independence from Portugal in 1822. It was an odd sort of independence. The Portuguese royal family had taken refuge in Brazil some years before (because of turbulence in Portugal), and Brazil had become for a while the center of the empire. When King João VI returned to Portugal and tried to make the colony subordinate to its colonizer, his son, Pedro, declared independence for Brazil, setting himself up as emperor of the colony. Although Brazilians, used to the Portuguese heritage of monarchies, did not object to this new form of government, they thought that Dom Pedro I was despotic. Once João VI died, domestic and international pressures forced Pedro to abdicate in 1831.

His son, Pedro II, was then nominally put at the head of the Empire, at the age of five. The regency that governed during Pedro II's youth lacked the support of the legislature, which, in effect, staged a coup d'état by declaring the majority of Dom Pedro II in 1841.

Despite his youth and inexperience, from 1850 on, Dom Pedro II was an effective monarch. The imperial court became centralized in Rio de Janeiro, and the liberal and conservative parties, although always under the control of the emperor, shared power almost equally, since they had no significant political, economic, or ideological differences.

The revolts that marked the regency (1831 to 1841) had almost completely subsided by the end of the 1850s. The country entered a period of great political and economic stability, owing, in large part, to the strong position Brazil maintained in the international coffee market. Rio de Janeiro coffee producers enjoyed great financial success, and after 1850 São Paulo coffee plantations also became major players in the business. With this growing financial health and political stability, Brazil entered one of its finest periods.

But by the mid-1870s the sociopolitical environment had begun to change quickly in Brazil, and threats to the government seemed present everywhere. The pleasant sense of tranquillity that had marked the early years of Dom Pedro II's reign had ended. In the first place, it had become clear that slavery's days in Brazil were numbered. In 1850 the slave trade ended, and in 1871 the first abolitionist law was passed. Known as the "*Lei do ventre livre*" [Law of the free womb], it was rather ineffectual, since it granted freedom only to children subsequently born of slaves.[2] Moreover, the slave owner had the option of either retaining the right to his human property until the slave reached adulthood, or receiving reimbursement for his loss when he freed a slave. Given this choice, the slaveholder usually chose to retain the freed slave until the slave reached the age of twenty-one. The impact of the law was not great—it did not bring an end to slavery—but the responses to the measure revealed the importance of the slavery issue and the need for meaningful reform. During this period an abolitionist movement took shape, and despite being equable and nonviolent, it would remain a focus of opposition to the Empire until at least 1888, the date of the abolition of slavery in Brazil.[3]

In the meantime, runaway slaves and slave rebellions became more frequent, and the debate that resulted undermined the nation's equilibrium. Despite pressure from England to end slave labor, until the 1870s slaves continued to be the primary source of labor in each of the 643 imperial municipalities of Brazil. As the coffee plantations grew and developed, forced labor became ever more scarce and costly, and plantation owners had to find new means to get their work done.

At the same time Europeans were migrating to Brazil in ever-increasing numbers, and many headed straight to the coffee plantations. The newcomers, it was hoped, would fill the growing void left by the end of the slave trade and the enactment of the first abolitionist laws. But the new solution created new problems. From the beginning, coffee plantation owners contracted with workers directly in their home countries, loaning them money for travel costs, housing, and incidental expenses. As a result, the European immigrants were essentially indentured servants, obliged to work and live side by side with the other slaves until they worked off their debt.[4] Some immigrants felt that the plantation owners had gone back on promises of property and, inevitably, their dissatisfaction led to acts of violence and flight to the cities. The government tried to correct the injustices suffered by immigrant workers, and it officially stepped in to take control of all contractual arrangements with succeeding immigrants. But great damage had already been done, and the leadership of the nation had yet another disaffected group with which to reckon.

Other scenes in the national drama also affected the history of this nation of mixed races. There was the disastrous Paraguayan War, at the end of which (in 1870) three fourths of the male population of Paraguay had died. We need not go into the details of the conflict here, nor whether the result was a victory or a stalemate, but the internal effects of the war in Brazil are relevant. Specifically, the nation's army acquired increased social and political power, and the abolitionist campaign gained momentum. Until then the military arm of the Empire had been the National Guard, composed of large landholders (*latifundiários*), businessmen, and politicians charged with controlling order and maintaining the agrarian aristocracy. The regular army had had neither social nor political power before the war, and it had been made up of freemen, few of whom were landowners. They were men who needed work or had been conscripted as punishment for crimes they had committed. When the war broke out, the Empire realized that it had to step up its recruitment efforts and form an army capable of dealing with the much more powerful Paraguayan army. The new army was made up primarily of slaves, both those sent in place of their masters and those freed in order to go to war. Despite being poorly provisioned, the army returned victorious and eager to accept the accolade of "the nation's saviors." The army's newly acquired high status put it in a position to exert its will against the Empire, and it expressed its opposition by refusing to fulfill what had been its primary function: pursuing runaway slaves.

Another group that was especially critical of the monarchy in the 1870s was the Partido Republicano Paulista [São Paulo Republican Party]. During this time the center of Brazilian coffee production had changed from the Paraíba Valley in the province of Rio de Janeiro to the western part of the province of São Paulo, and along with this relocation of economic power came a reallocation of political power. Coffee plantation owners and liberal professionals from the province of São Paulo, empowered by the São Paulo Republican Party, expressed their dissatisfaction with the monarchy, the power of the Church, and the two ruling political parties. In particular, the São Paulo landowners and liberals believed that the two dominant parties were overly beholden to the Rio-based imperial court and lacking in any social conscience.

It was within the context of a critique of the privileged classes, the union of Church and State, the persistence of slavery, and an awareness of the generalized absence of equality that the idea of a republic began to take form. Slavery was abolished in 1888, and the republic was founded in 1889.

The republic based its platform on a liberal discourse centered on the need to correct social and political inequalities. But there was a fundamental paradox: if freedom for slaves was finally becoming reality, and if citizens were beginning to have a true voice in the government for the first time, also taking root in Brazil at the same time were models of social analysis that viewed the races as ontologically different and essentially unequal. It was as if it were possible to beckon the slaves to freedom with one hand and, armed with scientific justification, to halt them from progress with the other. In fact, the hybridization of the races in the context of such thinking meant "chaos," as the daily newspaper *The Province of São Paulo* would conclude in 1887.

In newspapers and in the censuses, quantitative data reaffirmed Brazilians' theoretical fears regarding the makeup of the population. According to the 1872 census, while the number of slaves had dropped dramatically (in 1798 the slave population was 48.7 percent of the whole; by 1872 it was only 15.2 percent), the black and mestizo population was growing (55 percent of the whole). From the same perspective, the data of 1890 were even more "alarming." In the southeast the influx of European immigrants meant that the white population was predominant (61 percent of the whole), but the trend in the rest of Brazil was in the other direction, with mestizos totalling 48.5 percent of the population and whites only 36 percent. (See Table 1.)

Observed with care by foreign travellers, analyzed with skepticism by American and European scientists interested in racial issues, and feared by a good part of the local intelligentsia, the question of the effect of the mingling of races was understood to be key to comprehending the nation's future, and numerous theories arose between 1870 and 1930 to explain it.

Although already widespread in Europe in the mid-1800s, racial theories arrived late in Brazil. These ideas nevertheless

Table 1 1890 Census Figures

RACE	SOUTHEAST	OTHER REGIONS	BRAZIL
White	2,607,331/61.6%	3,694,867/36.5%	6,302,198/44.0%
Mestizo	1,024,313/24.6%	4,909,978/48.5%	5,934,291/41.4%
Black	583,359/13.8%	1,514,067/15.0%	2,097,426/14.6%
TOTAL	4,215,003	10,118,012	14,333,915

HASENBALG, 1979:149, BASED ON THE DEMOGRAPHIC CENSUS OF 1890.

received an enthusiastic reception, especially in scientific institutes of research and teaching, which at the time were the most important focal points for Brazil's small intellectual elite. The arrival and acceptance of these new interpretations were not, however, isolated occurrences. In fact, the 1870s saw a series of phenomena that coexisted uneasily. Brazil experienced the rise of faddish new philosophies and scientific theories, such as positivism and evolutionism, in which models of social analysis based on race played a fundamental role.* This period was also characterized by a strengthening and maturation of certain national centers of education, such as ethnographic museums, schools of law and medicine, and institutes of history and geography, all of which from that time on assumed their own identities and established alternative models of social and racial analysis.

In light of the developments of the 1870s I will examine the introduction and rebirth of racial theories in Brazil, especially their effects on liberal political models and the notion of the state. As a curious paradox of the time, liberalism and racism were embodied in two primary theoretical models that, although they were contradictory, enjoyed equal levels of acceptance in Brazil. The first one was based on the idea of individual rights and responsibilities. The second withdrew attention from the individual to focus on the achievement of the group, viewed biologically.

Many studies have dwelled on the importance of liberalism in fin de siècle Brazil (Viotti da Costa, 1977; Schwarz, 1977; Faoro, 1977). Few works have considered as carefully the influence

* Given the positivist slogan on the Brazilian flag, "*Ordem e Progresso*" ["Order and Progress"], it is difficult to think of Brazil apart from positivist philosophy. French philosopher Auguste Comte (1798–1857) is credited with the development of positivism, a system that is based on the belief that social and political phenomena may be grouped under and understood by scientific laws. More specifically, it holds that humanity passes through distinct and successive stages of thought. Evolutionism is a scientific model of analysis that sees humanity as a single unit that has evolved in a unique, progressive, and predictable manner, with Western civilization being its finest example.

that racial models had on the scientific and cultural production of the period or the parallel use of these two fundamentally exclusive models. First considered "subscience" and then unauthorized copies of European imperialism, enduring racial theories were condemned before they were understood in detail and within the scope of their era.

If social scientists took some doctrines seriously, such as positivism, which exerted its primary influence in countries under military leadership (Torres, 1943; Nascimento, 1989; Cruz Costa, 1967; Lins, 1964), racial theories were not given the same level of consideration. Scholars lampooned the content of determinist models, and they emphasized the malice implied by the broad acceptance of these doctrines within the country.

Analyzing all the Brazilian works that delved into European racial theories, contemporary scholars have concerned themselves more with the form of the works than with their content and have concluded that their authors together made up a "prehistory of the social sciences" (Santos, 1978: 26) and that the theorists and schools that predated the founding of universities in Brazil were the creators and reproducers of spurious copies of imperialist theories and models that were based on realities essentially unlike Brazil's.

Some authors have adhered to this type of interpretation more closely than others. In the well-known work by Nelson Werneck Sodré, *História da literatura brasileira* [History of Brazilian literature] (1938), the author established clear correlations between determinist racial theories and the European imperialist movement. For this historian, the use of such models "was linked much more to external influences than to imperatives of the national environment," and was, "therefore, the result of a European process and its influences" (1938/1982: 357–58). An organizing principle for Werneck Sodré's study of racial doctrines was the theme of imitation, and his conclusion was, "where there is formal imitation, neither originality nor autonomy can exist" (Sodré, 1938/1982: 19).

In *O Caráter Nacional Brasileiro* [The Brazilian national character] (1954), Dante Moreira Leite took positions similar to those already mentioned, stating, "the racial theories used here would be a reflection of the doctrines used by imperialistic ideologists, justifying European domination of all other nations" (Leite, 1954/1983: 362). His conclusion was that the acceptance of such doctrines was a consequence of the inadequacy of the scholars of the era, as if the local environment were not sufficiently mature for the scholars to go beyond mere repetition:

> One way to explain the apparent contradictions would be to say that they absorbed the theories of the era, and since those theories were fatally flawed they would produce contradictions when applied to concrete cases. . . . Apparently they didn't have the intellectual resources to oppose their European teachers, and this compelled them to repeat assertions that reality repeatedly contradicted. (1954/1983: 204)

This theme acquired greater visibility with João Cruz Costa's analysis, *Contribuição à história das idéias no Brasil* [The contribution of ideas in Brazil to history] (1956), in which the issue of racial determinism assumed a new complexity, for Cruz Costa established connections between the penetration of these new ideas and their application among upwardly mobile urban groups. Nevertheless, the author did not sustain an attempt throughout the book to find internal coherence among racial theories in Brazil. In his conclusion Professor Cruz Costa returned to the prevailing interpretation: "Summarizing what I have said, what impressed me when I tried to study evolution and philosophy in Brazil was the prolonged and varied importation of contradictory ideas and doctrines in the course of our history" (Cruz Costa, 1956: 413).[5]

In 1976 the Brazilianist Thomas E. Skidmore took up the question again. Having first intended to do a study of "representative figures of the years between 1870 and 1930" (1993: xxi), he settled on an analysis of the predominant racial theories during that time. In his conclusions Skidmore joins the ranks of those who rejected the merit of racial theories within the Brazilian context:

> The issues of race (and the related ones of climatic determinism) *were,* however, being discussed in Europe, and Europeans did not shrink from expressing themselves in unflattering terms about Latin America, and especially Brazil, because of its large African influence. Brazilians read these writers, usually uncritically. . . . Derivative in their culture, self-consciously imitative in their thought, mid-nineteenth century Brazilians, like other Latin Americans, were ill-equipped to argue about the latest social doctrines from Europe. (1993: xii–xiii)

In his critique Skidmore does not try to contextualize this kind of racial theory and imperialist practice. Nor does he try to define racial theory in terms of a single issue, but as a web of ideas that reflect an era. What is at issue is the presumed audience of works about racial theories. The public's engagement with the texts of the period was inseparable from the contexts of these writings, (Candido, 1978: 68), and political realities were sufficient to explain their entire production.[6] Thus, as long as the works stand out as clear reflections of and as direct references to their defining context, the authors' analyses emerge as immature.

In the meantime, the very contemporary critics who pointed out the traps present in nineteenth-century social theory fell into those traps themselves. They revived arguments of the era that suggested that "imitation [was the country's] greatest downfall . . . together with the mania for trying to pass for what we are not" (Romero, 1910: 114).[7] If one can consider the theories of those scientists as being the result of a specific moment, it is also necessary to comprehend them in terms of their unique and creative activity, emphasizing how the ideas were used within national boundaries. After all, to call such models "prescientific" is to resort to a kind of reductionism and dismiss the activities of renowned intellectuals of the era. It is also to ignore the importance of a moment in history in which the correlation between scientific production and social movement emerged clearly.

In the following chapters we will treat a portion of the social history of these ideas of a century ago, or "a constructivist history of science" (Stepan, 1991; Kuhn, 1962; Darnton, 1990), reconstructing not only concepts and models but also the backdrop from which these theories emerged. In so doing we will reveal new interpretations. It will be useful, therefore, to understand the political and historical construction of the racial argument at the end of the 1800s, as well as the concept of *race,* which, in repudiation of its biological definition, acquired an essentially social explanation. Prior to taking on the trappings of a defined, rigid, and ingrained concept, race was an object of study, and its meaning was constantly being tested and negotiated within a historical context, in which biological models of analysis were so influential.

Brazil's intellectual elite not only consumed accounts using racial theories; they made them their own. The models were different, and the theoretical consequences were diverse. In a country that was in the midst of the decline and dissolution of slavery and the establishment of a new political design, racial theories offered themselves as sound theoretical models for making sense of the tangle of interests that were taking root. In addition to the more pressing problems of finding manual laborers to replace slaves, or even preserving the rigid social hierarchy, it seemed necessary to establish differentiated criteria of citizenship.

It was under these circumstances that the racial models, despite their negative implications, established a successful foothold as a means of explaining social differences. But the immediate adoption of these theories was impossible. On the one hand, the racial models seemed to provide traditional organizations and hierarchies with scientific justification just when, with the end of slavery, the fairness of these structures was first being questioned in public. On the other hand, because of their pessimistic view of the future of people of mixed races, such theories would undermine a national venture that had barely begun.

In the middle of this paradox lies the contradiction between accepting the existence of innate human differences and praising racial blending, and it is here that Brazilian scientists first demonstrated their originality by adapting several racial models whose theoretical roots were fundamentally different. Social Darwinism bequeathed the assumption of racial differentiation and its intrinsic hierarchy, laying the groundwork for arguments on the negative implications of miscegenation. The principles of social evolutionism underscored the notion that the human races were not static but in a state of constant change and "improvement," refuting the idea that humanity was essentially one.*

The chief characters of this story are those now shadowy "men of science" in Brazil who, at the end of the nineteenth century, took up the quixotic task of defending within their own organizations a determinist science, using it to sustain their leadership and provide a basis for their sorties in pursuit of the nation's destiny. Mixing science and politics, research and literature, the academic and the evangelical, these intellectuals moved in the uncomfortable circles to which the models led them: between the acceptance of foreign theories that condemned racial blending, and their adaptation to a nation that was already highly interbred.

Many of Brazil's scientists discussed, produced, and circulated their ideas within their various institutions,[8] and thus they came

* According to the social Darwinists, different races are ontologically different and are, in effect, separate species. Social evolutionists judge the apparent differences between peoples as mere "inequalities," since they view humanity as a single species, differentiated only by separate stages.

to represent both their institutions and the intellectual discourse associated with them. Becoming familiar with these diverse organizations is critically important to understanding the different concepts they produced, for the institutions also gave a voice to a different kind of intellectual, one who had gone unrecognized for his own work but whose ideas are nonetheless crucial to building a new interpretation of the era.

"Le Brésil a aujourd'hui un peuple" [The Brazil of today has one people], said the French traveller Gustave Aimard toward the end of the 1800s, *"il n'a encore qu'une nationalité factice; ce qui fait le peuple, c'est la race"* [it is no longer an artificial nationality; what makes a people is race] (1888: 255).

The interpretations of a small group of scholars that made determinist science fashionable now seem dated, but the fact remains that racial theories were widely accepted at the time, for they seemed to offer an answer to a question constantly raised but rarely answered: *What is this country, after all?* The racial explanation was widely disseminated, and the predictions and scientific analyses for the future of Brazil were all pessimistic. It therefore fell to the "men of science" to intervene in the narrow confines that the theories allowed them.

The discussion of race assumed a central role in various Brazilian institutions and generated contrasting theses. From the phrenology of the ethnographic museums to the close reading of the "Germanics" at the Recife School, from the liberal analysis of the São Paulo Law School to the "Catholic-Evolutionist" interpretation of the institutes that served the "eugenics" model of the medical schools, we can follow the various paths that racial theories took.[9]

The challenge in understanding the enduring appeal and absorption of racial theories in Brazil does not lie in tracing and defaming their ingenuous use. Rather it lies in examining the originality of Brazilian racial theory, which was created by adapting foreign models and modernizing them by integrating what applied and discarding what was problematic.[10]

São Paulo Museum, or the Ipiranga (Ypiranga) Museum, São Paulo

Emilio Goeldi Museum of Belém, Pará

National Historical Museum, Rio de Janeiro

Recife School of Law, Recife

Bahia School of Medicine, Salvador

São Paulo School of Law, São Paulo

National School of Medicine, Rio de Janeiro

One can reconstruct the distant world of nineteenth-century Brazil by studying the logic of the models that mark the end of the Empire and the predicaments of the Old Republic.* This world was witness to a decisive moment in Brazilian intellectual history, with the importation of doctrines full of openly racist assumptions that today we roundly renounce. After the 1930s, the decline of social evolutionalism, which had informed and shaped many of Brazil's intellectual institutions, coincided with the growing frailty of many of these institutions. At the same time, the founding of the country's first universities had threatened the authority and autonomy of these very institutions. As a professor of the Recife School of Law would say in 1927, "the times changed, everything changed, the spirit could not stay the same."

But the moment that defines the beginning of this book is different. Far from the critiques of the evolutionists' postulates and the praise of the cultural relativists' viewpoints, which were to come decades later, scientists at the end of the nineteenth century operated from their institutes in the certainty that they would define their nation's destiny. With this we return to the 1870s to find these men in their institutes with their models and concepts of race. The notions they developed of citizenship, people, and nation help us to understand yet another moment in which Brazil was rediscovering itself.

* The period referred to as the Old Republic (1889–1930) was famous for its insincere political conduct. The Old Republic was also called the "República do café-com-leite" [Coffee and Cream Republic] due to the political alliance of the coffee-producing state of São Paulo and the dairy-producing state of Minas Gerais. With the power consolidated in these two states, this alliance was known for its electoral authoritarianism, its governmental elitism, and its economic pragmatism, and it governed the country as though it were a great coffee plantation.

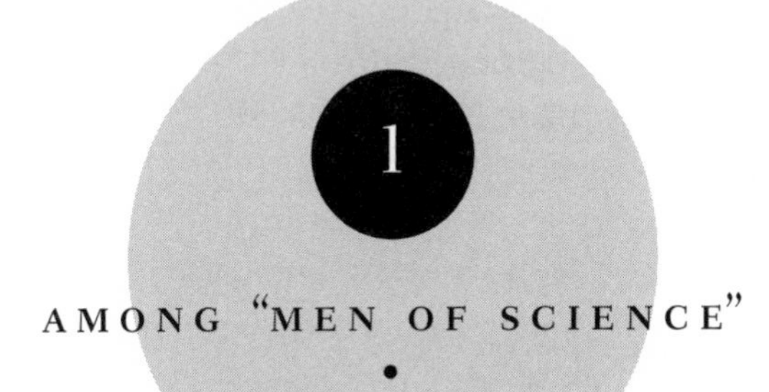

1 AMONG "MEN OF SCIENCE"

In the era of electricity and steam
the decade overshadows the century.
—*Journal of the Historical and Geographical Institute of Brazil* 22 (1859): 683.

THE ARRIVAL OF THE ROYAL FAMILY
The Dawn of a History of Educational Institutions in Brazil

It has only been within the relatively recent past that Brazil has been able to boast of a stable network of educational institutions. Teaching in the Portuguese colony was under Jesuit control and was limited to elementary schools. There were no centers of research or higher education.[1] This situation prevailed until the beginning of the nineteenth century, when Dom (or King) João VI, fleeing invading Napoleonic troops, left Portugal, one step ahead of Junot's French army, and arrived in the South American colony in 1808. He brought most of his court with him, as well as his sovereign Portuguese authority.

Dom João wanted to establish educational institutions that would help unify the colony, institutions that would mirror exactly those back home in Portugal (Corrêa, 1982; Azevedo, 1956; Carvalho, 1980). The bestowing of schools on the colony was motivated by a desire to centralize power, by a need to respond to the crisis of the Portuguese monarchy taking up residence in Brazil, and by the predicament produced by Dom João VI's sudden and impulsive decision to govern the Portuguese Empire from one of its colonies.[2]

With the arrival of Dom João VI's court, Brazil's first cultural institutions began to appear, and a new era of Brazilian institutional history began. The institutions that date from this era—the Royal Publishing House, the Library, the Royal Gardens, and the Royal Museum—helped transform the colony into not only the provisional seat of the Portuguese monarchy but also a productive and reproductive center of Portuguese culture and national memory.

At the same time an "enlightened national class" was emerging (Corrêa, 1982: 17), and paradoxically these Brazilians depended on the institutions that were created with the goal of ensuring the greatest Portuguese control over the colony. Closely tied to these Portuguese models were the first centers of learning, which further showed Brazil to be first a mirror of the mother country, and second a dependent and servile extension of the Portuguese court.

The process begun by Dom João VI was resumed under his son Dom Pedro after the Portuguese court and the outbreak of a liberal revolution back home forced the monarch's unexpected return to Portugal. While maintaining his father's initiatives, Dom Pedro advanced the foundation of new educational institutions, particularly after Brazil declared its independence in 1822. For instance, the law schools, created five years after Brazil's separation from Portugal, sought to create not only an original code, distinct from the colonial legacy, but also a more autonomous national intellectual elite.

The foundation of the first historical and geographical institute in 1838 was also a response to conditions associated with the political emancipation of the country. Headquartered in Rio de Janeiro, this institute was linked to a powerful local oligarchy, associated financially and intellectually with an "enlightened monarch" who sought to ensure strong, centralized control. In this cultural center

Dom Pedro had assumed the responsibility for creating the nation's history, for inventing the memory of a country that from that time forward should have been pursuing its own destiny, apart from the emperor's European homeland.

THE 1870s
Or "A Flock of New Ideas" (Silvio Romero)

The first group of Brazilian intellectuals were closely linked to the economic and financial elites of the country, and until the middle of the nineteenth century they were largely homogeneous in terms of education and careers (Carvalho, 1980). From that time forward certain regional and even professional differences appeared.

First, with the rise of coffee production during the 1850s and the concomitant shift of the country's economic axis from the northeast to the southeast, an analogous change occurred among the various scientific institutions of these regions; that is, those institutions located near the country's new economic centers were increasingly favored over those in regions whose wealth was declining.

Second, because of the tendency for academic fields to evolve differently, over time the nation's intellectual elites increasingly grew apart. Most of the Brazilian "enlightened class" were educated in Coimbra, Portugal, or less often in other European universities, and they then moved to a bureaucratic career. But by the 1870s the professions became more specialized, reflecting the differences that were emerging in their various institutions.

Fernando Azevedo concisely summarized the era's intellectual progress:

> During a period in which mathematics acquires new vigor with Otto Alencar, the Museum of Pará, founded by Emílio Goeldi in 1855, begins its activity. In 1893 Hermann von Ihering is hired to direct the Paulista Museum, an event that

> confers a strong scientific cast to the institution. Barbosa Rodrigues reorganizes the Botanical Garden, and in Bahia Nina Rodrigues undertakes a study, for the first time rigorously scientific, of the Afro-American element, a sizable segment of our population. This is in addition to the National Museum which undergoes a great transformation under the direction of Batista Lacerda. (Azevedo, 1956: 166)[3]

Other institutions helped to create an even more diversified intellectual panorama. Such was the case with the São Paulo and Recife Schools of Law. Although the intellectuals at both schools were concerned with the development of national standards of law, they made use of different tools. In São Paulo the intellectuals mostly adopted liberal models of analysis; whereas in Recife the analyses of the scholars followed the racial thread present in Haeckel and Spencerian models of social Darwinism. In the field of medicine, the Manguinhos Institute, under the direction of Oswaldo Cruz, became an important research center, specializing in the problems of yellow fever and urban sanitation. The historical institutes gathered together the intellectual and economic elites of different provinces under the sponsorship of Dom Pedro II; together these groups began to write the official history of this young country.

Various intellectual groups matured during the reign of Dom Pedro II. The members' educational backgrounds were diverse, and their professional aspirations varied according to the particularities of their specializations. For this reason, to identify the members of these institutes by a single socioeconomic profile becomes a progressively more complex proposition.

Indeed, we know little about the social origins of these intellectuals. Some investigators emphasize the distinct ties that existed between groups such as the agrarian aristocracy and the imperial state (Prado Jr., 1945; Nogueira, 1977); others consider the intellectuals to be representatives of "new urban constituencies in clear conflict with the traditional landholding bureaucracy" (Cruz Costa, 1967: 127). Perhaps the best way to define these thinkers is to observe their behavior closely, as Mariza Corrêa suggests (1983). If the enlightened elites were not primarily from the poorest classes, neither did they speak to the interests of nor were they wholly derived from the dominant classes. In short, despite the distinct kinship ties that bound certain intellectuals to landholding families, the intellectuals' activities played out within an urban context and thus were separate from their social origins (Corrêa, 1982: 23). At the same time the elites tried to legitimate or defend their positions scientifically, without reference to their class.

Not only were intellectual groups becoming more complex during Dom Pedro II's reign, the rate of change in Brazilian society as a whole was beginning to accelerate. Urbanization and migration to the cities[4] were as undeniable as the simultaneous development of political and financial elites, whose interests differed considerably. There were traditional landowners in the northeast, living off their last sugarcane harvests and their slave-based economy, and from the middle of the century onward there were coffee barons from Rio de Janeiro whose proximity to the emperor ensured them powerful political influence. To complicate the equation further, the burgeoning "São Paulo aristocracy," the economic heirs to this new "coffee empire," did not enjoy the same political influence as did the landowners of the province of Rio de Janeiro (Prado Jr., 1945; Faoro, 1977).[5] At stake were both the construction of a new political regime and the preservation of an entrenched social hierarchy that set the rural landed and slave-owning elites against the minuscule urban middle class. The end of the Paraguayan War in 1870, the "Law of the Free Womb" in 1871, and the influx of immigrant workers from Europe all contributed to the turmoil.

This broad range of predicaments obstructed Brazilians' efforts to design a new nation that could be free from attachments to the Empire. There was no clear political strategy to resolve the country's problems. In this sense the 1870s are a touchstone for various observers. From the most traditional historians, such as Capistrano de Abreu, to the most radical contemporary critics, such as Silvio Romero, everyone has agreed that the 1870s was a decade of innovation and the beginning of a new era:

> Until 1868 the commanding presence of the Roman Catholic Church had suffered not the slightest upset amid those plagues, and spiritualist philosophy had not met the slightest opposition. Neither had the authority of monarchical institutions borne any serious assault by any social class, nor had the institution of slavery and traditional feudal rights encountered the most isolated attack, nor had Romanticism, with its deceptive conceits and charming meditations, revealed the most subdued quarrel. . . . Suddenly an underground movement appeared from far away, the instability of our totality revealed itself, and the plight of the Empire appeared in all its clarity. . . . The foundations of the political world began to tremble. In the realm of theory the grappling was even more fierce since the potential for loss was horrifying. A flock of new ideas fluttered above us, converging from all points on the horizon. (Romero, 1926: 23–24)

Despite the overstatements that are to be expected from a scholar who was wrapped up in the moment he described, the fact is that everything did seem new in the 1870s: the political models, the attacks on religion, the conditions of work, the scientific theories, and the responses in the literature. In fact, during this period there emerged a new professional elite (employees of the new institutions) that incorporated liberal principles into its rhetoric and favored the adoption of a scientific evolutionist discourse as a model for social analysis. This type of evolutionist and determinist discourse was broadly employed within European imperialistic politics. When these theories entered Brazil it was hoped that they could effect rigorous social reforms in the 1870s by providing the means to account for national inconsistencies. Adopting a kind of "internal imperialism," the country passed from the object of discussion to the subject of discussion. At the same time, social differences began to be equated with racial variations. Known from that time on as "dangerous classes," Negroes, Africans, workers, slaves, and former slaves were, in the words of Silvio Romero, becoming "objects of science" (preface to Rodrigues, 1933/1988).

In the Era of "Science"

"Nothing perturbs a man of science, one devoted only to science, that is not science," wrote the Brazilian novelist Joaquim Maria Machado de Assis in the voice of his illustrious character, Simão Bacamarte, a psychiatrist who treated an entire town (1882/1989: 26). Formalizing disputes, and sometimes even sarcastically criticizing commonly held beliefs, Machado de Assis used Bacamarte to sketch a profile both of himself and of his environs. In fact, the novelist captured the spirit of the period, when science was viewed not only as a profession but as a kind of priesthood that valued the life of the mind over tangible productivity.

The focus on science and its social implications in this era was, of course, a worldwide phenomenon and not unique to Brazil. Historian Eric Hobsbawm points out that the broad fin de siècle "world of science moved along its intellectual railway tracks" (1975: 255). Wolf Lepenies mentions how the eighteenth-century scientist "had long since ceased to be a mere virtuoso whose objectives included the provision of amusement; yet the conviction still reigned that science was a calling and confession rather than a professional occupation" (1988: 2). Finally, historian David Knight designates the period between 1789 and 1914 as an "age of science," an "age of innocence and faith" (1986: 3). It was a time of both faith in the results of experiments and innocence in the near blind faith in scientific diagnoses and uncompromising prophecies.

Therefore, if during the eighteenth century "science had become something to talk about" (Knight, 1986: 2), few could make a living at this profession or translate research work into their primary source of income (Darnton, 1990). It was only in the second half of the nineteenth century that the "scientist" would achieve eminence and, more important, greater independence. That was the era of specialization, of the great syntheses, including the laws of thermodynamics and the theory of evolution, and of the partition of areas of knowledge.

It was amid these developments that the clash between literature and the social sciences erupted. In order to seek recognition as disciplines, areas of inquiry such as sociology sought to distance themselves from "the early literary forms of their own discipline, whose purpose was rather to describe and classify than to analyse and reduce to a system" (Lepenies, 1988: 7). This was the moment when Emile Durkheim introduced sociology into France, with his *De la division du travail social* [*Division of Labor in Society*] (1893) and *Les règles de la méthode sociologique* [*The Rules of Sociological Method*] (1895), claiming autonomy and individuality for this new science. Through the work of this new field society would no longer be understood as the mere sum of individuals, and social phenomena would be studied as "things" that were "external and coercive," and therefore befitting a scientific analysis in sociological terms. Following Durkheim a break with extra-social determinism occurred, since according to the new science, the "social phenomenon" could be explained only by the social dynamic itself.[6] In 1901 Marcel Mauss, Durkheim's student and nephew, positioned himself in relation to the birth of sociology: *"Mais si l'on doit admettre sans examen préable que les faits appelés sociaux sont naturels, intelligibles et par suite objets de science, encore faut il qu'il y ait des faites que puissent être proprement appelés de ce nom"* [But if one must accept without proof that these phenomena are natural, intelligible, and therefore possess scientific qualities, one must also call them by their proper name] (Mauss, 1901/1969: 141).

After the introduction of the theory of evolution, a similar process occurred in the natural sciences, wherein scientists were subject to a process of specialization and uncustomary appraisal, and biology became the primary model of analysis. The divisions of natural science such as geology, botany, and zoology soon asserted their independence, and new branches of inquiry emerged, deriving directly from new scientific research. At the beginning of the twentieth century the German physicist Max Planck established the bases of quantum mechanics, and the Dutch botanist Hugo de Vries developed his theories of mutations, questioning previous beliefs about the evolutionary process of biological species. Scientists in the field of neurology also made great strides with research and findings surrounding our understanding of the human nervous system.[7] Everywhere modern research and experimentation were effecting fundamental change upon entrenched scientific concepts.[8]

"We Live and Breathe Science in Brazil"

The "science" that came to Brazil at the end of the century was not so much experimental science or the sociology of Durkheim or Weber.* Brazil was taking in evolutionist and social Darwinist models first popularized and theoretically justified in the service of imperialistic domination.[9]

Avid readers of the literature produced in Europe and in the United States, the Brazilian elites would not escape untouched by the precepts that came from the outside. The country was making an effort to distinguish itself from other Latin American republics by fashioning itself on European models of learning and civility. It became apparent in its institutes, newspapers, and novels that in those last years of the nineteenth century, Brazil was trying to portray itself as a modern and scientific society.

* The title of this section is based on a quote from the *Academic Journal of the Recife School of Law,* 1893.

Dom Pedro II (with the white beard) in Cairo. In the center, the Viscount of Bom Retiro

But at that moment in Brazil more important than original scientific research and progress was the pursuit of a kind of scientific ethos, an indiscriminate and vague "scientism."* Brazilian researchers consumed far more scientific manuals and handbooks than monographs or original research. Science first appeared as a fashion and only much later as a discipline to practice for producing original results.

One notes an early example of this posture in the temperament and deeds of Dom Pedro II, who was celebrated as a "patron of science." Besides the political influence he wielded and the unifying role he exercised, the emperor also regularly attended national and international expositions, expeditions, and

* Scientism was not a coherent philosophy but a belief, deriving from positivism, that science and scientific methods possessed important truths and ways of knowing that one could profitably apply to all areas of thought and endeavor.

gatherings on scientific themes. Dom Pedro II was fond of saying, "I am science" (*Journal of the Historical and Geographical Institute of Brazil* [*JHGIB*]: 1878), a clear affirmation of his position, even though it was also a gentle parody of Louis XIV's celebrated words, *"L'état c'est moi"* [I am the state]. Nevertheless, his words are a faithful portrait of a chief of state who chose science as a touchstone, almost a standard of behavior, for an emperor noted for his "rare enlightenment" (Queirós, 1878/1987: 85).[10]

With an emperor who was familiar with the latest in science, especially when the science was of European origin, and with the elites pulling together (that is, when they saw some social advantage in it), the external image of the country changed quickly. With a concern for appearances foremost in their minds, Brazilians must have exported a very carefully fashioned image. With this logic one can understand how the Brazilian Empire portrayed itself in its celebrated "universal expositions."[11] Brazil was already known to travelling naturalists as an extraordinary destination, and at these events the country donned newly pressed academic robes. No longer just "jungle and savagery," the nation's new calling card bore a modern, industrious, civilized, and scientific image.

The newspapers of the time were particularly adept at promoting this image of the local society. The newspaper *The State of São Paulo,* founded in 1875 by the region's most affluent citizens under the original title *The Province of São Paulo,* assumed a "modern" journalistic identity, the fruit of a "progressive, scientific, and hardworking city." Providing daily coverage of European mavens such as Darwin, Spencer, and Comte, the newspaper gave voice to an entire evolutionist-positivist outlook, as if concepts such as science and modernity walked, perforce, hand in hand.[12]

Naturalist novels of the era also reveal a heavy application of determinist scientific models. This was the era when "the writer bore the standard of science" (Paes, 1986: 9), and writers wrapped their works in scientific thought in hopes of gaining approval for their supposed "literary objectivity." In fact, it was through literature and not science per se that the science wave

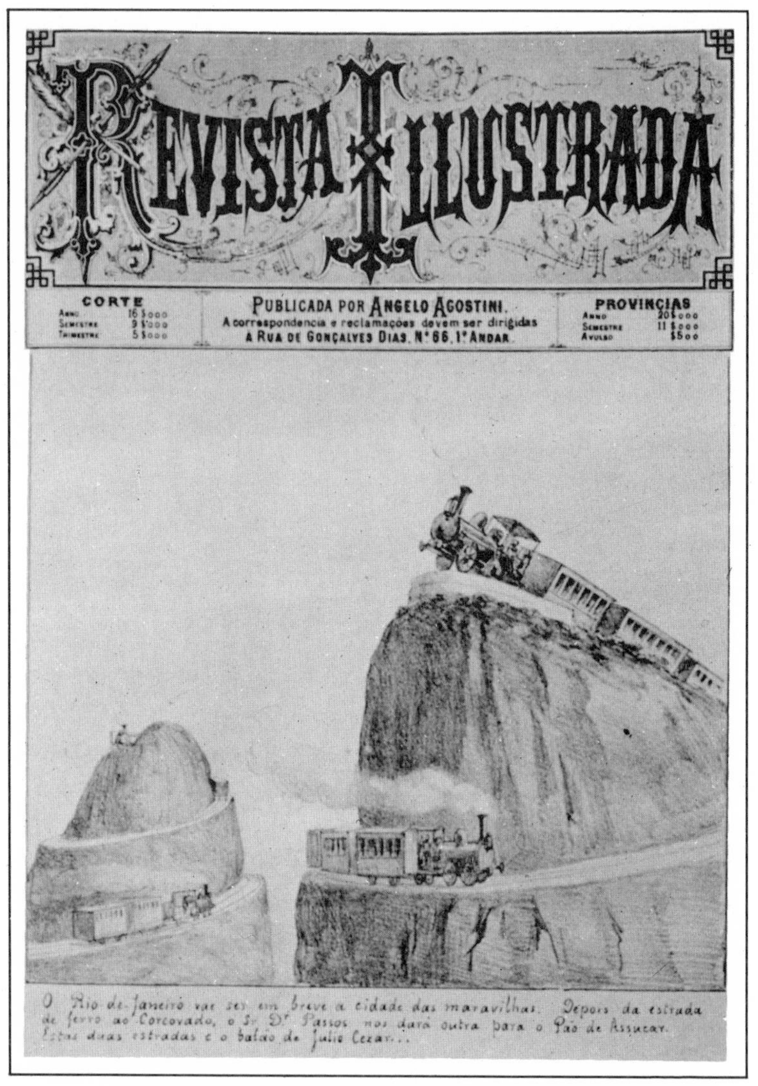

Angelo Agostini ironically portrayed the arrival of progress to the city of Rio de Janeiro
(*REVISTA ILLUSTRADA* [ILLUSTRATED REVIEW], 1882)

swept over the country. The principles of Darwin and Spencer along with the pessimistic conclusions of scientific racial theories of the times were worked into the plots of novels, and determinist doctrines shaped the characters. Lenita, the heroine of *A carne* [Flesh], was described as a "Herbert Spencer in skirts" (Ribeiro, 1888: 67); the naturalist Hartt is cited in *O Ateneu* [The Athenaeum] (Pompéia, 1889–1976); and the work *A esfinge* [The sphinx] concludes with a speech that adds nothing to the main text and is nothing but a treatise on "competition and struggle for improvement of the natural imperfection" of the nation (Peixoto, 1911: 473). Indeed, the characters and plots of these novels seemed to reflect the authors' interest in the tenets of evolutionary science more so than their literary imagination.

A number of works conformed to this model, but one in particular seems to integrate all the characteristics of the scientistic* style into the literary environment. It is *O chromo: Um estudo de temperamentos* [The chromo: A study of temperaments] (1888) by Horácio de Carvalho. An extreme example of what were termed "scientific novels," this is a minitreatise of novelistic physiology whose pages include footnotes, cosmographic figures, and characters whose behavior derives fully from the theories of polygenist anthropology.† The hero of the novel, Teixeira, is portrayed as "Darwinianly superior," the fruit of "a wave of spermatic evolution" (233); whereas Tonica, a supporting character, is understood as "one of the best products in Nature to move anthropological evolution forward" (336). Expressions lifted from the scientific theories of the day are sprinkled amid the most romantic moments of this novel's plot. Esther writes vows of love to Teixeira, revealing her scientific erudition as well as a fairly

* *Scientifism* is a term the author uses to signify the tendency of nineteenth-century writers and scholars to sprinkle science, or scientific-seeming methods, into their work.

† Polygenist anthropologists believed that the different human races had different origins; monogenists believed that all human races descended from a single source.

broad familiarity with contemporary scientific models: "What is there among us today that can hinder the great law of the survival of the fittest, in the words of our dear Darwin?" (354); "Today I would trade the most precious page of science for just one of your words" (349).[13] In the absence of any real scientific research or production in the country, rhetorical scientifism, exemplified by *O chromo,* permeated Brazilian thinking.

In the cities, Brazil's diffuse scientifism gave rise to public health programs in which bureaucrats tried to bring a new scientific understanding to high-density urban centers, launching projects with the flavor of eugenics and with the goal of eliminating illness and eradicating madness and poverty.[14] The "Vaccination Revolt" (1904) suggested the public's reaction to the intensity with which these public health projects were pursued. Despite the value of obligatory vaccinations, the force of the popular opposition suggests the rift that existed between the cities' scientific programs and the people's understanding of them.[15]

What we see in these and other examples is not concern that specialized scientific work be taken up in Brazil but the wish that the country adopt the widespread application and validation of the era's determinist theories, practices, and conclusions. One must understand, however, not only the penetration of these scientific views but also the peculiar national logic that made their acceptance possible. One must understand why these "men of science" chose racial theories of analysis over other successful models of the time. The justification is not obvious. That is, if it is certain that the Brazilian intellectual and political elites comprehended and accepted these evolutionist and social Darwinist models, that they led the nation to believe that Europe and Brazil were not unlike each other, and that these elites were confident in the inevitability of their progress and civilization, at the same time they were not entirely comfortable in applying these theories to racial issues. Paradoxically, the introduction of this new scientific outlook also exposed the details and fragility of a country that was already heavily crossbred.

Caricature from 1905 that treats the public reaction to obligatory vaccination
(*O MALHO* [THE HAMMER])

What, then, were the elements of the debate in Brazil? Who were those "men of science" who within their institutes assumed the arduous task of reflecting upon the nation's future and its vicissitudes?

"Men of Science" Studying Race and Its Effect on the Future of Brazil

According to Manuela Carneiro da Cunha, "the Portuguese were fascinated by the Orient and gave little thought to the New World. Brazil was not a subject of study or an object of reflection, nor were the Portuguese even particularly covetous of it. Brazil went almost unnoticed for the first fifty years after contact" (Cunha, 1990: 91). In fact, compassion did not accompany the Portuguese settlers. They rarely embraced the myth of the "noble savage," and their chiding view of the South American colony was one based on the specter of cannibalism or on the pessimistic opinion of the Jesuits who concerned themselves with the management of souls.[16]

In truth, although pessimism has colored the thoughts of Brazilians for many years,[17] this attitude dates from the middle of the nineteenth century, when for a number of travellers Brazil represented a nation "debilitated by the mixing of races." This was the observation of Henry Thomas Buckle (1821–62), who, projecting the fate of a people based on climate, condemned Brazilians to decadence owing to the country's teeming vegetation: "Nowhere else is there so painful a contrast between the grandeur of the external world and the littleness of the internal. And the mind, cowed by this unequal struggle, has not only been unable to advance, but without foreign aid it would undoubtedly have receded" (1865: 76). Buckle, who dedicated ten pages of his vast work on English civilization to the Brazilian condition, concluded that the "most abundant" nature in Brazil left little space for humans and their works.

Both the Argentinean philosopher José Ingenieros (1877–1925) and naturalist Louis Couty[18] insisted on similar grounds that problems would accrue to a country with "miscegenized races." Like these writers, various other travellers such as Louis Agassiz and Count Arthur de Gobineau reminded Brazilians of the dire consequences forecast by European racial theories, and applying these concepts to the conditions that they found in Brazil, these foreign observers commented on the precariousness of a country composed of mixed races. Thus, although there was no consensus on how Brazil was seen from abroad, one must recognize the strength and relevance for the country of the kind of pessimistic commentaries that saw in Brazil's racial and ethnic composition a "model of backwardness and failure."

Nevertheless, it is not enough to limit ourselves exclusively to the impressions that foreign theorists had of that "mestizo republic of European scientists" (Broca, 1956: 107). One must consider the local interpretation as well as analyze the homegrown texts and authors. In fact, starting toward the end of the 1870s, groups of a certain type of intellectual were increasingly found gathered in various research institutes. In these settings these thinkers enjoyed social acceptance, but they also found the necessary atmosphere to initiate a more independent discussion of racial issues and to work untrammelled by the dominant classes, which were then umbilically linked to the agrarian sectors of the economy.

These men were the first in a line of specialized professionals. Avid readers of scientific literature, preferably European, these intellectuals were scattered among the various institutes and saw themselves as "men of science." They were far from homogeneous, although the fall of the Empire had had the levelling effect of unsettling them all.[19] Their professional, economic, and regional interests ranged widely, but their scientific activities gave them credentials to assess and discuss the dilemmas and prospects that confronted the country. This enlightened elite, somewhat reduced in number after the birth of the new state, ended up circulating among various centers of learning and establishing cultural exchanges.[20] Thus the group shared a common profile that on one hand guaranteed them a certain level of recognition and on the other hand brought them a certain multidimensionality, which in this case concealed their minimal specialization and even the limited scope of their areas of knowledge.

With this background we have set the scene for the beginning of a veiled dispute between "men of science" and "men of letters." The philosophies of these adversaries were brought out in the open by the quarrel that erupted between the jurist Silvio Romero and the writer Machado de Assis. The polemic had its roots in an essay Machado de Assis had written on the "new generation," published in 1879, in which he analyzed his era's emerging writers. In the course of this survey he criticized Silvio Romero in particular for the jurist's work in literary criticism and his sermonizing scientific analysis of poetry. Even more strident than Machado de Assis's criticism was the response by Silvio Romero. Having been attacked precisely for what he believed was his greatest contribution, the master of the Recife School reacted virulently with a piece entitled "Machado de Assis, estudo comparativo de literatura brasileira" [Machado de Assis: a comparative study of Brazilian literature] (1897), in which Romero compared two writers of the period, Tobias Barreto and Machado de Assis, employing ethnographic and evolutionist criteria. Without going into the details of the dispute, the most important thing to note is that, in Romero's very unscientific judgment of Machado de Assis,[21] the kernels of another polemic emerged: the controversy between "men of science"—who identified themselves in terms of their association with scientific institutes and with a unique, activist, and interventionist posture—and "men of letters"—who, in the view of men like Romero, were out of touch with the most pressing issues of the day.[22]

Caricatures began to appear of the "men of letters," whom the "men of science" accused of engaging in activities that suggested an aversion to some of the country's more immediate and pressing social and political issues. On the other side, calling themselves intellectuals, the "men of science" struggled "for the scientific progress of the nation" (Lacerda, in *Archives of the National Museum,* 1876: 26). Yet they found themselves in a paradox. While they condemned the absence of original scientific research in their country, they possessed an influential public presence, made possible by their position and participation in their institutes of research and higher learning. But highly influential persons, such as Joaquim Nabuco,[23] did not exploit their association with the academy for political gain.

A caricature of Afrânio Peixoto, a "Man of Letters," by K. Lixto
(*A MAÇÃ* [THE APPLE], 1922)

The "men of science," ensconced in their institutes, saw themselves as key players in redeeming the age and in finding solutions to problems plaguing Brazil, as well as charting the course of their country. Their proposals were often radical and considered "alien," given the sense of alienation that their ideas aroused. These intellectuals did more than merely experience a moment of high visibility and relative autonomy; they also sought to devise global models and pioneering studies in an attempt to reveal, for the first time, a blueprint for the entire nation.

Deeply interested in the literary tastes of the period, the "men of science" tended to adopt evolutionist and particularly social Darwinist models, by this time generally discredited throughout Europe, which had as their focus the study of race and the

Manoel de Oliveira Lima (1865–1928), Archeological and Geographical Institute of Pernambuco

Francisco José Oliveira Vianna (1883–1951), Historical and Geographical Institute of Brazil

Tobias Barreto (1839–89), Recife School of Law

Euclides da Cunha (1866–1909), Historical and Geographical Institute of Brazil

Edgard Roquete-Pinto (1884–1954), National Museum

Herman von Ihering (1850–1930), São Paulo Museum

Silvio Romero (1851–1914), Recife School of Law

João Baptista Lacerda (1846–1915), National Museum

Raimundo Nina Rodrigues (1862–1906), Bahia School of Medicine

Oswaldo Cruz (1872–1917), Rio de Janeiro School of Law

Miguel Pereira (1871–1918), National Academy of Medicine

A. A. de Azevedo Sodré (1864–1929), Rio de Janeiro School of Medicine

validation of its unique contributions.[24] In fact, for these intellectuals the era's scientific models showed a new way to comprehend the world that was secular, materialist, and modern. On the other hand, "while they were autodidacts, these people were more responsive to bookish and erudite philosophism than to the spirit of philosophy in a broad sense" (Holanda, n.d.: 223), consuming above all manuals and handbooks, which were often poorly received in European circles.[25]

Famed Brazilian anthropologist Antonio Candido fittingly called these intellectuals the "cultural nouveau-riche" (1988: 30). Increasingly linked to urban activities, they would claim as their intellectual mission eclecticism and interpretations of positivist, social Darwinist, and evolutionist textbooks and manuals.

Without going into the convolutions of the kind of racial and social theory these men advocated, it is of interest to point out that it served an important function among the mass of authors who were eclectically exploited by the intellectuals of Dom Pedro II's regime. According to Sérgio Buarque de Holanda, Brazilian authors and researchers seized upon various concepts, sometimes inconsistent one with the other, that took the form of "battle strategies, that permitted the comprehension of and even gave solutions to concrete social and political problems in Brazil" (n.d.: 321). They had no interest in reviving the original debates, in recovering either the underlying logic of the theories or the context in which they were created; instead, they wanted to dismiss what sounded odd to them and adapt whatever "suited" them, from the justification of a kind of natural hierarchy to the verification of the inferiority of broad sectors of the population, primarily when their chosen theories explored the theme of the "misfortunes of miscegenation."

The challenge then is to explore the "originality" of Brazilian racial and social theories, and to examine the elasticity of evolutionist doctrines—for such elasticity can help to explain the varied acceptance of such theories in disparate contexts.

Several elements orient this course of thought. First, it is possible to verify that when the theory of "racial peculiarities"

(Schwarz, 1987: 41) arrived in Brazil it was already widely discredited in Europe. Second, what one observes is not the chance translation of foreign thinkers but rather an effort to select particular texts over others. As Cruz Costa concludes, "it is not the philosophy of Kant, Fichte, or Hegel that prevails, but a Germanism of the second order represented by Noiré, for example, a Monist who assumed the airs of an oracle" (Cruz Costa, 1967: 284). Therefore, the European racial theories adopted in Brazil seem not to have been just a matter of chance. Introduced in a critical and selective manner, they became a conservative and even an authoritarian instrument in the definition of a national identity (Ventura, 1988: 7) and in the service of social hierarchies that were already well established.

But before analyzing the absorption of these models in Brazil, it is necessary to return to the "source." The racial theories came primarily from Europe and the United States, and it is in these settings that the next chapter begins.

RACIAL DOCTRINES IN THE NINETEENTH CENTURY

•

A History of "Differences and Discrimination"

Prior to 1870, philosophical theories such as positivism, evolution, and Darwinism were unknown in Brazil. The sudden and simultaneous entry of these new doctrines into the country in the ensuing decades had a powerful influence on contemporary Brazilian thought. But these philosophies did not find wholesale acceptance, nor did these singular views of the world coalesce into a unified vision. Instead, scholars from the different institutions used these new theories selectively to inform their own distinctive ideas.

Nineteenth-century racial theorists referred constantly, but not uniformly, to ideas expressed by eighteenth-century writers.[1] Some cited humanistic literature, with Jean Jacques Rousseau at the forefront as a primary defender of the notion of a single humanity; opponents cited authors such as American lawyer Cornelius De Pauw and French naturalist Georges Louis Leclerc, Comte de Buffon, as powerful voices in the argument to justify the belief in the essential differences between the races.

BETWEEN GLORIFICATION AND DEFAMATION

The age of discovery, in the late fifteenth and early sixteenth centuries, ushered in a period of momentous change in Western history. The conquest of previously unknown lands led to new beliefs and perspectives and constant debate and reflection on the differences among humans, although information was more often spread by hearsay than by eyewitness accounts. In travel narratives, which blended reality with fantasy, the "new people" were frequently described as having unusual natures and strange customs (Mello e Souza, 1986; Holanda, n.d.; Todorov, 1983; Gerbi, 1982).

It was not until the eighteenth century, however, that "uncivilized people came to be known and characterized as primitive" (Clastres, 1983: 188). They were called primitive because they appeared to be primal, at the origins of humankind. Indigenous Americans occupied a special niche within a new perception of human beings as a species, with a unique evolution and a potential for "perfectibility."

"Perfectibility" is a key concept in Rousseau's humanistic theory. Together with the sense of "freedom" either to resist or to acquiesce to the laws of nature, this term described a particularly human condition (1775/1992: 26). In light of the theory of perfectibility, and contrary to nineteenth-century evolutionist ideas, humanistic thought held that human beings possessed a unique and inherent capacity to transcend themselves. The Genevan philosopher affirmed that there is another very specific quality that distinguishes people, about which there can be no argument: it is the capacity for self-perfection. But "perfectibility" did not guarantee access to a "civilized state" or to virtue, as nineteenth-century theorists supposed.

> It would be sad for us to be forced to agree that this distinctive and almost unlimited faculty is the source of all man's

> misfortunes; that it is this faculty which, by dint of time, draws him out of that original condition in which he would pass tranquil and innocent days; that it is this faculty which, bringing to flower over the centuries his enlightenment and his errors, his vices and his virtues, in the long run makes him the tyrant of himself and of Nature. (Rousseau, 1775/1992: 26)[2]

The humanistic tradition raised concerns about human diversity, and, because of the political legacy of the French Revolution and the teachings of the Enlightenment, the eighteenth century was stirred with interest in notions of human equality. Once people presumed that freedom and equality were natural, they began to think about the unity of humanity and the universality of equality, both of which were also understood to be natural. The leaders of modern nations wrote the principles of equality into their constitutions, conferring a "morally neutral" (Dumont, 1966: 322) value to "differences," and presuming that all human beings are born equal, although they stopped short of a full definition of the nature of humans.

Rousseau's notion of the "noble savage" is consistent with this line of thought, and aboriginal Americans became logical models for analysis. Rousseau did not expect that to return to a "natural state" was to return to an original paradise. Instead, he embraced the notion as a basis for analyzing Western society and its own "state of civilization."

> I ask which, Civil or natural life, is most liable to become unbearable to those who enjoy it? We see around us practically no People who do not complain of their existence, even many who deprive themselves of it insofar as they have the capacity; and the combination of divine and human Laws hardly suffices to stop this disorder. I ask if anyone has ever heard it said that a Savage in freedom even dreamed of complaining about life and killing himself. Let it then be

judged with less pride on which side genuine misery lies. (Rousseau, 1775/1992: 34)

The "otherness" of these "new men" logically emerged as a counterpoint to the Western experience. As Rousseau concluded on the origin of inequality among men, "the goodness suitable for the pure state of Nature was no longer that which suited nascent society" (1775/1992: 48). A stranger in his own land and abandoned in the midst of a seemingly hostile world, the celebrated philosopher of the Enlightenment found the indigenous people an ideal model of a morally superior "other," so unlike the products of Western civilization.

Coming to grips with his vision of opposites, Rousseau began to distance himself from the Enlightenment. His "compassion"[3] and identification with the "other" led him to seek the most advantageous way to understand that human being who was so distinct from the Western experience.

But even if Rousseau's idyllic vision had broad appeal and influence throughout the eighteenth century (Holanda, 1985: xxv),[4] one must also mention the more negative interpretations of his ideas. As the historian Laura Mello e Souza noted in *O diabo e a terra de Santa Cruz* [The Devil and the earth of Santa Cruz], the views that derogated the New World intensified in the second half of the eighteenth century, corresponding directly to the colonization and greater understanding of these new territories (1986: 42). At that time the inherently innocent savage became the inherently bad savage: "because of the alleged physically inferior continent, and from the subsequent natural debility of its species . . . all [were] condemned by nature to an inescapable decadence, to a fatal corruption" (Gerbi, 1982: ix).

Various thinkers propagated this more negative vision of America and its native peoples, but two of them deserve our attention: Comte Georges-Louis Leclerc de Buffon, with his thesis of the "infancy of the continent"; and Cornelius De Pauw, with his theory of "American degeneracy."

The renowned French naturalist Comte de Buffon (1707–88) proposed a general "human science," whose appellation was later revived by Michel Foucault (1966). Buffon identified a tension between a negative image of both nature and Native Americans and the positive representation of the natural state offered by Rousseau. He characterized South America as a place of privation, thus breaking with Rousseau's depiction of a paradise. The small stature of its animals, its sparse population, the absence of body hair on its humans, and the proliferation of reptiles, insects, and other small species all seemed to corroborate Buffon's assertion that this land was frail and immature (Buffon, 1834). Therefore, despite the continued popularity of the idea of the oneness of humanity, a distinct sense of hierarchy emerged, accompanied by a highly ethnocentric conception of culture and identity.

The debate became highly polarized when the jurist Cornelius De Pauw introduced the notion of "degeneracy." Aboriginal Americans, according to De Pauw, were a *degenerate* species; they were inferior because of their less complex structure. Before De Pauw, the term *degenerate* referred to changes of form, but with the impact of his arguments the word soon came to describe "a pathological detour from the original form."[5] Taking Buffon's arguments to the extreme, De Pauw argued that Americans were not only "immature" but also "decadent," confirming De Pauw's central thesis of "faith in progress and lack of faith in human goodness" (Gerbi, 1982: 66). A conspicuous anti-Americanism glimmered through the cracks of De Pauw's evaluations of "New World nature, frail due to its corruption, inferior due to its degeneracy" (De Pauw, 1768, quoted in Gerbi: 1982).[6]

Therefore, within the intellectual context of the eighteenth century, certain new perspectives stood out. On the one hand, the French Revolution popularized its humanistic vision of the equality of mankind, but on the other hand it introduced thoughts, timid though they were at first, on the fundamental differences among humans. Over the course of the nineteenth century, however, notions of difference assumed far greater importance, and genetics, intellectual aptitude, and moral inclinations became inextricably linked in racial theories.

ENTRENCHING THE DIFFERENCES
The Appearance of "Race"

By the end of the eighteenth century, the egalitarian tradition introduced by the French Revolution had established a lingering optimism, based on viewing diverse human groups as "peoples" or "nations," and never as races that differed in their genetic origins and anatomy (Stocking, 1968: 28).

In fact, when the French phrenologist Georges Cuvier introduced the term *race* into the literature, he inaugurated the idea of inherited physical traits that are characteristic of the various human groups (Stocking, 1968: 29).[7] The outline of an idea was emerging, colored by the differences between sixteenth-century chroniclers and nineteenth-century naturalists, "to whom it fell only to narrate, classify, order, and organize whatever he encountered in his path" (Sussekind, 1990: 45).

With the new theories on human groups, an intellectual reorientation took place, a backlash against the Enlightenment. This change took the form of an assault on the egalitarian assumptions of bourgeois revolutions. Racial discourse emerged as a variation on the theme of citizenship. Within these new models ran threads more associated with a biological group's limitations than with the will of an individual, which came to be understood as being contingent upon the attributes specific to one's race (Galton, 1869/1988: 86).

Thinking about Origins: Monogenism versus Polygenism

Although the terms of the discussion were new, the debate surrounding race derived from a long-standing question concerning the origins of humanity. This time-worn theme assumed a more defined role in the nineteenth century, when racial issues appeared to threaten society's illusions.

Among the accounts that fed Western curiosity at this time were the extraordinary stories of the "wild child" or children lost in exotic Asian forests and raised by wolves. One might speculate at length about the truth of these stories,[8] but it is more fruitful to consider the role that these strange events played in the thinking of the time. The living examples of these wild children seemed to personify and establish limits, albeit tenuous limits, that separated the world of nature from the world of culture; and the public's persistent interest revealed much about the extent of its fascination in the cases.[9]

In this era, there were two primary schools of thought on the question of man's origins. The *monogenist* vision was dominant until the middle of the nineteenth century and attracted the most support. Its proponents, who took their cues from Biblical scripture, believed that humanity was one. Humans had come from a common source, and the different types of humans were merely products of acclimatization: "Everything . . . proves that if they are willing to submit to the necessary sacrifices, all human races may live and prosper in almost every climate" (Quatrefage, 1857, quoted in Stocking, 1982). Embedded in their belief was the notion of *virtuality*. Humankind's uniform origin would guarantee a development similar in form but not in degree. Humanity was perceived to be a gradient that would run from the most perfect (those closest to Eden) to the least perfect (those who had degenerated from Eden). At the beginning, the monogenist approach did not assume a unique evolution for the races.[10]

From the middle of the nineteenth century, the growing sophistication of biological sciences led to a plausible alternative to the monogenist dogma of the Church. The proponents of this *polygenist* hypothesis believed that human creation had various sources, which explained racial differences.

The interpretation of contemporary biological and natural laws encouraged polygenists to analyze human behavior. This kind of bias was especially encouraged by the simultaneous birth of *phrenology* and *anthropometry*, new "sciences" that evaluated human capacities by measuring the size and proportions of the heads of different peoples. Simultaneously, a new *technical craniology* appeared, which was based on the measurement of the cephalic index (the ratio of the breadth to the length of the head). Developed by the Swiss anthropologist André Ratzius in the middle of the nineteenth century, this method facilitated the development of quantitative studies on the varieties of the human head. The more a path of analysis departed from humanistic models, the more strongly it rebounded, establishing rigid correlations between internal and external knowledge and between physical appearance and spiritual profundity.

Still following this polygenist model, a new hypothesis was gathering strength. It focused on the observation of the "biological nature of criminal behavior." Proponents of *criminal anthropology*, chief among whom was Cesare Lombroso, argued that criminality was a physical and hereditary phenomenon (Lombroso, 1876: 45) and, as such, it was an element that was objectively detectable in different societies. Criminal anthropology research also profoundly influenced the treatment of mental illness. One of the first areas to which phrenology was applied was psychopathy, where the science was used to explain the "moral" treatment of psychopathics and to justify conclusions that linked individual insanity to racially based degeneracy.

The practice of phrenology gained wide acceptance throughout the Western Hemisphere. Phrenology-inspired games of self-exploration appeared, courses proliferated, museums opened, and new artistic forms such as caricature, which also found a lot of inspiration from the study of phrenology, gathered strength as well. According to the Italian historian Claudio Pogliano, the renowned dictum "know thyself" acquired diverse uses in light of

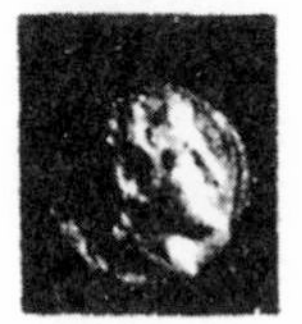

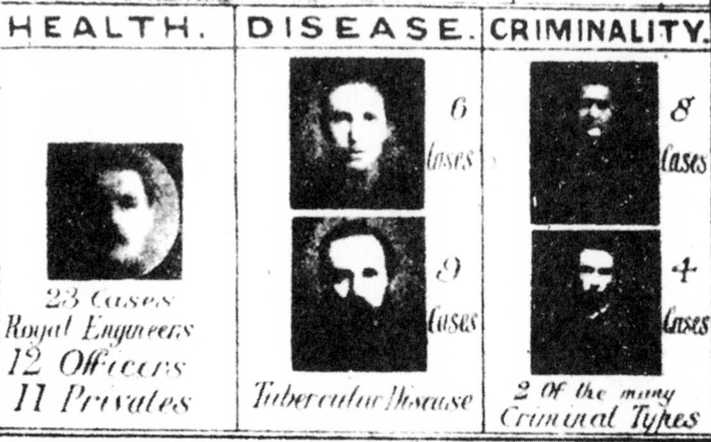

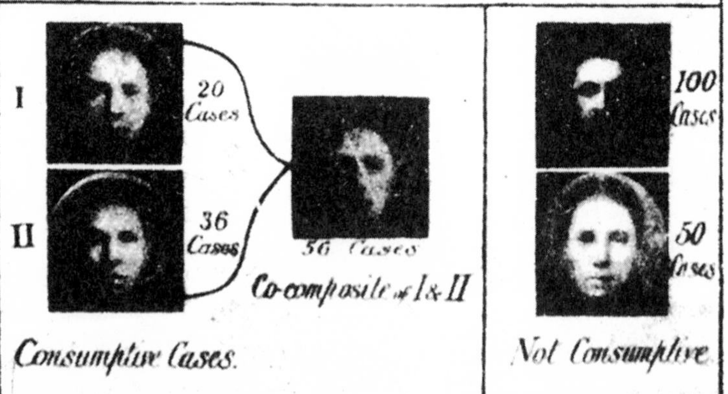

Examples of composite photographs for use in criminal studies
(FRANCIS GALTON, 1889)

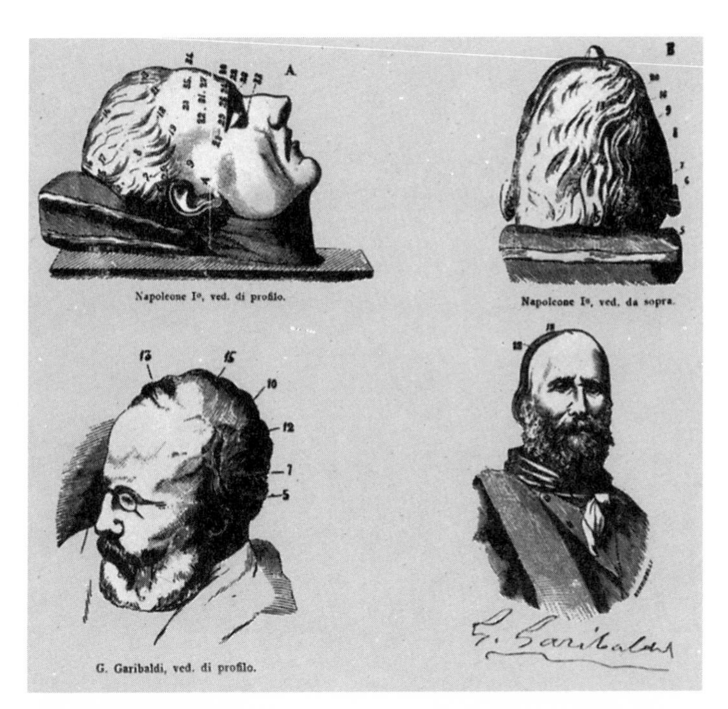

Physical characteristics aided in defining not only the criminal but also the genius, according to studies by Cesare Lombroso on Napoleon and Garibaldi

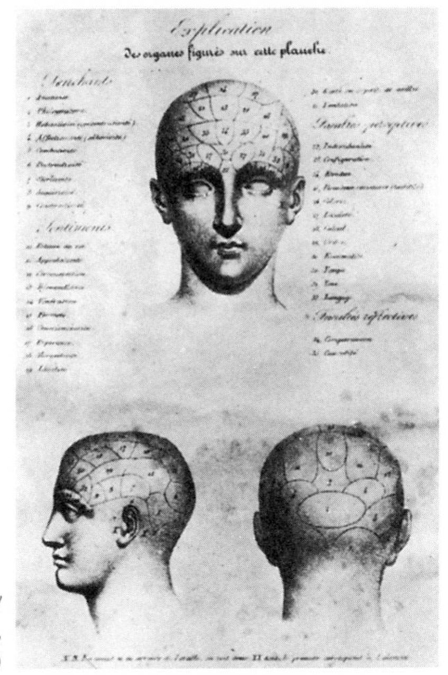

Studies on technical craniology (COURSE IN PHRENOLOGY, 1836, BRUSSELS)

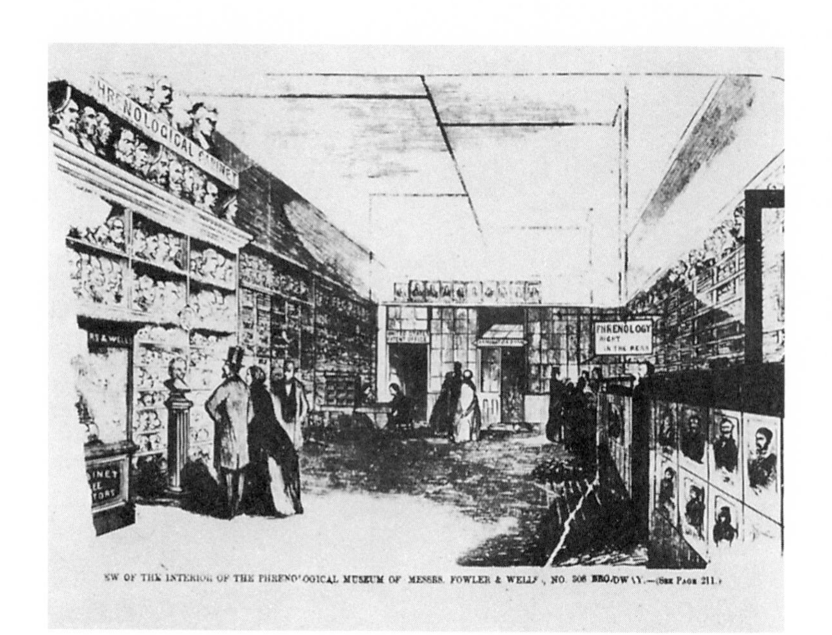

Museums of Phrenology

Example of a game deriving from phrenological studies

the new theories, more or less related to its original scientific function (1990: 193).

Reverting to Hippocrates, the proponents of polygenism insisted on the idea that different human races constituted "different species," specific "types" that through crossbreeding or adaptations could not be reduced to a single humanity. In the words of Hannah Arendt, polygenism marked the end of "the idea of the natural law as the uniting link between all men and all peoples" (1966: 177). This model rejected the notion of the "perfectibility" thought to be possible in the "noble savage," in the same way that the Enlightenment questioned the idea of "voluntarism," that is, the uniquely human ability to choose to submit to nature.

Questions surrounding the divisions of like disciplines were seen in debates that pitted monogenism against polygenism. *Anthropological studies,* for example, originated in connection with the physical and biological sciences and favored polygenist interpretations. *Ethnological analyses,* on the other hand, originated in the humanities and favored the monogenist tradition. Anthropology, thus understood as a branch of the natural sciences, dedicated itself above all to craniometric measurement, a method of study considered most fitting for the analysis of peoples and their contributions. Sol Tax, late professor of anthropology of the University of Chicago, referred to the dispute between these two schools of thought as "the thirty years war between ethnology and anthropology: 1830–60" (Tax, 1966: 10). This tension not only shaped the distinct sciences but also led to the demarcation of specific practices.

Rival societies appeared. For example, there was the "Anthropological Society of Paris," founded in 1859 by Paul Broca, a renowned anatomist, craniologist, scholar of human biology, and defender of polygenist theories. Broca postulated that observable human differences were a direct result of differences in racial structure. He and his colleagues of the "French Craniological School," including Franz Josef Gall and Paul Topinard, believed in the thesis of the "immutability of races" and made cases for their beliefs, citing parallels between the infertility of mules and the possibility of mulatto infertility (Broca, 1864). For them the primary element of analysis was the cranium; by studying the human skull one could prove the interrelation between physical and mental inferiority. Because of the belief that "miscegenized species" were sterile, human hybridization was thought to be condemnable. Broca hoped to arrive at the reconstruction of racial "types," or "pure races."

Samuel George Morton, a scientist in the "American School of Polygenism" and a disciple of Louis Agassiz, made similar arguments. After analyzing cranial data from various samplings of craniums from the United States and Egypt in his two studies, *Crania americana* (1839) and *Crania aegyptya* (1844), he established both physical and moral parallels between the populations of the two countries.

During the same era ethnological societies were founded in Paris, London, and New York. These associations adhered both to monogenism and to the philosophy of Rousseau. Their goals were both social and political and reflected their roots in the first French centers that grew out of the egalitarian models of liberal revolutions.

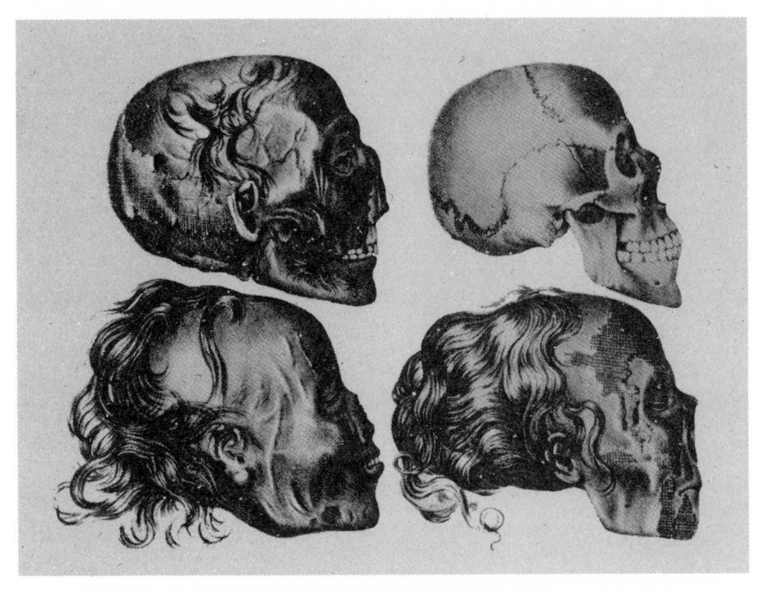

Craniums from Egyptian catacombs
(G. MORTON, 1844)

The fundamental differences in how these rival institutions defined and understood humanity were that while the "anthropological societies" preached the notion of the "immutability of human types"—and the notion of the limits of societies themselves—the "ethnological" groups remained loyal to the hypothesis of the "evolutionary perfection of the races."[11]

Evolution as Paradigm

It was only with the publication and dissemination of *On the Origin of Species* in 1859 that the controversy between polygenism and monogenism began to subside. Charles Darwin had made good use of his predecessors' ideas, as well as those of other like-minded people who supported the key points of his theory.[12] Indeed, the impact of the publication of his work was such that his theory came to serve as a kind of paradigm for the era. In so doing, it had the effect of tempering old controversies.

On the one hand, adherents to monogenism such as the French naturalist Quatrefage, satisfied with the evolutionist assumption about the single origin of humanity, continued to create hierarchies of peoples and races based on different intellectual and moral measurements. On the other hand, however, polygenist scientists accepted the evidence of common prehistorical ancestors but declared that the human species had been separate for enough time to have produced diverse genetic legacies. The novelty lay not so much in the fact that the two schools of thought incorporated the evolutionist model for their own purposes but that both applied to the concept of race an original connotation that departs from the realm of biology and delves into questions of political and cultural content.

Darwinian tenets were slowly becoming obligatory reference points, signifying an agreed upon theoretical reorientation. In the words of Richard Hofstadter:

> Many scientific discoveries affect ways of living more profoundly than evolution did; but none have had a greater impact on ways of thinking and believing. . . . The Darwinian era seized upon the new theory and attempted to sound its meaning for the several social disciplines. Anthropologists, sociologists, historians, political theorists, and economists were set to pondering what, if anything, Darwinian concepts meant for their own disciplines. (1975: 3–4)

Darwin's book reached a wide public despite its original narrow focus on biology, mainly because he employed an accessible writing style. "This preservation of favourable individual differences and variations, and the destruction of those which are injurious, I have called Natural Selection, or Survival of the Fittest" (1859/1963: 60), he declared after analyzing mutations occurring in plant and animal species.[13]

There are many interpretations of *On the Origin of Species* that depart from the outline originally sketched by Charles Darwin and use the basic concepts and propositions of the work for analyzing behavior in human societies.[14] Concepts such as "competition," "survival of the fittest," "evolution," and "heredity" have been applied to the diverse areas of knowledge: in psychology, with H. Magnus and his theory of colors, which assumed a natural hierarchy in the organization of shades of color (1877); in linguistics, with Franz Bopp and his search for the common roots of language (1867); in pedagogy, with studies on child development; and in naturalist literature, with the introduction of characters and plots created to be consistent with the determinist theories of the era. And this list does not even include the evolutionist sociology of Herbert Spencer and the determinist history of Henry Thomas Buckle.

For the political world, Darwinism provided a theoretical basis for conservatism. The links that joined this model to European imperialism are well known. Darwinism in this context employed the notion of "natural selection" as an explanation and justification for domination by the West, which was "stronger and better adapted" than other cultures (Hobsbawm, 1975 and 1987; Néré, 1975; Tuchman, 1966).

This application of natural selection to other disciplines also influenced social thought of this period, giving a new tone to old theoretical debates. While cultural ethnographers were adapting the monogenist point of view to new evolutionist claims,[15] social Darwinists were reviving polygenist perspectives from the beginning of the century with renewed vigor. Thus it became necessary to consider how long the process of "natural selection" had been occurring in human history, as well as how it related to the new reality that announced itself: racial blending.

The mixing of races in the polygenist view presented a fundamental question and was viewed as a recent phenomenon. According to this interpretation, mestizos were the embodiment of the fundamental difference between the races, and they personified the "degeneracy" that would develop from the crossing of "different species." A broad range of arguments coexisted beneath the umbrella of this notion. While Broca wrongly and naïvely defended the idea that, like the mule, the mestizo was infertile, determinist theorists such as Arthur de Gobineau and Gustave Le Bon argued the inverse, lamenting the extraordinary fertility of those populations, and that people of mixed race always inherited the most negative characteristics of the blended races. The relatively recent appearance of New World miscegenation seemed to fortify the polygenist thesis, while revealing hitherto unknown facets of it. In total, the human races, as "diverse species," were to see their hybridization as a phenomenon to be avoided.

It was sufficient to the followers of polygenism and its biology-based models to minimize the importance of common origins and acknowledge determinist tenets, present within Darwinism, that emphasized the importance of natural laws and designs.[16] Within polygenism, the notion of *natural selection* implied belief in *social degeneracy*. Likewise, *natural laws* appeared ominous and tinged with determinism, above all when they dealt with the impact that racial mixing would have on the experience of different nations. A single theory laid the foundation for the diverse interpretations of race at Brazil's institutes of higher learning, and these institutes fought for the honor of speaking for the era.

Cultural Anthropology: Inequality Explains Hierarchy

Cultural anthropology, also known as *social ethnology,* employed the perspective of evolutionism in its primary mission, which was the study of culture. For cultural anthropologists such as Lewis H. Morgan, E. B. Tylor, and James George Frazer, who at the time were also labeled social evolutionists, the primary concern was comparing the cultural development of various peoples. Through their studies they hoped to capture the rhythm of human sociocultural growth and, by means of analogy, to fashion schemata of broad applicability that would explain the common evolution of humans throughout history.

Civilization and progress, period buzzwords as they were in Brazil, were not understood as goals that were unique to a particular society; they were universal models. According to the social evolutionists, culture had evolved everywhere in successive stages, characterized by specific economic and social organizations. Since all peoples had to pass through them, these evolutionary stages were understood to be specific and obligatory, and human cultures followed a determined and immutable path from one stage to the next, always progressing from the most simple to the most complex and differentiated. On the other hand, the comparative method that the cultural anthropologists used worked as an organizing principle for their efforts, in that it supposed that each element could be separated from its original context and then inserted into a determined phase or stage of humanity. Without trying to exhaust the characteristics of this social evolutionist model, at this point it is sufficient to recall the optimistic principles of this way of thinking, which understood progress as being obligatory and held fast to the notion of a single humanity.[17]

Social Darwinism: Humanity Bound

Two great determinist schools exerted their influence in parallel with social evolutionism. The first was the *geographical determinist* school. Its primary spokespeople were Friedrich Ratzel and Henry Thomas Buckle, who argued that the cultural development of a nation was wholly conditioned by its physical environment. For the authors of this school, analyzing the conditions of each country was sufficient to make an objective evaluation of its sources of wealth and consequent "causes of civilization": "wealth . . . will be found to depend entirely on soil and climate. . . . [and] there is no instance in history of any country being civilized by its own efforts, unless it has possessed one of these conditions in a very favourable form" (Buckle, 1865: 33).

Another school of determinism, *racial determinism,* gathered strength at the same time.[18] Called "social Darwinism," or "racial theory," this new perspective disparaged miscegenation, holding that acquired traits were not transmitted, not even by means of social evolution; that is, that the races constituted finished phenomena, immutable results, and every hybridization was, in principle, a misstep. Social Darwinism had a dual effect in branding the products of miscegenation: "pure racial specimens" enjoyed an exalted status reserved for those not "tainted" by the process of miscegenation; and crossbreeding acquired a stigma defined as degenerate, not only in racial terms but in social terms as well.

In opposition to humanistic notions and the conclusions of ethnological schools, racial determinism had its roots in three basic propositions upheld by the teachings of a biological model of anthropology.[19] The first tenet affirmed the reality of the races, between which loomed the same distance to be found between the horse and the ass; this tenet also presupposed a condemnation of racial mixing. The second tenet established a necessary connection between physical and moral character, determining that the division of the world by races would correspond to a division by cultures. The third tenet pointed to the influence of the ethnic or "racio-cultural" group on the behavior of the individual based on a doctrine of collective psychology that denied the idea of individual free will.

Underlying these theories about the races was a "political ideal," a prognosis for the submission or even the possible elimination of the presumed inferior races. This ideal led to eugenics, the goal of which was to intervene in the reproductive processes of populations. In 1883 the British scientist Francis Galton coined the term *eugenics,* derived from the Greek words *eu* [good]

ANTHROPOMETRIC LABORATORY

For the measurement in various ways of Human Form and Faculty.

Entered from the Science Collection of the S. Kensington Museum.

This laboratory is established by Mr. Francis Galton for the following purposes:—

1. For the use of those who desire to be accurately measured in many ways, either to obtain timely warning of remediable faults in development, or to learn their powers.

2. For keeping a methodical register of the principal measurements of each person, of which he may at any future time obtain a copy under reasonable restrictions. His initials and date of birth will be entered in the register, but not his name. The names are indexed in a separate book.

3. For supplying information on the methods, practice, and uses of human measurement.

4. For anthropometric experiment and research, and for obtaining data for statistical discussion.

Charges for making the principal measurements:

THREEPENCE each, to those who are already on the Register.
FOURPENCE each, to those who are not:— one page of the Register will thenceforward be assigned to them, and a few extra measurements will be made, chiefly for future identification.

The Superintendent is charged with the control of the laboratory and with determining in each case, which, if any, of the extra measurements may be made, and under what conditions.

[illegible]

Announcement from Francis Galton's Anthropometric Laboratory, offering persons the opportunity to determine developmental defects through craniological measurement

(DISPLAYED IN THE INTERNATIONAL HEALTH EXPOSITION IN LONDON, 1884) and *genus* [birth, origin, race]. Galton was best known at the time for his work as a naturalist and as a geographer specializing in statistics. He wrote his first essay on human heredity in 1865 after having read *On the Origin of Species,* and in 1869 he published *Hereditary Genius*. With that book he founded the study of eugenics. Using a statistical and genealogical method, Galton sought to prove that human capacity was a function not of education but of heredity: "I propose to show in this book, that a man's natural abilities are derived by inheritance [and to suggest that] it would be quite practicable to produce a highly gifted race of men by judicious marriages during several consecutive generations" (Galton, 1869/1972: 45). Eugenics would thus seek to identify precisely the physical characteristics associated with certain social groups. Then prohibitions would be placed on interracial marriages, and restrictions would be imposed on "alcoholics, epileptics and lunatics" with the aim of producing a more "perfect" population, with greater genetic equilibrium.

Transformed into a vigorous scientific and social movement in the 1880s, eugenics pursued several goals. As a science it promoted a new understanding of the laws of human heredity, and through its application the population would see "desirable and controlled births." As a social movement, eugenics promoted marriages within explicit groups and, perhaps most important, discouraged certain unions considered detrimental to society.

At the same time the eugenics movement stimulated a scientific and rational treatment of heredity and introduced a new social politics of intervention that featured deliberate social selection (Stepan, 1991: 1–2).[20] The determinist social politics of eugenics was evident, and it also revealed incompatibilities between cultural evolutionism and social Darwinism. Indeed, this aspect of eugenics brought the evolutionist hypothesis back to earth. Adherents to the eugenics movement believed that civilization was humanity's fate, since the term *degeneracy* gradually took the ground previously occupied by the concept of evolution as the best metaphor to explain the paths and detours of Western progress.[21] For the social Darwinist authors, progress applied only to "pure" societies, those untouched by miscegenation. In these societies evolution was relentless.

Citing examples from world history to reinforce their arguments, the eugenists believed that the positive development of a nation was primarily a result of the racial purity of its people. European evolution, especially Aryan, represented for theorists such as Arthur de Gobineau an extreme case in which racial refinement had proceeded along a straight course that led directly toward civilization.[22] On the other hand, according to Samuel George Morton (1844), because of the widespread miscegenation that took place beginning in the ninth century B.C., Egypt had already known a period of decadence.

The polygenist assertion also had bases in biological science. Although it gathered strength from Darwin's theory, in truth, polygenist thought subverted its origins.[23] These determinists declared that the offspring of a hybrid marriage would always be more frail or degenerate. Even worse, that offspring would bear the defects but none of the virtues of either of the forebears.

Although it acquired multiple meanings, the hoary eighteenth-century notion of "perfectibility" persisted into the nineteenth century. This idea touched on not an intrinsic human quality but an attribute characteristic of "civilized races" that lean toward civilization. On the other hand, the concept acquired a unique and directed sense, since it appeared that only one model of "perfectibility" was possible, and that any other course led to degeneracy.

Other concepts of the time underwent redefinition as well. *Inequality* and *difference,* terms that common sense accepts as synonymous, came to represent diverse positions and principles of analysis. The notion of inequality implied the continuity of the humanistic concept of an indivisible human entity, marked only by accidental and random dissimilarities. Human diversity was perceived as transitory and mutable either over time or through cultural contact. The concept of difference was used in connection with the suggestion that ontologically diverse human species existed, races that did not share a single evolutionary line. Based on this theory, the differences observed in human peoples would be, therefore, definitive and permanent. Equality wouldn't be worth discussing anymore, because it would be like comparing apples and oranges.

These terms and concepts also differed according to how they served the two schools of the period. For the social evolutionists, humans were "unequal" among themselves or, rather, humans were hierarchically unequal in their global development. For the social Darwinists, humanity was divided into species that were forever marked by their "differences" and into races whose potentials would be ontologically dissimilar. Therefore, within this context and with the growth of the debate, one can discern two clearly defined groups. Gathered around the ethnological societies, on the one hand, were the social ethnologists, also called social evolutionists or cultural anthropologists, who were exponents of monogenism and of the unitarian vision of humanity. Affiliated with centers of physical anthropology, on the other hand, were the social Darwinist researchers, who were loyal to polygenism and to the notion that humanity consisted of fundamentally different species.

Contrary to the tenets of the Enlightenment, and electing the notion of "difference" as a key concept for analysis, the racial theorists proposed a rereading of the history of peoples. There were several polygenist authors at the time who spanned the gap between social Darwinism and racist doctrines. Among them, four scholars stand out as representative of the theories of the time: Ernest Renan, Gustave Le Bon, Hippolyte Taine, and Arthur de Gobineau.

For Ernest Renan (1823–92) three great races existed, the white, the black, and the yellow, each of which had a unique origin and evolution. According to him, the black, yellow, and mixed races "were inferior peoples, not because they were uncivilized, but because they were uncivilizable, imperfectible and not given to progress" (Renan, 1872/1961). Applying the notion of "imperfectible races," Renan crafted a radical theory that negated Darwinism to the extent that it wrote off not only the common origin of humans but also the possibility of imagining a compatible future.

Gustave Le Bon, who was a great popularizer of other people's ideas (Todorov, 1989: 129), contributed his thoughts on a theory that correlated animal species with human races: "Based on anatomical criteria such as the color of the skin and the shape and size of the cranium, it is possible to establish that humankind consists of many distinct species, which in all probability possess very different origins" (Le Bon, 1902: 209). In Le Bon's writings the word *race* began to replace the word *species,* and, likewise, concepts contrary to the Christian idea of monogenism began to achieve broader acceptance. A scholar of the so-called "social psychology," Gustave Le Bon believed that "the substitution of the individual's conscious activity by the group's unconscious action" (1902: 13) was the principal characteristic of the era. The group, understood as a whole, determined individual human behavior.

Another major determinist prophet was Hippolyte Taine (1828–93), for whom no phenomenon occurred without an external stimulus. Taine believed in an overarching determinism, into which any and all human manifestations would fit. He became known, even in his own time, for the contentiousness of his conclusions: *"cette cause donnée, elle apparaît, cette cause retirée, elle disparaît"* [if the cause is present, the phenomenon appears; if the cause is withdrawn, the phenomenon disappears] (1923: 11). In his analyses he turned the opinion of the philosophers of the Enlightenment upside down in that he viewed the individual as being the immediate consequence of his or her group.

Taine was also one of the racial theorists who were partially responsible for transforming the notion of race during the end of the nineteenth century: since it had already assumed a biological explanation, the racial concept then grew to equate race with the idea of nation. Taine complicated the debate further by introducing a more comprehensive determinism. He declared: *"J'entends les nationalités, les climats et les tempéraments, comme un doublet de race"* [I understand nationalities, climates, and temperaments as reflections of race] (1923: 41).

Arthur de Gobineau (1816–82), author of *Essai sur l'inegalité des races humaines* [Essay on the inequality of human races] (1853), was also a believer in an absolute racial determinism, one that granted free will to no individual, one in which "volition held no sway" (1853/1983: 1151). While he shared social Darwinist assumptions, he introduced the idea of "racial degeneracy," which he understood to be the consequence "of the blending of different human species." In fact, Gobineau cut his remaining ties with the monogenist and social evolutionist interpretations to the extent that in his argument he foresaw the impossibility of progress for some societies made up of "mestizo subraces incapable of civilization."[24]

"Interbreeding is always detrimental," said Gobineau, expressing his negative prognoses of polygenism. According to him, the idea of a single and general social evolution appeared to be a mistake, since the "fixed and existing characteristics of the different races" determined the necessity of the perpetuation of "pure strains," unaltered by miscegenation. Therefore, if "civilization" was a stage that could be reached by few races, what was one to say to the mestizos, those of a "decadent and degenerate subrace"?[25]

For Gobineau, if one could not hope for much from certain "inferior races," it was not necessary to fear them. But his view of nations of mixed race was radically different. Compared with the people of pure race who were immutable, the unstable populations derived from the interbreeding of different races were, he believed, "unbalanced and decadent."[26] "A highly gifted and frustrated nobleman," in the words of Hannah Arendt (1966: 170), Gobineau seemed more than anything else a high priest of racism. If, with his extreme pessimism, Gobineau inspired few

European scholars to further research in the agonizing last years of the century,[27] the same cannot be said of his impact in other societies where miscegenation was not mere speculation or an exercise of the imagination but a living reality.

Therefore, according to Arendt, doctrines such as Gobineau's were more important in the shaping of nations than for explaining innate cultural differences: "They [the racists] were the only ones who consistently denied the great principle upon which national organizations of peoples are built, the principle of equality and solidarity of all peoples guaranteed by the idea of mankind" (Arendt, 1973: 161).

Thus miscegenation was becoming a great dividing line between the monogenist concepts of the ethnological schools and the polygenist interpretations typical of the era's physical anthropology studies. Through this oscillation one notes that there was nothing new about the perception of "differences." The only novelty was the "assimilation" of these ideas. That is, it was only in the nineteenth century, with the proliferation of racial theories, that apprehending "differences" between peoples became a theoretical project with universal and globalizing application. "To assimilate the differences" meant to establish rigid correlations between physical characteristics and moral attributes. In the midst of this grandiose project, which aspired to remove human diversity from the uncertain realm of culture and place it within the secure haven of nineteenth-century determinist science, little room was left for individual volition. Powerful models emerged from biology, and it was with the laws of nature that adherents to these theories classified human diversity.

Such models were certainly not the only explanations for the behavior of societies at that moment. One can say, however, that determinist racial models were broadly accepted, especially in Brazil.[28] Racial theory was used in Brazil in an uncommon way in that the social Darwinist interpretation was combined with the evolutionist and monogenist perspectives. It served to explain differences and hierarchies, but, once certain adjustments had been made to the theory, one was not prevented from imagining the survivability of a mestizo nation. This suggests, however, a debate that presumes reflection on how faithful Brazilians were to their sources and how the specifics of theory were present in the national mind, subjects I will examine later.

However, because determinist theory became a vernacular common to the 1930s, a study of all Brazilian intellectuals who worked on the racial question becomes almost impossible. I have chosen, therefore, to treat the authors not separately but as individuals connected to their respective institutes, which represented, in turn, a larger context of intellectual discourse. In these research centers "men of science" enjoyed an environment that was conducive to the production and dissemination of their ideas and theories. One should bear in mind that at the end of the nineteenth century these institutes of higher learning were both highly selective and venerated for their intellectual status. Despite how diverse these institutes were in their internal characteristics and how distinct they were in their functions, studying them helps one to build a broad panorama of the Brazilian intellectual elites of the era, to understand the range of philosophies and thinkers, as well as to reconstruct the logic of their racial models.

Finally, the internal publications organized by the different institutes are a fundamental source for studying the issue of race in Brazil. Serving the function of "calling cards," scientific reviews, which were wellsprings of communication between the various institutes, were essential to establishing a profile of each center, as well as for distilling the intellectual debates of the moment.

In the ethnological museums, historical institutes, and schools of law and medicine, the discussion of race assumed a pivotal role, and analyzing these centers, from which dissenting though contemporary voices emerged, provided fertile ground to work. Through their appraisal one can review the meandering routes that the racial doctrines roved.[29]

3

ETHNOGRAPHIC MUSEUMS IN BRAZIL

"Clams Are Clans, and Mollusks Are Men as Well"

The end of the nineteenth century has been called "The Age of Museums" because that era saw a series of ethnographic museums flourish, all of them closely linked to biological criteria of investigation and to evolutionist models of analysis (William Sturtevant quoted in Stocking, 1985). From 1870 to 1930 the national museums—the São Paulo Museum, the National Museum, and the Emilio Goeldi Museum of Pará—played important roles in ethnographic research and the study of the so-called natural sciences.[1] Toward an understanding of the roles of these museums, we will focus not only on the specific development of each of these museums but also on the broader intellectual context of the era. The discussion of the institutes will provide insights into the debate that the ethnographic museums established with the nation's other centers of higher learning.

THE "AGE OF MUSEUMS"

> Our project is an encyclopedic museum that gathers evidence from the whole of human knowledge.
> —*Herman von Ihering (1885)*

Museums derive their name from the muses of ancient temples, but the configuration of the Brazilian ethnographic institutes under consideration here is associated with another moment and definition. According to Jacques Le Goff (1984: 37–39), the museums of the late nineteenth and early twentieth centuries were linked to the written and figurative memory of the Renaissance and to the logic of a new self-documenting civilization. The nineteenth century would see a new seduction of memory, an explosion of the commemorative spirit.

Two trends were noteworthy at this time: at the same time that the scientific movement embraced the idea of the recovery of national memory, national monuments to memory proliferated. The French Revolution spawned the National Archives, the creation of which, on July 25, 1874, served in large part to help define the nation's character. A similar process occurred in other countries as well, with the establishment of centralized archives in Turin, Saint Petersburg, Venice, and Florence, for example.

This era saw the launching of a series of museums whose character, unlike that of earlier museums, was wholly commemorative. The Louvre (1773) and the Prado Museum (1783) are examples of the beginning of the "era of public and national museums." These first institutions, better known as *cabinets de curiosité* [curiosity cabinets], served, as the term suggests, more as settings for displaying objects for public admiration than as institutions for teaching and scientific research.

Ethnographic museums dedicated to the collection, preservation, exhibition, study, and interpretation of material objects appeared only in the nineteenth century. The Renaissance curiosity that had marked the exploration of Asia and the New World found a home in these new museums, which were evolving into centers of an embryonic anthropology.

The British Museum, founded in 1753, was the first such institution to touch on this new anthropological purpose, primarily with its collection from the expeditions of Captain Cook. But it was not until the nineteenth century that the museum trend gathered rapid momentum, with the near simultaneous creation of a series of museums and societies including the Saint Petersburg Ethnographic Museum of Sciences (1836), the National Museum of Ethnology in Leiden (1837), and the Peabody Museum of Archaeology and Ethnology at Harvard University (1866). From that time forward one sees two distinct models for these institutions. Some followed the Peabody example, which focused on prehistory, archeology, and ethnology. Others, primarily the continental European museums, were created as centers of national and popular culture (Stocking, 1985: 8).

These museums developed slowly, however. They began to flower only after 1890, after they established norms and operating procedures and redefined their mission statements. The ethnological museums soon became well-ordered collections of a canonized culture subject to evolving schools of thought. Comparison and classification became the goals of their scientists, true "philosopher travelers,"[2] who, with the financial backing of scientific institutions, set off for distant lands in search of representative collections of flora and fauna as well as insights into and evidence of human ethnology.

If the first museums were a product of the Enlightenment, the ethnographic institutes dated from an era when European imperialism was waning. Ironically, the same moment that marked the weakening of colonial dominion favored the creation of these museums, which preserved artifacts of the non-European world.[3]

Similar museums appeared in Brazil, and, like their European counterparts, these centers existed to fulfill specific roles. As copies of their European models, they were to establish a relatively isolated realm of influence in relation to the other national scientific institutes, and they communicated primarily with European and North American museums. On the other hand, as they adopted evolutionist and social Darwinist models, they began to take part, in a very specific way, in the debate that was being waged over the future of this young nation.

The 1890s, the "Brazilian age of museums," coincided with the peak of other international institutions. Although their founding dates differ—the National Museum began in 1808, the Emilio Goeldi Museum of Pará in 1866, the São Paulo Museum in 1894—the periods of their creation are basically the same.[4] During the "age of museums," the museums created rules and procedures, identified collections, and established their professional presence.

Even before the advent of scientific museums, Brazil had already been the destination of innumerable expeditions and research projects by foreign naturalists. Beginning most notably in the nineteenth century, Italians, Spaniards, French, Germans, and Americans travelled throughout the country in search of specimens for their collections. Since these travellers believed that the cultures they were studying would soon be wiped out, the order of the day was to save as much as possible so that the "remains" of these cultures might be preserved in metropolitan museums.

It is important to underscore that the creation of local museums in Brazil was linked to external intellectual pressures. Long before a debate began about the establishment of institutions of higher learning in Brazil, the country was already considered an exceptional site for gathering collections and the raw materials necessary for European museums. Once the Brazilian institutions were in place, they served as a refuge for travellers financed by foreign museums and for the development of an embryonic anthropology.

Until the middle of the nineteenth century, all scientific research in Brazil was carried out by non-Brazilians who came for the sole purpose of collecting. According to the Brazilian educator Fernando Azevedo, neither the government nor Brazilian institutes of higher learning had the interest or the resources necessary to finance expeditions. In his words, "we were in a period of improvisation and dilettantism" (1956: 367). But beginning in the 1870s the intellectual environment in Brazil began to change. At the same time that new scientific models were appearing, various centers of research and teaching were gathering strength, and by association the national museums also derived benefit.

THE NATIONAL MUSEUM OR THE ROYAL MUSEUM
"A National Scientific Museum"

> Each century has a mission to fulfill, just as each person has his or her role to play in the theater of life or in the fabric of society. The mission for this century is to universalize science and amalgamate its peoples.
>
> —*João Batista Lacerda* (1876)

The National Museum in Rio de Janeiro became profoundly associated with Dom João VI because the museum was founded in the same year that the king fled Portugal and installed his court in Brazil. The museum was part of a package of cultural measures implemented by a decree of the Portuguese monarch on July 6, 1808,[5] and its function was "to stimulate botanical and zoological studies in the area."

Installed in the building now occupied by the National Archive, the museum housed a small collection donated by Dom João VI, consisting of artworks, engravings, mineralogical specimens, indigenous artifacts, stuffed animals, and natural products. Although it was enriched by further donations, the museum suffered, as did the other institutions created by the monarch. The National Museum was an "institution by decree," without deep roots to sustain it, and it was far removed from the scientific methods of European institutions. Its role was primarily commemorative; it was an archive of collections and curiosities, exhibited without any method of classification.

The museum defined itself as an institution dedicated to the disciplines of zoology, botany, and geology, as is evident in Article 1 of the "Museum Regulations": "The National Museum is dedicated to the study of natural history, with special attention to Brazil, and to the teaching of physical and natural sciences." The museum favored the employment of Brazilian scientists, and this fact underscores its nationalistic perspective. Whether reflecting its preference for filling the directors' seats,[6] or its favoritism in selecting articles to appear in its journal, with this posture the National Museum introduced a new variable into this "world of museums."

In the view of João Batista Lacerda, the National Museum was slower to develop than its contemporary counterparts in Europe for two main reasons: Brazil had no colonies to conquer and pillage to establish collections, and the country had limited financial resources to allocate to the National Museum. It was only with the administrations of Ladislau Netto (1874–93) and João Batista Lacerda (1895–1915) that the museum adopted structures like those of the great European centers.[7] In 1876 Netto reorganized the museum, and at the same time he founded a journal, *Archives of the National Museum*. Published three times a year, this journal was necessary for communicating and collaborating with foreign museums.

A New Museum and a New Journal

> Fortunate is the museum that receives the strength necessary to confront evil and defeat it . . . thus it will avenge once more that collective organization . . . its far-spreading and lamentable lethargy. . . . Practitioners of science weary of the wait have fallen asleep. . . . With its new and auspicious constitution, the National Museum prepares from this time forward to join the scientific societies and congresses of civilization. (*Archives of the National Museum*, 1876: 1)

With this solemn address, Ladislau Netto heralded the museum's renewal and at the same time inaugurated its new journal. His words pointed to the institution's new scientific stance and signified its entry into the world of museums, into a circle of intense dialogue generated primarily by publications.

The first issue of *Archives of the National Museum,* published in 1876, listed, even before its formal introduction, the journal's advisory board.[8] Of the forty-four people named, only three were Brazilians (the Viscount of Bom Retiro, Thomas Coelho de Almeida, and D. S. Ferreira Penna). Among the other names there appeared such foreign notables as Paul Broca, Charles Darwin, Armand de Quatrefage, and L. R. Turlaine, all of whom helped lend credibility to the museum and its journal within the international scientific community. Consistent with the style of other publications of national museums, in its opening pages the journal recognized foreign naturalists and thereby established the museum's contact with foreign intellectuals and also declared that the institution and its journal were fully engaged in international scientific debate.

Next came the introductions of the three members of the publication's board,[9] with a listing of their specializations, and a general overview of the subject areas of the journal: "(1) Anthropology, general and applied zoology and animal paleontology; (2) General and applied botany and plant paleontology; (3) Physical sciences: mineralogy, geology and paleontology."

An analysis of the breakdown of the journal's contents over the first twenty-four years (1876–1930) reveals the limited space devoted to anthropology, contrasted with the absolute dominance of articles about the so-called natural sciences (77 percent). More specifically, while essays on zoology totalled 44 percent of all texts published in the journal, those on botany made up 19 percent, followed by those on geology, with 14 percent of the total. The remaining articles were on anthropology (14 percent) and archeology (9 percent); in addition to being quite short, these articles appear to be rather uncontroversial. (See Table 2.) The articles on

Table 2 Distribution of Articles in the Archives of the National Museum *by Discipline and Year of Publication*

YEAR	BOT.	ZOO.	GEO.	ANTHRO.	ARCH.	TOTAL
1876	3	1	1	3	5	13
1877	1	4	1		1	7
1878		2	3			5
1879		3	2	3		8
1880	1					1
1885			1	2	1	4
1887		1				1
1892	4					4
1895	1		2			3
1897	1	1		1		3
1901	1	1			2	4
1903		7	3	2		12
1905	1	4				5
1907		5				5
1909	1	4	1			6
1911		1				1
1915		1				1
1916	5	1		1		7
1916(b)	1	2		2		5
1917/18		1		1		2
1918/20	3	5	3	2	1	14
1923/25	1	11	1	1	2	16
1926	1	4	1			6
TOTAL	25	59	19	18	12	133

Key: Bot. = Botany; Zoo. = Zoology; Geo. = Geology; Anthro. = Anthropology; Arch. = Archeology

ARCHIVES OF THE NATIONAL MUSEUM, 1876–1926, VOLS. 1–23.

archeology covered primarily methods and vestiges of material culture that were of little importance, while the essays on anthropology presented physical evidence, founded on models of craniometry. Indeed, the museum considered anthropology to be a branch of the biological and natural sciences.

An analysis of the authors of the journal articles is also illuminating. Brazilian scientists, and especially naturalists who held prominent positions in the museum, dominated the journal. Particularly prolific authors were João Batista Lacerda, Ladislau Netto, and, after 1907, Alípio Miranda. (See Table 3.)

The Study of the New "Anthropological Science"

Because of the credentials of the journal's writers, and despite the museum's formal title, the institution bore more relation to a museum of natural sciences than to anything else. Even the few journal articles that embraced social themes did so from a biological and physical perspective. Such is the case with the essays written by João Batista Lacerda about the "anthropology of indigenous races in Brazil."

When the National Museum was the first institution in the country to offer a course of study in anthropology, it revealed its ideas about what constituted the discipline. The focus of the program was the study of human anatomy, which should come as no surprise since João Batista Lacerda, the museum's head since 1877, had affirmed that "psycho-anatomical knowledge forms the basis of anthropology" (*Archives of the National Museum,* 1877: 110). In this discipline the measurement of craniums was of primary interest.

In the very first issue of the museum's journal, Lacerda chose to study the Botocudos, a central Brazilian Indian tribe. He used eleven brains, deposited in the museum long before, as "samples of the tribe." His article began with a long introductory digression about "world anthropology" and its contributions:

Table 3 Distribution of Articles in the Archives of the National Museum *by Author and Year of Publication*

YEAR	NETTO	LACERDA	HARTT	MULLER	MIRANDA
1876	2	3	2		
1877	1	3		3	
1878		1		1	
1879		2		3	
1880					
1885	1	1	1		
1887					
1892				3	
1895					
1897					
1901		1			
1903		1			
1905					4
1907		1			4
1909		4			1
1911					1
1915					1
1916					1
1926					1
TOTAL	4	17	3	10	13

ARCHIVES OF THE NATIONAL MUSEUM, 1876–1926, VOLS. 1–23.

It has been a century, at the very most, that anthropology, the youngest of the sciences, has offered a new scholarly field of investigation. Within this period Blumenbach has accumulated a great deal of craniometrical research to establish the differences between human races, and Buffon has established the bases of natural human sciences and defined ethnography or the description of societies.

> Following this line . . . Retzius, Pritchard, Wagner . . . have competed to strengthen their positions in anthropology. (*Archives of the National Museum,* 1876: 47)

In this way Lacerda not only listed the principal proponents of the new "anthropological science," which he considered to be a branch of biology; he also launched a frontal attack on social ethnography, which was characterized at the time as an unscientific practice whose primary interest was the mere description of societies. But Lacerda did not limit himself to a critique of European work. After lamenting the absence of Brazilian research, he turned his attention to North American scientists such as Morton and Moreno, whose research examined the physical characteristics of human subjects and affirmed what was seen as the unyielding fact that humans are essentially different.

Then, using Broca's French phrenological resources, Lacerda described the difficulties in working with this kind of material:

> One must struggle against the superstitious ideas of the Indians on one hand and with the scruples of the missionaries on the other . . . in order to procure an indigenous skull, [and Lacerda concluded that] because of their limited capacity, the Botocudos should be placed on a level with the New Caledonians and Australians, among the races most notable for their class of intellectual inferiority. Their aptitudes are indeed quite limited, and it would be difficult to assimilate them into mainstream civilization. (*Archives of the National Museum,* 1887: 53)

In this manner the author joined the evolutionist fray that was endeavoring to find "missing links" among isolated cultures, evidence that would reveal "civilization's infancy." Reiterated several times, the conclusion was inevitable: "We are dealing with a very low level on the human scale, and we can equate

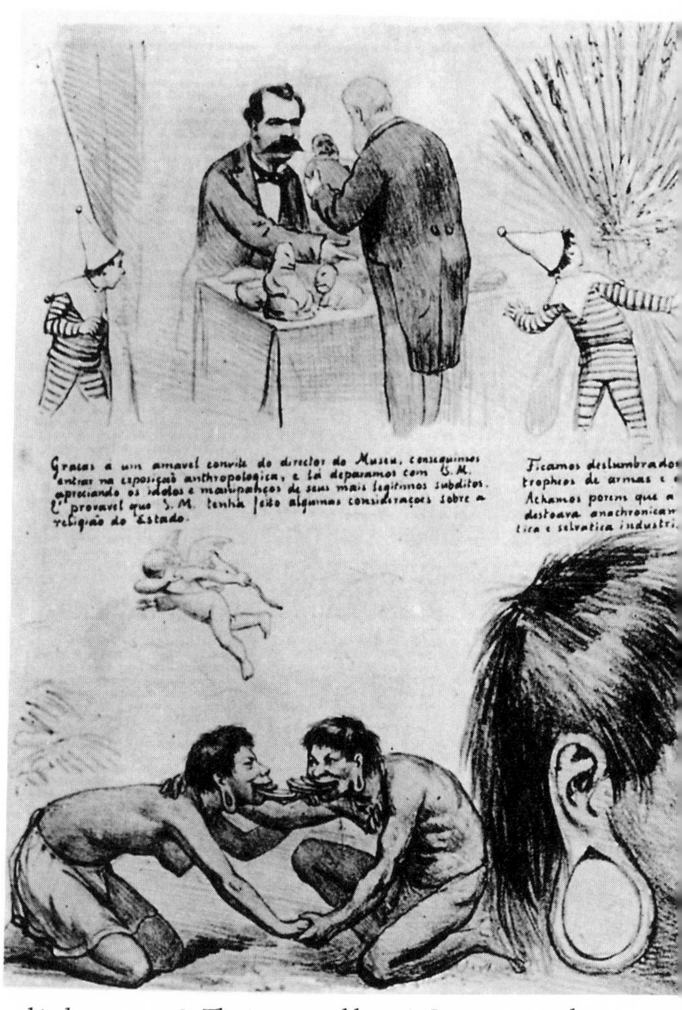

1. *Thanks to a kind invitation from the Director of the Museum, we managed to enter the anthropological exhibit, and we met with S.M. admiring the idols and fetishes of his most genuine subjects. It is likely that S.M. had drawn some conclusions about the state religion.*

2. *The innumerable artifacts of arms and indigenous objects astonished us. We thought, however, that the imperial cloak clashed anachronistically next to the savage native handicrafts.*

3. *It seems to us that if our imperial host added some feathers to his imperial regalia of toucan breast feathers he would certainly look the part of a fine imperial chief.*

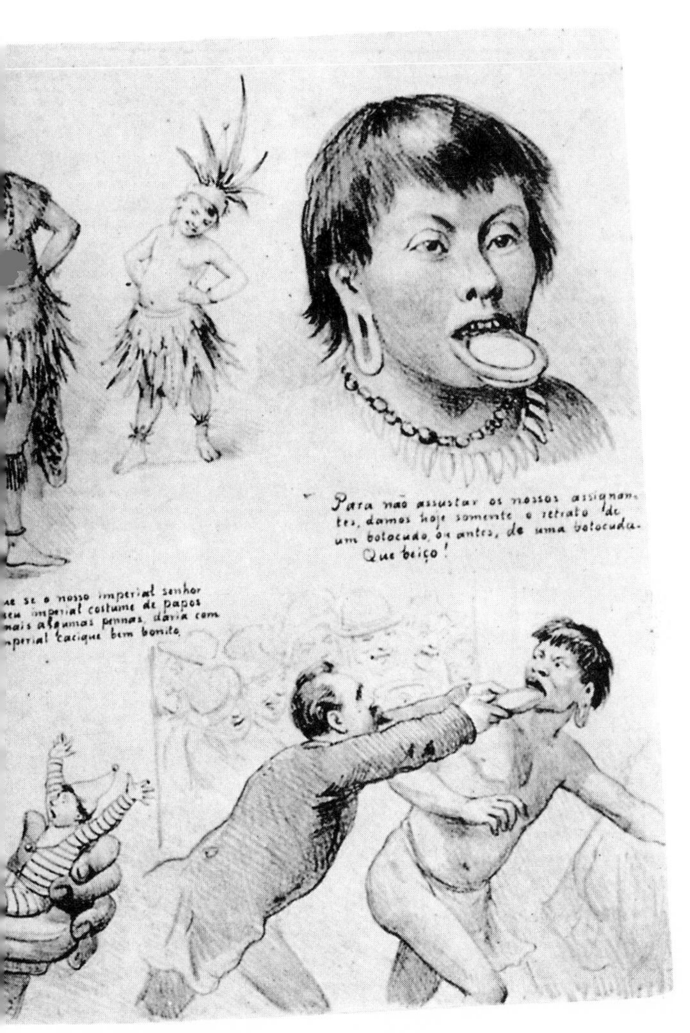

4. *So as not to frighten our subscribers, today we offer the portrait of just one Botocudo or, more precisely, a Botocudo woman. What a lip!*
5. *Imagine two Botocudos in love, and kissing! How lovely!*
6. *But when we recall that they placed a poor Christian on a plate the size of a lip and they gobbled him up as though he were a bean and sausage stew! . . . How horrifying!*
7. *But who could say! These cannibals feared being consumed by public curiosity. Only with some effort did the Museum Director keep them from running off.*

these peoples to other savage societies about which we know today" (*Archives of the National Museum,* 1885: 185).[10]

Here Lacerda departed dramatically from the Romantic notion of the Indian. The Indians of coastal Brazil, known as the Tupi, had been held up as living evidence of Rousseau's "noble savage." In contrast, Lacerda presented what he called the "savage" Botocudos. As "Indians of science," as favorite objects of study, this tribe came to represent the lack of civilization, the base of the human pyramid that had been erected according to evolutionist ideals.[11] It is also interesting to note how he combined theories that were fundamentally inconsistent with one another. Lacerda,[12] an ardent advocate of polygenism, believed in the existence of various sources of human creation (*Archives of the National Museum,* 1887: 75), but he continued to suppose that evolution moved only in the direction of civilization.

Reinaugurated in the mid-1870s, the National Museum represents one example of a national professional museum that structured itself in the image of foreign centers of higher education. Adopting these ideas only in part, and weakened by its lack of personnel, the Rio de Janeiro museum was a complex institution whose traits will emerge more clearly when they are compared to other similar institutions.

THE SÃO PAULO MUSEUM OR THE YPIRANGA MUSEUM
"Science Comes to São Paulo"

We have no university today in our country, nor even an academy or school of natural sciences. Under these conditions it is not difficult to explain the backward state in which we find the study of natural sciences in Brazil.

—*Herman von Ihering (1895)*

According to the official version, the creation of a museum in São Paulo was first associated with the idea of erecting a grandiose monument in honor of Brazil's independence. Following the commemorative ceremonies on September 7, 1824, Lucas Antônio Monteiro Barros, in his capacity as provincial president, and with the approval of Dom Pedro I, solicited voluntary contributions for the new museum. The local political elite, not recognizing any practical use for such a center, withheld both its support and its contributions. Because of a financial shortfall the project did not go forward. New efforts to finance the museum through lottery proceeds began in the 1870s. This was the era of the "Ypiranga Lottery," whose goals were destined to be unattained once the Provincial Assembly began to redirect profits to address "social ends of most pressing need" (Gomes, quoted in Paiva, 1984: 10).

Nevertheless, with the growing economic wealth of the region, the idea of founding a museum in São Paulo gathered support. The presence of such an institution would link the region to the capital and symbolize the entry of this up-and-coming province on the national stage. Finally, in March 1885, in honor of the emancipation of the Brazilian slaves, and by approval of Dom Pedro II, José Luiz d'Almeida Couto contracted the Italian architect Tommaso Gaudenzio Bezzi to begin the project.

The construction of the museum was completed in 1890 despite countless misfortunes. But the building remained unoccupied for a while. Designed in a pompous classical style, the edifice looked more like a palace than a museum, and it was wholly unsuited to the needs of an educational institution. Conducting scientific and pedagogical activities in the building was impractical, and the only function that the São Paulo Museum served was as a historical monument.

In 1893 the São Paulo Museum acquired the Joaquim Sertório collections, consisting of specimens of natural history, pieces of furniture, newspapers, and indigenous artifacts, and the museum was inaugurated with these items on July 26, 1894. In the same year, and at the suggestion of Orville Derby (director of the State Geographical and Geological Commission), the museum hired as its director the zoologist Herman von Ihering, known for his achievement in international debates.[13] With his leadership a new museum emerged, whose objective was, in von Ihering's words, "the study, by scientific means, of the natural history of South America and, in particular, of Brazil."

A Museum "Built on a Truly Scientific Basis"

Using evolutionist knowledge as a base, and following the biological sciences model of classification, von Ihering invested the São Paulo Museum with a professional character, derived from and consistent with the great European institutions. In 1895 the first issue of the *Journal of the São Paulo Museum* appeared, reflecting both the museum's character and the individualized program of its director. Part of that program was an "encyclopedic museum" project with the goal of assembling samples of the whole of human knowledge (Paiva, 1984: 13).[14]

In addition to featuring an illustration of the museum's façade, the cover of that first issue of the journal listed von Ihering's brief résumé:

> Doctor of Medicine and of Philosophy, Director of the São Paulo Museum, honorary member of the Italian Anthropological Society, the Córdoba Academy of Sciences, the Bremen Geographical Society, the Berlin Anthropological Society, the Philadelphia Academy, the Moscow Society of Naturalists, the Berlin Society of Ethnology, the Leipzig Museum of Ethnology, and the Chilean Scientific Society.

The publication displayed, therefore, even on its frontispiece, not only its mentor's credentials and area of expertise but also a strong hint of international intellectual exchange.

The first issue revealed a great deal about the journal and the museum. Whereas the two first articles dealt with the history of the museum, portraying the institution as a "monument to the glory of São Paulo," von Ihering's article considered the institution's new image. He used this piece of writing as his address at the museum's inauguration:

> Most of the world's museums have their origins in private collections which become government property when they outgrow their space and resources. . . . Examining the history of this museum, we can see that it has developed along the lines of its analogous institutions. . . . Allow us to celebrate with Your Excellency the creation of a museum built on a truly scientific basis, which until now did not exist in Brazil. . . . The objective of our collections is to demonstrate the fascinating nature of South America and Brazil and especially of the South American man. . . . We intend to work with scientific classifications. . . . In this sense we have done little, if anything, to this point. . . . I cannot fail to mention that outside of São Paulo another prosperous countryman created a museum with scientific personnel and upon a foundation even broader than our own. I am referring to the Pará Museum . . . under the able direction of my friend Dr. Goeldi. (*Journal of the São Paulo Museum,* 1895: 19–24)

Beyond the announcement of the driving interest of the museum, von Ihering was proclaiming in his speech a rift among museums. When he stated that the only museum founded on scientific principles was the São Paulo Museum, and when he praised only the Emilio Goeldi Museum of Pará, the zoologist was in effect denouncing the work of the National Museum staff, who at that very time were modernizing their institution.

The response of the National Museum was swift. Lacerda angrily referred to von Ihering's words:

> Dr. von Ihering had his sights on us when in order to establish the scientific rigor of his museum he sought to deceive all innocents as to the value of the Rio de Janeiro Museum, which he deems unworthy of comparison with the São Paulo Museum and the Emilio Goeldi Museum of Pará. . . . Dr. Ihering most certainly hopes for a miracle, given the scant state resources available to him and the museum's small aggregation of collections purchased from a private party. (*Archives of the National Museum,* 1895)

Flouting the meager material circumstances suffered by the São Paulo Museum compared to the magnitude of its visionary mission, the director of the National Museum did not hesitate to comment on the political agenda that emerged through the words of the German scientist: "Of course Dr. von Ihering hopes to bestir the people of São Paulo and to extol his incomparable services to the powers that be. He did well in his work *pro domo sua* [for his own house]."

Beyond the personal quarrels, the importance of the debate centered on the perspective that von Ihering inaugurated—the establishment of a diverse field of endeavor and a new professional presence. As he affirmed: "The museums of this century cannot simply continue the work of those of the last century. Their goals were different, not just with reference to the collections they exhibited but also with reference to their scientific character" (*Journal of the São Paulo Museum,* 1907: 448). In forging this new scientific image, von Ihering chose to use the European and North American institutions as models.

As we have seen, the journal reflected von Ihering's leadership and the character of the museum. But it is important to know that the foreign presence in the journal was profound. The journal itself was fundamentally a collaboration of European naturalists. Brazilian scientists wrote but 1 percent of the articles, and most of the essays appeared in their original language, either English, French, or German. The power of von Ihering's personality was also evident, since during his administration he was responsible for a remarkable 40 percent of the articles published in the journal.

On the basis of the authors' profiles, one can see the complete domination of the journal by the natural sciences. Of the 254 articles catalogued, 180 (70 percent) of them were primarily concerned with zoology—von Ihering's specialization. Because of their heavy use of color plates, zoological studies always merited the most prominent positions within the journal. They appeared so frequently that little space remained for other disciplines: anthropology (10 percent), botany (5 percent), biographies (4 percent), geology and archeology (4 percent).[15] (See Table 4.) As for the journal's quality of scientific publication, in the fields of anthropology and natural sciences it reviewed research and included articles that met high professional standards.

Evolutionism and Controversy

Soon after the São Paulo Museum began operation, anthropology began to emerge as a discipline in Brazil, conforming to the parameters and models of the natural sciences. Studying "primitive man" was not much different from studying local flora and fauna. Indeed, from the official perspective of the São Paulo Museum, the study of humanity was clearly subordinate to certain strains of scientific thought, especially biology; only insofar as anthropology reflected scientific thought did it attract attention. Recognizing the importance of this association, von Ihering declared his certainty that "the evolution one found in nature was exactly identical to that one might apply to humans" (*Journal of the São Paulo Museum,* 1897).

For the purposes of the museum and its journal, anthropology as a discipline was understood to be a branch of zoological and botanical studies, so much so that anthropological themes often appeared in the midst of articles on local flora and fauna. This is what von Ihering suggested when on describing the evolution of Tertiary mollusks he concluded: "in fact, what is important for animals and the natural world is also important for humans in

Table 4 Distribution of Articles in the Journal of the São Paulo Museum *by Theme and Year of Publication*

YEAR	BOTANY	ZOOLOGY	GEOLOGY	ANTHROPOLOGY	ARCHEOLOGY	BIOLOGY	DIVERSE	TOTAL
1895		5			1		4	10
1897		7		1		1		9
1898	2	7	1	1				11
1900		11			1	1		13
1902		6				1		7
1904		6		4	2			12
1907		4	1	3			1	9
1911		14	1	2	1	2		20
1914	1	17				3		21
1918	5	16	1	4	2		3	31
1919		10			2			12
1920		16	1	3				20
1922	1	15	3		1		1	21
1926	1	15	1	1		2		20
1927		20		2		1		23
1929	2	11		4				17
TOTAL	12	180	9	25	10	11	9	256

JOURNAL OF THE SÃO PAULO MUSEUM, 1895–1929, VOLS. 1–16.

their evolution" (*Journal of the São Paulo Museum,* 1902). The assumption was that the biological evolutionist model could serve as a basis for explaining all living things on earth, and in particular for explaining human evolution. Thus von Ihering was working with a social evolutionist interpretation the basis of which was not religious but scientific and positivistic.

But if the dominant tendency in the essays published at the turn of the century was toward this brand of evolutionism, one cannot say the same about later periods. After this, one notices the appearance of social Darwinist authors, whose names can be found in the journal more as bibliographical references than as regular contributors. But, in fact, the influence of social Darwinism is present in von Ihering's position, if more in his public behavior than in his scientific work as such.

The controversy in which the director of the São Paulo Museum became involved in 1911 is well known. The bone of contention surrounded statements that von Ihering published in the newspaper *The State of São Paulo* about the Kaingang Indians, a tribe that lived in the area through which the Northeastern Brazilian Railroad wished to lay track. The zoologist viewed the tribe's presence as an impediment to the "development of civilization and progress" (*The State of São Paulo,* 1911), and he made a public appeal for its extermination.[16]

Despite the control that von Ihering exerted over the museum's journal, he did not express his controversial opinions in that medium, and his reluctance to do so is worthy of note. Even though von Ihering departed from his field of specialization to do battle with social issues in *The State of São Paulo,* his determinist interpretations did not enter the pages of the *Journal of the São Paulo Museum,* at least not in an explicit manner. The defense of a social evolutionist interpretation appeared in articles of anthropology and in analyses of craniometry, but none of this writing extended to social applications.

Von Ihering's piece in *The State of São Paulo* was perhaps the first instance of a "museum scientist" using the newspapers to advocate on behalf of social issues using social Darwinist models as theoretical justification. As a professional scientist, he was the very image of the "pure scientist," immune to the passions of an era when Brazilians were engaged in a process of self-redefinition. Von Ihering introduced in his São Paulo publication the same positions he would submit in the *Journal of the Historical and Geographical Institute of São Paulo* (1911). So if in the latter publication the issue of the extermination of the Kaingang appeared rather more cloaked in historical and scientific garb, in *The State of São Paulo* the irate intellectual showed himself clearly in favor of eradicating a barbarous and degenerate group.[17]

THE EMILIO GOELDI MUSEUM OF PARÁ
"The Light of Science in the Very Midst of the Amazon Jungle"

Throughout the nineteenth century the north of Brazil, and in particular the Amazon Basin, was the site of a series of foreign scientific expeditions. If it was a kind of "naturalists' paradise" for foreigners, the Amazonian region remained, surprisingly, virgin territory for Brazilian scientists.

In 1866 several interested scientists from the state of Pará called for the creation of a national museum of natural history and sought backing from Domingos Soares Ferreira Penna, then secretary of the State of Pará. On October 6, 1866, the Associação Filomática do Pará [Pará Association of Science] was founded with the support of Domingos Soares Ferreira Penna, Jonas Montenegro, and Ladislau de Souza Mello. Ferreira Penna was a geographer, an ethnographer, as well as a regional journalist and politician, but the others had no scientific training.

The association became a museum, located in Belém, with its original members providing governance, led by Ferreira Penna. According to its director, the museum would serve as an academy, since the city did not have any institutions of higher learning or other science-oriented centers. The primary goal of the museum was to study the flora and fauna, the geology, the geography, and the history of the immense Amazonian region (Cunha, 1966: 8).

The process of the institution's founding was not original, but, in this case, the people seeking to create a scientific institution in the middle of the Amazon jungle faced unique difficulties and challenges. The museum met with various misfortunes, and its administrative control passed to the provincial government in 1871. Despite the best efforts of Ferreira Penna, during this transition several scholars resigned, citing insufficient operating budgets and resources, and in the last years of the Empire the museum became a simple public bureau. Finally, representatives of the Legislative Assembly closed the museum's doors in 1888.

But the museum was reinaugurated, owing not only to the "rubber boom" and the economic renewal of the region but also to efforts to transform Belém into a kind of "Paris of the Tropics." The institution as it had been constituted by the state's governor, Dr. Justo Leite Chermont, and its director of Public Instruction, José Veríssimo de Mattos, suffered from its former insufficiencies: a lack of financial resources, institutional objectives, and qualified personnel.

In 1893 Lauro Sodré, then governor, learned that the Swiss naturalist Dr. Emilio Goeldi had resigned from his post at the National Museum, and Sodré decided to hire him. Goeldi became head of the Pará institution on July 9, 1893, and on the next day he mapped out a new framework for the museum. He began by reorganizing the institution into departments of zoology, botany, ethnology, archeology, geology, and mineralogy. He added a library with specialized collections in natural sciences and anthropology, as well as zoological and botanical gardens adjoining the museum.

From that time forward Goeldi tried to make the museum a faithful copy of its European cousins. Toward this end he brought in a series of European naturalists, including Jacques Hubert (botanist), Friedrich Katzer (geologist), Gottfried Hagman (zoologist), Adolph Ducke (zoologist and botanist), Joseph Schonnann (taxidermist), Curt Nimuendaju (ethnologist), and Ernst Lonse (lithographic artist). He also organized two journals: *Boletim do Museu Paraense* [Bulletin of the Pará Museum] and *Memória do Museu Paraense* [Memoirs of the Pará Museum]. At the end of the nineteenth century the museum gained a certain notoriety, partly because of its operations but also because of Goeldi's intervention in the litigation with France over the question of French Guiana, now part of the Brazilian State of Amapá.[18]

An analysis of the first ten volumes (1894–1949) of the *Bulletin of the Pará Museum of Natural History and Ethnography* (from 1906 the *Bulletin of the Emilio Goeldi Museum of Pará*) reveals an extraordinary publication as compared to the journals of similar institutions, and it points to the strengths of the museum's mission.

One takes immediate note of the *Bulletin of the Emilio Goeldi Museum of Pará* both because of its brevity and because of its insistent declarations of its "modesty" in comparison with its peer publications. At the same time these characteristics were associated with the museum officials' intention of making the bulletin a vehicle for entry "into the circle where the international scientific and literary movement operated" (*Bulletin of the Emilio Goeldi Museum of Pará*, 1894: 2). The first page of the journal is curious in this regard. The bulletin begins with a short article, written in English, asking for an "exchange of publications." The article specifies themes of particular interest and reaffirms the journal's request for intellectual exchange, repeating the request in several languages: *"Prière déchange de publications; Bitte um Schriftenaustausch."* By seeking contributions from scientists associated with foreign institutes, the museum underscored its interest in increasing the exposure of its own work. On the second page of the publication Goeldi made a long digression on which language the journal should use, concluding that "since this is a Brazilian publication it should wear our nation's dress. They will say that Japan reflects its progressiveness in its use of French and English; but we respond on our behalf that the

Russians, the Hungarians, and the Danish tend ever more to publish scientific works in their own language."

Besides declaring his desire to contribute to the "development of natural sciences and ethnology in Brazil and South America in general and in the states of Pará and Amazônia in particular," Goeldi concluded by affirming that, in addition to regional studies, the Emilio Goeldi Museum of Pará would "remain fully informed of developments conducted elsewhere, in distant locales . . . by foreign naturalists" (*Bulletin of the Emilio Goeldi Museum of Pará,* 1894: 2). The museum and its journal embraced, therefore, a perspective similar to that of the other museums, its primary focus being on the natural sciences. Regional studies were at its core, but they were colored by the work and concerns of European and North American naturalists.

The general director's inaugural address, published in the first issue of the museum's journal, not only equated the study of science with civilization but also praised travellers to Brazil:

> To maintain a Museum properly . . . is a consequence, even a duty in our civilization. . . . The capital of this region, which the celebrated scientist Bates termed a paradise for naturalists, which from La Condamine to Hartt was scrutinized by scholars and travellers of the highest caliber such as Lacerda, Wallace, Humboldt . . . and Agassiz, to cite only the most notable . . . draws greater and greater attention of scientists the world over.

But the address did stop at applauding foreign scientists. Goeldi also cited his most notable colleagues and their regional specializations.[19] Then he put the importance of the work of his institute into a scientific perspective. This is, in fact, the essence of the second part of Goeldi's statement:

> Gentlemen, in this part of America there has occurred one of those murky and equivocal dramas that vex the inquiries

> of the wisest scholars to have issued from the breast of Humanity since time immemorial. In this region races, whose origins and filiations are unknown and whose history is a closed book, have existed, lived, struggled and left their mark. . . . Gentlemen, who knows if here we do not have the key to one of the most stirring enigmas to provoke scientific inquiry today: the origin of the American man. (*Bulletin of the Emilio Goeldi Museum of Pará,* 1894: 6–7)

Goeldi's goal seemed to be to maintain control over regional research and thereby take part in the great intellectual debates of the era. Although he was a naturalist, the director of the Emilio Goeldi Museum of Pará was above all a devout evolutionist. He defended the idea of human "perfectibility," as defined in the nineteenth century, which presumed that humans would achieve equality to the extent that they were able to transcend themselves and, in the case of the more primitive people, attain a civilized state. But as a scholar he seemed seduced by the conclusions of the proponents of polygenism who apprehended the existence of various races or human species scattered over the globe. He saw that the international success of the museum could be linked, therefore, to future discoveries in this field that would prove "the origin of the American man" and the "essence of his character and backwardness."

But Goeldi was never able to produce solid studies to back up his theories, and he ended up referring to the material conditions of the museum with a querulous tone: "The museum should cease to be a depository of curiosities, . . . and it should become a systematic and scientifically classified collection. . . . To place potsherds at the side of cranial fragments suggests a lack of unity" (*Bulletin of the Emilio Goeldi Museum of Pará,* 1894: 7 and 15). He wished "to get rid of certain collections of furniture more appropriate to a historical gallery" (*Bulletin of the Emilio Goeldi Museum of Pará,* 1894: 17). He lamented the museum personnel: "[W]e must have fewer administrators and more work. The museum must cease to be a public bureaucracy and become a scientific enterprise" (*Bulletin of the Emilio Goeldi Museum of Pará,* 1894: 18). He agonized over existing regulations: "[I]ts administrative offices give the impression of complete detachment from notions of the organization of other world museums and of something more akin to paging through Medieval legal manuscripts" (*Bulletin of the Emilio Goeldi Museum of Pará,* 1894: 19).

Yet the attention to be devoted to anthropology and to polygenist interpretations, as outlined in Goeldi's inaugural address, seems not to have remained of fundamental concern as the journal evolved. There are few articles on archeology, and studies of anthropology are notably absent (0.4 percent), and those that do appear deal with indigenous language and vocabulary. All of this indicates either that Goeldi found insufficient material to support his suspicions or that he dedicated himself exclusively to research connected to his professional expertise. In fact, studies by natural scientists made up 95 percent of the journal's essays, and they reflected the same divisions found in the *Journal of the São Paulo Museum*. The greatest number of articles were in zoology (48 percent), followed by botany (36 percent) and geology (10 percent). (See Table 5.)

Given what we know about the natures of the National Museum and the Emilio Goeldi Museum of Pará, their shared dispute perhaps can come into focus. This episode reveals something of Goeldi's conflicting ideas about his museum. Without getting into the details of this controversy, one can detect Goeldi's irate tone both in his reaction to the "hoary museum" (*Bulletin of the Emilio Goeldi Museum of Pará,* 1897) and in his condemnation of the National Museum's methods of enriching its collection.

> The manner by which the National Museum gained its wealth not very long ago is also well known. It was at the indisputable expense of the Emilio Goeldi Museum of Pará, with the inordinate number of precious objects it took from Marajó and from other Amazonian areas. This brought

Table 5 Distribution of Articles by Theme and Year of Publication in the Bulletin of the Pará Museum of Natural History and Ethnography/Emílio Goeldi Museum of Pará, *1894–1949*

YEAR	BOT.	ZOO.	GEO.	ANTHRO.	ARCH.	TOTAL
1894	2	9	2	1		14
1897	8	11	6			25
1901	10	12		2		24
1904/6	11	8		1		20
1907/8	9	7	1			17
1909/10	3	1		1		5
1910	2	1	1	1		5
1914		1				1
1934						
1949		11	3	1		15
TOTAL	45	61	13	7		126

Key: Bot. = Botany; Zoo. = Zoology; Geo. = Geology; Anthro. = Anthropology; Arch. = Archeology

> under its control, in the guise of a loan and with the pretext of providing greater depth to one or another anthropological exhibit in the Brazilian capital, the better part of what Pará possessed. They returned nothing, and they gave nothing in exchange. (*Bulletin of the Emilio Goeldi Museum of Pará*, 1894: 16)

On the one hand, Goeldi sought to portray his museum more along the lines of the professional model of the National Museum. On the other hand, he lamented the manner in which the other museum operated. Behind his criticism was also the censure of the scientific work of the National Museum, which, according to von Ihering and Goeldi, boasted of accomplishments it had not achieved.[20]

Nevertheless, both museums espoused goals that were more grandiose than the realities under which they were operating, given their shortage of resources and personnel.

The Emilio Goeldi Museum suffered from its own internal fragility at the same time that it was expected to play a role in making Belém a center of power consistent with the wealth that the rubber industry brought to the area. In the end, Goeldi stated: "[W]ait, be patient, Rome could not be built in a day, much less a museum of National History and Ethnography at the mouth of the Amazon" (*Bulletin of the Emilio Goeldi Museum of Pará,* 1897: 17). So remote from the other cultural and political centers of the nation, where other museums brought, in effect, civilization to their regions, this museum found that its first order of business was to bring civilization to itself through the arduous task of assembling its collection.

As a result, one might measure the scientific importance of the museum at that moment more in terms of the influence that foreign institutes exerted on it than by its native intellectual production. The Goeldi museum's journal, for example, consisted primarily of articles written by scientists outside the museum, if we exclude Goeldi's essays, which seemed tailored to fill any empty spaces. Moreover the museum served as a security blanket for foreign travellers inexperienced with Brazil and a market for the exchange of precious collections. It was with some weariness that Goeldi referred to such services:

> First they ask us information about this animal, then they want details about that plant, an ethnographer wishes information about some indigenous tribe, and then we receive a letter from an anthropologist begging for help in obtaining the skulls of certain Indians. (*Bulletin of the Emilio Goeldi Museum of Pará,* 1897/2: 17).

Even if the Emilio Goeldi Museum was not the best equipped museum, and even if it did not have among its staff the most famous scientists, it was certainly the best situated for what it sought to do.

THE NATIONAL ETHNOGRAPHIC MUSEUMS
"From Curiosity Cabinets to a False Front Building"

It is hard to understand how a country distinguished by only slight scientific activity could support three ethnographic museums. In fact, the images these institutions conveyed clearly were inconsistent with their practices. Perhaps a closer look at the origins of these institutions can shed some light on the matter. For instance, besides having its beginnings linked to a Portuguese monarch in Brazil, who struggled with the vicissitudes of an empire that had had to move to the colony, until the last quarter of the nineteenth century the National Museum was fundamentally tied to the government and, in particular, to the image of the emperor.

On the other hand, in its first years the São Paulo Museum stood out as the most extreme example of a "curiosity cabinet" in the service of and in homage to the local elites. The combination of the desire to build a "great and imposing work" and the longing of the São Paulo elites to project a sense of culture was reflected in the monument itself, which seemed little like a museum. The museum was built far from the city, and because of its location it understandably suffered problems of communication.[21] But the museum would, nevertheless, wield influence in the era's stunted cultural atmosphere.

The Pará museum in its early days operated in similar circumstances. The institution seemed to exist to glorify local constituents and to serve the roles of "gateway to the jungle," symbol of the strength of rubber, and repository of miscellaneous museum objects.

Before the 1880s a blueprint did not exist for establishing common standards and for giving a new meaning and presence to the national museums. It was only in that decade, when the museums brought in new professionals and equipped their institutions with a view toward meeting new scientific objectives, that they entered an exceptionally rich period. This new era marked a moment of greater correlation between the national museums, a fact that transcended the strong temperaments of their directors. The museum's directors organized collections, classified materials, hired personnel, edited journals, and wrote most of the articles. As Simão Schwartzman stated, each museum "relied heavily on a charismatic leader," whose efforts guaranteed institutional survivability (1979: 139).[22]

The 1880s was also the beginning of a time when the museums turned their closest attention to other countries. "Looking at Europe, but with an eye on Brazil" (Pontes, quoted in Miceli, 1989: 363), may be perhaps the best way to think about the perspective that united the national ethnographic museums at this productive time. Although the National Museum was particularly interested in local issues, it restructured itself according to the new models of European scientific museums. The museum at Rio de Janeiro was a constant presence in international expositions and thereby carried abroad some of its country's eccentricities.

It was the Emilio Goeldi Museum of Pará, however, that played the most strategic role in the new era. Although far removed from the nation's capital, the Pará museum lay in the heart of the "naturalists' capital," at the very entrance to the jungle's mysteries, so it welcomed foreigners who dared to confront the Amazonian wilds. Belém was an excellent location for hosting a debate that challenged other museums.

Far from both the forest and the glitter of the capital was the São Paulo Museum. Sustained by a powerful economic elite and directed by a rather isolated German scientist, the institution seemed more like a "false front building." The São Paulo Museum was a copy of other existing institutions and possessed all of the requisite characteristics, but it did not have the wherewithal to live up to its objectives. Its journal depended wholly on its director. Unfortunately he failed to deliver what the local public expected.

But beyond the specifics of each of the museums, one can say that all of them filled an important role in encouraging Brazilian studies and research in natural sciences and physical anthropology. They also embodied the scientific and objective ideal that people of the era so highly esteemed. As Schwartzman wrote: "[I]t was the only environment in which science was practiced for the sake of science, unlike the other institutes where practical applications were a sine qua non" (1979: 84).

Far removed from the political debates of the era, the museums sought to examine Brazilians in a very specific way. Coming to humans by way of the flora and fauna they gathered, analyzed, classified, ranked, and displayed, the museums endeavored to bring a little science and order to an environment devoid of like intellectual activity.

Concerning a Certain Kind of Order: Race, a Local Issue

> A museum should observe, collect, classify,
> and make known all objects of nature.
> —*Emilio Goeldi* (1894)

To speak of Brazilian museum practices at the end of the nineteenth century is to recall what Michel Foucault described as "general theories as to the ordering of things, and the interpretation that such an ordering involves" (1973: xxi). As Roberto da Matta has stated

> [M]useum collectors had a true obsession for classification, as did our colonial administrators and Victorian evolutionist anthropologists. In fact, they conceived the science of man

> as a kind of art of classification. They saw their work as obtaining samples typical of periods through which humankind had travelled in its progress toward our time and especially our society. (1983: 8)

The ethnographic museums had adopted the principles of social evolutionism and with them a particular manner of classification that presupposed a rigid biological analogy that viewed living organisms as being interchangeable with social groups. The primary interest of the social evolutionist museum anthropologists lay in the idea of the cultural development of humanity as a whole and not the development of a specific society. They sought to capture the rhythm of human growth and, by means of comparison, to devise concepts of broad applicability. True to their principles, these scientists seemed to understand the country as a great "archive" of original and primary documents for the verification and study of "periods of humanity's arrested development," or of the "lost moments in the history of humanity" (Lacerda, in *Archives of the National Museum,* 1885). Their primary role was to take part in a debate that was playing out in other foreign scientific establishments.

The Brazilians working on the study of man's cultural development viewed social evolution as directly associated with the problem of race and its possible implications. According to the literary critic Antonio Candido, during that era there was a great effort that

> related to a dramatic existential position within the collective Brazilian intellect. Within a context dominated by the century's obsession with biology, it nervously inquired of its own future, the fruit of an inbred people, marked by fear of an alleged racial inferiority, which at the time had gained acceptance as a scientific postulate. (1978: 29)

Accepting the dominant racial determinist theories of the times meant confirming the future insurvivability of the nation, and reconciling this fact with the dominant reverence for science proved a major struggle for the country's institutions of higher learning.

Debates on the issue of the implications of race for the country's future were not limited to an inner circle. Foreign museums also saw Brazil as "a great racial laboratory." The Brazilian museums were staffed primarily by foreign scientists who often also maintained strong ties to other parts of the world. The remote locations were considered scientific outposts for the collection of ethnographic materials, whether for phrenologists interested in the analysis of the skulls of local indigenous populations, or for anthropologists in the observation of the behavior of these "strangely miscegenized" peoples.

But if the three institutions generally took part in a relatively focused debate, it was in relation to the racial issue that their views diverged, with matters of local interest defining the terms of the dialogue. After classifying and ranking "the local human species" (*Journal of the São Paulo Museum,* 1902), and after seeking within the plant and animal kingdoms models for understanding the human being, these institutions ended up swelling the number of determinist analyses that were then appearing.

Far from having sympathy for the image of Rousseau's noble savage, the museums' scientists were hoping to find not just examples of underdeveloped cultures but populations turned feral from the blending of such diverse races. Despite the limited space the museums allotted to the work of anthropologists, their specialists rediscovered the "American man," making use of naturalistic and racial criteria. Borrowing from the natural sciences model, they applied the theories of evolutionary development of animal and vegetable species to human species, first as metaphors and later as illustrative examples, whether they were classifying purebred or hybrid types. For instance, in a footnote to a text on zoology, von Ihering pondered: "One can observe relatively easily in groups of humans the decadence presented by hybrid types. . . . Far removed from the purebred, local miscegenation should be studied with care" (*Journal of the São Paulo Museum,* 1902). As part of a debate taking place in Brazil's own backyard but extending beyond its borders, the museums helped to disseminate racial theories within Brazil that questioned or puzzled over the future of a "young mestizo nation" (Lacerda, 1911).

Racial theories did not cease to be sources of interest to the inveterate social evolutionist museum scientists. "One must understand the decadence of the human race so as later to predict a future evolution," said von Ihering as he strayed from the arena of zoology to refer to human beings (*Journal of the São Paulo Museum,* 1908). As a scientist and as a specialist in the theory of evolution, Lacerda discovered in the Botocudos the finest example of human inferiority, and in the face of the inevitable need for racial purification he pointed to whitening the race as the great national solution.

The outcome of the museums' work, however, was something else. Understood as "science sites" (von Ihering, in *Journal of the São Paulo Museum,* 1895), the museums seemed to work to calm the turmoil that ideas of race brought to their context. In the First Universal Races Congress (1911), for example, Lacerda's speech sounded hopeful. Evolutionary science promised whitening, and contrary to the demographic census, Lacerda foresaw a country growing ever whiter. The museum scientists conformed to a cliché in that, secure in their theoretical foundations, they disregarded the surrounding evidence and worked with only the models and doctrines they had adopted.

According to the Brazilian political scientist José Murilo de Carvalho, at a time when "a door was opening for the government to an enlightened authoritarianism, based on the real or imagined expertise of its technicians" (1980: 35), the ethnographic museums fulfilled an unforeseen local function. While they helped to define the backwardness of their indigenous peoples or reaffirmed the inferiority implicit in miscegenation and in developing races, they also in the end renounced the era's debates of ideas involving the effect of racial mixing and racial makeup on the nation's destiny.

The Demise of a Stated Mission

The 1920s marked the end of the "era of national museums." From that time on, the Brazilian ethnographic museums lost more and more of their original comprehensive ambitions, and their strategic importance to foreign museums diminished. They were emerging more clearly as institutions dedicated entirely to the natural sciences.

Several factors influenced this shift. In the first place, the public had become aware of the frailties of the institutions and suspicious of their dependence on their directors. All of the museums lacked sufficient resources. In 1890 the National Museum issued a directive that required its staff to work exclusively on its behalf, with the result that several of its scientists resigned, including Orville Derby, S. Scheacke, and even João Batista Lacerda. Another indication of the National Museum's privations was both the less frequent publication of its journal and its growing dissociation from local issues. Disappointed with these turns of events, Lacerda stated frankly: "Detached from the world of politics, men of science want only to work in peace and quiet" (*Archives of the National Museum,* 1921: 11).

The São Paulo Museum, which had existed in the shadow of its director until his departure in 1916, subsequently underwent a profound transformation. Under the direction of the historian Alfonso D'Escragnolle Taunay, the museum continued to conduct research on natural history, but it abandoned the more comprehensive scientific mission it had pursued under von Ihering. The new director humbly described the São Paulo Museum's situation: "we have enough to do, and we work on various collections, some exquisite, others modest, and yet others rudimentary" (*Journal of the São Paulo Museum,* 1915: 17).

Rocked by the rubber crisis and by Goeldi's departure, the Emilio Goeldi Museum of Pará entered a period of notable decline as well. During the directorships of Jacques Hubert and Emília Snethlage, both of whom were former colleagues of Goeldi, the museum remained active, primarily because of the contributions of foreign scientists. The museum's journal, however, was the very embodiment of instability. Volume 8 was published in 1914, but the next volume did not appear until 1934, and when it did it relied on contributions from people who were not associated with the museum, since by that time the museum's technical staff had dwindled to almost nothing.

The decline of these institutions was also linked to a broader national trend. According to Schwartzman, the development of applied sciences was gaining new support, especially on the local level.[23] "In the area of technical education and in the achievements realized in agriculture and livestock, applied science in Brazil appeared to have attained its zenith in the first decades of the century" (Schwartzman, 1979: 143). Regional institutes with universal aspirations dedicated to the development of "a pure science removed from daily concerns" (*Archives of the National Museum,* 1926), at that time the museums produced not only meager but also unrealistic research of little useful application.

It was under these inauspicious circumstances that Dom Pedro II, "catalyst and champion of the sciences," departed, and the museums lost their most generous benefactor and enduring defender.[24]

During the 1920s there was even more evidence of the decline of the museums. In Lacerda's words: "We lacked resources, young empirical scientists, and sufficient background in experimental methods. In addition, our grudging government paid our scientists a lower wage than that of a second-rate traveling salesman" (*Archives of the National Museum,* 1914: 73).

The advent of the 1930s marked the end of the "era of ethnographic museums" as a worldwide phenomenon. The original model for these national museums, associated with a pragmatic scientific perspective, had failed. The museums were coupled with the radical critique that surfaced then in opposition to the evolutionist paradigm, and they became mired for a time before they reorganized themselves on other theoretical bases.

After losing a large portion of its technical staff the Emilio Goeldi Museum of Pará became part of the Instituto de Pesquisas da Amazônia [Institute of Amazonian Studies]. In 1927 the São Paulo Museum saw its biology division first transferred to the recently created Institute of Biology and then in 1935 incorporated by the University of São Paulo as a "complementary institution." In 1939 its zoology division became the Department of Zoology of the State Secretary of Agriculture, which more recently became the University of São Paulo Museum of Zoology. The National Museum, in addition to sustaining the loss of a significant part of its technical staff, suffered a lack of resources and qualified personnel. Even in the last years of the 1920s and in the 1930s the National Museum entered the limelight once again. In 1929 the museum's director, Edgar Roquete-Pinto, served as the president of the First Brazilian Eugenics Congress.[25] Roquete-Pinto, as an anthropologist, took the opportunity to play an important public role. He opposed the powerful racist position held by most of the Congress participants, who defended the application of a radical eugenically based political strategy and the theory of the "devolution of racial mixing." Influenced by Mendel's teachings of genetics and by Franz Boaz's North American cultural relativism, Roquete-Pinto advanced the argument that the "Brazilian problem was a matter of hygiene and not of race."[26] He also took a position in favor of Japanese immigration, opposing the majority opinion of medical researchers, such as Miguel Couto and Renato Kehl,[27] who insisted on the introduction of eugenics laws that would restrict the entry of Asian labor. In this way the National Museum broke with its history of support for biological and phrenological models. The institution began to convene a tenuous intellectual avant-garde that directly opposed the contemporary and well-entrenched scientific racism.[28] (See Table 6.)

By the end of the 1920s the national museums were dismembered and suffered a loss of autonomy. After all, science no longer supported the thesis that humanity consisted of races or species that responded to unique evolutionary processes. Both the work and the theories of these museums were dated. Because the comprehensive mission of the universities with which the museums became associated clashed with the universities' own pursuits, for some years the museums were limited to working in the natural sciences. Only relics of formerly active entities, the ethnological museums of the 1930s bore little resemblance to the institutions that had been framed by evolutionist theories. Working with plants and animals was not the same as pondering the development of human beings. The museums had lost the distinction that their ideas had formerly conferred on them. After all, men aren't mollusks. Mollusks are mollusks.

The shining era of the ethnographic museums has receded so far into the distance that over the years these institutions have lost their original designations and missions. Lest all their work be lost in the midst of so many major changes, one should keep in mind the naturalist's logic of classification that these "museum men" possessed. Biology guaranteed "order" in the midst of "disorder."

Table 6 Anthropological Profile of Brazilian Races, Organized According to Official Census Figures of 1872 and 1890, Showing Roquete-Pinto's Prediction of Racial Whitening

YEAR	WHITES	AFRO-BRAZILIANS	INDIANS	MESTIZOS	TOTAL
1872	38.1	16.5	7	38.4	100
1890	44	12	12	32	100
1912	50	9	13	28	100
2012	80	0	17	3	100

At these sites, where communities of men simply applied the laws of biology, and where nature's order domesticated the capriciousness of culture, it seemed possible to reverse the sense of insecurity that racial issues generated elsewhere, such as in the schools of law and medicine.

While they helped popularize abroad the image of Brazil as an enormous racial laboratory and as an example for the world, the nation's ethnographic museums held on to their own distinctive view of the naturalist as one who classified plants, animals, and humans collectively. "Human perfectibility will play out its role in Brazil as long as nature does not stop exerting influence on plant and animal species," declared von Ihering, who held out hope of an evolutionary improvement among the country's discredited indigenous and mestizo populations.

Immersed as they were in the extremes of their logic, however, the museum scientists became lost amid a crush of rules of evolutionist science that made sense to an ever decreasing number of initiates. It is perhaps for this reason that the ethnographic museums suffered most from not adapting themselves to the new scientific theories and the restructuring of scientific study that took place in the 1930s. They became obsolete.

Nevertheless, the idea of where science was practiced, a site composed of a professional group single-mindedly dedicated to its mission, became fixed. The care with which they selected their scientists distinguished the ethnographic museums from other scientific institutions of the day. One notes this especially in the case of the historical and geographical institutes, where leadership positions were doled out based on social roles, to the detriment of the work of the institutes.

4

HISTORICAL AND GEOGRAPHICAL INSTITUTES

•

"Guardians of the Official Story"

"Kindred organizations in Europe and America joyously celebrated the arrival of their new associate which, like a rugged Indian from the jungles of Brazil, steps boldly forward, eager to struggle tooth and nail for the greater glory of his tribe" (*Journal of the Historical and Geographical Institute of Brazil,* 1839/1: 177).[1] It was in this way that the pioneering Brazilian Historical and Geographical Institute was introduced in 1839.

Located in Rio de Janeiro and created shortly after Brazil became independent from Portugal in 1822, this institution fulfilled the role for which it and other similar historical entities were created: to construct a national history, to re-create a past, to codify fundamental myths, and to put facts in order so as to achieve a measure of consensus about the nature of Brazilian events and people. Loosely modelled on their Old World counterparts, the Brazilian historical and geographical institutes proposed to meet a monumental challenge: "To gather, to systematize, and to preserve" (*Journal of the Historical and Geographical Institute of Brazil,* 1839/1) documents, facts, and names, with the goal of creating a national history for this vast country that lacked an official history even as it lacked firm territorial boundaries.

National unity required the construction of a consensual past, even though the influential social and economic groups that made up the various institutes were bound to shade the history with their own interpretations. With a social makeup similar to that of the European academies of the Enlightenment, whose members were selected on the basis of their social standing, the Brazilian institutes were markedly provincial, despite their cosmopolitan pretensions.

When momentum built for a program to create a consolidated and official history of Brazil, a country divided by regional disputes, it fell to the Historical and Geographical Institute of Brazil to define the nation's regions and to gain the confidence of its people. The other institutes that were founded in its wake worked to confirm regional characteristics and to define, whenever possible, a region's cultural uniqueness.

The nation's historical and geographical associations were founded at widely different times and in dramatically different regions, so a full analysis of them as a group is impossible.[2] Nevertheless, it will be useful to take a global view of them as places that produced historical knowledge in the nineteenth century but were different from other centers of higher learning, such as museums and schools of law and medicine. Not only did the economic backgrounds of the historical associations' members differ from those of the scientific and academic centers; they were also organized differently. Subsidized by the emperor, or by the historical association members themselves, these organizations had the appearance of courtly societies, specializing in the production of knowledge bearing an official stamp of approval.

The three centers under examination are the Historical and Geographical Institute of Brazil, the Archeological and Geographical Institute of Pernambuco, and the Historical and Geographical Institute of São Paulo. The first association, located in

Rio de Janeiro, is one of the most enduring and pioneering of the museums and became the model for most of the other institutes founded in Brazil in the nineteenth century. The other two institutions are in some ways typical examples of historical and geographical institutions that adapted the museum model to local conditions. The distinct regional profiles of these two institutions also help illuminate the regional political disputes of the Empire and the Old Republic that were played out in these regions.

Of course, the most interesting characteristic of all three centers is their brand of official scholarship, which started to be distorted by racial discourse only toward the end of the century. As we shall see, in many ways scholarship at institutions that assembled an intellectual elite alongside an economic and financial elite experienced notable constraints.

THE HISTORICAL AND GEOGRAPHICAL INSTITUTE OF BRAZIL
"Courtly History Is National History"

"Pacifica Scientiae Occupatio."
[A career devoted to knowledge gives peace.]
—*Journal of the Historical and Geographical Institute of Brazil* (1839): 10

On February 28, 1827, the Sociedade Auxiliadora da Indústria Nacional [National Industrial Auxiliary Association] celebrated its inauguration in Rio de Janeiro. The goal of the association, which was founded in principle years before by Dom João VI but put into operation only in 1838, was to help develop the nation's agriculture and livestock production. Similar to other organizations created during the period, this one was designed to help manage the centralization of the state.

Nearly ten years after the association's inauguration, the idea of creating another scientific association dedicated to historical and geographical studies came from the National Industrial Auxiliary

Association itself. Therefore, "on Sunday, November 21, 1838, at eleven o'clock in the morning, twenty-seven distinguished gentlemen of the local association gathered in the modest hall of the National Museum with the intention of inaugurating a new organization dedicated to historical scholarship" (*Journal of the Historical and Geographical Institute of Brazil* [1839]: 20).

The nature of the membership of the newly founded organization was one of its most characteristic features, one that it would sustain throughout its life: members were recruited based more on social concerns than on professional qualifications. The institute avoided the rules governing the academic world, since the selection criteria for its staff did not particularly reward competence in the institute's chosen areas of specialization (Guimarães, 1988: 7).

Another dominant feature of the Historical and Geographical Institute of Brazil was the web of personal relations connecting the administration of the institute to the state, and especially to its enlightened imperial core. Examining the profile of the twenty-seven founding members, one notes that twenty-two of them occupied high-ranking positions within the internal hierarchy of the state. For example, the first president of the Historical and Geographical Institute of Brazil, José Feliciano Fernandes Pinheiro, Viscount of São Leopoldo, became a senator as well as a counsellor, an honorary title bestowed on him during the Empire.* As another example, Canon Januário da Cunha Barboza, first secretary of the institute and one of the members responsible for the institute's intellectual design, was also "official sermonizer and Imperial chronicler." Among the founding members were also voting members of the Supreme Court, solicitors, appellate court judges, and heads of the secretariat of imperial trade. No fewer than ten state counsellors, six of whom were also

* The office of counsellor (or member of the State Council) was a lifelong appointment, made by the emperor himself. Counsellors were the emperor's closest advisers and confidantes.

senators, were members of this institute. These were the imperial elite, a large percentage of whom had been born in Portugal and were loyal defenders of the House of Bragança, the royal family brought to Brazil by Dom João VI.[3] The group taken all in all closely resembled a courtly association.

In addition, not only did the state supply 75 percent of the institute's budget from the outset, but in the 1840s the emperor began to attend the members' meetings assiduously.[4] On the occasion of his last meeting with the institute and as evidence of his support, in November 1889 he remarked: "I give thanks to the Institute and say nothing more as the Institute is well aware of my commitment to it."

Despite the formal description of the Historical and Geographical Institute of Brazil as a "scientific-cultural association," the traces of an official involvement were highly visible. In the hands of a powerful local oligarchy linked to an enlightened monarch, in both private and public debates the institute tended to express itself in an official style, punctuated by other statements that were less partisan in nature.

Internal Hierarchies: "A Courtly Society"

"And always allow the reflective genius of the foreigner to write our history? . . . Try also to awaken Americans from the contemptible obscurity that afflicts us" (*Journal of the Historical and Geographical Institute of Brazil,* 1839). Expressing the synthesis of a broad range of goals, this was the central theme of Januário da Cunha Barboza's address at the inauguration of the Historical and Geographical Institute of Brazil. At the center of the association's stated goals was a desire to found an original and national historiography, to teach and disseminate knowledge, and to frame a history that, like its European models, would be devoted to exalting the glories of the country.[5] In fact, many of the literary romantics, such as the poets Gonçalves de Magalhães and

Gonçalves Dias, were members of the institute and embraced its goals with a sense of patriotic duty. Within this generation there was no place for a meddlesome intellectual pecking order, and science and the arts enjoyed an equal allure and veneration. The institute's members wanted to construct a comprehensive intellectual life as a means of creating knowledge and, consequently, gaining distinction for the country (Candido, 1959: 10).

The era in which the institute began is of some importance. Established some years after the beginning of the country's movement for independence, in a certain way the institute was at the core of an emerging zeitgeist. "Independence has a decisive role within the romantic ideal," affirmed Antonio Candido when he characterized this period in which literature became a valued national resource, whether it copied European models or expressed a distinct and local reality (Candido, 1959: 9–11). More than just accumulating documents, the Rio association foresaw work as existing to affirm a theoretical outlook. To write the homeland's history was above all an exercise in exaltation. The institute achieved its commemorative intention not only through the texts produced and published by its journal but also through the enterprising production of monuments, medals, hymns, slogans, symbols, and uniforms that were unique to the establishment. Remember to commemorate, document to celebrate. Thus the function of the institute was twofold: it existed for the veneration of the local elite and for the production of a fundamentally regionalist history.

The profile of the members of the Historical and Geographical Institute of Brazil was not inadvertent either. The bulk of the members were politicians and landowners. There were also men of letters and renowned scholars, such as the historian Francisco Adolfo de Varnhagen, the poet Gonçalves Dias, and, in later years, the jurist Silvio Romero and the writer and journalist Euclides da Cunha. The composition of the internal leadership of the institute bespoke the function of the institute. Beginning with the membership, one can observe the following subdivisions: (1) *efetivos*

Selos, espada e uniformes do IHGB
(Revista do IHGB, *1888*)

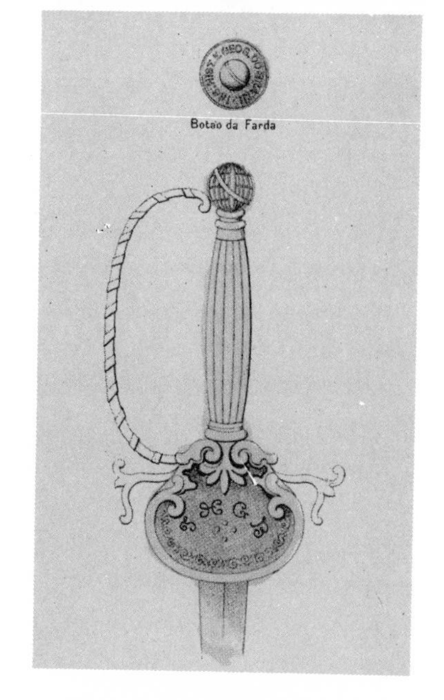

Seals, sword, and uniforms
of the Historical and Geographical Institute of Brazil

[active members], for whom residence in the federal capital was obligatory, and whose specialization was Brazilian history, geography, or ethnography, and whose literary abilities were of some importance; (2) *correspondentes* [correspondents], of whom was required either the same level of intellectual expertise as the first subdivision or the contribution of a "substantial donation" for the use of the institute's museum; (3) *honorários* [honorary members], who, as conditions for recognition, had to be of "respectable age" and to possess "consummate knowledge and distinguished presence"; (4) *beneméritos* [meritorious members], active members who received their due recognition for having contributed valued service to the institute, or for having made donations in an amount greater than 2,000 milreis (a former Brazilian monetary unit) in cash or other articles of value; and (5) *presidente honorário* [honorary president], conferred only upon the emperor or the head of a foreign nation.[6]

One can see, therefore, that there were flexible and diverse preconditions for the admission and absorption of new members. In this way the association played different roles for different people: for some it represented a locus of intellectual projection, and for others it was a place for personal self-promotion.[7]

Meanwhile, what attracts one's attention is not the credentials and duties of the members in themselves, but the logic of their distribution among the membership. The position of president was strictly reserved for renowned politicians and generally involved fulfilling figurative functions, convening sessions, or delivering proceedings that had previously been decided; whereas those members who joined the institute on their academic merits primarily occupied positions as secretaries and orators, yet they fulfilled the more productive roles.

Surveying the biographical data on some of the members of the Historical and Geographical Institute of Brazil, we have arrived at an idea of its composition. Between 1838 and 1930 the association elected eight presidents, all with relatively similar backgrounds. The first, José Feliciano Fernandes Pinheiro,

Viscount of São Leopoldo, was better known in his previous post as a statistician, and not so much as a distinguished scholar. But as a minister, he was well equipped to advocate on behalf of the need for the institute. In like manner, the second president of the institute, the counsellor Cândido José de Araújo Vianna, Marques of Sapucahy, elected president of the institute on August 12, 1847, fulfilled only official functions. "Gentleman of the Imperial House of the Emperor's Council, Former Minister of the Supreme Court of Justice, Dignitary of the Order of the Southern Cross, Knight of Christ and the Rose, Great Cross of the Portuguese Order of the Tower and the Sword," he took a seat in the assembly as representative of the state of Minas Gerais in 1823. In 1839 he was named senator for the states of Alagoas and Maranhão and served as trustee of the Ministries of Commerce, Justice, and the Empire.

Other prominent political personalities, about whom much could be said, also served as presidents of the Historical and Geographical Institute of Brazil. Among them were the Viscount of Bom Retiro, who was a senator and counsellor; Olegario Herculano, who was a counsellor and the president of the federal Supreme Court; the Marques of Paranaguá, who was president of the provinces of Piauí, Maranhão, and Pernambuco; and finally José Maria da Silva Paranhos Júnior, the Baron of Rio Branco, who is best known for his work in the Ministry of Foreign Relations. There was a rationale behind the similarities among all those who occupied this position. The president was always the person who advertised and represented the institute and who, because of his charge, at the same time established links between the association and the broad directives of official politics in the state.

For their part, the secretaries were responsible for the institute's day-to-day activities. They took charge of meeting agendas and proceedings, directed research, organized the journal, proposed competitions and tributes, assisted with the business of the library as well as its collection, and established guidelines for inducting new members. In short, they were responsible for the whole range of institutional work and goals. Keeping this kind of role in mind, one might imagine the typical profile of the secretaries. Very few of the members ever worked in anything but an amateur capacity, and the fact that the meetings of the Historical and Geographical Institute of Brazil took place on Sundays reveals much about the devoted nature of the staff.

Januário da Cunha Barboza, a canon, sacred orator, poet, and biographer, served as the first secretary of the Historical and Geographical Institute of Brazil. He was primarily responsible for the first six years of the institution's life. Canon Januário founded and directed the *Revista do Instituto* [Journal of the Institute], organized the first set of bylaws of the institute, and tried to spread the organization's name throughout European historical centers by circulating the journal and the institute's research outside the country. In addition to his internal activities, he wrote scientific treatises on "American antiquities" seeking determinedly "to save our past from a lethal silence." In his work Canon Januário epitomized the future secretaries. He worked as one who believed in and sought to sustain an institution whose chances for survival were still uncertain. He was also the very image of the intellectual who made the advancement of the group his primary activity.

In fact, the secretaries of the institute tended to depart somewhat from the profile of the other members of the Historical and Geographical Institute of Brazil, and for the most part occupied positions that prescribed less involvement. Many of them were dedicated to teaching and to writing biographies of their peers for the institute, preserving their memory without remuneration.[8]

But not all the secretaries lived in the shadows of the politicians. Francisco Adolfo de Varnhagen, Viscount of Porto Alegre, elected May 23, 1851, is an example of a secretary who achieved wide recognition. Although he served at the institute for only half a year, during this period the famous historian, biographer, geographer, and mathematician compiled the general alphabetical *Indice* [Index] of memoirs and biographies. Characterized by José

Honório Rodrigues as a "monarchist, sycophant, conservative, and dignitary," Francisco Adolfo de Varnhagen represented the "typical" intellectual of this institute, at least during the imperial period.

A devoted admirer of the House of Bragança, in his various articles Varnhagen defended the monarchy and colonization. He found slavery defensible, believing that there was no recourse "so that we do not have to wait for Indians to act civilly and cease declaring war on those who refuse to submit and cease occupying by force those fertile lands that they are stealing from civilization" (*Journal of the Historical and Geographical Institute of Brazil*, 1850). Considered by many to be the first national historian, Varnhagen played an exemplary role within the institute through his efforts to write the history of Brazil. With his monarchist bias, he wrote a history that contrasted sharply with the republican sympathies so prevalent in other South American nations. His was also a conservative history, given that it was profoundly linked to the ruling rural aristocracy and to the Empire itself.[9]

Joaquim Manuel de Macedo, the novelist who gained fame as the author of *A moreninha* [The little dark girl],[10] and Max Fleiuss were other notable secretaries of the Historical and Geographical Institute of Brazil. As secretary of the institute beginning in 1905, during the first republican period, Fleiuss functioned much as his colleagues had done during the previous regime. He was above all an "institutional professional," a correspondent member of the Pernambuco Institute of Archeology and the Historical Institute of Minas Gerais and Bahia, an active member of the Rio de Janeiro Geographic Society, and an associate of the Royal Academy of Madrid. He was, indeed, an enthusiastic advocate of the institute model.[11]

Traditionally the plenary sessions of the institute had been held on the day that the emperor had first participated in the organization, but in 1905 Fleiuss changed the date of the plenary sessions to November 15 to honor the shift from empire to republic. Fleiuss did not wish to forget Dom Pedro II, and the monarchy in general, which was considered the "perpetual protector" of the Rio de Janeiro organization, but at the same time he guaranteed a new alliance with the representatives of the republic, which from then on gained a more formal access to the institute.

Respected and high-profile intellectuals also filled the position of orator. Often former secretaries, such as Varnhagen or even Macedo, filled this position. Perhaps weary from the duties of the demanding role of secretary, they turned to this new, more prestigious and less arduous position. There were also other associates who distinguished themselves as orators, among them Alfonso d'Escragnolle Taunay, who began working in the Historical and Geographical Institute of Brazil in 1869. He was a scientist, novelist, poet, and journalistic social commentator, the celebrated author of *Retirada da laguna* [Retreat from the lagoon], and a tenured member of the Brazilian Academy of Letters (which had forty members).[12] Taunay brought with him his name, lending greater recognition for the institute, as well as the qualities required of the institute's orators: sufficient prestige to leverage the establishment and the commitment to create a national history.

The presidents, as influential politicians, and the secretaries and orators, as respected intellectuals, were responsible for giving shape to the institute. All in all the institute emerged as an organization devoted to a unified mission and strictly wedded to creating an official interpretation, whatever that might be.

Underwritten by the members themselves and by generous donations from the emperor, the staff of the institute met every other week, on Sunday mornings. The meetings followed a well-defined agenda with the members reviewing the minutes of the previous meeting, and reading letters and the list of donations received, and the orator giving an address on a previously selected historical, geographical, or ethnological topic. A range of subjects was covered, such as the peculiarities of indigenous customs, chronicles of the city of Rio de Janeiro, current events, announcements about the new members, or memorials to institute members who had recently died. The participants would contribute responses and then work together to select the topic of discussion for the next session. The orator would conclude the session, first by praising the emperor, then by repeatedly praising the work and the importance of the Historical and Geographical Institute of Brazil.

To these usual activities the members added various other, less ordinary, ones. Some examples were generating enthusiasm and funding for collecting national historical documents, hosting competitions, promoting conferences, organizing expeditions to the country's interior, and sponsoring foreign research, especially at Spanish and Portuguese archives.

Despite the social role that the Historical and Geographical Institute of Brazil played, it is important to understand that this association sought to bring to the documentation of Brazilian history a rigor previously unknown. The creation of a quarterly journal in 1839 helped make these goals manifest.

Creating Their Journal: Fulfilling Institutional Goals

> Give me a map of a country, its configuration, its climate, its waters, its winds, and the sum of its physical geography; tell me about its natural resources, its flora and fauna, and I will describe *a priori* that country's man.
>
> —*Journal of the Historical and Geographical Institute of Brazil,* 1839

The *Journal of the Historical and Geographical Institute of Brazil* was created in 1839, and until 1864 it continued as a quarterly publication, an annual numbered volume with continuous pagination.[13]

It was the custom to use seals and inscriptions in the journal. Until 1889 the publication used a circular official emblem, surrounded by the Latin inscription *Laus Virtuti Ubique Quandocumque* [Praise for virtue always and everywhere]. In the center of the emblem were two young people who symbolized, respectively, history and geography. From time to time other images, such as books, quills, or a large image of the Earth, replaced this emblem. The symbol remained inconsistent until 1889, when the Historical and Geographical Institute of Brazil introduced a new symbol—a circular emblem that encloses the image of a stone upon which a crowned and winged humanlike figure is inscribing the number 21. At the top is written *Auspice Petro Secundo* [Under the auspices of Dom Pedro II] while at the bottom is *Pacifica Scientiae Occupatio* [A career devoted to knowledge gives peace]. This new seal, which corresponded to the image on the commemorative coin minted by the institute on the occasion of the abolition of slavery, joined several motifs that would appear repeatedly. As a symbol it praised knowledge and affirmed loyalty to Dom Pedro, a sentiment that would grow inexorably during the first years of the Old Republic.

The internal organization of the journal was reasonably predictable. It was divided into three parts. The first consisted of articles and documents that dealt with issues relevant to the institute's purpose, for example, interpretations of historical events and texts concerning territorial disputes and geographical boundaries. The articles that treated indigenous ethnography revealed the influence of the romantic movement within the institute. The second part of the journal featured biographies of Brazilians who were "distinguished in letters, arms, and virtue." These short biographies were a highly specialized form of historical writing, a history organized by peerages and genealogies, a history created for the agrarian elites who were hungry for titles that would link them to the old European aristocracies. The final part of the journal consisted of proceedings of the institute's biweekly meetings, which reproduced day-to-day business.

Including all of the regular and special volumes of the journal,[14] a grand total of 1,862 articles were published.[15] Certain characteristics of the publication emerge upon examination of the data in Table 7. Historical articles clearly dominated the publication,

Table 7 Distribution of Articles in the Journal of the Historical and Geographical Institute of Brazil

DISCIPLINE	NUMBER OF ARTICLES	PERCENT
History	844	45%
Geography and geology	326	18%
Biographies	295	16%
Anthropology and ethnology	86	5%
International relations	48	3%
International contributions (trans.)	41	2%
Reviews	27	1%
Indigenous languages	170	1%
Miscellaneous topics	25	9%
TOTAL	1,862	100%

POPPINO, 1953.

making up nearly half of all journal items. Geographical articles also played a very specific role in the journal, although they accounted for only 18 percent of all articles. As this was an era when many legal actions arose surrounding territorial and boundary disputes, the journal understandably gave these events ample attention. An example of this was the famous "Acre Issue" pleaded by the Baron of Rio Branco, an active member of the Historical and Geographical Institute of Brazil.

The third most numerous category of articles, totalling 16 percent of the whole, were biographies. Within this category there were distinct groupings. The first type were biographies of great figures from Brazilian history; these fulfilled a primary institutional goal. Among the most frequently recurring names that were featured were the Emperors Dom Pedro I and Dom Pedro II, the Portuguese navigator and explorer Pedro Álvares Cabral, the politician José Bonifácio, the nineteenth-century Portuguese government official Marques of Pombal, and the entrepreneur and politician Viscount of Mauá.

The purpose of the shorter biographies of the institute's members was quite different. These short articles, which were meant to be read aloud by the president, were a primary institutional activity, designed to legitimize and recognize the organization's members. A fairly rigid idea governed the preparation of these biographies, and there was a clear correlation between the position a member occupied in the organization and the number of biographies written about that person. For instance, eleven biographies were written about Viscount of São Leopoldo. But *quantity* was not the only distinction. People also kept score of "who wrote about whom." Baron Homem de Mello and Joaquim Manuel de Macedo, for example, wrote biographies of the Viscount of São Leopoldo. And Francisco Adolfo de Varnhagen, the subject of five essays, had his name associated with eminent personalities such as the historians Pedro Lessa and Oliveira Lima. The biographer was clearly linked with his subject. The latter had the distinction of seeing his name immortalized among the institute's ranks; the former had the honor of rubbing shoulders with great personalities; and both enjoyed belonging to the inner circle in a game of reciprocal self-promotion. As Antonio Candido stated, "[I]t was a kind of patriotic resurrection ritual . . . the stimulus of a desire where everything excelled: to establish a distinguished past, to deal the cards of nobility to our intellectual life, even if with some sacrifice of accuracy" (Candido, 1959: 380).

Doing Anthropology: "The Redeemable Indian, and the Negro as an Impediment to Civilization"

As disciplines, anthropology and ethnology assumed increasing importance within the *Journal of the Historical and Geographical Institute of Brazil,* to the extent that they even became separate fields of inquiry. One may note, however, that the journal and thus the institute maintained a dubious position with respect to racial issues. Although the institute was essentially a project for national unification, the work of the institute was based on ideas that effectively excluded Indians and Afro-Brazilians.

The positions on these two groups as expressed in the journal were not identical, however. Articles about the Afro-Brazilian population clearly stated that evolution was possible within the population. The vision was determinist, nevertheless, regarding the "race's potential for civilization." "Negroes are an example of a group incapable of civilization," affirmed one article published in 1891. "Negro populations occupy the lowest rank of human civilization," declared an essay from 1884. Needless to say, the journal's articles were thus less than optimistic about the chances for Afro-Brazilian integration.

Issues surrounding the Indians of Brazil provoked such disparate responses that even within the institute one could find a positivist and evolutionist perspective, a Roman Catholic perspective, and a romantic view of the Indian, who in the minds of most Brazilians was beginning to take on the dimensions of a national symbol. The combination of an evolutionist view and Catholic doctrine yielded a position that, while censurable, offered solutions:

> One could then foster the education of these wretched forest children, while at the same time inuring them to the mild yoke of labor, rendering them useful to themselves and their country. It would be at the same time the test of and the solution for a perfect civilization. Humanity and civilization, therefore, could still have hope. (*Journal of the Historical and Geographical Institute of Brazil,* 1854: 272)

Those who espoused this point of view—primarily Jesuits and people linked to the military sector, such as Colonel José de Machado Oliveira or Domingos Alves Moniz Barretos—believed that they could save the indigenous population through catechism. Instruction would deliver the primitive people from their "barbarous and errant" ways and usher them into civilization, which the Catholic evolutionists understood to be an eminently Caucasian phenomenon. Advocates of this point of view held the same theoretical stance with regard to the Afro-Brazilian population: even though the Afro-Brazilians were considered by some to be of an "even more inferior" race, they remained human. The social evolutionist and monogenist model held firm, consistent with the powerful Roman Catholic influence of the area.

The winning essay in a contest sponsored by the institute in 1844 to recognize the best project on "How to Write the History of Brazil" illustrates the Catholic evolutionist position well. Karl Friedrich Philipp von Martius, a German naturalist and correspondent member of the institute, won the prize with a thesis focused on the specifics of the trajectory of the tropical nation, created and inhabited by three mixed races:

> Anyone who would endeavor to write the History of Brazil, a country so full of promise, should never lose sight of which elements vie for the development of its people. These people, however, are the result of a convergence of three races and are diverse in the extreme. (*Journal of the Historical and Geographical Institute of Brazil,* 1844: 389–90)

The winning project proposed, therefore, a "formula," a means of understanding Brazil. The idea was to correlate the development of the country with the desired improvement specific to each of the three races that populated the nation. According to von Martius, the races possessed fundamentally different characteristics. Whites would play the role of civilizers. Indians would do what they must to retrieve their original dignity, which would enable them to climb the stairs toward civilization. Afro-Brazilians would serve as the whipping boys and represented an impediment to the nation's progress: "There is no doubt that Brazil would have had," wrote von Martius, "a very different evolution had those miserable Negro slaves not been introduced"

(*Journal of the Historical and Geographical Institute of Brazil,* 1854).[16]

Brazilians drifted back to von Martius's racial interpretation some years later, although they altered the tone of his argument.[17] In any case, the notion of racial hierarchy remained:

> I will begin by saying that the Negro trunk was the first on earth . . . then came the red and finally the white, which probably coincided with the first Ice Age. . . . I also believe that nature will proceed in the same manner in their order of disappearance. The Negro trunk will disappear before the red, then followed by the white. (Domingos Alves Moniz Berreto, *Journal of the Historical and Geographical Institute of Brazil,* 1873: 389–91)

From then on, two lively and clearly distinct schools of thought became apparent. While the Afro-Brazilians bore the stigma of the impossibility of adaptation, the Indians were still enveloped by a romantic vision. Although the idealistic view of the Indians was equally unscientific, the status conferred on this group was substantial. Influenced by well-known Brazilian literary romantics such as Gonçalves de Magalhães and Gonçalves Dias, the idealized view of the Indian inherent in literary Indianism contributed to a national sense of self and became part of the Western literary tradition. According to Antonio Candido, from this romantic depiction of the Indian emerged the "writer with a mission," the poet-spokesman of greater truths and deeper feelings (Candido, 1959: 20–22).

Scholars of the Historical and Geographical Institute of Brazil opposed the historian Francisco Adolfo de Varnhagen, because he endorsed massacres of the indigenous population, and they urged that the image of both Indians and Afro-Brazilians be restored, because these scholars considered both races to be, in the words of Gonçalves Dias, "capable of civilization . . . and able to build an enlightened society" (*Journal of the Historical and Geographical*

Institute of Brazil, 1876). In the 1890s this idea would take deeper root when the problem of the "adaptation of diverse races" would be viewed through a scientific and determinist lens.

Historical Discourse: An Official Voice

Surveying the journal's articles on historical subjects, what immediately stands out is that 40 percent of all of the collected essays are devoted to colonial history (the period from 1500 to 1808). (See Table 8, where historical articles are arranged by period.) This bias probably reflects the Brazilian self-perception at the time. Concerned with probing events in the interest of creating a national identity, the scholars writing for the journal found ideal materials in the most distant moments of the country's history.

A good example of the association's interest in the colonial past is shown in the articles devoted to the "discovery" of Brazil by Portugal in 1500. The subject attracted such influential authors

Table 8 Historical Subjects of the Journal of the Historical and Geographical Institute of Brazil

PERIOD	PERCENT
Before 1500	1%
1500–1580	7%
1580–1654	9%
1654–1750	10%
1750–1808	13%
1808–1823	12%
1823–1845	14%
1845–1889	14%
1889–1893	14%
Unclassified	6%
TOTAL	100%

POPPINO, 1953.

as Varnhagen, Gonçalves Dias, Alfonso Taunay, and Gonçalves de Magalhães, to name just a few. The political emancipation of 1822, understood almost as a second discovery, was also the inspiration for a series of studies within the institute. Written some decades after the fact, most of the articles served as justifications of their authors' patriotic convictions and sense of duty. The chronicling of Brazil's political independence was also fundamental to establishing a historical chronology and to shaping a national identity.

Interestingly, however, it seems that writers were not given the benefit of the doubt in terms of being objective in writing accounts of their own time, as the following comments on historical philosophy reveal:

> The wisest plan is the one organized by the decade system in which one relates the facts occurring only within specific periods. . . . It seems appropriate that history be thus confined, in order that no national historian need introduce contemporary history and subject himself to irresponsible judgments and other aggravations. Archive the documents, and the time will come. (*Journal of the Historical and Geographical Institute of Brazil,* 1882: 159)

To write history in this fashion was to glean documents, as if one were mining gemstones. The historians selecting facts were presumed to be working with the same impartiality found in the sharp-sighted workman who separates the good stones from the bad, or even from those stones that offer only minimal luster to the eye.

An Era of Pessimism

Political analysis was at the center of most of the historical articles, as one can see in Table 9. Themes such as Brazilian independence and its different agents, conspiracies, colonial invasions

Table 9 Themes in the Journal of the Historical and Geographical Institute of Brazil

TYPE OF HISTORY	1839–1864	1865–1889	1890–1914	1915–1938
Political	47%	43%	25%	18%
Social	15%	27%	44%	55%
Religious	23%	15%	10%	11%
Military	8%	8%	9%	8%
Economic	7%	7%	12%	8%

POPPINO, 1953.

and their consequences, the discovery of Brazil, and the removal of Dom João VI with the Portuguese court to Brazil were frequently treated in the *Journal of the Historical and Geographical Institute of Brazil,* with the emphasis being on the political consequences of these events, and the conclusion always being that the events had been inevitable.

In the 1890s, however, this laudatory slant began to change. With ever greater frequency, texts on "the nation's problems" began appearing, which, taken as a whole, revealed a disheartening view. The year 1908 was a particularly significant benchmark, because in that year three articles appeared in a single issue that announced new viewpoints for the institute.

The first of them, written by Euclides da Cunha, an active member of the institute, was titled "From Independence to Republic." The objective of his article was to present a lofty account of the period 1822–89. The originality of this piece lay not so much in its theme as in the author's theoretical and critical stance:

> The new currents, formative forces from Littre's comfortable positivism to all of Comte's orthodox principles

> and schools, and from Darwin's restrictive conclusions to Spencer's daring generalizations—in fact, what they have given us is not their abstract principles, or laws incomprehensible to the vast majority, but the great conquests sketched out during our century. (*Journal of the Historical and Geographical Institute of Brazil,* 1908: 70)

After introducing a new methodology, the author concluded his argument in a somewhat pessimistic tone, suggesting the beginning of a new era for the republic. It signalled the end of acquiescence for the institute, the end of wishful thinking and idyllic views.

Euclides da Cunha, author of *Os Sertões* [Rebellion in the backlands], was not alone in offering a less than glowing historical account. In this same issue was an article titled "Social Brazil," by Silvio Romero, also an active member of the institute. The literary critic from the Recife School of Law began his article with a declaration of his methodology: "What Brazil needs most is social criticism, preferably individual psychological criticism . . . which leads to an understanding of temperament and character" (*Journal of the Historical and Geographical Institute of Brazil,* 1908: 105). Striking a balance between the strains of modern anthropological literature, which included works by Le Play, Preville, and Herbert Spencer, Silvio Romero gave his conclusions about the overwhelmingly deterministic influences involved in the formation of each race and the consequences of the mixing of the races. Beginning with the assumption that whites played a fundamental role in the civilizing process, Romero, instead of lamenting the "barbarism of the Indian and the ineptitude of the Negro," went on to seek original solutions to the problems of race. In light of the country's state of decline, he saw an opportunity in racial blending, and it was on the mestizo, as a local phenomenon well adapted to the environment, that the author pinned all his hopes.

Although the third article printed in this same 1908 volume did not seek to overhaul national history in the manner of

Euclides da Cunha, nor did it even trace Brazil's racial profile, it did point to an important revision of contemporary historiography. In "A história antes e após Buckle: reflexões sobre o conceito de história" [History before and after Buckle: Reflections on the concept of history], Pedro A. Carneiro Lessa presented a vast panorama of world historiography up to the determinist model of history, which he considered "the only scientific one." According to this barrister from the São Paulo School of Law, the famous English historian and geographical determinist Henry Buckle was relevant for "elevating the important branch of historical research to the level of that of the natural scientists," which would confer on the discipline the certainty that its directions would be "governed by consistent laws" (*Journal of the Historical and Geographical Institute of Brazil,* 1908: 195–285). Through his writings, Lessa introduced to the institute the interpretations of Buckle, the author of *History of Civilization in England,* a work known in that era for its defense of the unequalled influence of geographical factors on history, as well as for its conclusions about the deficiencies of Brazil and its people: "The governing factor is nature: a thousand years of discipline would not alter the character of the Negro or of the Chinaman. The former would not lessen his vulgar and violent passions, and the latter would not unchain himself from his traditions and his habits" (*Journal of the Historical and Geographical Institute of Brazil,* 1908: 216).

Although Buckle's work had come late to the institute, it had a powerful effect. The use of a determinist and scientific discourse, which combined the credibility of axioms with the objectivity of a science whose parameters were established by the observed predictability of natural phenomena, seemed to constitute the ideal formula for wrestling with complex regional issues in Brazil, according to Lessa: "The will of individuals should be limited by laws that conform to the principles of determinism and by ideas that effect advantage and the betterment of the species" (*Journal of the Historical and Geographical Institute of Brazil,* 1908: 285).

Thus, as the twentieth century began, a new way of understanding history began to prevail. To write national history was to take part in a debate on contemporary problems and the uncertainties of the future as well as to integrate the era's scientific advances.

On the other hand, on the racial issue, von Martius's comprehension of history, dating from the first years of the institute, began to acquire new vigor. As we have seen, through the use of a formula von Martius sought to emphasize the uniqueness of a country defined by the presence of three formative and unequally capable races. He believed that the black populations were typified by "utter deficiency," even in regard to the ability for religious or cultural expression, and that the forces of evolution would eventually lead to the demise of the black man:

> We are in the presence of an example of the application of the great law of adaptation to one's environment and of natural selection in the struggle for life. . . . It is precisely because of their incompatibility with Romanism and with civilization that the fetishistic African practices are destined to disappear completely. . . . Besides, the Caucasian race is relentlessly absorbing the Negro. Therefore, within days the fetishes will have no more worshipers. *Les dieux s'en vont* [The gods are leaving]. (*Journal of the Historical and Geographical Institute of Brazil,* 1912: 195–260)

Loyal to its original project, which was to construct "a national history as a way of uniting and transmitting a unique and articulated system of interpretations" (Guimarães, 1988: 17), the Historical and Geographical Institute of Brazil embraced its peers while at the same time it excluded "the foreigners on Brazilian lands." These aliens were, of course, the Afro-Brazilians who were considered to be a "factor in the backwardness of civilization." In this way the institute weighed in on the determinist debate taking place in other intellectual circles of the era using the model of a patriotic and Catholic history, imbued with evolutionist discourse and tied to sanctioned political views.

At this point it is useful to note how the determinist model functioned in other institutes that were alike not only in name but also in their notions of what constituted the writing of history.[18]

THE ARCHEOLOGICAL AND GEOGRAPHICAL INSTITUTE OF PERNAMBUCO
"The Lion of the North"

> The fine example of Pernambuco is worthy of recognition and worthy of imitation for all that stirs us in our love of history, our foundation of patriotic sentiments and nationalistic temper.
> —*Journal of the Archeological and Geographical Institute of Pernambuco,* 1904: 333

The Archeological and Geographical Institute of Pernambuco was founded "[o]n January 28, 1862, on the forty-first anniversary of Independence and of the Empire of Brazil and anniversary of the deliverance of Pernambuco from Dutch dominion" (*Journal of the Archeological and Geographical Institute of Pernambuco,* 1863/11: 332). The solemn session that inaugurated the institute was accompanied by all manner of pomp and circumstance befitting the creation of the second historical institute in Brazil, and the first such institute in the northeast. The event gathered a large part of the region's economic and intellectual elite, and forthwith Joaquim Pires Machado Portello, a well-known local landholder, was named interim president.

All the speeches delivered at this first meeting underscored two of the institute's primary functions, which were writing the nation's history and demonstrating that Pernambucan history in particular was relevant within the context of the country's history. One of the speeches revealed this regional pride:

> Pernambuco, already one of the glories of Brazil, stated before Parliament that it had a history of its own, that because of its geographical location, its outstanding natural gifts, the virtues of its children, and the pride of its residents, it has played roles in all of the nation's epochs, and it has without doubt always tendered abundant material for the extensive pages of the annals of Brazil. (*Journal of the Archeological and Geographical Institute of Pernambuco,* 1863: 5)

In fact, in this Pernambuco association the regional focus was so marked that texts devoted to the study of the area amounted to 67 percent of all the articles published in the institute's journal from 1870 to 1930.

The Archeological and Geographical Institute of Pernambuco was responding to the political and cultural aspirations of the province of Pernambuco, which hoped to maintain its hegemony at least over the interior of the northeastern region. Until 1820 Pernambuco had been responsible for 50 percent of Brazil's export income from the sale of sugar and cotton. Since the beginning of the nineteenth century, however, the region had experienced a conspicuous economic decline as a result of international competition and the subsequent drop in price of its primary export products.[19]

The region fell further behind after 1870, when fundamental shifts in the equilibrium between Brazilian regions began to occur. Not only did changes in prices and incentives for agricultural products provoke regional discord, but the politics surrounding European immigration, which was facilitated in the south but inhibited in the north, introduced the phenomenon that the abolitionist and historian Joaquim Nabuco called "the two Brazils."[20]

With a survey of the relations between the agrarian north and the Empire one can make a critical reflection on the situation of the great northeastern agricultural enterprise and the state of Pernambuco. "The truth," stated the historian Sérgio Buarque de Holanda, "is that the empire of plantations, but only of those plantations in more developed areas, begins only with the Republic, because the other areas were in inexorable decline" (Holanda, 1951). Pernambuco's institute was, therefore, the fruit of a decadent traditional rural elite. Because of the insecurity caused by economic reversals, the region's rural elite enjoyed "the reassurances of cultural romanticists seeking to preserve the past as a shield against an uncertain future" (Levine, 1978: 72).

The fact that new members of the institute were accepted purely on the basis of personal connections corroborates Levine's assertion. For example, a candidate did not have to furnish proof of scientific work or even intellectual competence to become an active member. The only prerequisite was that a member of the institute formally submit a candidate's name for approval.[21] The traits of the institute already tended somewhat toward the extreme, but the organization's recruitment practice only made the situation worse. The wealthy, self-selected society at the institute concerned itself with unearthing facts and luminaries of the local history in order to better define the image of the local agrarian elites. This helped guarantee self-perpetuation.

The socioeconomic profile of the membership could not have been more homogeneous; the membership tended to be composed of large local landholders, Church officials, and a few professionals, the latter of whom were usually graduates of the Recife School of Law. Even this mild diversity was only apparent, however, because the agrarian aristocracy traditionally supplied the "countryside, the Church, and the legal profession" with its offspring. The Recife School of Law educated and prepared almost every person who would go on to join the northeastern ruling elite.[22]

The institute's first board of directors reflected the ambition of the Pernambucan elites. Among the names associated with the center's first years are representatives of the Church, such as

Monsignor Dr. Francisco Muniz Tavares, as well as personalities from the local reigning landholders, such as the Baron of Livramento or Major Salvador Henrique de Albuquerque. Through the institute's leaders the importance of northern Brazil within the scope of Brazilian history would be evident, even in the midst of a period that saw a transition of money and power from the northeastern to the southern regions.

The institute's name was different from that of its peers, and more than signifying a nominal dissimilarity, this difference seemed to reveal a distinct theoretical perspective. Archeology, for the Archeological and Geographical Institute of Pernambuco, was the discipline that "studied antiquities and geography, in all their facets, insofar as they applied to Pernambuco" (*Journal of the Archeological and Geographical Institute of Pernambuco,* 1863: 22). This was the extent of the organization's interest in archeology. In fact, articles rigidly defined as covering archeology and dealing with prehistorical Brazil amounted to only 2 percent of the journal's texts.

Despite its unique name, the institute adhered to statutes similar to those established by Rio's Historical and Geographical Institute of Brazil, although with a special emphasis on Pernambuco:

> Article 1: The goal of the Archeological and Geographical Institute of Pernambuco is to collect all available or reported historical documents, monuments, and traditions possible. It will afford special attention to the history of the old colonial provinces of Pernambuco and Itamaracá from the Age of Discoveries until today. (*Journal of the Archeological and Geographical Institute of Pernambuco,* 1863: 23)

If in the case of Rio's institute one can detect a strong leaning toward regional studies, in the Archeological and Geographical Institute of Pernambuco local history occupied almost the sum total of the works and activities undertaken by the institute.

From the coins to the monuments, epigraphs, or celebrations, Pernambuco was always proudly on display in the work of the institute.

Visits to Recife by Dom Pedro II in 1859 and Francisco Adolfo de Varnhagen in 1861 had wounded provincial pride, bringing into focus the region's perception that its past had been relegated to oblivion. It was only with the founding of the Archeological and Geographical Institute that Pernambuco gained an institutional structure for preserving local memory. The founding of the institute was, therefore, linked to the need to define the Pernambucan version of official history and to avoid using foreign criteria to write that history, such as had been done in Varnhagen's *História geral do Brasil* [General history of Brazil].[23] When Monsignor Muniz Tavares, himself a participant in the Pernambuco Revolt of 1817, proposed the creation of an association in Pernambuco, it became clear that a goal was to diminish the historiographical hegemony assumed by the Brazilian Historical and Geographical Institute in Rio de Janeiro.

Despite their initial sense of inferiority, members of the Archeological and Geographical Institute of Pernambuco eventually developed a tone different from the one they first boasted. The institute soon resembled an "antiquarian society" devoted to issues unique to the region,[24] and the view of the institute's members became, for the most part, moderate.

Journal of the Archeological and Geographical Institute of Pernambuco: "The Pride of Being Pernambucan"

In the first meeting of the Archeological and Geographical Institute of Pernambuco its members decided to create a "quarterly pamphlet" that would include "at least thirty-two printed pages." In accordance with institutional statutes, the journal "would publish proceedings of meetings, historical works, members' memoirs judged interesting to the history of Pernambuco and Brazil, as well as announcements of works on the history of

Pernambuco written by other associations or literary persons" (*Journal of the Archeological and Geographical Institute of Pernambuco,* 1863: 22). But the stated intentions were only partially realized. As of 1894 the quarterly publication was an annual, and the text of the journal consisted primarily of proceedings and historical speeches whose function was mainly commemorative, leaving little space for essays dedicated to original studies of history or geography.

These and other characteristics of the publication can be better understood by analyzing the first thirty volumes, from 1863 to 1930. As one can see in Table 10, the distribution of themes covered in the journal is similar to that of the journals of the other institutes. In addition, the articles reflect the predominance of patriotic and commemorative history within the association.

Works on Pernambuco accounted for 83 percent of all the articles published in the journal. Furthermore, the themes and events chosen were covered repeatedly. For example, the journal published sixty-four articles (51 percent) on the Dutch invasion,* all of which interpreted the incident similarly. While on the one hand the writers lamented what was described in one piece as "the ignominious foreign yoke" (*Journal of the Archeological and*

* In the late sixteenth century, Portugal was not known for its international aggression. But with the unification of the Iberian Kingdoms of Portugal and Spain in 1570, Portugal effectively inherited Spain's enemies. Among these enemies was Holland, which had recently gained its freedom from Spain. This nation presented a problem for Brazil. Because of Holland's powerful merchant fleet, Portugal had earlier contracted the Dutch West Indies Company to trade and distribute Brazilian sugar. But Dutch presence in Spanish-controlled ports had been banned since 1590, and Holland had to withdraw from Brazil. These factors help explain why the Dutch invaded Pernambuco, one of Brazil's primary sugar-producing areas, in 1624. The Dutch occupied Pernambuco until they were driven out in 1645, by which time Portugal was free from the Spanish yoke. Although the Dutch expulsion has traditionally been enthusiastically celebrated by Pernambucans, many recent studies have documented the positive impact and even the strong popularity of the "invasion."

Table 10 Distribution of Articles in the Journal of the Archeological and Geographical Institute of Pernambuco

DISCIPLINE	NUMBER OF ARTICLES	PERCENT
History	124	46%
Geography and geology	51	16%
Biographies and genealogies	57	18%
Anthropology and ethnology	10	3%
Literature and bibliography	5	1%
Natural science and archeology	8	2%
Miscellaneous	44	14%
TOTAL	299	100%

Geographical Institute of Pernambuco, 1863: 73), on the other hand they praised the heroic response of the "valiant and patriotic" citizens of Pernambuco (*Journal of the Archeological and Geographical Institute of Pernambuco,* 1868: 461).

The Pernambucan journal's articles on history covered topics similar to those covered by the other institutes, including articles whose focus was primarily political, followed by works that dealt with social or cultural issues within the province (see Table 11).

Table 11 Themes in the Journal of the Archeological and Geographical Institute of Pernambuco

TYPE OF HISTORY	NUMBER OF ARTICLES	PERCENT
Political	70	55%
Social/cultural	29	23%
Military	18	14%
Religious	6	4%
Economic	5	3%
TOTAL	128	99%

These articles, in turn, ushered in a brand of carelessly written articles that became typical for the institute, in which the authors combined historical data with local folklore. One piece after another retraced the history of the Pernambuco anthem, studied traditional theater, described historical monuments, or gathered local legends of remote origins. Such a link between the institute and folkloric studies was unexpected, and it seemed even to match the profile of the few scholars associated with the institute, such as Miranda de Souza Gomes or Barboza Viana, who remained in Pernambuco and became absorbed by local themes and issues.[25]

"A Pernambucan Race"

As a discipline, anthropology also received special treatment at the institute, as it was through this study, as well as archeology, that the institute's members sought to determine the existence of a "Pernambucan race":

> To a number of travellers it seemed that Pernambuco had already been occupied by a people of more advanced civilization than anywhere else in Brazil. What a stir it would provoke if we postulated that there had been a time when America, now so disfigured, had heroic feats the likes of which we celebrate today. (*Journal of the Archeological and Geographical Institute of Pernambuco,* 1898: 172)

Not all the articles on anthropology confined themselves to a search for a "local race." A good part of them theorized on the inherent differences of humans, exalting the superiority of whites and condemning the resident indigenous and black populations:

> In terms of the internal culture, the savage is the equivalent of the beggar, and as for external culture, he is the slave moaning under the superstitions of his passions. Just as the

> botanist must study not only edible plants but poisonous plants as well, the ethnologist must study the aberrations and transgressions of the savage too. (*Journal of the Archeological and Geographical Institute of Pernambuco,* 1922: 194)

One might say that the Archeological and Geographical Institute of Pernambuco was, perhaps, the only one of the historical and geographical institutes to point to concrete solutions, betting on the notion of "whitening" as a resource for regional development:

> Without the influx of whites, the northern region is condemned to stagnation and monotony, because it is known in biological philosophy that, without the rejuvenating influx of racial melding, a single hereditary racial ancestry will not prove immutable but fatally decadent. (*Journal of the Archeological and Geographical Institute of Pernambuco,* 1869: 187)

In spite of their radical racial analyses, the institute's historians still found room to glorify the Biblical model of monogenism: "the wonderful concept of the author of creation, *Philosophia Quaerit, Religio possidet, Veritatem*" [While philosophy seeks the truth, religion possesses it] (*Journal of the Archeological and Geographical Institute of Pernambuco,* 1891: 268). Through these and other articles, the Pernambucan institute's writers arrived at the same solution that Rio's institute discovered. Writers in Rio had deftly combined the "era's modern racial-scientific thought" with the precepts of Biblical scripture and monogenism. The result was the acceptance of a "good miscegenation" in view of the "racial decadence" of the region.[26]

Pernambucans held an ambiguous view of miscegenation. Although miscegenation was a threatening idea, it was considered a moderate solution, compatible with the orderly image of society held by the Pernambuco elite. Therefore, despite the institute's use of polygenist analytical models to assess local conditions, monogenism and the theory of evolution prevailed.

Shaping the Pernambucan Identity

Despite the fact that Pernambucan historians' sense of history resembled that of other institutes, their objectives were usually notably different in that distinct historical themes had relevance for them only when those themes were interwoven with a local focus, as can be seen in the institute's treatment of abolitionism:

> Gentlemen, in everything that I have read about this subject, whether from the political, historical, juridical or philosophical perspective, the name of our legendary and heroic province has been forgotten and sidelined, either literally or figuratively. It is time to take back our rightful share and proclaim out loud the role we have played in abolition. . . . If there be a man uninspired by our noble plan, he is not a Pernambucan. (*Journal of the Archeological and Geographical Institute of Pernambuco,* 1891: 268)

Therefore, whether through the presentation of facts about Pernambuco or through the presentation of episodes pertaining to national history, the position of the Archeological and Geographical Institute of Pernambuco was always the same: to glorify the special role the province had played, even if doing so required exaggerating the truth.[27]

The invasion and occupation by the Dutch thus became a kind of creation myth for the region, a defining point for the Pernambucan identity, and the primary characters in the story emerged anointed as heroes of the land:

> It was an unequal battle, but such virtue, heroism and selflessness had never before been seen. Each Brazilian was a

> hero, each hero a history, each history an eternity! . . . but the most brilliant miracle was not the power of man but of God. It was a sacred history: Moses was Vidal, Gideon was Vieira, Samson was Henrique Dias, Joshua was Camarão. To them we owe our freedom, our religion and our country. . . . The Archeological Institute of Pernambuco is the symbol of an adoring public, and it is here that we proffer two cults: to Religion and to Country. (*Journal of the Archeological and Geographical Institute of Pernambuco,* 1868: 460–61)

Pernambucan historians advanced religion and patriotism as defining elements of the Pernambucan. Traits such as valor, selflessness, and patriotism became the core of their identity. These historians also persistently recalled the Revolt of 1817 against Portuguese rule,* an event viewed as a herald of the "Pernambucan avant-garde," referring to the incontrovertible defense of national liberty: "Pernambuco, Lion of the North, cradle from which issued the first cries for liberty and the Brazilian Republic" (*Journal of the Archeological and Geographical Institute of Pernambuco,* 1916: 431).

The Pernambucan institute showed a clear preference for studies of colonial history, as one can see in Table 12. The expulsion of the Dutch and the Revolution of 1817 were the subjects of many of the articles of this period, and there were even whole volumes devoted to such events. There were no articles written on the republican period, and there were few relating to the Empire.

In spite of the model provided by Rio de Janeiro's institute, the Archeological and Geographical Institute of Pernambuco retained the characteristics of the society that surrounded it and the elite group that supported it. As historian Robert Levine wrote, "For the northeastern society, the life of the rural planter represented the pinnacle of history, tradition and order" (1978: 50). The firm

* A republican and abolitionist revolt inspired by the French and American Revolutions, but put down easily by the government.

Table 12 Historical Subjects of the Journal of the Archeological and Geographical Institute of Pernambuco

PERIOD	NUMBER OF ARTICLES	PERCENT
Colonial	99	78%
Empire	28	22%
Republic	0	—
TOTAL	127	100%

desire to preserve a regional identity and an emphasis on order and stability helped to sustain the Pernambucans' pluralistic vision of the country, which, according to Levine, tended to mature after 1889. The republic arrived in the northeastern province that year without much fanfare and received the support of liberal and conservative political leaders. A year later the institute discovered its own methods and official credos within republicanism and federalism and lent its support as well.

But if the new political administration did not alter the institutional profile, one cannot say that the new regime had no effect on the region's sense of place. With the end of northeastern hegemony an alliance was established between political conservatism and regionalism in Pernambuco. At the same time, interest in the theme of the Dutch domination enjoyed a renaissance, to the extent that the revival helped to create a large part of the region's identity. According to Pernambucan historian Evaldo Cabral de Mello, the Dutch played a central role in the nativist Pernambucan ideology, from its conception until the middle of the nineteenth century. Over the course of the next two hundred years, however, "nativism would have to accommodate changes to the colonial economy, changes to altered power relationships among local groups and among these groups and the cities, and, finally, changes to the appearance of dominant ideologies" (Cabral de Mello 1986: 15). Inherited from the Luso-Brazilian chronicles, the nativist imagination tended to read the period's history from an experiential perspective, selecting topics that were consistent with contemporary perceptions.

Two important events in the province pointed toward its permanent integration into the Empire. One was the Equatorial Confederation (1824), a republican and abolitionist revolt in Pernambuco, which, like the uprising seven years earlier, was easily put down by government forces. The other was the Praieira Revolt (1848–49), another unsuccessful Pernambucan insurrection, which, despite its failure, was significant for the broad social class support that it had.

In sum, according to Evaldo Cabral de Mello, these events led to the demise of nativism as a political force, "whose meaning from then on would be reduced to little more than the ideological underpinnings upon which the Institute was founded in 1862" (1986: 15).

We now turn to an exploration of how this same regionalist attitude coexisted not with local elites in obvious decline but with Brazilians in a state that used economic progress as a springboard for regional glorification. As the last example of the institutes, let us now examine the São Paulo Historical and Geographical Institute.

THE SÃO PAULO HISTORICAL AND GEOGRAPHICAL INSTITUTE
"The Bandeirante *Model"*

> The history of São Paulo is the history of Brazil itself.
>
> —*Journal of the São Paulo Historical and Geographical Institute,* 1895: 1

The following note appeared on the first page of *The State of São Paulo* newspaper on November 10, 1894:

> Messrs. Jaguaribe Filho, Antônio Pizza and Estevan Leão Bouroul invite all men of letters of this capital to a meeting at noon today in the Academy salon, which the Baron of Ramalho has graciously provided. The purpose of this meeting is to discuss the creation of the São Paulo Historical Institute.

Five days later, in the same newspaper, there was another reference to the sixty-nine people who had participated in the first meeting of the institute, as well as a message of congratulations:

> With numerous persons in attendance, the new association was instated. . . . We congratulate the organizers of such a useful institution, and in the name of the State we congratulate them for achieving such an important deed for our historical and literary life.

It was with pride that São Paulo received the new institute, its members drawn in large part from the state's limited number of intellectual elite, most of whom were already associated with the São Paulo Museum and the Academy of Law.[28]

The new institute had two distinct goals: to follow the model envisioned by the Historical and Geographical Institute of Brazil and to attract particular attention to São Paulo. "The history of São Paulo is the history of Brazil" was certainly a catchy phrase, but it was also one which, when it appeared in the first volume of the São Paulo journal, was clearly designed to provoke. The São Paulo institute's mission was clearly a challenge laid at the door of the Carioca* association, which through its title had designated itself, in effect, "The Brazilian Institute." With the inauguration of the São Paulo organization Rio de Janeiro's apparent hold over the whole of Brazil became increasingly fragile.

* *Carioca* is a term that refers to Rio de Janeiro or, especially, to residents of Rio de Janeiro. Here, it refers to the Historical and Geographical Institute of Brazil.

The self-assurance of the São Paulo institute was evident in the total absence of references to the Carioca institute, which was not even among the associations with whom the São Paulo institute had official communication. Ancient disputes,[29] where only the details differed, reappeared. And, not limiting themselves to institutional concerns, they rekindled quarrels among the dominant elites of both states. With the burgeoning of the coffee-producing areas of the state of São Paulo and the concomitant decline of the prodigious plantations in Rio de Janeiro's Paraíba Valley in the 1880s, a shift was already beginning to occur in the nation's balance of power. At the end of the nineteenth century São Paulo was the most dynamic state, owing not only to its economic success but also to its internal consolidation, made possible through its extensive railway system.[30] This new order would not be immune from those institutional machinations that would tend to produce and reproduce internally the dilemmas occurring in political and economic spheres.

It remained for the São Paulo Historical and Geographical Institute to rewrite Brazilian history, holding before itself its own examples and trajectory: "Let us pull together as an Institute, so that through the past lustrum of our beloved guild may reign the glory of the State of São Paulo, of Brazil, of Civilization, of Science" (*Journal of the São Paulo Historical and Geographical Institute,* 1914: 13). The work of the organization was a matter of seeking historical facts and figures relating to the state of São Paulo that would be sufficiently representative to create a decidedly regional history but that at the same time would tell the history of the country as a whole.

A theme that the institute's members believed warranted special attention as unique and regional was the colonial expeditions, or *bandeirismo*:* "Let us go to work, esteemed and distinguished

* The word *bandeirismo* and its associated word *bandeirante* are terms that derive from the Brazilian colonial expeditionary forces that searched the interior of the territory for riches, including slaves. The words refer, respectively, to the

members, and let us pull together as an Institute as if we were the soldiers of a regiment from years past, for we are truly members of an expedition from the Past, which seeks to execute, in multiple and continuous forays, a raid in search of historical truths" (*Journal of the São Paulo Historical and Geographical Institute,* 1897: 85). The nation's media made regular reference to the "era of expeditionaries," reclaiming it as a symbol for the pioneering state of São Paulo, but ignoring that, although these men did extend the country's frontiers, they also plundered the indigenous populations and committed acts of cruelty and violence against them.

Despite the unfortunate choice of *bandeirismo* as a symbol, the institute grew and developed. At the same time, São Paulo enjoyed a period of political and economic might and invested the São Paulo Historical and Geographical Institute with the task of returning the symbols of "culture and civilization" to the state, symbols that until then had resided with the Crown.

Creating a São Paulo History

> One of the noble features of the Institute is the perfect replication of a dominant trait of the São Paulo land: its generosity, its sublime hospitality, . . . the highest expression of human solidarity. Tradition is the rule here: São Paulo has never fit within its borders.
>
> —*Alfonso d'Escragnolle Taunay* (Journal of the São Paulo Historical and Geographical Institute, *1912: 97*)

The rules, regulations, and committees that would govern the activities of the new association were decided at the institute's first meeting. Based on how the organization represented itself in its journal, the institute's basic idea was consistent with that of

---

expeditionary phenomenon and to the adventurer himself. These words derive from the Portuguese word *bandeira,* or flag, which the *bandeirantes* carried into the wilderness.

the Historical and Geographical Institute of Brazil, which was to emphasize the patriotic and civic consciousness of the nation:

> There is a need for an association to promote the means to study documents with which one can know the origins of the most important facts of our ancestors, or emend mistaken notions, or fill in gaps in our knowledge. . . . The die has been cast . . . that our history be the faithful interpretation of events and the practical account of our patriots. (*Journal of the São Paulo Historical and Geographical Institute,* 1895: 1)

The São Paulo institute's mode of operation was similar to that of its Carioca counterpart: the members met every other week, and the profile of the institute's hierarchy was the same as in the other associations. The president was always a public figure for show, and the secretary was the true "performer" within the organization. For example, on the institute's first board of directors, elected in 1895, Antônio Toledo Pizza, a researcher and historian at the São Paulo museum, held the position of secretary, and Dr. Cesário Motta Júnior, an eminent figure in the republic because of his work as minister of law and jurisconsult, was named president of the institution. Canon José Valois de Castro represented the Church, and the republic of Brazil's president, Prudente José de Moraes Barros, was proclaimed honorary president. Over the years other secretaries were the historians Couto Magalhães and Afonso de Freitas and, in 1932, the anthropologist Plínio Ayrosa. It was common to have *meritorious members* in the institutes because they could be useful on the national level (examples of these at the São Paulo institute were the Baron of Rio Branco and Counsellor Rui Barbosa). The presidents of the São Paulo Historical and Geographical Institute had first been serving as meritorious members when they were chosen for the job; for example, Manuel Antônio Duarte de Azevedo (1897–1912) was a *catedrático,* or distinguished professor, in the School of Law, a conservative party congressman, Minister of the Navy and Minister of Justice, a counsellor of the state and, during the republic, a senator. Altino Arantes (1916–22), who presided over only plenary sessions, was also president of the state of São Paulo and of the São Paulo Academy of Letters.

On the outside, the activities of the São Paulo institute did not significantly differ from those of the Historical and Geographical Institute of Brazil. Public ceremonies, the issuance of seals, the minting of coins, the commemoration of São Paulo historians, opinions on border difficulties between São Paulo and other states were considered fundamental undertakings of both institutes.

But beneath their exteriors the two institutes differed in important details. When the institutes were founded, political circumstances at the national level created distinct loyalties. That is, at the time it was established, the Historical and Geographical Institute of Brazil sought through its work to legitimize the imperial state, and later the republic; from the beginning the São Paulo Historical and Geographical Institute as a whole supported the new republic through its journal. So, for example, whereas the Historical and Geographical Institute of Brazil traditionally commemorated its "anniversary meeting" on the date of the emperor's first participation at an association event, the São Paulo Historical and Geographical Institute from the very beginning named the president of the republic, Prudente de Moraes, as its honorary and meritorious president.

On the other hand, the committees as well as the debate at the São Paulo institute primarily centered on historical and geographical issues specifically pertaining to São Paulo. Observe, for example, the following list of topics for study agreed upon for 1895:

> The emblems of São Paulo, the influence of the Tietê River on the civilization of São Paulo, railways in São Paulo, medical geography in São Paulo, the flora and fauna of São Paulo, the influence of the study of law on the civilization of São Paulo and the nation, public funds in São Paulo, the

Portuguese language and its São Paulo variants, the press in São Paulo. (*Journal of the São Paulo Historical and Geographical Institute,* 1895: 168)

Although the São Paulo institute was yet another establishment that sought to aggrandize its regional assets, behind it was a powerful state that enjoyed a secure economy. The financial stability of the institute was guaranteed by the donations of its members, who happened to be wealthy landholders, members of the professional class, and elements associated with the Church, as well as by regular contributions made by the state government. The São Paulo institute, which had its own headquarters and resources,[31] was uniquely situated to struggle for supremacy over the other regional institutes.

Journal of the São Paulo Historical and Geographical Institute: São Paulo as Text and Pretext

The thematic distribution of articles in the *Journal of the São Paulo Historical and Geographical Institute* is similar to that in the publications of the other institutes, as is shown in Table 13.[32] Historical articles predominate, constituting 45 percent of the total, and the journal taken as a whole exhibits a notably elitist and São Paulo–oriented vision, as is demonstrated by this statement: "One cannot expect all layers of our society to manifest simultaneously the love we exhibit for our national and São Paulo past, an indisputable demonstration of a country's civilization" (*Journal of the São Paulo Historical and Geographical Institute,* 1898: 526). This elitism was manifest not just in the representation of the historian, viewed as one of the chosen few, but also in the journal's constant glorification of the special role of São Paulo in Brazil's national history.[33]

The geographical and geological studies carried in the journal reflected a profile similar to that found in the journals of other

Table 13 Distribution of Articles in the Journal of the São Paulo Historical and Geographical Institute

DISCIPLINE	NUMBER OF ARTICLES	PERCENT
History	169	45%
Geography and geology	60	15%
Biographies	85	22%
Anthropology and ethnography	44	11%
International relations	5	1%
Reviews	4	1%
Miscellaneous	15	4%
TOTAL	382	99%

institutes. First, these articles were in the distinct minority. Second, their primary role was pragmatic; they dealt in particular with matters concerning the borders between São Paulo and Minas Gerais, which were then in litigation.[34]

Biographies occupied even greater space in the São Paulo institute publication than in the journals of other like institutes. Their role in the scheme of the institute was noteworthy: the biographies consecrated people who had previously been unknown in São Paulo history, and these writings constituted true "São Paulo peerage books," in a region where economic supremacy had not yet translated into cultural distinction.[35] Written to be read in the association's plenary meetings, the biographies took on additional meaning as the institution developed. They clearly separated the people who were to be remembered and linked to the history of the institute from the rest of the participants, uncelebrated and relegated to the membership lists monotonously reprinted in each new issue of the journal.

The creation of a history in São Paulo as elsewhere was associated with the notion that the past was something remote, but the institute also pursued other related interests. A clear disciplinary division emerged: while historical studies presupposed distance in time, anthropological studies pieced together a more immediate social and political context.

Anthropology in the São Paulo Historical and Geographical Institute: "From the Noble Savage to the Merely Savage"

The São Paulo institute's journal devoted more space to anthropology than its counterparts did (11 percent of its articles). This characteristic is consistent with the orientation of the institute. In fact, according to Sérgio Buarque de Holanda, in São Paulo "the new positivists, whether orthodox or heterodox, the Spencerians and a few materialists would come to join our philosophasters and our legacies of doctrines recommended by the Church" (Holanda, n.d.: 330).

Scholars at the São Paulo Historical and Geographical Institute held to an evolutionist and racial determinist anthropology that was associated with an epic and positivist vision of history. Their articles oscillated between a polygenist vision of humanity and the monogenist conclusions of Biblical scripture. As we shall see, the monogenist and positivist worldview lost to pressures exerted by the suspicion and fear that the polygenist model engendered. A pessimistic tone consistent with a "degenerative" vision at times prevailed, giving rise to images that were no longer idealized:

> My eyes are now open, and I perceive that such men live no longer in paradisiacal innocence and that the theories of Jean Jacques Rousseau are mere dreams. . . . The Americans do not represent a savage race but a degenerate race that turned savage. . . . Thus, a few centuries will pass, and the last American will lie down to die. All the primitive peoples of the continent wither when faced with another race. (*Journal of the São Paulo Historical and Geographical Institute,* 1904: 53–54)

There was no consensus. The radicalism of the sentiments quoted here represented the views of only a portion of the institute's members. But the fact of their expression gives a glimmer of a debate on the potential for the suppression of an indigenous race by the civilization process at the hands of the "white colonizing group."

Paradoxically, this radical interpretation distanced itself from the positions taken in other institutes at the same time. For example, scholars at the Recife School of Law and the Bahia School of Medicine feared a future of mixed blood in Brazil, and such a position was not uncommon among the elite members of the institutes. The same São Paulo elite that belonged to the São Paulo Historical and Geographical Institute assumed for itself the task of promoting an immigration policy that encouraged Europeans but restricted the entry of persons of African or Asian origin, based on the belief that the "savages who had become degenerate" would eventually die out.[36] Reflecting the uncertainty of the era, in 1906 the writer of an essay on the country's labor problem, published in the newspaper *O Estado de São Paulo* [The State of São Paulo], affirmed that "one expects little of the Indians, and even less of the blacks and mestizos" (March 17, 1906).

It was in this very context that the director of the São Paulo Museum, Herman von Ihering, defended in the press the policy of exterminating the Kaingang Indians, "in order that civilization might hasten the work of nature" (*The State of São Paulo,* 1911). He also used the institute's journal to scrutinize the differences between the Tupi Indians from the time of the conquest and the traitorous Kaingang from the end of the nineteenth century (*Journal of the São Paulo Historical and Geographical Institute,* 1895: 253). In 1911 Herman von Ihering returned to the question, severely criticizing the humanitarian position of certain indigenists and affirming the racial inferiority of the Kaingang (*Journal of the São Paulo Historical and Geographical Institute,* 1911).

At the same time, there were those at the institute who still held to the monogenist theories, based on their spiritual and romantic inclination. As we've seen, there is no unalloyed theoretical coherence to be found on racial determinism in the São Paulo Historical and Geographical Institute. Like the other historical institutes, the São Paulo group managed to mix evolutionism and social Darwinism, polygenism and monogenism, scientific and religious conclusions, as is evident in Leóncio do Amaral Gurgel's positions on the indigenous Brazilians. After citing a series of race scholars such as Agassiz, Littré, Broca, Morton, Pritchard, and Buffon, best known for their denunciations of the monogenist model, Gurgel concluded his article by writing: "It is acceptable to say that, as a Catholic and, therefore, based on faith, I already adhered to the idea of monogenism long before my studies on the issue confirmed my beliefs with absolute certainty. Since humans are all essentially the same, they all have the same exalted destiny" (*Journal of the São Paulo Historical and Geographical Institute,* 1907: 321). Alongside the new racial theories, therefore, the axioms of Roman Catholic monogenism coexisted, and they seemed to be, even for the members of the São Paulo institute, difficult to overcome. "In theory we are Darwinists, but in our heart we believe in monogenism," concluded a less rigorous essay, published in 1902 (*Journal of the São Paulo Historical and Geographical Institute*).

The resulting theoretical approach, as Sérgio Buarque de Holanda wrote, was a kind of "spiritualistic eclecticism" that successfully accommodated diverse methods and postulates in the service of interests that for the most part possessed little theoretical basis (Holanda, n.d.: 321). History seemed to explain white dominance at a time when the end of slavery was still a fresh memory. "The image of the end of our odious slavery remains clear before our eyes, but the paths that show the order that reigns after its end are clear as well," and history seemed to guarantee a "civilized" future, even in the European manner.

The Bandeirante *Model*

Members of the São Paulo institute displayed the same dominant interest in the colonial period as did other like institutes (see Table 14). Each institute chose to highlight different images and events in an effort to draw attention to the contributions of its region to Brazilian history. As we have seen, São Paulo showed a clear thematic preference for the phenomenon of the colonial expeditions, its historians being responsible for the approbation and popularization of the image of the *bandeirante,* an enduring part of Brazil's official history. They sought to establish a connection between the courageous and tireless exploits of the romantic and fearless adventurers who tamed the wilderness and the ascendant destiny of the state of São Paulo. In other words, they hoped to gain legitimacy for their region by establishing its origins in the actions of its early heroes.

According to historian Joseph Love, "if these historians have laid a foundation for the myth of the *bandeirantes'* almost Faust-like quest for adventure and opportunity, the mythmakers have accompanied the historians pari passu, linking São Paulo's current greatness with its 'ancient past'" (1980: 5). Without returning to the debate on the origins of the "São Paulo myth," it is useful to stress the publicity that the institute gave to this representation of

Table 14 Historical Subjects of the Journal *of the São Paulo Historical and Geographical Institute*

PERIOD	NUMBER OF ARTICLES	PERCENT
Colonial	106	71%
Empire	39	26%
Republic	5	3%
TOTAL	150	100%

the region's history. Demonstrating their intention to compete with the federal capital, the São Paulo elites chose a symbol that was a guaranteed São Paulo original and won them the right to extensive display. In defense of racial whitening and in the choice of the *bandeirante* as the region's symbol, the institute arrived at different assessments on the future and the past. The São Paulo historians laid claim first to a prescribed future, and second to the stability conferred by a shared and noble origin, and in the process they conjured up a glorious past for a fledgling elite.

Despite their diverse contexts, the Brazilian historical and geographical institutes, old "bodyguards to the emperor," retained their first and primary function: they were always the official, unifying, and optimistic voices in the midst of the myriad critical and pessimistic opinions that were characteristic at other establishments that we have studied.

AN INSTITUTIONAL MODEL: AN OFFICIAL AND OPTIMISTIC VISION

> The Historical Institutes are not private associations, but guilds for the national welfare, because they are the archives and the museums that hold the relics, the fruits, of our ancestors.
> —*Journal of the Archeological and Geographical Institute of Pernambuco,* 1866

According to the Brazilian historian José Honório Rodrigues, the notion of creating a chronology of the nation's history appeared only after the foundation of its institutes of history (1957: 152). Until then, isolated efforts to write Brazil's history showed little concern for the systematization and construction of a theory of national history.

Beyond their political and regional particulars, the historical institutes worked to establish a nomenclature and an agenda, with people and facts, from which many historians strayed very little. Confined to an encyclopedic project that found order and connection where before there had been only isolated events within a regional experience, and with a bead on the present, the institutes' scholars committed themselves to the creation of a national history.

The project to develop a national history was not unique to Brazil but took place in the context of a broader trend. Throughout the nineteenth century the study of history infiltrated universities and defined itself as a discipline. The historian soon lost his identity as *un homme de lettres* but gained the status of a scholar on a level with his intellectual peers (Darnton, 1990). Brazilian historians were adept users of foreign models, which served as points of departure for analyzing their own local history. As a result their heroes had the look of figures taken from Western culture.

But if, as Hobsbawm states, "all invented traditions, so far as possible, use history as a legitimator of action and cement of group cohesion," at the same time it is impossible not to consider the links between historical memory and the concept of nation (Hobsbawm and Ranger, 1983: 12). In Brazil, in particular, this process was linked to the idea of founding a national project on the basis of history. Like most scholars, the historians working on this cloaked their work in a veil of objectivity. Their accounts were deliberately orchestrated with episodes and figures that were expeditious to the project, goals that were viewed as necessary as materials otherwise more appropriately intellectual. It was with this pretense of impartiality that they tried to make these institutions "sites of knowledge":

> Gentlemen! We find ourselves in neutral territory, where politics does not intrude with its subtleties and evasions. Outside, both night and day, rage raucous, antagonistic and discordant interests. . . . Here [is] meditative silence, peace and quiet of the soul's labor to honor the good name of the

> nation. . . . Here is the calm of devoted scholars who place the transmission of truth above all else. (*Journal of the Historical and Geographical Institute of Brazil,* 1890: 192).[37]

The historical and geographical institutions revealed some original characteristics from the very beginning. Personal relationships constituted the criteria for membership, and thus members were from the rural elite, with a class consciousness, to be sure. Furthermore, the work that was produced at these institutes was notably different from that of the other research centers. In the historical institutes the highest expression of intellectual activity was the biography, which functioned as a means of classifying and ranking the excellence of the members.

When we consider historical texts, we note the use of a single model of analysis and single image of the nation. When unity and indivisibility constituted political dogma,[38] as during the imperial era, one wrote Brazilian history as if one were presenting the nation's portrait before a committee of specialists. This approach to the writing of history presumed the existence of a previously defined epistemological field, once one understood the "nation" as having no history. Thus the classification of history based on defining events, for instance that proposed by those who believed that the country began at the moment of the Portuguese "discovery," is comprehensible. After all, on the one hand this episode seemed to embody the Brazilian myth of origin, from which one could date a white European local history, although this means overlooking the people who predated the Portuguese. On the other hand, such an approach also reveals shared ideas that presupposed the existence of a thing called Brazil, preceding its role as a land that was conquered and colonized by Europeans (Santos, 1986: 9).

In the meantime, the homogeneous profile that was presented profoundly camouflaged diverse realities and discourses. In the Historical and Geographical Institute of Brazil, for example, all intellectual production was intimately associated with the imperial state, which was believed to be "the last bastion of the nation's political unity facing the malevolent specter of anarchy" (*Journal of the Historical and Geographical Institute of Brazil,* 1840: 505). Praised constantly, the monarch was represented as personifying the only solution when the nation was faced with the peril of political disintegration, as is indicated in this bit of verse: "And if the nation suffered uncurbed civil war, / it invoked the angel of Brazil in heavens far" (*Journal of the Historical and Geographical Institute of Brazil,* 1841: 39).[39] Born amid a struggle for the nation's sovereignty, the Historical and Geographical Institute of Brazil identified with the era's political moderates, maintaining from the beginning that explicit goal of constructing a "national memory" in such a way that scholarship and power relations would be so compatible that there would be no room for discord.[40] The members of the Historical and Geographical Institute of Brazil were "imperial guardians." They knew how to guarantee their place within the new political order by justifying the preservation of internal unity. This unity was the prime source of a state "that was born an empire," and it was discussed under the cloud of potential discord. The sentiments of the institute on the advent of the republic appeared graphically in the proceedings of a session that Dr. Prudente de Moraes, the first civilian president of the republic, attended:

> Moved by his exceptional humbleness and graciousness, the president inquired as to who usually sat at the head of the table. When he learned that it was the place of honorary presidents, and that the Count D'Eu would sit there only in the absence of Dom Pedro II, he said that he wished to sit at the side of the honored members of the institute, leaving unoccupied the place of honor. (*Journal of the Historical and Geographical Institute of Brazil,* 57, 1894: 395)

It was different at the São Paulo Historical and Geographical Institute. Founded during the republican era, the São Paulo institute bore the imprint of the new era and viewed itself as the "legitimate son" of the existing government.[41] The main difference did not derive from political squabbles but from the revealing discourse that emanated from the institute from the very beginning. The members disseminated a regionalist perspective, characterized by professing "on one hand, acceptance of the existence of a larger political unit, but on the other hand, [seeking] favoritism and decisional autonomy from the larger unit on economic and social policies, even at the risk of jeopardizing the legitimacy of the prevailing political system" (Levine, 1978: xix). The São Paulo institute chose the symbol of the *bandeirante* to help solve the problem of its loyalty being divided between the state and the nation.

The Archeological and Geographical Institute of Pernambuco, in turn, fulfilled a similar role for the northern half of the country. Representing the "Lion of the North," the bastion of the old sugarcane-growing regions, this institute was a true defender of the interests of Pernambuco and the northeast. By focusing on episodes such as the expulsion of the Dutch or the Revolt of 1817, the institute helped to consolidate and project an image of a region that had been marginalized by the new official history produced by the regions of the nation's southern axis when economic and national trends favored those regions. Especially when compared to the circumstances of São Paulo, Pernambucan regionalism retained its uniqueness. It tended to uphold the decadent elites who held on to a glorious past but was living in a depressing present.

While the institutes wrestled among themselves, a common goal began to emerge: it was to create a Brazilian history or, more exactly, to give a past to the country and generalize the histories of certain influential regional groups. In fact, the institutes complied to the letter with the dictum that "one must forget a great deal in order to remember well," even if this tack implied a rigorous process for selecting peers, so as better to define the nature of those regions whose histories the institutes would exclude.

In these centers the membership's position on the racial issue seemed to help to construct a white, Eurocentric history for Brazil, but once again the likeness was not exact at the various institutes. Evolutionist and monogenist theories appeared alongside the supposed social Darwinists and polygenists, as if models originally considered incompatible could somehow commingle. Evolutionist conclusions justified white supremacy and a rigid social hierarchy, which explained the belief in the "natural whitening" of the people through a process of sociobiological Darwinism. Yet it was the racial determinist theories at the institutes that helped to prove that the country was suffering from a certain backwardness, because these theories condemned the nation's racial mixing.

Despite the admiration that the racial determinists seemed to enjoy in Brazil, they served more as a point of reference than as inspiration for the forming of original interpretations. Their conclusions were a source of great optimism, as if the task of writing the official history of the nation could not admit pessimism or predictions of social change. Von Martius's project, presented in the first years of the Historical and Geographical Institute of Brazil, was still the foremost model. According to von Martius the history of Brazil consisted of the history of its three formative races, living together in an orderly way and respecting biological hierarchies and inequalities. Silvio Romero revived the outline of the German naturalist's thesis in mid-century, once again exhorting the three separate national races to action, and encouraging the "good miscegenation" that was occurring in the country.

Far from the pessimism of the Bahian physicians, the skepticism of the Recife School professors, and the scientifism of the ethnology museum naturalists, the historical and geographical institutes persisted in a positive interpretation of reality. The future would be undeniably white, predictable, and secure. In an atmosphere beset by insecurity about the future and flooded with discouraging prognoses, the historical institutes offered another powerful point of view.

Table 15 Themes in the Journal of the São Paulo Historical and Geographical Institute

TYPE OF HISTORY	NUMBER OF ENTRIES	PERCENT
Political	90	64%
Social/cultural	31	22%
Military	10	8%
Religious	5	3%
Economic	5	3%
TOTAL	141	100%

"Collect to preserve well. Preserve to serve well" were mottoes of a certain breed of establishment that remained until the 1930s. After that time the three institutes we have examined began to show obvious financial and organizational strains, and the frequency with which their journals were published diminished.

"Nothing can resist the wave of modernism and convenience," declared an author in a 1929 article in the *Journal of the Archeological and Geographical Institute of Pernambuco* (62), attesting to the growing discrepancies between the institution's profile and the social conditions evolving around it. Within this new setting state resources and interests seemed to migrate to other areas of educational competence and cultural expression, leaving the historical associations with less financial support from their members and their more loyal followers.

Yet the decline of the institutes did not spell their immediate collapse. Indeed, their members constituted the first professional cadres of the new schools and universities created during the 1930s. The continued presence of the institutes today seems to indicate that they represent something more substantial than the mere vestiges or perpetuation of an anachronism. Guardians of their own memory or, more properly stated, of a certain type of history, today the historical and geographical institutes accommodate those who have resisted time and seek to create history based on long genealogies, historical personages, and insistently reworked events. Although this historical model became obsolete, it persisted in books, particularly officially sanctioned schoolbooks. One can see vestiges of the institutes' patriotic mission, as well as traces of the "history of Brazil's history," in Table 15.

SCHOOLS OF LAW, OR THE NATION'S CHOSEN

•

It is essential that our youth, who are the hope of the future, be convinced that this great country neither created schools nor founded institutes like these to prepare only amanuenses and district attorneys but primarily to prepare discerning men through study and learning to guide and elevate her with their wisdom.

—*Academic Journal of the Recife School of Law,* 1894: 9

Written at the end of the nineteenth century, the passage that introduces this chapter tellingly illustrates the attitude of the nation's two great law schools from their first years of existence.

The creation of these institutions was closely tied to the logic and dynamics that marked Brazilian political independence in 1822. The law schools seemed to respond to the need to create a local intelligentsia and carry out an academic agenda designed to help meet the nation's peculiar problems. But a particular responsibility would fall into the hands of these jurists as well—the dual task of founding a new self-image for the country and inventing new legal models for a nation that had just separated from colonial rule, but, uniquely, retained a Portuguese monarch. According to one writer for the law journal at the Recife School of Law, it was necessary to prove "for the world and for ourselves" that imperial Brazil was truly independent and so needed "not only new laws, but also a new conscience" (*Academic Journal of the Recife School of Law,* 1922/1826: 91).

The masters of unquestioned erudition who founded the law schools proposed to create an elite group, unfettered by the cultural ties that bound the country to the European metropolis. The goal was to replace foreign hegemony, whether French or Portuguese, with a system crowned by high-quality institutions of learning, such as law schools, which would take responsibility for the generation of their own judgment and would give the nation a new Constitution.

This was the logic behind the government's approval on August 31, 1826, of the plan to create two centers dedicated to the study of law; the decision was signed into law on August 11, 1827. The two schools were designed to serve the two different parts of the country, although there were numerous disputes about where exactly they should be located. A school situated in Olinda (it would move to Recife in 1854) would serve the north, and one in São Paulo would serve the south.[1]

When the law schools opened their doors in 1828, the prestige of both the legal profession and the *bacharel** in Brazil began to mount. The source of the prestige lay not in the course of study, nor in the law profession as such, but in the symbolic mandate of legal professionals and in the political possibilities that beckoned. In fact, from the ranks of these two schools would emerge many of the country's great politicians and thinkers, including ministers, senators, representatives, and governors, who would chart the nation's course. The obtaining of the degree became synonymous with achieving social prestige and political power;

* The Brazilian *bacharel* degree is the rough equivalent of a highly specialized bachelor's degree in the United States. Areas of study include either traditional undergraduate disciplines, such as history, economics, and biology, or professional studies, such as law and pharmacy. Because history first ties the Brazilian *bacharel* to the study of law, for many years the degree was synonymous with the study of law. In nineteenth-century Brazil the term became a symbol manipulated by those who held high social positions.

thus the *bacharel* became a distinctive figure in a country eager to create its own intellectual and political elites. As an alumnus would say in 1831, in Brazil there are "two aspirations: to secure a rank in the National Guard and to acquire the degree of *bacharel* for at least one of one's offspring" (*Academic Journal of the Recife School of Law,* 1904: 17). The *bacharel* was becoming the renowned intellectual of local society, drawing attention to the eclecticism of ideas and the pragmatism for which the degree stood,[2] and the law schools were rapidly transformed into centers of the ruling rural elites.

From their very first years the law schools encountered difficulties inherent in institutions of higher learning that begin their activities without a group of highly trained educators to sustain them or a staff that possesses the intellectual wherewithal to guide them. There were accounts, dating to the first days of the schools, of disrespectful students and powerless professors working in a setting that was not appropriate for study and reflection.

The image of the intellectual that was beginning to form depicted an eclectic thinker who emerged "with the taint of a controversial academic life, troubled and heterogeneous, that had been erected in the institutes and academic associations, and that had its most formidable opponent in the press" (Adorno, 1988: 79). In fact, intellectual debate occurred not in the classrooms or in the daily contact between undisciplined students and unmotivated professors but primarily in the newspapers and journals of the two schools.

To remark on the low quality of teaching and to assess the intellectual production of both of these profoundly different schools requires detailed analysis. Their similar institutional façades cloaked significant dissimilarities in both theoretical orientation and professional profiles. The liberal political model exerted strong influence on the São Paulo school, while the evolutionist and social Darwinist position reigned at the school in Recife, Pernambuco, a region where racial problems were more evident. Also the highly doctrinaire faculty at Recife contrasted sharply with the more politically pragmatic faculty at São Paulo.

One cannot hope to fully understand nineteenth-century Brazilian *bacharelismo* by studying the history of these two centers. But examining each school separately can shed some light on the phenomenon and particularly on the relevance of racial discussion at the law schools. Because of the volume and complexity of intellectual production at the two law schools, an analysis of their scholarly publications is crucial. These journals fulfilled a noteworthy role in these institutions, serving to certify and promote new intellectual groups. To understand the role of these institutions more fully, this chapter turns to the example provided by the Recife School of Law, where the racial discussion had more importance and complexity than it did in São Paulo.

THE RECIFE SCHOOL OF LAW: *"The Mestizo Is the Nation Coming of Age"*

The First Phase: The Transience of Olinda

Pernambuco, the northeastern province chosen to be home to one of the nation's two law schools, was not known for its passivity or for its deference in politics. Indeed, many studies were conducted into the advisability of the choice at the time of the school's founding. Did the founders of the school make the choice "on the basis of a certain revolutionary and intellectual spirit" within the region, or were they trying to punish and control the "republican intransigence of Recife" (Documents of the Recife School of Law, 1827)? This is a difficult question, but what was certain was that in 1828, the year of the inauguration of what would become the Recife School of Law, the embers of three separate and failed political rebellions, fought in 1817, 1821, and 1824, were still smoldering. In fact, Pernambuco maintained the same republican pride and the same ambition to lead the northern region of the country that it had had in previous years.[3]

Pernambuco's law program, begun on May 15, 1828, at the São Bento Monastery in Olinda, did not, at the start, enjoy the autonomy the Pernambucans expected. On the contrary, Olinda's legal curriculum represented a clear continuation of old Portuguese ideas. Provincial isolation made the school dependent on Portugal for its customs, most of its professors, and even some of its students. But the Olinda school still represented a welcome opportunity for the people of the northern half of the country.[4] A law of August 26, 1830, essentially gave full accreditation to the law school, and the relaxed standards for admission did not fail to attract students eager to avoid the rigorous entrance exams for the University of Coimbra, Portugal's most famous university, or, to a lesser degree, the University of Paris.

Everything about Olinda resembled the Portuguese metropolis the Pernambucan city opposed so vigorously. The school's course of study was identical to that of Coimbra, as were the traditions, even for dress. Even in the midsummer heat "it was common to see academics wearing a tall hat, dress coat and black overcoat" (*Academic Journal of the Recife School of Law,* 1925: 303).

During the Olinda period, both of Brazil's law schools suffered from all the problems attendant upon a hasty establishment and a lack of qualified personnel. The most important influence in this period was the Church, which had offered the use of its monastery and whose clergy had had an active role in teaching the first courses. The "1904 memoirs," or yearbook, mockingly recalled clergymen such as Father Chagas, professor of the first-year law course:

> At the foot of the chair from which he lectures, Father Chagas keeps a bag stuffed with books, from which he retrieves delicacies fit for the finest palate as he ponderously reads entire pages from treatises. If, after the class, students

> inquire of the point that he has made, he is sure to have a fit. (*Academic Journal of the Recife School of Law,* 1904: 10)

On the other hand, the other professors, often poor and poorly paid, were said to be living in a "state of relaxation" (Bevilacqua, 1977: 42). Many explained their frequent absences from classes by citing the distance between their home in Recife and the law school, but this kind of abuse reached an extreme in the case of Dr. Francisco de Paula, who "in a year's time gave fewer than twelve classes" (*Proceedings,* Recife School of Law, 1830). The jurist Clovis Bevilacqua added,

> When Francisco José de Almeida wished to defend his doctoral thesis, he asked that the director, Lopes Gama, inform him how many professors were on the staff. The secretary declared that Dr. Manuel Maria do Amaral had been absent from the law school for three years in service as a representative to the General Assembly, that Dr. Francisco de Paula had been on leave for more than a year, that Dr. Pedro Autran was practicing law in Bahia . . . as were several other colleagues, leaving available only four professors and a substitute. (Bevilacqua, 1977: 44)

In light of these conditions, the students followed a less traditional and less rigorous model of behavior than was customary in most other law schools. There were countless incidents of disrespect, such as the case of a fourth-year student, Inocêncio da Silva Paula,

> who, having completed his examination, for which he received a grade of F, approached the platform and, instead of thanking the professor-observers as dictated by the Statutes, uttered very clearly and distinctly that there was no reason to thank them because he thought their conduct

> unbecoming. (*Academic Journal of the Recife School of Law,* 1832/1924)

The examples compound, revealing the minimal importance of both intellectual endeavors and poor student performance at the school. In 1914 classmates enjoyed reading the work of the students of 1831: "Why are coins in general round?—Because everything in nature tends to become plump.* What is the primary jurisdiction of the minister of war?—Public education" (*Academic Journal of the Recife School of Law,* 1914: 39). They were also amused by the results of a French exam in which a student translated *cependant* [during] as "this pendant," and *les boeufs de Dieu* [God's cattle] as "God's hags," both ironic plays on words.

The students with their shortcomings, the professors and their absenteeism, the unsatisfactory physical structures, indeed, everything about the Olinda school seemed impermanent. The São Bento convent was the "provisional location" for twenty-two years. Then the "Casarão do Hospício" [Hospice Manor] housed the school from 1852 to 1854, when the building was abandoned after a great fire routed the small core of people who regularly attended classes. A student wrote an anonymous and humorous poem as testimony to the misfortunes of the school:

> *There were some who in their dedication*
> *Came to class and saw but ruination*
> *Chairs and tables, books upon the ground*
> *Ashes taking notes to wind the only sound.*
> (Academic Journal of the Recife School of Law, *1904: 104*)

Whether through what one may surmise by the anecdotal evidence, or through the lack of tangible scholarship, it is clear that there was little innovative intellectual production during the

* Unfortunately, in translating *se arredondar* as "becomes rounded" one loses the sense of the pun intended by the original, which also means "to amass a fortune."

Olinda period. Primarily there were rigid course structures, copies of foreign legal books, and the deep roots and influences of the religious masters and Catholic natural rights. It was a Catholic science, committed to divine revelation and protected by the immutable character of the monarchy.

The school's move to Recife in 1854 signalled a change both geographical and intellectual. It was only after the move that the school became involved in original research and evolved into a truly creative center for ideas and a gathering place for intellectuals engaged with the problems of their time and country.

A New Beginning in Recife

When the School of Law moved the short distance to Recife in 1854, certain members of the teaching staff had much to celebrate. Some had complained of how isolated Olinda was, and, in particular, how far it was from Recife. Unfortunately, the new accommodations were not much better. The building in Recife was also inadequate for the purposes of an institution of higher learning, and it came to be known as the "*pardieiro*" [hovel, dump]. In 1860 negative criticism of the facilities surpassed any praise for other aspects, as can be seen by this sample: "[It is] a big old house inferior in its accommodations and hygienic conditions to any of our military barracks. When it rains, it becomes a lake. When the sun shines, it becomes a Sahara without an oasis. When the wind blows, tuberculosis and pneumonia are close at hand" (Documents, Recife School of Law, 1860).

But if the move did not succeed in bringing about an improvement in physical surroundings, the same cannot be said of the levels of scholarship. At Recife a new group of intellectuals collected at the school; they were men whose work would transcend the narrow regional confines of their predecessors.[5]

The first step in the academic reform undertaken in 1854 was to enforce discipline and to put an end to the disobedience that had reigned in Olinda. The school made the preparatory exams more rigorous and enacted a strict class calendar, extending from March 15 to October 15. Further, it defined the length of class sessions and established a system of Saturday review sessions, called *sabatinas* (Articles 53, 69, 70, and 75). The new rules limited the number of classes a student could miss, and also reduced the number of allowable failures. A student who failed two courses would not be allowed to return to the school (Article 80). Finally, in an attempt to control the dismal relations between students and professors, the school instituted a rigorous system for punishing student misconduct ranging from a mere reprimand to expulsion from the class by order of the professor or, in the event of more serious infractions, even imprisonment from one to eight days, by order of the school director (Articles 111–27).

In the ensuing decades other proposals for curricular reform also stand out. A good example is the 1879 reform that established what came to be known as "free schooling," a reform that limited obligatory curriculum, abolished required attendance, and divided the school's program into two distinct sections: "legal sciences and social sciences." Subsequently the "legal sciences" program consisted of courses in natural, Roman, constitutional, civil, and criminal law; legal and theoretical rights; and procedural practice. The "social sciences" program, with some apparent overlap of subjects, consisted of courses in natural, public, universal, constitutional, ecclesiastical, personal, administrative, public hygiene law, and economic and political law.

The reform that took place at the Recife School of Law was not an isolated phenomenon. Pernambuco especially was a site for reform; as already discussed, the Archeological and Geographical Institute of Pernambuco was founded in 1863 as a response to the historiographical hegemony exercised by the Carioca institute. On the other hand, a theoretical shift also began to emerge at the law school at this time, much heralded by the very scholars who were engaged in it and who sought to give a "scientific statute" to the legal system, apart from the religious and metaphysical influences that were then dominant.

There are various pieces of evidence that point the way to this change. In 1870 Silvio Romero wrote a famous preface to law professor Tobias Barreto's book in which, with a nearly prophetic tone, he singled out his archenemies—Roman Catholicism, the monarchy, and romanticism—and proclaimed the beginning of a new era:

> In all of the nineteenth century, the years that span 1868 to 1878 are the decade that most dramatically represents our spiritual life. . . . Suddenly we have witnessed the immutability of things. . . . A *flock of new ideas* has overflown us from all points on the horizon. . . . Positivism, evolutionism, Darwinism, religious criticism, naturalism, scientifism in poetry and the novel, new methods of literary history and criticism, and the transformation of instruction in law and politics. Everything is in flux, and the Recife School has sounded the alarm. (Romero, 1926: 23–24)

In 1875 Romero was defending his doctoral thesis on political economy when a significant disagreement erupted between him and a member of the examining committee, Coelho Rodrigues, the two men representing opposing political camps. The solemn occasion quickly deteriorated into political theater. Then the incident detonated when Rodrigues (the detractor) complained about what Silvio Romero was doing to metaphysics, to which the doctoral candidate responded, "That is not a question of metaphysics, but logic."

"Logic does not preclude metaphysics," responded the detractor.

"Metaphysics no longer exists. If you didn't know that, know it now," rejoined the doctoral candidate.

"I didn't know that," retorted the other.

"Well, go study up and observe that metaphysics is dead."

"Were you, sir, the one who killed it?" the professor then asked him.

"It was progress; it was civilization."

Prolonging the performance, the *bacharel* Silvio Romero seized the books lying on the table and declared with a triumphal pose, "I cannot bear anymore this mob of blockheads who know nothing about anything" (*Proceedings,* Recife School of Law, 1875; Bevilacqua, 1977: 144).

Whether metaphysics was dead or alive, the temperament of the new generation had changed, and many among the younger scholars had by then assumed some of the most influential positions within the institution. This second generation, so to speak, sought to obliterate the old models, always in the name of civilization, and with the new models, they introduced a set of evolutionist jargon that found broad acceptance in Recife, primarily after Tobias Barreto's readings of the German philosophers Ernst Haeckel and Henry Thomas Buckle and following the circulation of authors such as Spencer, Darwin, Littré, Le Play, Gustave Le Bon, and Arthur de Gobineau, among others. After that decade, in the words of Professor Phaelante Câmara, "Darwinism felt at home in the congregation and among the academic ranks" (*Academic Journal of the Recife School of Law,* 1904: 17), and the Recife School of Law assumed such an identity that the group of Tobias Barreto's Germanists began calling themselves "the Recife School renovators" (Documents RSL, 1875).

Praised by its contemporaries, the school's theoretical position of the 1870s, even up through the first years of the twentieth century, was understood as a wondrous intellectual revolution.

> Our school has had two decidedly distinct moments. The first was a pugnacious empiricism from years past, with deep roots in religious preconception and in the monarchical prejudice of divine right. The second was the meticulous study of the social mechanism of ecological conditions, heredity, human atavisms, and of physical, anthropological, and social factors without which one cannot comprehend the true science of Law. (*Academic Journal of the Recife School of Law,* 1904: 22)

Although one needn't accept all the excesses and celebration expressed in these accounts, it is important to note that this period did usher in a new concept of law. The "scientific" notion with which the discipline emerged made legal studies an ally of evolutionary biology, the natural sciences, and physical and determinist anthropology. Simultaneously, while law was affirming itself, it was also moving away from the other human sciences, seeking to link itself to areas governed only by laws and certitudes. "Is it not true that by examining the laws that govern a people one can be sure to find and judge the level that its civilization has attained? Of course," concluded a law student from the class of 1900 as he justified the role of legal scholarship in the practice of the sciences (*Academic Journal of the Recife School of Law,* 1900: 88).

The insistence on scientifism and specificity in the practice of law was such that perhaps the best definition for the emerging specialist in law was found by Laurindo Leão, professor of criminal law in the Recife School. Wielding an explanation from the anthropologist Paul Topinard, Leão defended the existence of "three orders of character: the observers, the creators, and the composites. The creators give us artists, the composites give us philosophers, and the observers give us scientists. In Brazil, these give us unequivocal law" (*Academic Journal of the Recife School of Law,* 1900: 42).

"Far from metaphysics" and "removed from subjectivism," the law school's intellectuals lived the certainty that they were constructing not only new theories but also a new nation. Having come mostly from sectors of an urban middle class that was steadily becoming less subject to rural domination, Recife intellectuals shared the feeling that "there was nothing science couldn't do" (*Academic Journal of the Recife School of Law,* 1894: 195), and that they had a true calling, a mission to accomplish. In Olinda the law students had belonged mostly to traditional families in the region who were linked to agricultural concerns; whereas in Recife the social makeup of the student body was more diverse, representing the region's rural families but also the upwardly mobile urban middle class (Bevilacqua, 1977).

Whether because of the affirmation of law, or because of the negation of the other disciplines, the most important thing about this new generation, led by Tobias Barreto and, after the 1870s, by Silvio Romero, was that it began to define itself as the herald of a new era, as the nation's best and brightest. "Brazil depends wholly on us and is in our hands. The future belongs to us," declared the valedictory speaker of 1900, as if to affirm a right previously assumed but never before granted.

"Science Felt at Home Here": Naturalism

According to several critics, the "1870s generation" was responsible for the introduction of "cultural modernity" to Brazil, at least to the extent that the leading intellectuals of the time proposed a break with religious thought (in the case of the law schools, there was a break from the theory of Catholic natural rights) in favor of a secular vision of the world.[6] In fact, from that time onward the theory that gained momentum was based on the belief that the social order was absolutely rigid and immutable.

Deterministic scientific theories introduced a secular and temporal discourse that, in the Brazilian context, would be used as a weapon within a number of established institutions. At the Recife School of Law, after the simultaneous introduction of evolutionist and social Darwinist models there was a nearly immediate attempt to adapt the law to these theories, to apply them to the national reality.

It was perhaps in Recife that the era's racial determinist doctrines adhered most doggedly, consistent with the mounting scientific ethos. Although they were far from the country's centers of political decision making, the Recife scholars at least lived with the assurance that they represented the Brazilian scientific avant-garde. More than "science," with its different theories and interpretations, they discussed a scientific posture, or rather, they disseminated "scientifism" or a "scientific attitude" that would explain all human endeavor. In a speech on sociology, Joaquim Pimenta declared in 1910: "Science is a simple fact of life." In the same year Professor Octávio Tavares exhorted in a speech to his colleagues: "Let us learn to be men of our time, let us learn to be scientific" (*Academic Journal of the Recife School of Law,* 1910).

The examples are many, and in their aggregate they clearly demonstrate that the attachment of the Recife scholars to the new set of determinist and evolutionist ideas was so strong that scientific practices extended to the personal level. In Recife determinist principles began to appear in literature and literary criticism, and novelists, "in the name of a 'realist' literary criticism, [began to] use scientific methods ever more exacting" (Bosi, 1972: 186) in the creation of a naturalist literature. Naturally, several intellectuals of the Recife center viewed racial determinism as a fierce assault on literary romanticism.

The naturalist novels that appeared, many of which were written by jurists and other law school faculty, essentially consisted of strings of quotations and grand shows of erudition. The heroes and other characters mouthed a determinist science that informed and shaped their plots. Barbosa, the protagonist of *A carne* [Flesh] (1888), by Júlio Ribeiro, describes marriage as "a sociological institution in evolution, as it relates to the individual" (1888: 112). Teixeira, in *O chromo* [The chromo] (1888), is described as "Darwinianly superior," since "he comes from far away, across a thousand generations and boisterous centuries, genealogically anonymous, passing from womb to womb on the wave of spermatic evolution. . . . one of Nature's best designs to urge on anthropological evolution" (Carvalho, 1888: 336).

Carvalho's novel assumes naturalistic tones when the characters and the plot itself are reduced to scientific categories and surrender to "the natural laws" that limit their horizons. The "literary jurists" went so far as to introduce references to the era's great scientists in their writing. In this way they created the necessary bridge that made the novels almost literally scientific. For instance, in his novel Raul Pompéia made references to Ladislau Netto, who was then the director of the National Museum (Pompéia, 1889: 76). Júlio Ribeiro sprinkled in his writings the precepts of Darwin, Haeckel, and von Martius, among others. Horácio de Carvalho quoted the physicians Charcot and Berheim (Carvalho, 1888: 105).

Often heroes and heroines would expatiate on the era's scientific conclusions in asides that were unrelated to the novel's plot. "It doesn't have the world's best climate," wrote Afrânio Peixoto, a well-known lawyer of the Recife school, at the end of his novel *A esfinge* [The sphinx], "and it's not the world's richest country . . . but one day competition will right these natural imperfections, and that day the fight will begin" (Peixoto, 1911: 473). In Graça Aranha's *Canãa* [Canaan], Milkau, the protagonist, praises white European immigration:

> Frankly speaking, the key to the civilization of this land is the immigration of Europeans, but each one of us has an obligation to lend a hand at governance and administration. . . . And in the distant future the mulatto era will become again the age of the new whites . . . who will recognize and accept the heritage of their mestizo forebears who will have left a legacy, as nothing passes from the world without leaving its mark. (Aranha, 1912: 67 and 211)

Here Aranha was reflecting theories that were prevalent in the Recife School of Law, where he was then enrolled as a student.[7] Through literature Recife's legal scholars disseminated their theories and interpretations, which otherwise would have remained restricted to more academic circles of debate.[8]

Governed by the same laws and principles, literature was becoming both similar to and subordinate to science: "the law that governs literature," wrote Silvio Romero in *O naturalismo em literatura* [Naturalism in literature], "is the same one that drives history in general: transformative evolution. . . . If the poet chooses not to do science, he should at least make use of it in order to be consistent with the times. . . . The poet owes it to science to observe its goals and conclusions so as not to write foolishness" (1882: 35). With the method proposed by Silvio Romero for his school, in his mind it became possible to have "a certain esthetic refinement, that considered the work of art a kind of meteorite, accessible only through an intrinsic proof unrelated to the work itself . . . In lands where biographical, historical, and sociological criteria had become essential to the appreciation of a literary work, the work could no longer sustain an intense presence" (Holanda, 1951).

The focus moved from the text and reverted to the context. According to Antonio Candido, this was the "greatest sin" of these determinist currents, whose exaggerations can be explained by the "very atmosphere of the era, of the century of biology" (Candido, 1988: 102 and 114). As they constructed principles from science, which would then extend to the most diverse branches of knowledge, Recife intellectuals introduced to Brazil positions and models that until then were relatively unknown. The general belief was that it was necessary to give the nation another form, "to challenge it with the scientific form" (*Academic Journal of the Recife School of Law,* 1898), a task that implied not only the absorption of foreign interpretations but also their use as matrices of thought. As "men of science," the law scholars found themselves disposed to adapt the new ideas and to invent a scientific solution for the nation. This was the profile that Silvio Romero filled as a polemicist, and because he fulfilled this role so well he would bind together a generation that later in the 1920s would continue to celebrate him. Although Romero was not the "father" of the generation, he was at least its shepherd, and it would be wrong not to "give him his due."

Silvio Romero and the "Mestizo Soul"

If there was anyone we could call passionate about shaping his life as a "man of science" it was Silvio Romero. An intellectual of many extreme positions, and one who found himself both on and off the mark,[9] Romero was above all a man of his time who viewed science as the whole solution to a complex national reality.

More than anything else, Silvio Romero was a great agitator. Self-taught and little concerned with what he called "pure speculation," he used the most recent developments in science and philosophy to struggle directly with national problems. In truth, the different theoretical matrices in the air only interested him to the extent that they helped focus his thinking about local issues and about the meanings of nationality.

Romero stood out for the radicalism of his positions and for his adherence to evolutionist naturalism, in opposition to French positivism.[10] Borrowing previously unknown terminology from authors such as Haeckel, Darwin, and Spencer, Romero daringly advanced the notion that racial mixing was the best way to achieve national homogeneity.

The novelty of his idea lay not only in his terminology and argumentation but also in a theoretical position that many of the Recife professors shared. This position found in the "ethnographic criterion" the key that revealed the nation's problems. Everything was viewed in light of race, and if one sought to explain the nation's future, race was an unavoidable issue.

Although some scholars' positions on race softened with time,[11] Romero's thinking during the last years of the nineteenth century seemed to become ever more dogmatic. Following are just a few examples of the great importance that issues of race assumed for Romero and, by extension, for the entire school: "the people are who they are, and what they are is what their race has made it" (1907: 75). "Brazil is a mixed nation. It does no good to discuss whether this is good or bad. It's just the way it is"

(1888/1949: 104). And, finally, "all Brazilians are mestizos, if not in blood, at least in their ideas" (1888/1949: 85).

In fact, Silvio Romero, who had a reputation for being averse to "the undistracted contemplation of things" (1907: 64), withdrew from the purely theoretical models to find in the Brazilian mestizo "the white man's triumph." That is, because it had become obvious that one could not categorize the Brazilian nation as a distinct ethnic group, he concluded that his nation's race would ultimately become mestizo. Romero made use of his era's polygenist precepts in unorthodox ways. Consistent with the era's determinist theories, he deduced that racial blending was the consequence of the struggle for the survival of the species. Paradoxically, however, he did not follow the lead of the social Darwinists, who condemned racial hybridization. Instead, he found in this phenomenon the basis for the "nation's survival." Borrowing Silvio Rabello's expression, Romero's theory approximated an "Aryanism of convenience." It depended on the notion of natural selection and presumed the emergence of a stronger race. It did not denounce racial mingling as destructive. In this way the blending of the three formative races was becoming such a fundamental element that Silvio Romero even allowed himself the luxury of viewing the political reality with irony when he declared: "one day this will be a true mulatto country. The first emperor was deposed because he was not born here, and the second one will be deposed because he is not mulatto" (1895: 39).

Despite his praise for "racial blending," one should not come to the conclusion that Silvio Romero was a defender of equality among men. On the contrary, he believed firmly in racial determinism. In 1887 he said, "Let us not be prejudiced, but let us recognize the differences," as though he were announcing a moment in which polygenism constituted a truth as absolute as the celebrated equality declared by the Enlightenment. According to Romero, the debate over the single origin of mankind became a pseudo-problem when viewed against "an original inequality, born of nature's laboratory, where the character of and differences between the races appear as primordial facts before the lure of advanced ethnography" (1895: 37).

Without entering into Romero's labyrinthine theory,[12] it would be more useful simply to understand him as a kind of "founding father," and his beliefs as important influences in the development of racial thought in Brazil.[13] It was in his predilection for the theme of racial blending, in his adherence to the biological and ethnological determinist models, and in his radical and science-laden talk that we see the power of this teacher in his writings and their enduring legacy. After Romero, the study of law underwent an important shift in Brazil. It joined with anthropology, it declared itself a "science" in the determinist mold of the era, and it conferred on itself the right to address and determine the problems and the destiny of the nation.

Academic Journal of the Recife School of Law: The First Issue, a Scientific Periodical

We credit the Republican politician Benjamin Constant for enacting the law in 1890 that authorized and funded the *Academic Journal of the Recife School of Law,* which first appeared in 1891. The school's faculty was given primary responsibility for its publication, and in its inaugural issue the journal published its goals: "to provoke and stimulate scientific production yet underdeveloped in our country; to establish strong intellectual connections among various national and international nuclei; to strengthen the nation's schools of law" (*Academic Journal of the Recife School of Law,* 1891: 8). We will analyze the research that emerged from the journal's pages between 1891 and 1930 to get a sense of its authors' unique views of the issues facing the nation of Brazil.

Following the proclamation of the republic, Brazil viewed itself as a "nation in the process of becoming." Studies of criminal anthropology and penal law would play monumental roles. It was as if the great debates on the nation's destiny were made for disciplines such as the law. In the very first pages of the journal its organizers openly alluded to the difficulties that the discipline of law was undergoing, as well as the urgent need that it be "helped by ethnology and psychology to emerge from its metaphysical limbo" (*Academic Journal of the Recife School of Law,* 1891: 9). Even in its earliest days the journal tried to affirm its uniqueness and to guarantee "modernity" through its allegiance to certain models and authors. It is not just a coincidence that the journal's first article proposed "an evolutionary tableau for the law," establishing "the reality of evolution as unique and unyielding," but also enumerating the authors who would preside over the first thirty years of the journal. They would include Ernst Haeckel, Darwin, and Gustave Le Bon, as well as the Italian criminal anthropologists Cesare Lombroso and Enrico Ferri. One can perceive in this journal, as opposed to other journals we have discussed, a more immediate acceptance of the notions of evolutionism and of studies that considered race as a fundamental element of analysis.

The attention afforded to two of the cited authors, Lombroso and Ferri, who were noted for their studies in criminology, demonstrates the coverage racial theories were given in the law journal.[14] Most articles of this type relied on advances made in the "Italian school" and approached crime through an analysis "of the individual, of his physical type, and of his race" (*Academic Journal of the Recife School of Law,* 1891: 31).

As believers in an independent criminal law code, and pointing to specific kinds of delinquents, scholars at the Recife law school revealed a generalized fear of the "anarchy of the races" (*Academic Journal of the Recife School of Law,* 1892) in the country and their opinion on the need for appropriate legislation. Thus, in the inaugural issue one finds analyses that call for the creation of a penal code founded on both national and scientific bases: "We need new legislation, especially with regard to penal law. All such legislation must be rooted in our nation's reality and must conform to the character of the people for which it is created. But all legislation must have a basis in science, and science is what will determine and establish its basis" (*Academic Journal of the Recife School of Law,* 1891: 43).

With this first issue the professors responsible for the journal thoroughly summarized the publication's noble objectives. On the one hand they put forward their belief that the law was a scientific practice, although the science was linked to evolutionist and determinist models of analysis. On the other hand, they defined the lofty mission they meant to impose on their national legislators: the creation of an original legal code.

The *Academic Journal of the Recife School of Law* did not differ greatly from the other periodicals we have studied thus far. In addition to serving as a vehicle for publishing the in-house work of the professors, it was also a forum for exchanging ideas with both international and other national institutions, particularly the latter.

Similar to other publications of the era, in the *Academic Journal* one notes that most of the articles were written by professors who either occupied positions of authority within the institution or had distinguished themselves in a wider political sphere. Clovis Bevilacqua is a good example. In addition to writing 20 percent of the articles published, this eminent professor either introduced or concluded each issue.[15] Because he was well known outside the institution, the editors involved Bevilaqua routinely, as if his participation was necessary to establish the integrity of the publication.

The evolutionist thread that was common to the publications of the various other institutes can also be detected in this law review. As Bevilacqua noted, the stance was quite consensual: "[I]n the name of science, we no longer raise the spear of criticism to wound the theory of evolution. What do arise from time to time in scientific circles are different manners of understanding it.

One version might posit a single and universal evolution while another might advance a multiple version, but then it rests" (*Academic Journal of the Recife School of Law,* 1897: 117). The theories were subject to different interpretations, but the paradigm transcended criticism.

But if in many aspects the Recife law school's journal resembled other, similar publications, it also possessed a unique characteristic that warrants more attention. Although the *Academic Journal of the Recife School of Law* was considered a scientific periodical, the space it devoted to the nation's political and social problems was impressive. Exploring a theory was often merely the pretext for contemplating local issues, which were introduced at any time, despite the primary subject of any article.

The thematic breakdown of 294 articles published over forty years, from 1891 to 1930, is shown in Table 16. An analysis of these results reveals some interesting facts about the function and the orientation of the publication. First, of course, is the impressive number of articles about the Recife School of Law itself. To a certain degree these articles both served to document the institution's intellectual standing and helped create a history of its recent past.

Although, overall, articles about the law school were the most numerous, they were not the most characteristic of the publication. During its first thirty years the journal consisted primarily of book reviews, biographies, and articles on criminal law or criminal anthropology and civil law.[16] A broader thematic variety began to emerge only in the 1920s. From that point forward, articles on medical law, sociology, commercial law, public law, and customs law began to dominate the journal, shifting the editorial focus from criminal law and civil law.

The data on the journal's early years seem to point toward a correlation between the subjects of the journal's essays and the era's great topics of debate. Despite the diversity of themes and treatments that came up in the articles, the focus frequently

Table 16 Breakdown of the Thematic Content of the Academic Journal of the Recife School of Law

THEME	TOTAL
Recife School of law	61
Criminal law	51
Civil law	45
History of law	34
Medical law	22
Biographies	21
Reviews of literature	17
International law	14
Philosophy of law	10
Roman law	8
Comparative law	3
Administrative law	2
Customs law	2
Sociology	1
Public law	1
Commercial law	1
Family law	1
TOTAL	294

returned to the development of a single legal code and the establishment of fixed regulations that would govern the entire country. It was because of the attention that was brought to bear on codes and regulations that civil law and criminal law commanded a privileged status. These were necessary priorities in a new nation. If one must legislate first for people's rights and individuals' rights, one must then also fix the limits of their freedoms and establish penalties, or the perils of criminal behavior.

Still, the journal maintained a notable internal split. Clovis Bevilacqua wrote many of the essays on civil and international law, and a broad range of the school's professors, who repeatedly referred to themselves as "followers of Silvio Romero," wrote the rest. If Bevilacqua's analyses seemed more like theoretical presentations, far removed from the school's and the nation's most pressing needs, other essays, often of foreign authorship, forced an engagement with local debate and national problems.

In the journal's essays taken as a totality one finds clues that the institution was developing its own original profile, as well as the fruits of clearly unique interpretations. The preponderance of articles on criminal law does not, however, seem accidental. They form part of a specific debate, and the decision to feature particular authors and theories was calculated to draw attention to specific positions. In Recife, this effort resulted in the reconfiguration of the scientific models that were then available, with a special accent on the new area of criminal law and its racial determinants.

Criminal Anthropology

Society is a sea of crimes.

—*Academic Journal of the Recife School of Law,* 1913: 134

In Recife's law school journal the number of articles and book reviews published in the areas of criminal law and criminal anthropology stands out. This kind of article, constituting 47 percent of the journal's pieces, is not simply commonplace; it represents a commonly accepted view of what studies were of most import to Brazil at the time. "It would prove one's considerable mental insufficiency not to observe this transformation because one allowed modern criminal law to pass by unnoticed," declared Professor Tito Rosa in 1895 (*Academic Journal of the Recife School of Law,* 51), presupposing that others shared these views of the era. Faith was put in the leaders of the "new school," Lombroso, Garófalo, and Ferri, because, according to Tito Rosa, they represented "what was modern in the struggle of that murky

Introductory course on physiological types
(PARIS, 1895)

Classroom of Anthropometry
(PARIS, 1887)

Photographic studio of the Forensic Identification Service (PARIS, N.D.)

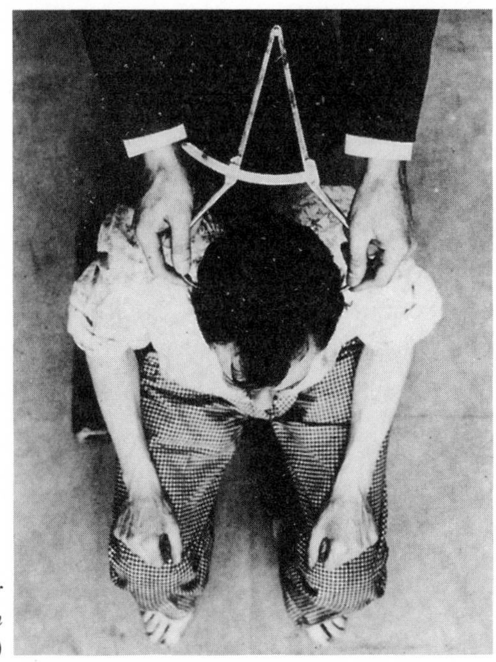

Cranial measurement for criminal identification (PARIS, N.D.)

phenomenon that went by the name of crime" (*Academic Journal of the Recife School of Law,* 1893: 42).

This transformation did not address the evidence of the phenomenon but the treatment accorded to it from that time forward. As an "anthropological phenomenon," it turned its focus from the crime itself to concentrate on the analysis of the criminal's character, which these writers understood to be the result of three distinct factors: the "physical, anthropological, and social" (*Academic Journal of the Recife School of Law,* 1895: 59).[17]

The interpretations of these factors of the criminal's character varied. For Lombroso the criminal represented the return to savagery. For Garófalo the criminal was a moral anomaly. And for Benedickt the criminal was a classic example of neurasthenia. In all cases, however, the general belief was that "to focus on the nature of the criminal resulted in a change in the concept of crime." The studies on criminal anthropology brought scientific criteria to the practice of law, and their authors used professorships in criminal law and disciplines such as geology, biology, and anthropology as bully pulpits for instructing the nation. They argued, for example, that punishment should be meted out to the guilty based on "the classification of the perpetrator, with his organic and physical flaws, and with an inherited and acquired preference for crime, who should be punished exclusively in accordance with these criteria" (Benedickt in *Academic Journal of the Recife School of Law,* 1907: 48).

Instead of resting on the concept of an individual's free will, these theories of criminality were based on beliefs that a universe ruled by physical, causal, and evolutionary laws provided no leeway for individual freedom. A person was the "sum of the physical characteristics of his race, the result of interplay with his environment" (*Academic Journal of the Recife School of Law,* 1913: 58). Consequently, the physical manifestation of the person, or the *phenotype,* came to be understood as "the mirror of the soul" (*Academic Journal of the Recife School of Law,* 1921: 71), in which were reflected both virtues and vices.

For some theorists, the criminal's physical type was so predictable that it was possible to depict him in objective terms. Cesare Lombroso, for example, devised a detailed table, subdivided into "anatomical factors" (cranial and facial asymmetry, occipital regions overbalancing the forehead, prominent superciliary arches, and pronounced prognathous jaws); "physiological factors" (insensitivity, muscularity, left-handedness, and ambidextrousness); "psychological factors" (undeveloped senses of touch, smell, and taste; senses of sight and hearing ranging from acute to slight; listlessness; inhibition); and "sociological factors" (tattoos on the body) (*Academic Journal of the Recife School of Law,* 1913: 68).

Although they may have agreed with Lombroso's characterizations, other scholars associated with this intellectual current, such as Ferri, limited themselves to discussing examples of "innate criminals," subjects who displayed anomalies and atavistic stigmata and who possessed "a personal predisposition to crime."

Garófalo's positions introduced further complexities. He disagreed with earlier delimitations and established not *one* anthropological type, but *three* classes of criminal: the thief, the assassin, and the violent person (Garófalo, 1885; quoted in Gould, 1981).

For the Recife professors, the potential for criminality seemed to be anywhere and everywhere, from the most unsuspecting places to the most distinguished persons. Laurindo Leão, professor of criminal law, made use of these theories in his celebrated list of madmen.

> The following were partially insane: Julius Caesar, Napoleon, Flaubert, Richelieu, Dostoyevsky, Byron, Pascal, Mozart, and Wagner. The following were insane, at least at the end of their lives: Comte, Newton, Nietzsche, and Molière. The following were paranoiacs: Rousseau and Haller. The following were psychotics: Balzac and Swift.

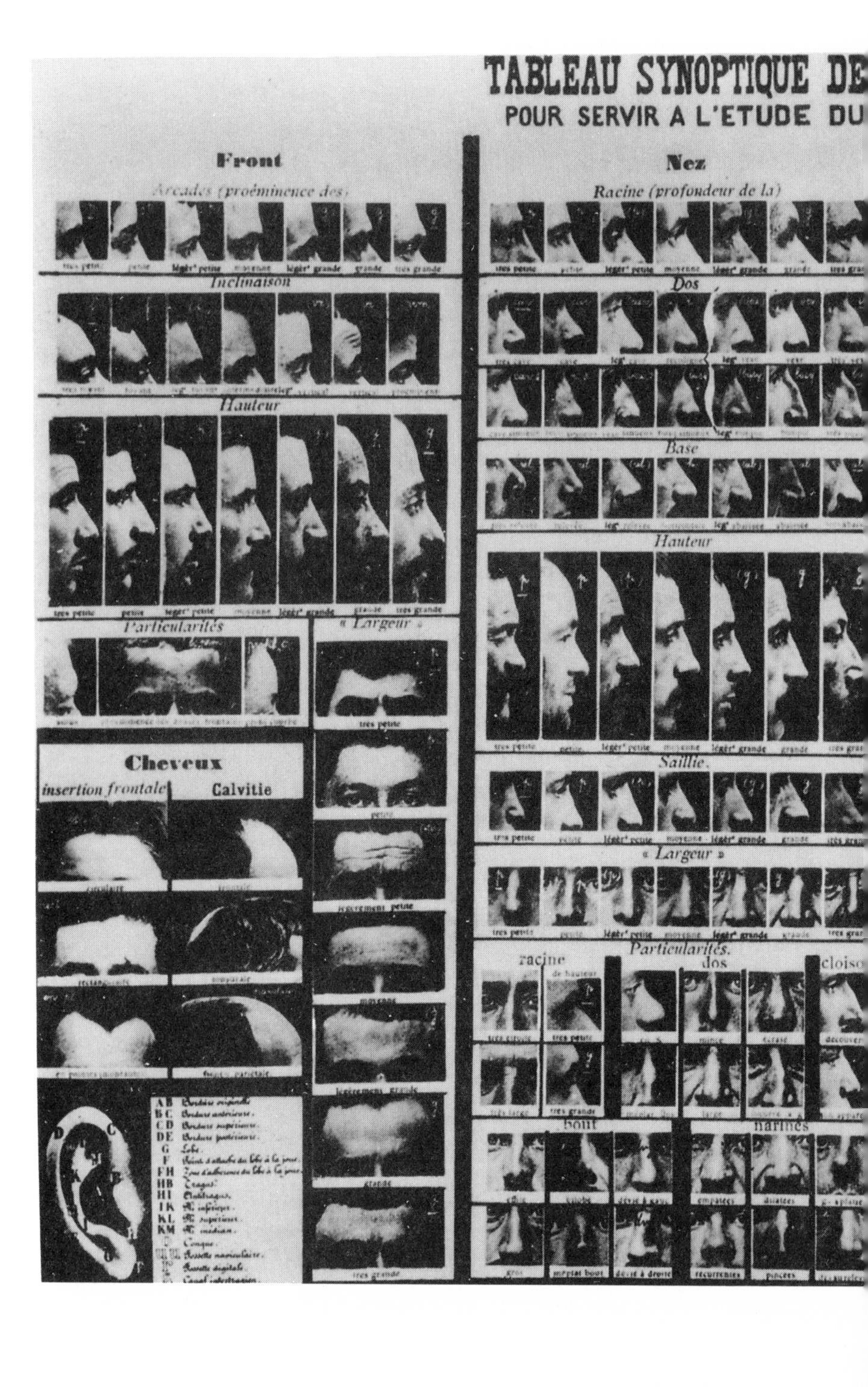

TABLEAU SYNOPTIQUE DE
POUR SERVIR A L'ETUDE DU
Front
Arcades (proéminence des)
Inclinaison
Hauteur
très petite
petite
légèr' petite
moyenne
légèr' grande
grande
très grande
Particularités
« Largeur »
très petite
Cheveux
insertion frontale
Calvitie
Nez
Racine (profondeur de la)
Dos
Base
Hauteur
Saillie.
« Largeur »
Particularités.
racine
dos
bout
narines

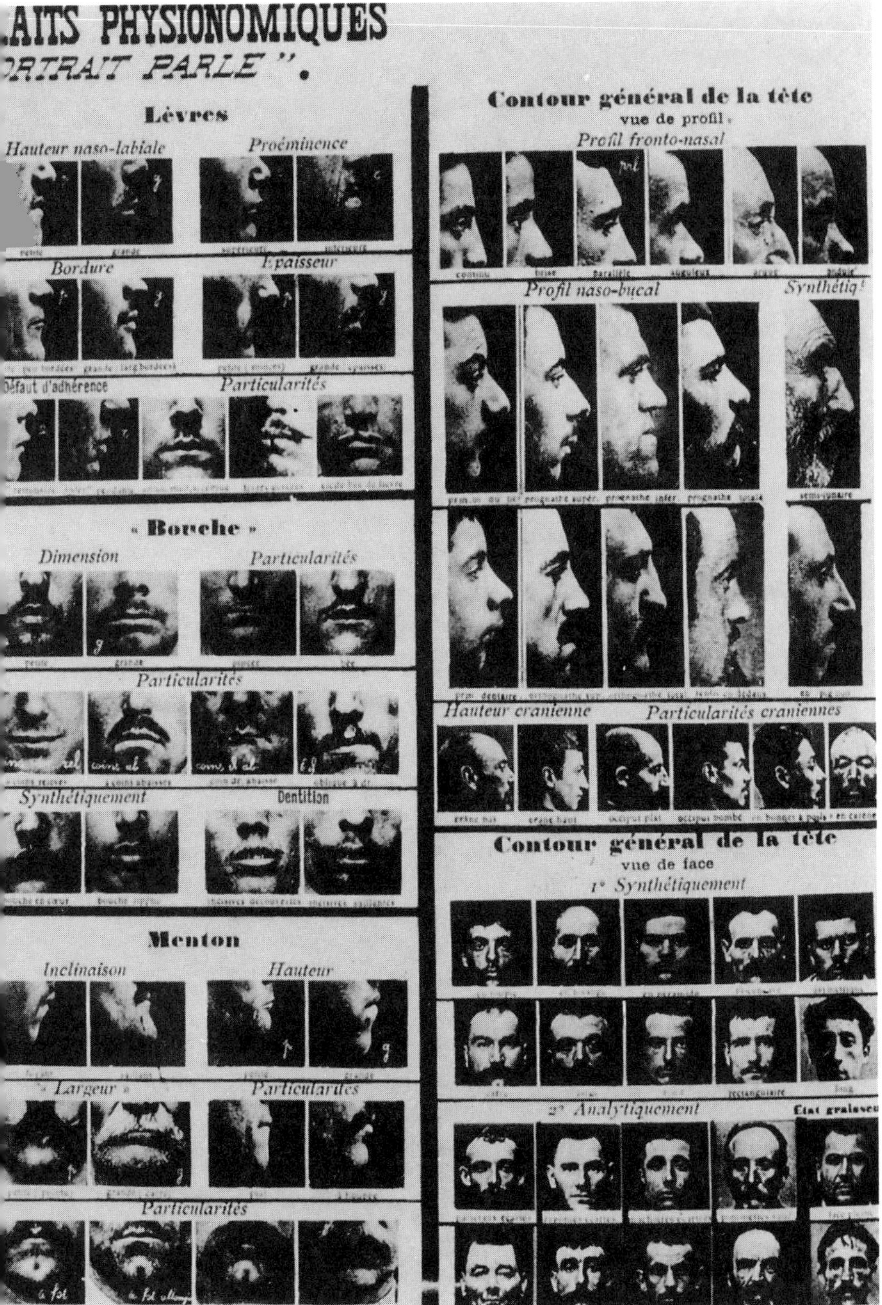

LAITS PHYSIONOMIQUES
ORTRAIT PARLE".

Lèvres

Hauteur naso-labiale

Proéminence

Bordure

Epaisseur

Défaut d'adhérence

Particularités

« Bouche »

Dimension

Particularités

Particularités

Synthétiquement

Dentition

Menton

Inclinaison

Hauteur

« Largeur »

Particularités

Particularités

Contour général de la tête

vue de profil.

Profil fronto-nasal

Profil naso-bucal

Synthétiq

Hauteur cranienne

Particularités craniennes

Contour général de la tête

vue de face

1° Synthétiquement

2° Analytiquement

Etat graisseu

Physiognomic characteristics chart for the study of human facial types

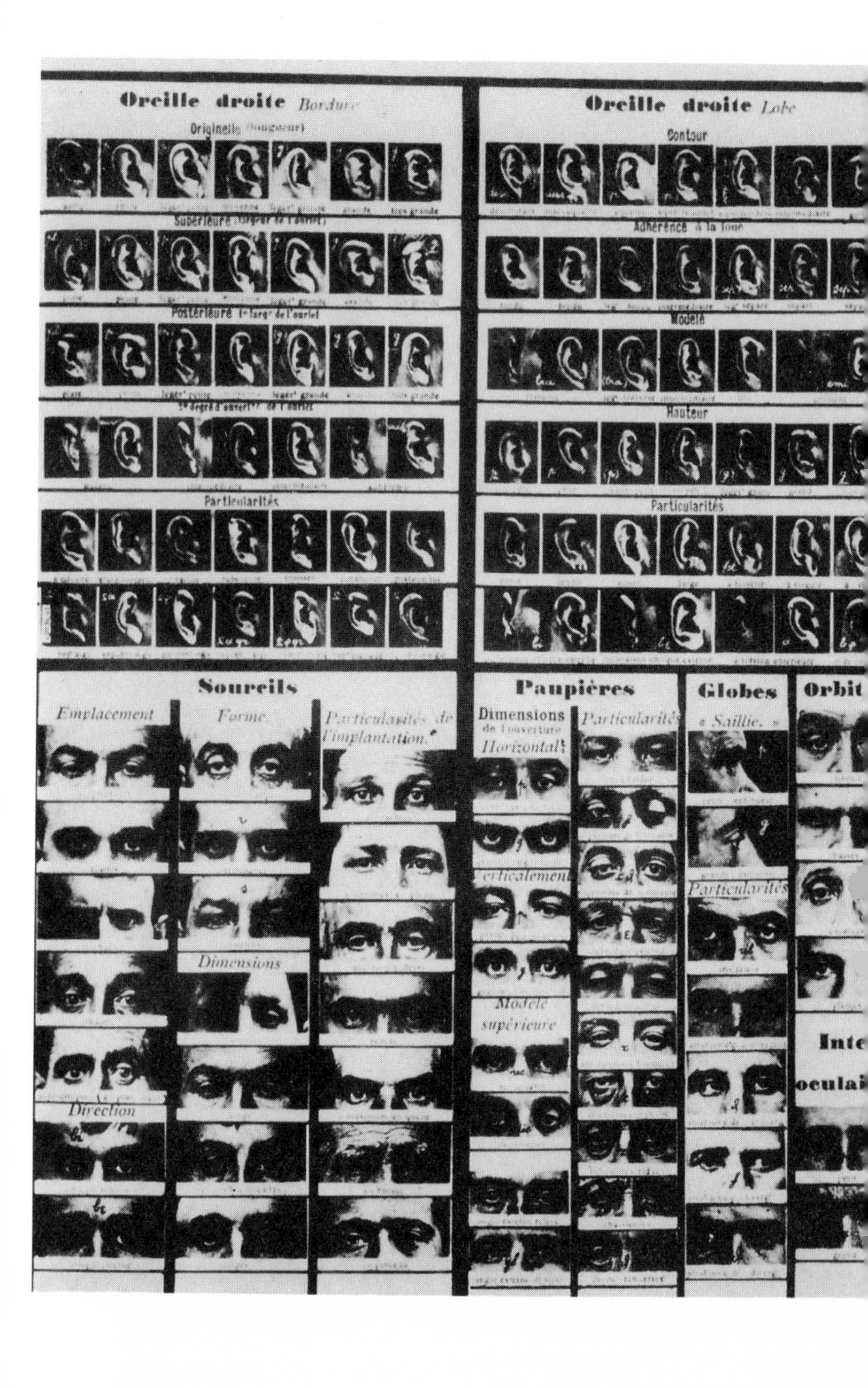
Oreille droite Bordure
Originelle
Supérieure
Postérieure
Particularités
Oreille droite Lobe
Contour
Adhérence à la joue
Modelé
Hauteur
Particularités
Soureils
Emplacement
Forme
Particularités de l'implantation
Dimensions
Direction
Paupières
Dimensions de l'ouverture
Horizontal
Verticalement
Modelé supérieure
Particularités
Globes
« Saillie. »
Particularités
Orbit
Inte
oculai

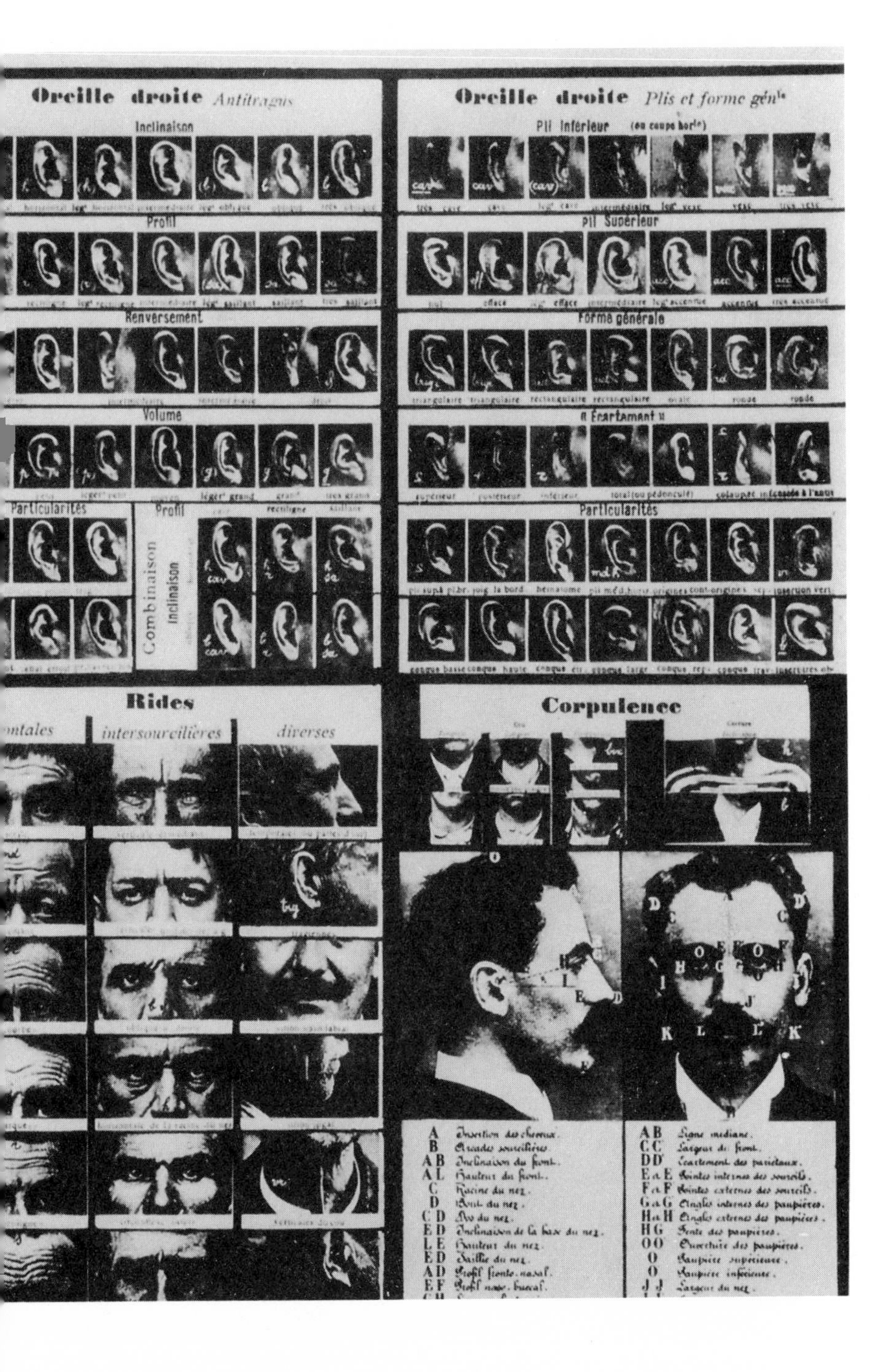

Oreille droite Antitragus
Inclinaison
Profil
Renversement
Volume
Particularités
Profil
Combinaison
Inclinaison
Oreille droite Plis et forme génle
Pli inférieur
Pli supérieur
Forme générale
« Écartement »
Particularités
Rides
intersourcilières
diverses
Corpulence
A Insertion des cheveux.
B Arcades sourcilières.
AB Inclinaison du front.
AL Hauteur du front.
C Racine du nez.
D Bout du nez.
CD Dos du nez.
ED Inclinaison de la base du nez.
LE Hauteur du nez.
ED Saillie du nez.
AD Profil fronto-nasal.
EF Profil naso-buccal.
AB Ligne médiane.
CC Largeur du front.
DD' Écartement des pariétaux.
E et E Pointes internes des sourcils.
F et F Pointes externes des sourcils.
G et G Angles internes des paupières.
H et H Angles externes des paupières.
HG Fente des paupières.
OO Ouverture des paupières.
O Paupière supérieure.
O Paupière inférieure.
J J Largeur du nez.

> The following were neurasthenics: Voltaire, Chateaubriand, Zola, Chopin, and especially Pasteur. There were other forms of madness as well: Tolstoy was a one-of-a-kind; Diderot was absentminded; Wagner was decadent; Beethoven was deaf; Goethe was a somnambulist; Victor Hugo was an egoist. . . . Of less concern is the insanity itself. Of more importance is the close relationship of degeneracy, insanity, and criminality. (*Academic Journal of the Recife School of Law*, 1913: 58–59)

By including a broad range of types Leão hoped to demonstrate the slender thread that separates the madness associated with creative ability from that of criminality.

Whether expressed by the broad strokes of an outline or through the enumeration of multiple details, these theories of human types were designed to identify and recognize a nation's criminality and madness, as well as its sources of potential success and failure, based on the physical characteristics of a people. An "objective criterion of analysis," the "anthropological method" offered these intellectuals a collection of certainties pertaining not only to the individual but also to the nation.

Silvio Romero's positions were reproduced, and sometimes radicalized, in the journal. He drew an obvious conclusion. Passing through a slow evolutionary process, the nation lacked a unique type, a defined race. Its population appeared to be subject to the temptations of crime and to the depths of madness. It was becoming apparent that the issue was how to reconcile a racial determinist discourse with the variables available to the Recife legal scholars. Seeking to find a connection between such theories and national reality, Laurindo Leão wrote, "A mestizo nation is a nation invaded by criminals." Summarizing the anxieties that seemed to issue from every quarter, Professor Joaquim Pimenta asked, "Are we, perhaps, who we are because we are a subrace, a nation of mestizos, a fusion of inferior ethnic elements, or because we are a nation in the process of formation, which would

O Espetáculo das Raças

"The Spectacle of the Races": Couple from the agrarian aristocracy; couple from the sertão; *hunter of runaway slaves; indigenous porter, all shown as mestizos*
(W. ADAMS, 1832)

The use of the technique of phrenology, with its cranial measurements and moral implications, furthered the craft of caricatures

Amazement at the potential of craniometry
(ARTIST UNKNOWN, 1850. FROM "ENTIRE FORM ET FONCTION" BY CLAUDIO POGLIANO IN *LA FABRIQUE DE LA PENSÉE*, 1990.)

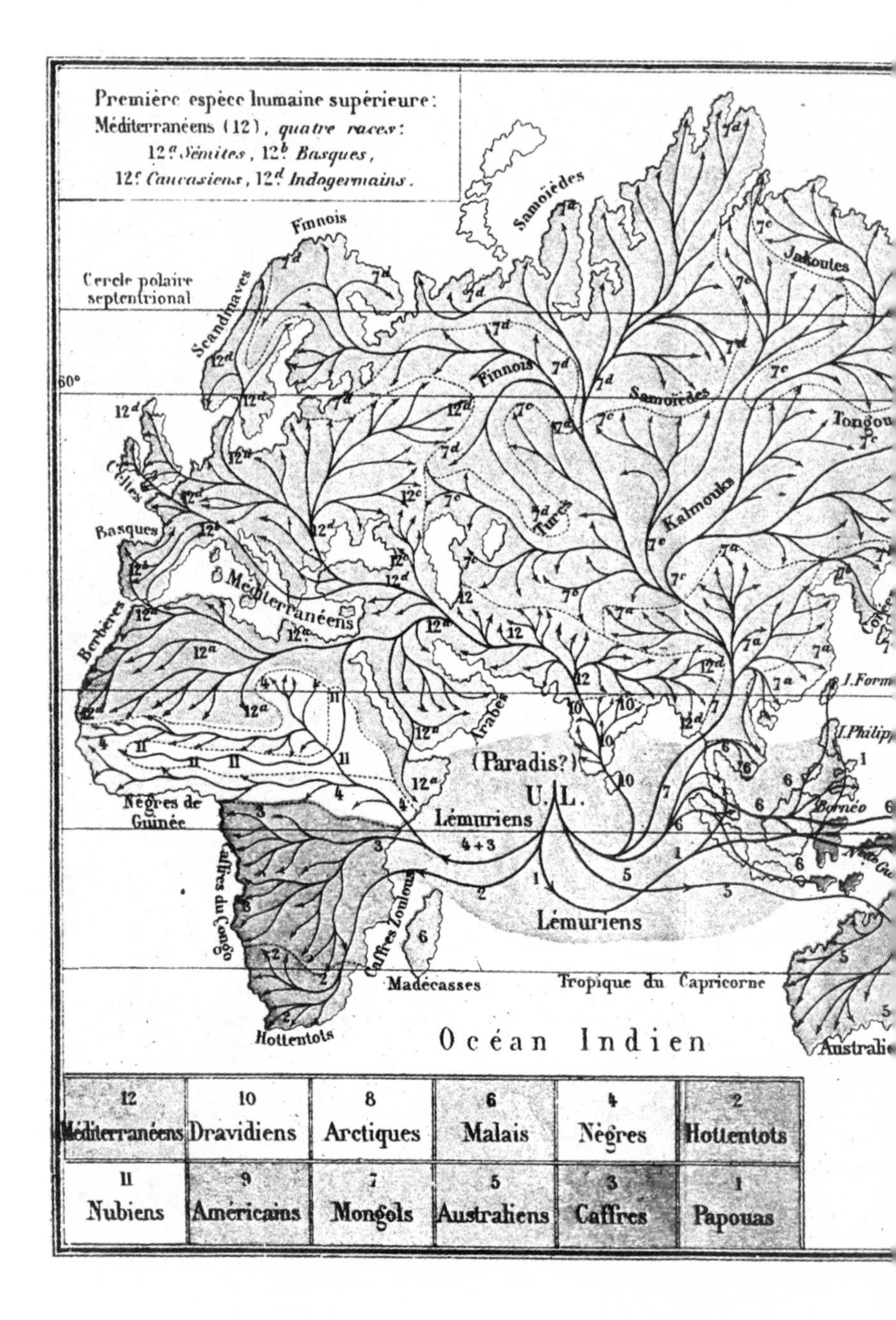

Première espèce humaine supérieure:
Méditerranéens (12), quatre races:
12a Sémites, 12b Basques,
12c Caucasiens, 12d Indogermains.
Finnois
Samoïèdes
Cercle polaire septentrional
Scandinaves
60°
Jakoutes
Finnois
Samoïèdes
Tongou
Celtes
Basques
Turcs
Kalmouks
Méditerranéens
Berbères
Arabes
(Paradis?)
U. L.
Lémuriens
4+3
Nègres de Guinée
Caffres du Congo
Caffres Zoulous
Lémuriens
I. Form
I. Philip
Bornéo
Madécasses
Tropique du Capricorne
Hottentots
Océan Indien
Australie
12 Méditerranéens
10 Dravidiens
8 Arctiques
6 Malais
4 Nègres
2 Hottentots
11 Nubiens
9 Américains
7 Mongols
5 Australiens
3 Caffres
1 Papouas

World map of the different human races,
illustrating the process of geographical determinism
(ERNST HAECKEL, 1884)

"Brazilian racial types," Afro-Brazilian and mestizo
(H. VAN EMELEN, 1927)

"Brazilian racial types," caboclo *[a term with many definitions, here representing an Afro-indigenous mix] and Indian*
(H. VAN EMELEN, 1927)

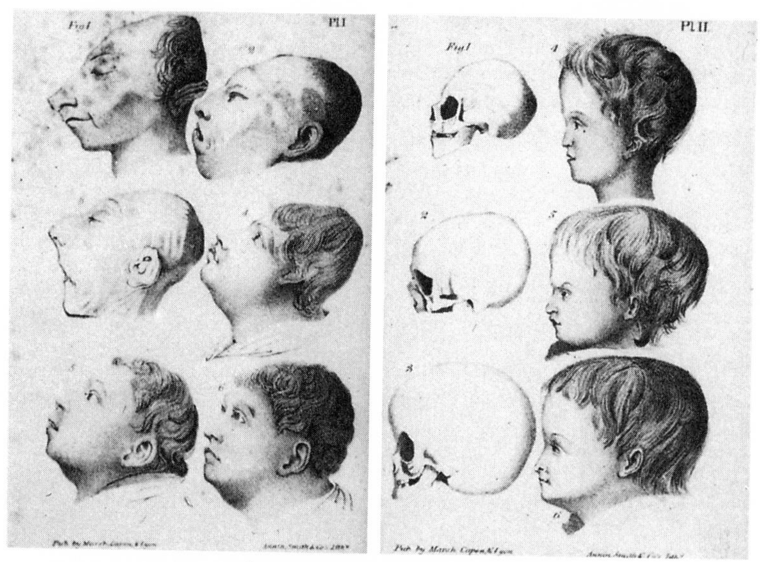

Phrenological studies of madness
(GASPAR SPURZHEIM, 1776–1832)

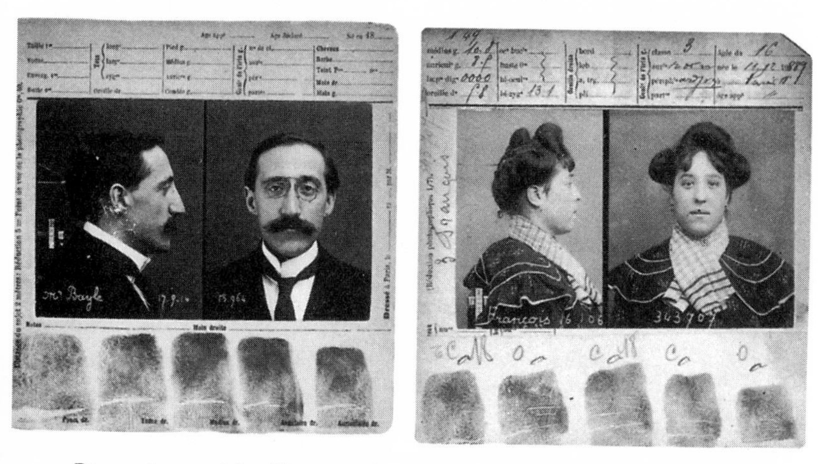

Pioneering models of forensic identification from the turn of the century
(FRANCE)

explain the state of social delinquency of the Brazilian people?" (*Academic Journal of the Recife School of Law,* 1919: 54).

Medical Law: "We Are an Ailing People"

Until the end of the 1920s, the views of race and criminality we have been discussing had dominated the journal. After that, a discourse that was critical of criminal anthropology and its determinist concoctions began to infiltrate the discussion. It began timidly, but it gathered strength as the journal moved from a narrow focus on the problems of race to expanded coverage of broader national problems.

As though it became necessary to find "a little evolution amid so much decadence," hygiene, health, and education became the most urgent themes in the journal in the 1920s. That is, without giving free rein to the evolutionist paradigm or to the era's anthropological theories, the journal more frequently featured a kind of article that investigated problems specific to Brazil, which could not always be explained by European determinist theories. In a 1927 issue of the journal, Professor Luís e Silva concluded: "With our diversity of environment and anthropological types, criminology in Brazil cannot be led by the same norms that pertain in Europe" (*Academic Journal of the Recife School of Law,* 44).

Although this rather subjective quotation reveals a reaction to the then-dominant pessimistic interpretation, it was, in fact, a breath of fresh air. From within this trend the hygienist and the expert specialist in legal medicine appeared as counterpoints to the figures of the anthropologist and the sociologist, who were seen as offering few solutions to the nation's problems: "The anthropological point of view offers our decadence as a decisive fact, . . . [and] rare are the sociologists who have not been seduced by Gobineau's anthropological novel" (*Academic Journal of the Recife School of Law,* 1919: 55).

"What is the answer?" inquired an article in 1919. "It is not because we are the shadow of a nation that we march with such a slow and tired gait along civilization's highway" (*Academic Journal of the Recife School of Law,* 58). This "national problem" persisted, although its continued presence could not have been the exclusive fault of ethnic or racial factors. As the new data suggested, perhaps hygienic and social issues were to blame; after all, until that time the nation had not delved into the effects of these problems: "80 percent of the population suffers from hookworm disease, precisely because 80 percent of us are uneducated, of whom only 29 percent know how to read with limited comprehension, and only 5 percent know how to write. Herein lies the depressing explanation for the difference between us and other nations" (*Academic Journal of the Recife School of Law,* 1919: 59).

A new argument was appearing. Giving health to the country and educating its people was the way to cultivate nature and perfect human beings.

> It is not because we are an experimental country that we march in the rearguard of other nations. It is because we are ignorant, badly educated, badly fed and because we have polluted nerves and weakened hearts, blood, livers, and intestines. More than the *race,* more than tradition, more than customs, it is the *law* that alters the race that makes tradition recede. (*Academic Journal of the Recife School of Law,* 1919: 60)

New theories mingled with those that had already been planted. The newer ones grew out of an interpretation of the nation that had been passed through the sieve of racial determinist theories. At the same time that a heated debate between law and medicine was gathering momentum, the racial issue began to recede before the force of new data from the hygienists.

Was law limited to legislation, and was medicine not to venture beyond diagnosis? These questions were perhaps the crux of the dispute that was mounting. "We are an infirm nation," declared the hygienist Joaquim Pimenta (*Academic Journal of the Recife School of Law,* 1919: 55). "We are a territory upon which nature has imprinted a creative but ambiguous race," declared Recife professor of criminal law Laurindo Leão (*Academic Journal of the Recife School of Law,* 1923: 52). Both men diagnosed the nation's illness similarly, but their cures involved very different medicines.

DECADENCE: "EVERYTHING CHANGED"*

"God save us from hearing anything else about foreigners. Everything about Brazil is great except for its people." Thus Professor Netto Campello concluded his analysis of the "national situation" (*Academic Journal of the Recife School of Law,* 1919: 60), revealing a consensus that was emerging at that time concerning how to think of Brazilians. Although they approached their problems from distinct angles, as "men of science," the jurists of Recife felt they were responsible for this difficult, formative nation. They sought in the study of philosophy the principles necessary for wrestling with the nation's problems of miscegenation, backwardness, poverty, and underdevelopment.

With a sometimes ingenuous conception of how Brazil depended on them, these legal scholars felt certain that they had to transcend their juridical expertise to confront the country's problems as a whole. Despite the gloomy predictions that surrounded Recife, the city approached the 1920s without the radical responses of other times, but its scholars still had not renounced the scientific models that they had adopted in the 1870s.

The solution to the nation's "situation" appeared to lie in creating a theoretical design that would reconcile theories by refining them. Glimmers of new thought began to emanate, and they

* The subtitle of this section is a quote from the *Academic Journal of the Recife School of Law,* 1925: 43.

were different from both determinism and the praise that surrounded the mixing of races. These new ways of thinking did not follow the social Darwinist model in lamenting the effects of racial blending, but they did seek a "good mixture" of the races, achieved through a greater "influx of white blood" in the population, as was suggested in one article:

> Through the accumulated heredity of different races, mestizos deriving from antipodal races are passionate and unstable by nature. Through their savage nature they kill, and through the effects of civilization they weep. But among us they are remorseful. We must have good racial mixtures to avoid nonsensical crime. (*Academic Journal of the Recife School of Law,* 1913: 83)

Even if the Recife legal scholars did not reject determinist interpretations, they uncovered unexpected loopholes to allow for a "good racial mixture" or, better yet, to allow for an evolution that did not necessarily lead to degeneracy. According to this way of thinking, "the science that proclaims that nature creates men different should attenuate it, where the strong should work in cooperation on behalf of the weak. This is good evolution" (*Academic Journal of the Recife School of Law,* 1918: 116).

By stripping racial models of their most radical tenets, legal scholars recast the models that had been difficult to apply to the Brazilian situation. Of course, portions of the determinist theories still survived. No one questioned, for instance, the notion of racial inequality or the notion of the necessity of an authoritarian solution. A 1923 article based on ideas found in Gumplowiz declared that "Racial struggle is the origin of the State. It is, therefore, a natural force of racial and sociological determinism, just as consciousness is a natural formation of biological determinism" (*Academic Journal of the Recife School of Law,* 1923: 146).

Although the degenerationist interpretation based on social Darwinism did not attract many followers, the same could not be said of the era's other theories. Evolutionist analysis, containing a hint of racial determinism, functioned as a model of inevitability. It was an authoritarian argument that omitted the discussion of social conflict in the face of a form of "naturalization of the State and society." The state was emerging as a "superior form of integration, . . . an integrating center of racial realities" (*Academic Journal of the Recife School of Law,* 1923: 147). Once the problems of miscegenation had been understood, it seemed to be just a matter of applying a necessary centralization to the phenomenon of disparate races. Opposing the "inefficient Liberal Republic, . . . the now celebrated government 'of the people and by the people,' an artful form of a failed dream" (*Academic Journal of the Recife School of Law,* 1927: 151), Recife's legal scholars sought new forms of government and unheard-of manners of intervention.

In this regard, although the racial theme had lost some of its pessimistic edge, it remained pivotal to their arguments. In the name of social evolution's exigencies, these scientists hoped the public would fall in line with their ideas.

With their anticlerical radicalism and with their applications of Darwin to law and of Haeckel to ethics, these men were above all satisfied with themselves, "imagining themselves the golden boys of the age of science" (Rabello, 1967: 95). "Men more of the present than of the future, irremediably dated" (Chacon, 1969: 56), they were above all children of their time, using the scientific techniques and technology that were available to them. Located as these men were far from the centers of political decision making, their blind faith in science enabled them to foresee a future, to imagine a nation as yet unknown.

The law school's publications began to show fewer signs of visionary thinking in the 1920s and 1930s. Writers began to question evolutionist models, and the famed advocates of these models soon became the butt of jokes. "*Les abeilles d'aujourd'hui sont exactement ce qu'elles étaient il y a dix siècles*" [The bees of today are exactly as they were ten centuries ago], declared J. H. Fabre, a professor who visited the Recife School of Law in 1924.

"But what about Darwin?" asked one of the more curious students. "*Oh! Celui-là! Ses observations même n'ont guère de valeur. J'ai essayé de le lire, mas j'y ai renoncé; c'est du roman*" [Oh! That one! His observations are scarcely worth a thing. I have tried to read him, but I gave up; he reads like a novel] (*Academic Journal of the Recife School of Law,* 1925: 331).

The intellectuals who only a short time before had blindly followed all the evolutionist paradigms began to dismiss these ideas as subjective and out-of-date. This alternation in course would affect the entire concept of law and the legal profession, as was reflected in one commentary:

> Today's student is a businessman, a reporter, a civil servant. He now wears a linen suit, not a Prince Albert. . . . The free play of ideas no longer stirs his emotions. He tends toward other things: a job to do, a function to serve. Everything has changed. The spirit of things could not remain the same. (*Academic Journal of the Recife School of Law,* 1925: 343).

Sounding like a lament or nostalgia for some bygone era, Professor Odilon Nestor recalled that not only the ideas but also the intellectual and social profile of the school's students had changed:

> The Academy is but a shadow of its former self. It has lost its old luster, it has ceased to be a focus of intellectual dissemination and a center of ideas. . . . The new generations have adopted a way of living that is different from the generations that preceded them. They possess a wholly modern quality that we now call "common sense." They have lost their joy, their spontaneity, and their originality. . . . With their more realistic and more practical view of life they have rejected undisciplined, bohemian, and exuberant ways. Literary and philosophical movements do not move our present students. They have set their eyes on other horizons as well: a job to

do, a function to serve. They have changed with the times, the laws, the professors, the courses, and the disciplines. Everything has changed. (*Academic Journal of the Recife School of Law,* 1927: 172–74)

Witnessing an era that they could no longer claim to dominate, the old Recife professors behaved as scribes of a period that was quickly becoming distant history. Despite its basis in science, their fervor had earlier taken on the shades of religion, but their passion was receding. "Modernity" went by the name of "common sense," and the law ceased to be a mission so that it could become a profession.

This was also the time during which the first debates were held on behalf of a full-fledged university, which was seen as "the only solution for the scientific education of our youth" (*Academic Journal of the Recife School of Law,* 1928: 44). Many felt that the School of Law was so dependent on a type of outmoded theoretical and professional model that its institutional collapse was inevitable.

For better or for worse, the Recife jurists were on the cusp of a new age. To the racial argument were added data from advocates of sanitation, educational models, and folkloric interpretations. As had happened previously, something new appeared. Suddenly the differences seemed overdue, and a "modern" view emerged to repudiate the earlier interpretations. "Everything has changed. The spirit cannot remain the same."

THE SÃO PAULO ACADEMY OF LAW
"Liberalism Goes Well with Evolution"

"São Paulo here, São Paulo there."

The São Paulo School of Law[18] also has its roots in the political independence of 1822. With independence, forming an elite core to chart the future of the nation became a national priority.[19]

The decision to found an institution of higher education in the province of São Paulo was not, however, without its detractors. Defended by some because of the province's "natural advantages and for reasons of simple convenience" (Parliamentary Annals, 1825), the choice generated lasting disagreement. The reasons were many. To begin with, the geographical location of the city of São Paulo made access difficult for students from the northern reaches of the Empire. There was also a serious shortage of student housing in the city. "That horrible highway from Cubatão" was enough to solidify one's impression of the region's poor highways. Many believed that the São Paulo dialect would "corrupt our children's speech," should they come to study there. These complaints had one unwavering conclusion in common: it was an injustice always to favor "this city over the other provinces" (Vampré, 1924/1975: 19).

"I don't know why the city of São Paulo should merit such preference. I don't know why we should always have thrust in our faces São Paulo here, São Paulo there. It's always São Paulo this, São Paulo that," bemoaned a politician in disgust over the negotiations, a year before the establishment of the school (quoted in Vampré, 1924/1975).

Despite the heated discussions, the city of São Paulo was chosen as the home of the future law school. The reasons cited for this choice were reported to be innumerable, including the city's proximity to the port of Santos, the region's low cost of living, the temperate climate, and, finally, the city's ease of access for students from the southern provinces and from the interior of Minas Gerais.

After the decision was approved on August 31, 1826, and made law on August 11, 1827, the São Paulo school was inaugurated on March 1, 1828. As in Olinda, the São Paulo program initially suffered problems. There were simply no appropriate buildings available, outside of some old convents. Because of its size and condition, the school first chose the Convent of São Francisco, which had been built in 1684. The government forced the friars to vacate most of the building, giving rise to extremely difficult relations between the friars and the school. At the students' insistence, the bell ringer sounded the hours of both the Franciscans and the academics. He did so with such enthusiasm that the frequent interruptions often greatly upset the professors (Dulles, 1984: 21). The friars also imposed some irritating conditions on the school. For instance, in order to keep the students out of the garden that surrounded the building, the friars demanded that the students enter the church only through the monastery.

In addition to the inadequate infrastructure, there were some serious problems with the quality of the school's teaching staff. The director was José Arouche de Toledo Rendon, a wealthy Brazilian Army general, seventy-one years of age, who, according to Almeida Nogueira, "seemed to know arms better than letters" (1977: 20).

The students, most of whom came from provinces in the southeast of the country,[20] suffered from the provisional nature of the accommodations. Many students were housed in cubicles owned by the monastery, and others were scattered throughout the city's neighborhoods, finding lodging in private homes that they called *repúblicas* [republics] (Bruno, 1954: 22). Wherever these students chose to live, their presence and lifestyle altered the patterns and customs of the peaceful city that was then São Paulo.

After it overcame the challenges of its first years, the São Paulo School of Law went on to become one of the nation's intellectual centers. Renowned for being self-taught, the professors of this institution did not limit their instruction to a narrow view of the law; on the contrary, their work was eclectic. They gathered under one roof the study of "political militancy, journalism, literature, advocacy, and above all activism in the law offices" (Adorno, 1988: 92). A favored source of recruitments for the state bureaucracy, the São Paulo Law School earned the right to this praise by Rui Barbosa in a speech in 1909: "in the study of law [in São Paulo], the academic world and the political world mutually infiltrate each other" (*Journal of the São Paulo School of Law,* 1909: 159).

As a final observation on the siting of the school, it is worthy to note that from 1870 to 1930, while Pernambuco went through a period of financial and political decline, for the first time São Paulo knew what it meant to concentrate economic and political hegemony in the same place.

In the midst of this boom the Historical and Geographical Institute of São Paulo and the São Paulo Museum were founded, in 1894. All the signs seemed to indicate that members of the ascendant coffee elite of São Paulo were preparing a new cultural scenario for their city, one that they deemed more consistent with the state's newfound status. It was necessary to create a local intellectual elite that would be alert "to the vicissitudes of the new São Paulo configuration" (*The State of São Paulo,* 1895). It was no coincidence that the coffee elite founded the São Paulo School of Law, established new departments, and published an official journal. To understand this better, let's take a look at the specifics of the São Paulo school's intellectual profile and trajectory.

Journal of the São Paulo School of Law

The founding of the *Journal of the São Paulo School of Law* is linked to the reform of Benjamin Constant. His Decree number 1159 of December 3, 1892, established the annual publication of periodicals in the nation's schools of higher education. The schools received this decree coolly, as a gift that brought with it additional work for professors and administrators. They did not view publishing a journal as a coveted triumph.

At the beginning, the objectives of the São Paulo journal were modest and focused on the internal workings of the institution. The journal originally sought "[o]riginal memoirs on matters pertaining to the courses taught at the institution and summaries of the decisions made by faculty leaders" (*Journal of the São Paulo School of Law,* 1893: 3). Five faculty members made up the journal staff, shifting their responsibilities annually. The journal clearly functioned as an internal organ for the school, published in service to the school. It certainly did not publish articles that were as combative as those of its Pernambuco counterpart.

One person did not dominate this publication, and this fact sets the São Paulo law journal apart from others we have studied. Pedro Lessa wrote many articles for the journal, but he contributed far fewer than, for example, Clovis Bevilacqua contributed to the *Academic Journal of the Recife School of Law,* or von Ihering wrote for the *Journal of the São Paulo Museum*. Also the São Paulo law journal did not seem to be the sole means for the school's professors and students to disseminate their ideas. The students had their own magazines and journals, and the faculty contributed constantly to the daily newspapers. Professors of the school wrote several editorials in the *São Paulo Post,* and, of course, in their comments they referred glowingly to the intellectual activities at the São Paulo School of Law (Schwarcz, 1987).[21]

The São Paulo professors of law profited from the advantages accorded them by a new political and economic climate. This environment together with the fact that the students came from the wealthy and politically influential southeastern elite made for a situation that was much more financially stable than that which their Recife colleagues bore. Given the proximity of the nation's decision-making centers, not only were the São Paulo professors able to use their social origins and association with the school as a springboard to political posts in the republic; they also had easy access to important agents of communication.

The school faculty considered the journal to be more an official and institutional periodical than a platform for the dissemination of ideas and polemics espoused by individual professors. Perhaps this unique characteristic explains the much more varied array of essays that appeared in its pages. Taken together, the body of writings reveals a certain didactic design and a thematic diversity whose purpose seemed to be to introduce the reader to the intricacies of the profession. (See Table 17.)

Table 17 Breakdown of the Thematic Content of the Journal of the São Paulo School of Law *(1890–1930)*

THEME	TOTAL
Civil law	32
São Paulo School of Law	26
Medical law	21
Criminal law	20
Philosophy of law	20
Commercial law	12
History of law	9
Biographies	7
International law	6
University	6
Roman law	4
Administrative law	3
Political economy	3
Industrial law	3
Family law	3
Constitutional law	2
Tax law	2
Public law	2
Private law	1
State law	1
TOTAL	183

"Only for the Chosen"*

The São Paulo School of Law was unique in its high regard for the practice of law as a social function. From the association between the supposed prominence of the profession and the

* The quotation in the title of this section comes from the *Journal of the São Paulo School of Law,* 1929: 286.

acclaimed "innate superiority of São Paulo," a publication resulted whose constant trademark references would be to one place—São Paulo—and one practice—the law. The province of São Paulo would always be characterized by a distinguishing feature; for example, "São Paulo maintains an aura for its civilizing role as the alma mater of our teaching of the science of justice" (*Journal of the São Paulo School of Law,* 1909: 104). At the same time, the work of justice was beginning to be portrayed as an impartial practice, which, it was believed, would be responsible for leading the nation away from barbarism toward civilization. The journal never failed to stress São Paulo's leadership and its presumed guiding role in this work.

The São Paulo institution found in itself, and only in itself, the nation's long-awaited model for progress: "It is a true messenger caravan of Enlightenment for the whole country, . . . the means of disseminating great ideas, a tireless sower of practical truths for our nation" (*Journal of the São Paulo School of Law,* 1913: 18), declared Almeida Nogueira. But it was not enough to underscore the importance of the school. The practice of law as a profession would help Brazil join the list of the world's civilized countries. Rui Barbosa commented:

> This country will survive if it believes in and sanctifies Justice and Law. If not, it will quickly pass from disarray to anarchy, from anarchy to chaos, and from chaos to barbarism and lawlessness . . . a lost race. There is no alternative. It will be either justice, peace and prosperity, or it will be dictatorship. North America and Europe are watching us. I am not exaggerating. I am telling you what will happen. I see this. (*Journal of the São Paulo School of Law,* 1909: 177)[22]

To ensure the success of their mission to create civilization, it always seemed necessary for a school of law to affirm the importance of science, while at the same time to reaffirm the preeminence of law.

> If science is indispensable to human life, and if only it elevates mankind and separates him from the animals, without Law and adherence to it nothing lasting can exist on earth. It is the science of Law that guarantees humanity's rights. The man of Law is, therefore, the arbiter of all social energies. As the physician studies the individual, the *bacharel* studies society, . . . with all other professions merely serving the man of Law. He and only he knows where one justifies legal action. It is he and only he because he has learned the scientific view of the realm of legal action. (*Journal of the São Paulo School of Law,* 1929: 169)

By establishing a clear division between the law and the other occupations, the journal's writers gave law a special importance within the journal, and this phenomenon resembled an act of hope:

> God gave us this fundamental mission to work for the benefit of mankind, and it has made our profession a truly exceptional one. Only the chosen should pursue it. What will you be? Lawyers, judges, diplomats, legislators, public administrators. Always men of Law, men of State. (*Journal of the São Paulo School of Law,* 1929: 169)

It was in this way that politics and the academy converged, the union of the two falling just short of a religious event. It was evolutionism with Catholic underpinnings. It pondered inevitabilities, but it appealed to the Divine. It conjoined a professional choice to a missionary calling. During this period the São Paulo law school rapidly became a center of the "chosen few," specially trained to guide the nation's destiny. Although São Paulo was far from the centers of decision making during the monarchy, since it had emerged during the republic as a regional economic power and represented a financially privileged clientele, the São Paulo School of Law gave great credibility to the country's new political game.

Criminal Anthropology and Public Medicine: The Critical View

Articles on criminal law appeared frequently in the first years of the journal.[23] Because of the numerous articles on the subject, it is clear that the theme and the discipline were of interest. By the journal's account, when Enrico Ferri, who was a professor of the Italian school of penal law, visited the school on November 14, 1908, the students received him with enthusiasm, and "they showered him euphorically with flowers and wild applause" (*Journal of the São Paulo School of Law,* 1909: 239). One notes, however, some equivocation when scholars tried to apply the theory to local conditions. In the end they condemned the racial determinism found in Italian thinking on criminal law, because, in the words of Pedro Lessa, they considered such beliefs "the result of a reactionary movement against humanitarian theories . . . Moral and racial development do not occur without certain conditions of social well-being" (*Journal of the São Paulo School of Law,* 1900: 178–79).

In defense of individual free will and in the interests of social analysis of the criminal phenomenon, scholars introduced determinist models into the São Paulo academic circles only with the greatest caution. What Recife accepted as avant-garde, São Paulo assimilated only with great care, with "the critical eye of those who recognize the truth of some concepts and who reject the extreme views of certain jurists" (*Journal of the São Paulo School of Law,* 1906: 67).

Beginning in the first decade of this century it is possible to discern this same line of thought in the debate waged over public medicine. The medical-hygienist perspective did not seem to present a threat within the São Paulo law school, since from the beginning the work of hygienists was consigned to a subordinate position: "Public medicine is an adjunct to help the lawyer discharge his duties. Good governments proceed from good laws. And to have good laws one must observe how, at least in this regard, medicine contributes to the teaching of law" (*Journal of the São Paulo School of Law,* 1907: 41). The assistance of the medical professional was important, but the autonomy and the precedence of the jurist were guaranteed, since the law always had the last word. An article about a lawsuit concerning a seduction concluded: "The jurist's mission is immense and is as noble as that of the physician. They walk a parallel road. The duty of medicine is first to prevent illness and second to cure it. The duty of law is first to prevent and resolve the crimes and second to punish those who commit them" (*Journal of the São Paulo School of Law,* 1908: 104).

On the one hand the jurists granted the importance of public medicine, and on the other hand they sought to restrict its validity. That is, if law and medicine together had a central role to play in the nation's progress,[24] the image the jurists held of the hygienist and the public physician was that of a technician, whose role was auxiliary and complementary.

The discussion of details specific to the practice of law can take one only so far. Looking beyond legal applications, one notes that racial determinist theories that informed both criminal anthropology and medical law were clearly in the process of being repudiated. Behind São Paulo's lack of confidence in these models there lay an adherence to other theoretical traditions, an investment in political liberalism, and skepticism about social explanations defined wholly by race.

But if the critique of racial determinism when applied to penal law was severe, one could not say the same of the school's response to physical anthropology: "Anthropology is the branch of natural history that deals with man and human races and the ethnology of peoples and tribes. . . . [Anthropologists] are the ones whose knowledge should inform the jurist's good analysis" (*Journal of the São Paulo School of Law,* 1899: 323). A good jurist was one who advised well and used "modern racial theories," yet when he made his conclusions he did not submit wholly to their designs.

In Praise of a Liberal State

São Paulo's "men of law" affirmed their supremacy "in the analysis of societies," exhibiting an autonomy that distinguished them from the law scholars at Recife (*Journal of the São Paulo School of Law,* 1929: 131). While they understood that their role was to reveal new models, they learned from the other sciences while still retaining their own identity.

The São Paulo jurists defended the liberal interpretation of the state, since it corroborated the arguments they affirmed. They censured what they considered to be "Recife's overly Germanic and ethnic spirit" (*Journal of the São Paulo School of Law,* 1906), and they adopted a model in which democracy merged with theories of evolution. In this model the negative aspects of the phenomenon of mixed races, so cultivated by the Recife academicians, were seen as a troubling element, but it was only part of a more comprehensive display of concerns.

> A society creates a means for its own governance, and it is the law, and the state regulates the exercise of the law. . . . The human aggregate, which is society itself, people, race or the nation, is a complex of individuals linked by traditions, manners, and customs, comprising a unit based on its historical conditions and political organization. (*Journal of the São Paulo School of Law,* 1930: 8)

The article quoted here haphazardly cites a series of points that show how the issue of race emerges in the midst of discrete factors of cultural and political character.

The state appears to be defined as "a natural and evolutionary result," a body organizing the different elements that coexisted until then in chaos: "Sovereign authority is the force that balances, unifies, disciplines, and drives social and individual forces through law. These are all fundamental characteristics of the state. The supreme authority is sovereign and necessary for a social order in which a nation, race, or people must live" (*Journal of the São Paulo School of Law,* 1930: 9).

The concepts of "nation, race, and people" occurred simultaneously and appeared to be essentially synonymous, all subjected to the action of a state that prevailed over every conflict: "Through its branches and powers the state does everything. The final stage of evolution is the form by which the nation, the people, will organize and harmonize" (*Journal of the São Paulo School of Law,* 1930: 9).

The São Paulo model reveals "a conservative liberalism" (Nogueira, 1977: 67) that was closer to the post–French Revolution approach, in which the concept of liberty appeared to be a function of the notion of order. Despite Anglo-Saxon influence, Raimundo Faoro also declared that liberalism came to the country "smelling of Bragantine* mustiness" (1977), which conveyed not only a conservative but also an elitist and antidemocratic image. This image emerged with clarity in Brazil, being derived from adaptations that allowed the country to reconcile imperial slavery and the plantation system, as well as government expansion and republican political authoritarianism.

The model proclaimed for São Paulo was as a harmonious state, untouched by social and racial differences:

> Far from being a liability, inequality is recognized among men born physically, intellectually, and morally unequal, and it represents an asset for the sovereign state. It is a stage in the progress of society, and the human force of will to cause it to disappear or recede is most powerful and stimulates production. (*Journal of the São Paulo School of Law,* 1923: 46)

The critique of racial determinism did not imply, however, a rejection of the evolutionist perspective. Humans remained

* A reference to the Portuguese royal House of Bragança.

unequal, although capable of "evolution and perfectibility" through the intercession of a state that was both sovereign and capable of overcoming economic and racial diversity.

In the 1930s there were again changes worthy of note. In defense of the liberal state, an appeal for democracy emerged. Employing the same logic of the harmonious state, intellectuals declared that representative democracy was the result of a foretold human evolution within Brazil:

> If we try to learn through human evolution what manner of state corresponds to man's deepest sentiments and to the vital needs of an educated society, we will find that it is democracy. We have here a social evolution that leads us to a representative democracy in which the people govern themselves. The federal republic is a spontaneous product of national evolution. (*Journal of the São Paulo School of Law,* 1929)

At the end of the 1920s new political tensions formed a backdrop to the discussions on the liberal state: Brazil was anxious about its future as the specter of war, fascism, and dictatorship loomed, and in the journal's pages a distinctly São Paulan model appeared. The notion was that through the analysis and interpretation of human races, "the truth about inequality among them" persisted. In addition, and despite the adoption of a liberal model, the evolutionist interpretation remained generally accepted and helped to justify a state that aspired to be "the fruit of an unswerving social evolution" (*Journal of the São Paulo School of Law,* 1929).

The *Journal of the São Paulo School of Law* was founded shortly after a military coup d'état in 1889 that overthrew the Empire and established the republic. The journal was an unremitting defender of states' rights, and it adapted a conservative liberal model to prevailing evolutionist perspectives. During the Old Republic (1889–1930), the combination of elitist liberalism and evolutionist theories at the São Paulo law school led to confidence in a centralized state, camouflaging markedly regional interests and class conflicts.*

The São Paulo School of Law reflected the vigor that São Paulo enjoyed during the Old Republic. Not only did the academy tend to justify the existence of an authoritarian and clearly manipulative state; it also sought in evolutionist theory the truth of its origins and the road to its future.

RECIFE AND SÃO PAULO

"In Brazil the Individual Has Always Been a Hollow Promise"

Law school academics in Recife and São Paulo never hid or disguised their disagreements. From the very beginning the differences between the two schools were always greater than their similarities. Perhaps the scholars at both locations shared the same high regard for their profession, as well as an evolutionist jargon that held sway until the 1930s, but, beyond these broad commonalities, the two law schools found very little about which they could agree.

Their dissimilarities varied in proportion and importance, and one finds a great range of contrasts from fundamental theoretical differences to the most minor details. Their language exams are a case in point. A candidate for admission to the São Paulo law school had only to pass an exam in English, but his Recife counterpart had to take exams in English, German, and Italian. This small detail suggests important bibliographic implications for the

* The reference here is to the period of the 1920s when movements of workers and *tenentistas* appeared. The *tenentistas* were military cadets and young officers who created an insurrection that had far-reaching implications within both the military and national politics.

school at São Paulo. Many of the social Darwinist authors, such as Haeckel and Buckle, whom the Recife scholars held in such high regard, were read in German; and masters of criminology, such as Lombroso, Garófalo, and Ferri, were read in Italian.

If on the admission exam the Recife school tested "anthropological notions," on São Paulo's exam candidates were tested on their knowledge of "psychology and logic." These details also reveal divergent values in the two programs. Recife adhered to studies of physical anthropology, informed by phrenology and racial determinism, while São Paulo leaned toward the philosophical view and a more oblique engagement with biological sciences. The curricular offerings of the two institutions were also different. Recife offered more courses in penal law, or "criminal anthropology." São Paulo emphasized the area of civil law.

In these few examples one can see the outlines of broad features that are, nevertheless, insufficient to characterize the powerful differences between the two institutions. The wider gulfs become apparent with an analysis of each institution's perception of itself and the objectives that it set for itself since its foundation. Recife educated and prepared itself to produce indoctrinators, or "men of science" as the era understood the term; São Paulo was responsible for training the region's great state politicians and bureaucrats.[25] The Recife school was more self-celebratory. It exalted "the creation of an intellectual center, a source of autonomous ideas" (*Academic Journal of the Recife School of Law,* 1908: 102). The São Paulo group was self-confident and, although the school's leaders recognized that their school had its weaknesses, they still spotlighted the institution's role in the nation's political leadership: "we are aware of our theoretical shortcomings, but they do not interfere with our long-term involvement in the leadership of the nation's destiny" (*Journal of the São Paulo School of Law,* 1912: 83).

Both camps drew their patriotic lines, revealing their well-flaunted theoretical differences, but to a certain extent other dissimilarities were well camouflaged. Beyond their intellectual differences, a most unusual kind of difference was appearing.

From Recife emerged theories and new models that São Paulo scholars censured as extreme. From São Paulo came political practices that were transformed into laws and measures.

Along this line it is interesting to consider the immigration restrictions Brazil placed on Asians and Africans. This issue provided a constant theme for debate in the House of Representatives and in other bodies during the 1880s. For example, São Paulo politicians strongly influenced the Central Immigration Society (1883–91), which at various times pointed to the "debilitated, corrupt, bastardized, depraved and, in a word, detestable [character] of the Chinese race" (Hall, 1976: 159). Following the abolition of slavery in 1888, Brazil suffered an immediate labor shortage, and states began seeking solutions for their dilemma, and loosening immigration restrictions was one solution. A law passed on June 28, 1890, opened Brazil to all healthy persons capable of work and not involved in legal processes against them in their countries of origin, "with the exception of Africans and Asians" (Decree of the Provisional Government, sixth fascicle, Rio de Janeiro, 1890). This kind of dialectic ebbed and flowed constantly in the House. In 1892 Senator Monteiro Barros prohibited the admission of Africans, but in that same year an open-door immigration policy was approved and authorized by Floriano Peixoto on October 5, 1892.

A stereotyped view of certain races, especially Asians, prevailed in both federal and state arenas, and it was certainly responsible for the country's generalized uneasiness about setting immigration policy. Believed to be "incapable of assimilation, bearers of languages and customs foreign to our own and practitioners of suicide and opium" (Nogueira, 1984), Asian immigrants were seriously restricted from entering the country.

São Paulo, the "most advanced province" in its defense of a liberal and modernizing program that would allow manual laborers unrestricted entry, did not live up to its reputation when it came to admitting Asian and African workers. For support of their position, São Paulo's decision makers turned to the eugenics models of intervention that Recife scholars defended so passionately. These studies provided the necessary arguments to support the paulistas' position on the "miserable quality" of these kinds of immigrants, as well as the justification to prohibit their entry.

On August 1, 1893, the Legislative Assembly of Rio de Janeiro discussed contracts with 15,000 European and 500 Asian workers. With the eventual arrival of this manual labor, Minas Gerais immediately declared its interest in the "entry of Orientals, although separate from the Europeans" (Compendium of State Laws and Decrees of the State of Minas Gerais: 94–95). São Paulo, on the other hand, demonstrated in practice just how susceptible it could be to racist social Darwinist theories. In addition to specifying that only workers from the European, American, and African continents would be permitted, the São Paulo legislative representatives went on to limit admission to only select people from these continents. From Europe they would admit Italians, Swiss, Germans, Dutch, Norwegians, Danes, English, Austrians, and Spaniards, and from Spain they would admit only those from the Canary Islands, Navarra, and the Basque provinces. From the Caribbean and North America, they would accept only Puerto Ricans and Canadians from the province of Quebec. From Africa, only residents of the Canary Islands, who were also Spaniards, were acceptable (Compendium of State Laws and Decrees of the State of São Paulo, 1895–96: 41).

These small debates on the "quality of immigration" reveal unsuspected facets of the thinking of São Paulo politicians and academicians. For instance, defended by "eminent jurists of the São Paulo School of Law whose positions and seats in the legislature were guaranteed" (Adjunct Document, 13) the prohibition of the entry of "chins" [chinks] was part of a São Paulo campaign led by the institution's scholars, who, through newspapers such as the *Correio Paulistano,* did not hesitate at that moment to adopt the concerns and programs defended by Recife. The *Correio Paulistano* of July 19, 1892, referred to the Chinese in the following way:

> Who are the Chinese? . . . the slaves with all their horrors and vices were not as pernicious as these contracted Chinese. . . . The Negro knew nothing more than to be a sensuous idiot, without the slightest idea of religion. . . . The Chinese are lascivious persons in the extreme, the scoria accumulated from countries with feckless customs. . . . They are all criminals, gamblers of the worst kind. . . . Admitting the possibility of introducing these lepers of body and soul, how much will the State of São Paulo spend in prisons with the increase of criminality?

Given that Brazil faced an acute shortage of manual labor after the prohibition of slavery, how else can one understand this manner of restriction except as a racist design to "purify the race and to cleanse the nation of the incursion of the foreign into white Aryan blood"? The immigration measures that were adopted reveal an even more complex mind-set. This was not merely a policy of rejection based on racial criteria; it clearly implied an acceptance of existing hierarchies in continental Europe. That explains why Central Europeans were barred from immigration. Indeed, most of the populations that were rejected were rejected merely on the basis of their Negro or mestizo composition. It is useful to recall that in the same era the first "return to Africa" projects were enacted, involving the return of black populations to their continent of origin (see Corrêa, 1983).

The issue of immigration policy, which branched into several others, illuminates a revealing practice. The Recife School of Law espoused a clearly determinist model, but São Paulo's liberal façade, which served as its calling card for official matters, coexisted with a racist discourse. These underlying positions and theories would emerge when it came to defending hierarchies and explaining inequalities. At such times it was very clear that although these jurists may have been speaking of democracy, they did not necessarily mean to extend the rights and obligations of citizenship to all. As Marco Aurélio Nogueira declared, "in the exercise of their finest principles, liberals reserved liberalism for the evanescent domains of rhetoric. . . . the politics they practiced was oligarchic and authoritarian, as well as supportive of state supremacy" (1984: 66–67).

It is helpful to recall that the absence of certain topics can reveal a lot about a journal's editorial role. In the pages of the São Paulo law school's journal one finds neither sordid attacks on Asian and African peoples nor truthful accounts of debates waged in other forums. Rather, what is present in abundance is the illuminating theory, the product of the intellectual who labors in isolation, "far from the passions and turmoil of the outside world" (*Journal of the São Paulo School of Law,* 1922: 103).[26]

The two law schools resembled each other in that they ignored the needs of individual Brazilians. São Paulo professor Braz de Souza Arruda lamented forlornly in an introductory class titled "A questão social" [The social question], that "in Brazil the individual has always been a hollow promise" (*Journal of the São Paulo School of Law,* 1914: 23). In Recife the individual had always been understood to be "a representative of his group." With the adoption of a more and more anti-democratic conservative liberalism in São Paulo, the question of citizenship nearly disappeared, and with it individual will. "After all, who cares," one jurist wrote (*Journal of the São Paulo School of Law,* 1914: 23).

If in Recife the adoption of a racist model resulted in an authoritarian program that categorically ignored the individual, at least the law scholars revealed their differences and conflicts, even if these conflicts were incorrectly named and racially based; for example, "The State is necessary. . . . It is a natural design, . . . and deriving from a social evolution, it imposes a direction on society. . . . Finally, that which gives birth to the State is the impulse that emerges in the struggle either between races or our heterogeneous groups" (*Academic Journal of the Recife School of Law,* 1923: 146). São Paulo liberalism avoided conflict, either in deference to the authoritarian state government, noted earlier by Marco Aurélio Nogueira, or because of its adherence to an evolutionist position. The view from São Paulo was as follows: "As the liberal democratic regime signifies and represents the evolution of popular will, revolution is not contained within it. Executed with loyalty, it will satisfy the people and bring peace" (*Journal of the São Paulo School of Law,* 1929: 358).

Evolving social differences at Recife and São Paulo could point toward newly diverging theoretical tracks as well as the need to address new and different issues of socioeconomic inequalities. In Recife the ranks of the school came to be dominated by people who were decreasingly attached to the rural oligarchic rule, whereas in contrast the nouveau riche were becoming increasingly powerful at the São Paulo law school. Cries of discontent, explained by the shift of the political and economic power axis, arose more keenly from Recife, while São Paulo soon moved from commentator to defender and became responsible for generating an official position for the state.

Despite their differences, both institutions managed to declare that "Brazil had a future." For Recife that future would come about by means of a racial blending that would shape and make the population uniform. For São Paulo racial evolution would occur because of the missionary efforts of a liberal state.

The figure of the jurist remained in the middle of this battle, almost untouched. Confident in their position as "missionaries," the Brazilian jurists sought to fashion for themselves an image that would distinguish them from the nation's other scientists. They were the ones "chosen" to direct the nation's destiny and to wrestle with the data that other academics would present. They saw themselves as removed from empirical medical work, the theoretical research of museum naturalists, and the eclectic and official vision of scholars at the historical and geographical institutes. They viewed themselves as masters in the process of civilization, guardians of the true way.

6

SCHOOLS OF MEDICINE, OR HOW TO HEAL AN AILING NATION

•

In her book *As ilusões da liberdade* [The illusions of liberty] (1983), Mariza Corrêa reconstructs the role and importance of medical practice in Brazil in the nineteenth century through an analysis of the careers of a select group of physicians who were members of what was called the "Nina Rodrigues School." This group gathered initially at the Bahia School of Medicine, which we consider today to be the birthplace of Brazilian medical law. Corrêa tells a story that includes not only the broad history of nineteenth-century Brazilian medicine but also the correlation of medical practice with anthropology, and the function of the physicians of the "Nina Rodrigues School" within the context of the state (especially their roles in regional disputes) and in specific medical and health projects.

In this chapter we will examine the "Nina Rodrigues School,"[1] from a different perspective and in a broader context than usual. Without denying the importance of these medical scholars, we will rethink the importance of this "school" by comparing it with other groups within the Bahia School of Medicine, as well as those within a wider medical community that includes the Rio de Janeiro School of Medicine and even other institutions such as law schools.

Through such an analysis we will have the opportunity to explore the medical debate at the turn of the century on several different levels. The tasks are to assess the emergence of medical knowledge in Brazil within an institutional setting, and more specifically, to try to gain a better understanding of a certain thematic metamorphosis that seems to have been part of the history of the Bahia School of Medicine, which, between 1870 and 1930, favored different approaches at different times.

These approaches were driven by social needs and by scholarly theories. Until the 1880s the discussion of public hygiene attracted a good part of the medical community's attention because there was considerable medical involvement in the daily life of communities beset by infectious diseases. The 1890s were a time of focus on medical law, with the appearance of the "expert," who, together with the police, explained criminality and defined insanity. It was only in the 1930s that these experts were replaced by the "eugenicist," who took on the task of isolating the diseased from the healthy.

By contrast, analyzing the scientific production of the Rio de Janeiro School of Medicine and comparing it with the Bahian school helps one see how medical debates acquired yet another dimension, when they were used in a struggle for control in medicine. Physicians in the Rio de Janeiro school sought to prove their originality and establish their identity by discovering cures for tropical diseases such as yellow fever and Chagas' disease, which they intended to eradicate quickly through "hygiene" programs. The Bahian physicians would do the same when they came to the conclusion that the mixing of the races was the nation's great source of trouble, but at the same time its towering uniqueness. In other words, while the Carioca physicians dealt in *diseases,* the Bahians turned their eye to the *diseased,* the ailing population as a whole. They would foretell insanity and anticipate criminality as the fruits of miscegenation, and in the 1920s their programs gave rise to "purification eugenics." If this description of the work of the discipline echoes other terminology, at least the focus was different.

But the debate extended beyond these two levels of analysis, which were limited to the internal workings of medical practice. When contrasted with the dialogue typical of the schools of law, the medical discourse was uniquely different. There was a more or less formalized polemic about areas of knowledge, professional projects, and even different interpretations about the nature of the country. From the medical perspective, the objective was to heal an ailing country. To do this, physicians devised a medical program based on the doctrines of eugenics, whereby physicians would amputate the nation's gangrenous limbs so that the remaining Brazilians would have the potential for "perfectibility." The "man of law" would be an adviser, making into law that which the medical expert might diagnose and in time try to heal.

In the schools of law and medicine the positions were practically reversed. It was the duty of the jurist to codify and to give a unified shape to the country; whereas it was for the physician to fulfill a technical role, to assist in implementing the exemplary efforts of these legal professionals. The discussion that came out of the two types of institutions seemed to be virtually the same, but by looking more closely one can detect nuances of difference.

The racial theme remains relevant since it integrates the theoretical arsenal of both medical schools. In Bahia it was race or, rather, racial mixing that was thought to explain criminality, insanity, and degeneracy. For the Carioca physicians (those from Rio de Janeiro), the simple intimacy of the different races that immigrated to Brazil, with their distinct physical constitutions, would bear primary responsibility for the appearance of disease and for the obstacles to biological "perfectibility."

With this approach, even if one becomes lost in a wealth of details, one gains a sense of the importance of medical discourse to the debate generated by the era's other elite practices.

A SHORT HISTORY OF THE MEDICAL PROFESSION: FROM "BARBER-SURGEONS" TO "PROFESSIONAL PHYSICIANS"

According to Michel Foucault, the nineteenth century saw the birth of two great myths: "the myth of a nationalized medical profession, organized like the clergy, and invested, at the level of a man's bodily health, with powers similar to those exercised by the clergy over men's souls; and the myth of the total disappearance of disease in an untroubled, dispassionate society restored to its original state of health" (1973: 31–32).

The second myth emerged as a result of historical reflection and understanding of the development of sickness, based on proof that illnesses differed with eras, individuals, and places. Following the French Revolution, doctors used new medical practices to intervene in epidemics, ascertain their nature, and produce a cure, rather than merely pronounce death. According to Foucault, "individuality in modern culture is bound up with that of death, . . . an obstinate relation to death" (1973: 197). This "obstinacy" was not a consequence of fear, however; it was partially a recognition that through monumental public interventions, the practice of medicine could alter the course of death and impede the biological debilitation of the populations.

Within this context the status of the physician grew dramatically. The practitioner ceased to be dependent for money on treating individuals, and he began to earn his living as a research scientist who, with a university education and the financial backing of the government, imposed himself on his milieu and transformed it.

Circumstances were different in Portugal. At the University of Coimbra, where most of the Portuguese and colonial physicians received their training, research and experimental work were still rare. According to some commentaries, the medical school professors were more concerned with reciting platitudes and theoretical conjectures than with observing patients or analyzing the course of an illness (Santos Filho, 1947; Souza, 1940). Even as of

1790, a student of human anatomy learned by working on the body of a sheep. The professor would display the animal's structures and organs, declaring, "This is a lung! This is the heart!" (Santos Filho, 1947: 190). An obscurantism typical of Portuguese and Spanish schools persisted in medical training and remained intact throughout the eighteenth century.

Medical Practice in Colonial Brazil

If anachronism and inefficiency were conspicuous in the medical schools of Portugal, one need only imagine the conditions in early Brazil. Barred by Portugal for three hundred years from founding institutions of higher learning, Brazil suffered a shortage of specialized medical and research personnel with up-to-date scientific backgrounds.

Until 1808, the year in which two medical-surgical courses were established after the arrival of the royal family, medical treatment was inadequate and did not meet minimal professional standards. Most medical care had been administered by herbalist "medicine men," who acquired their knowledge from African and indigenous sources, or by medical practitioners whose work was supervised by the kingdom's "surgeons-general" until 1872.

"Practitioners" and "proto-physicians" were no more than simple initiates. They were generally illiterate mestizos whose practice conferred on them no social prestige. They were a small minority in the midst of a crowd of medicine men, midwives, pharmacists, dentists, and bloodletters; there was a total absence of European-style physicians and surgeons. In 1789, for example, the Viceroy Luiz de Vasconcelos complained to his home government that there were only four physicians in the entire colony.

In 1872 Brazil's surgeon-general was replaced by a permanent council called the Proto-Medicato, which consisted of congressional representatives and nurses who had graduated from the University of Coimbra.[2] The council members had the responsibility of policing all therapeutic activities, as well as issuing "letters of authorization" to all those who wished to practice their "art." The requirements for obtaining this authorization were few: a certificate attesting to an apprenticeship under the supervision of a practitioner and a brief exam before the council, which more often than not approved the candidates (Aragão, 1923: 11; Schwartzman, 1979: 66).

The shortage of professional medical personnel was not, however, accidental. The obstacles to pursuing a medical career in Brazil were many. The importation of French books was prohibited, and access to medical books in general was limited. To illustrate the scarcity of written resources in early Brazil, in Rio de Janeiro there was one bookstore that carried theological works, and only one other bookseller that dealt in Portuguese medical texts. In addition, until 1800, Brazilians were barred from entering the medical profession. A Royal Edict was handed down on May 1, 1800, allowing four students, designated by the municipality of Rio de Janeiro, to continue their studies in Coimbra. Two of them specialized in mathematics, the third in medicine, and the fourth in surgery. All of these factors had the desired effect of keeping the colony dependent on Portugal.

Faced with such a shortage, unauthorized medical practices spread to such a degree that highly specialized personnel proliferated. Minimally trained *endireitas* or "straighteners" treated cases of dislocations and broken bones, and *barbeiros* or "barbers" performed minor procedures such as applying leeches, bloodletting, extracting teeth, and other surgical activities (Aragão, 1923: 14).

Such was the condition of Brazilian medical services when in 1808 the royal family disembarked at its American colony. The number of physicians and surgeons living in that immense territory was appallingly low. With the sudden arrival of a large part of the Portuguese court, hygienic and sanitary problems multiplied. Portugal had its hands full with Junot's invading Napoleonic forces at the time and could not spare medical specialists from Coimbra.

The solution was to establish schools in Brazil that could train medical personnel. One should take note that these new centers were meant to provide the colony with surgeons, but not with "physicians."[3] Only Coimbra was authorized to confer degrees in medicine, and thus Portugal was able to retain control over its vast domain in South America.

Therefore, if programs in legal education were not created until five years after Brazil gained its independence, only for reasons of force majeure would the regency government, made up of doctors and *bacharéis* of law, feel obligated to establish schools of surgery so early in the American colony.

The Arrival of Dom João VI and the Creation of the First Brazilian Medical-Surgical Schools

It was by means of a royal letter dated February 18, 1808, that Dom João VI, en route from Bahia, created the "School of Surgery," following the suggestion of the kingdom's surgeon-general, José Correia Picanço. The location chosen was the building of an old Jesuit school, the former site of the Military Hospital, in Rio de Janeiro. Two different courses were to be administered: "theoretical and practical surgery" and "anatomy and surgical procedures" (Santos Filho, 1947: 197). From the very beginning the practical applications of the new school were explicit;[4] likewise, the royal letter spelled out procedures for the school's operations. The surgical training would be a four-year course; classes would last an hour and a half; Thursdays would be holidays; and fluency in French would be a prerequisite for admission.[5]

Coming from Bahia, the regent arrived in Rio de Janeiro on March 7, 1808. On April 2 he inaugurated the school of surgery in Rio de Janeiro. The urgency of this task was reflected in the speed with which the school was put into operation and in the pragmatism that was expressed in the king's written decision: "It is absolutely essential that surgeons who are trained in the Military and Naval Hospital of this court also know the principles of medicine, by the application of which they can effectively treat the sick aboard ships and the people in the places that our diverse populations reside over the vast continent of Brazil" (Lobo, 1969: 13).

The royal decree of December 5, 1810, by which Dom João arranged for three students to be sent to Edinburgh, and then continue additional training with London surgeons, seemed not at all incidental. By all indications, the regent himself had little confidence in Brazilian professors, who had little experience and whose knowledge was out-of-date.[6]

It was only in 1813 that the schools of surgery were reorganized according to a project proposed by Dr. Manuel Luís Álvaro de Carvalho. The plan proposed the founding of three medical-surgical academies: one in Bahia, another in Rio, and yet another in São Luís do Maranhão. The third school never materialized, but the Rio academy appeared in the same year, and Bahia established its school in 1815.

The transformation of the two schools into academies implied a greater institutionalization of medical studies in Brazil. The schools reorganized and augmented their programs[7] and implemented new regulations. The most telling among the new regulations was a statute declaring that students who had passed their fifth-year exams would receive a certification of "approved surgeon," and that superior students who wished to repeat the fourth and fifth years of instruction would receive a diploma as "surgeon graduate," which corresponded to a kind of advanced degree in the field.

This new degree created a new network of hierarchies in that the surgeon graduate enjoyed a number of privileges that did not extend to the approved surgeon. Graduates of both levels of training, however, had to submit to evaluation and licensing by the royal surgeon-general. The existence of these academies and the credentials they conferred did not preclude uncertified medical practitioners from performing their work. On the contrary, the surgeon-general continued to authorize the practice of four different types of practitioners: the barber surgeon, the bloodletting surgeon, the approved surgeon, and the surgeon graduate.[8]

Despite various improvements and the fact that the two medical schools sustained an uninterrupted flow of graduates, the shortage of surgeons continued. There were efforts to correct the scarcity, the most important of which involved extending special academic honors to Brazilian students returning from Portugal's University of Coimbra, granting these graduates the same privileges normally reserved for those who had studied at Paris or Montpellier. This step was taken on August 26, 1830.

These efforts notwithstanding, conditions at the academies were precarious. The academies had been created in the image of their Portuguese models, about which the student Francisco de Sales Torres Homem would say in 1828, "if they were famous in Portugal, they were unknown in the rest of Europe" (*Annals*, 1828). From Rio came complaints about the laxity of professors and the lack of official and material support. In Bahia, where student enrollment was significantly lower than in Rio,[9] the instruction was irregular and inefficient. The Bahian academy suspended classes for a whole semester when Brazil declared its independence in 1822, and as of 1829 the school was still holding classes in the hallways of the Santa Casa building. The Bahian school endured a Franciscan poverty, going without furniture or equipment for its core classes. The clamor for academic reform in imperial Brazil had become deafening by the end of the 1820s.

The Bahia and Rio de Janeiro Schools of Medicine

The process of defining the practice of medicine as opposed to the healing then being practiced by barbers, bloodletters, and practitioners led to the foundation of Brazil's Society of Medicine in 1829. Organized along the lines of the French Academy, the society first sought to analyze the different proposals for the reform of medical education in a legislative session (Schwartzman, 1979: 69). Out of this group came the reforms that were made law in October 1832.

In addition to transforming the medical-surgical academies into "schools" or "faculties of medicine," the government's decree abolished the diploma granted for bloodletting and gave the nation's two medical schools the right to grant the degrees of Doctor of Medicine, Doctor of Pharmacy, and Doctor of Obstetrics. It is interesting to note that this decree did not consider the matter of dentistry. "Odontological arts" in Brazil were still within the purview of bloodletting barbers; the specialization in dentistry was not established in Brazil until 1884.

Going beyond the initial adoption of Parisian school regulations, in the ensuing years after 1832 the Brazilian schools chose to strengthen their laws and statutes. They divided their training into three parts: collateral sciences, medicine, and surgery. Together these areas comprised fourteen subjects, each one led by a director and two substitutes. The faculty was guaranteed autonomy in making decisions and in developing the school's internal regulations. The professors qualified for retirement after twenty-five years of service. The course was lengthened to six years, and at the time of enrollment the candidates had to demonstrate knowledge of Latin, French, logic, arithmetic, and geometry. Examinations became an annual event, and to obtain the degree a student had to defend a thesis in Portuguese or Latin.[10]

Even with these advances, the schools continued to suffer from economic constraints and disorganization. In 1832 the professors, for the most part from the lower end of the economic scale and poorly prepared to assume their new stations, became doctors by decree and were the objects of ridicule for their monotonous classes, not to mention the hardly scientific means by which they were qualified and assigned to teach at the academy: "patronage in the process of selection for employment is repugnant: sons succeed their fathers, brothers-in-law, nephews and uncles; it is the principle of monarchical succession, the only one that the nation recognizes" (Santos Filho, 1947: 180).

The socioeconomic profile of the students also tended to improve in direct proportion to the degree to which the profession was rising in estimation. Economically advantaged students generally attended the Carioca school, and they tended to have little respect for the faculty, who were mostly mestizo and dark-skinned (Santos Filho, 1947: 278), tended to come from the lower social strata, and were often the children of barbers and bloodletters. The professors of the school complained that students did not tip their hats to them, and that at times students threw stones and other hard objects at them. There was no shortage of disruptive student strikes, such as the one that occurred at the end of 1831. Provoked by the passage of "new examination regulations," students armed themselves with fruits, vegetables, and eggs they pilfered from neighboring bars, tore stones from the pavement and, wielding clubs and canes, locked themselves within the school building and held hostage an unlucky professor they had encountered. They occupied the building for two days and ceased their revolt only after the police surrounded the school and cut off the students' supply of food and drink. The government forced them to take their exams, but it did not punish them ("Historical Account of the Year, 1832"). In addition, the students were well known for their frequent hazing rituals, as described by student Antônio Henrique Leal: "There were eighty-something of us first-year students . . . it was true pandemonium! Kicks, whistles, rude bellowing reminiscent of so many animals. . . . Some of us had our coattails cut off, others lost our neckties, and received some well-placed kicks . . . no one was untouched" (Santos Filho, 1947: 246).

The student-faculty relations in Bahia were not much different, being aggravated by a shortage of teaching materials and professors and the lack of simple professional competence.

For the first forty years the Brazilian medical schools focused their primary efforts on their organization and operations, to the detriment of original scientific research. The exams lacked rigor, the professors were unqualified, funds and appropriations were always in short supply, and complaints of student disrespect abounded. Historians are unanimous, however, in identifying the 1870s as a turning point in terms of the profile and the scientific production of Brazilian medical schools. New courses and publications appeared, and interest groups began to coalesce.

It is also important to take note of the state of the public's health during these years. The epidemics of cholera, yellow fever, smallpox, and many other diseases underscored the physicians' "mission of hygiene." In addition, numerous sick and wounded were returning from the infamous Paraguayan War, and the demand for surgeons was immediate. Together with the disorderly growth of cities, crime rates, mental health problems, and drunkenness were increasing among the population. Finally, the medical profession was gaining an understanding of what diseases could be considered endemic among certain groups of immigrants. For instance, the correlation between the rise of the incidence of yellow fever and Italian immigration was well-known at the time (Chalhoub, 1993).

In the face of these changing circumstances, the nation's medical profession was in the process of redefining itself. This was the era of the appearance of the "medical missionary," resolute in his intent to intervene and heal. It was also the time during which the specialist in medical law developed, based not so much on the crime as on the flaws and deficiencies of the criminal. The growth of this specialty then gave rise to a discussion within the medical profession about defining the limits and possibilities of the practice of medical law.

Medical journals became highly influential. They were perfectly suited to summarize the broad characteristics of Brazilian medicine, as well as to profile the new medical professional, at the end of the nineteenth century and the beginning of the twentieth century.

THE MEDICAL PRESS IN BRAZIL

According to historian Jean Clavreul, medicine is characterized as "a practice detached from what people say about it." In other words, medical books have proven absolutely ineffective in conveying the dynamics of medical practice in a strict sense. They are discourses about medicine, but the practice of medicine is something wholly different, governed by its own laws and the consequences of always varying deliberations and applications of logic (1983: 29).

Perhaps the ineffectiveness of medical books in conveying the dynamics of medical practice explains the existence of two parallel phenomena in Brazil: there were very few books written on the subject of medical practice, but the conditions were favorable for the production of medical journals. By the middle of the nineteenth century, scientific journalism emerged as a new avenue for medical professionals, enabling them to depend less on the daily press and providing opportunities for the publication of their own specialized materials such as reports, monographs, articles, lectures, and communiqués. Soon, with the increased availability of pharmaceutical products, advertising entered the formula, and the new medical journals acquired the means to publish on a more reliable schedule.

The wide variety of nineteenth-century Brazilian medical journals was notable.[11] Although these periodicals were published, for the most part, in the principal medical centers of the Empire, they were of limited circulation and short duration. The two journals that are presented in this chapter, the *Medical Gazette of Bahia* and *Medical Brazil,* however, were unusual not only because of their wide circulation but also because of their longevity.[12]

Notwithstanding editorial differences and thematic variations, both publications have certain qualities in common, the most outstanding being the free interchange of information. From Bahia came primarily studies on "medical law" and, from the 1920s forward, on "alienation and mental diseases." From Rio came articles on "public hygiene," models for combatting the great epidemics that were sweeping the nation.

Since they were scientific journals, the two periodicals tried to distinguish themselves from other publications; while at the same time they struggled to achieve a common identity. The "impartial and distant character" of this kind of journal, as well as its supposed retreat "from literature uncommitted to reality and from those journals moved by political passions" (*Medical Brazil,* 1902: 206) would set it apart from the journals of other disciplines we have discussed. In the medical journals the most pressing political events, such as the Paraguayan War, the abolition of slavery, or the proclamation of the republic, were mentioned only in passing in articles that concentrated primarily on medical themes. All of these journals found their "identity" in their shared search for an original national medicine, a way of elevating the medical profession's work in Brazil to the level of the other "evolved nations":

> Brazilian science remains in the vague, indefinite, and sleepy dawn, galvanized by foreign imports, bereft of any originality. There is nothing genuinely Brazilian, in the same way we say that chemistry is a French science, psychology is English, anatomy is German, and criminology is Italian. We lack a space we can all our own. Our mission is thus laid before us. (*Medical Gazette of Bahia,* 1896: 390)

The peculiarity of the nation's features—its climate, race, physical geography, even its "degree of civilization"—were all potentially interesting elements from which one could fashion the discovery of an original Brazilian science.

But the characteristics that the two journals had in common did not stop there. The articles made full use of a medical vocabulary, but their coverage of topics surrounding social conditions eclipsed that of topics more narrowly focused on medicine. Through the efforts these publications made to discuss social conditions they came to define society as "an ailing body." It was the responsibility of the physician to "cure it of its ills, cure it of its most deeply rooted sicknesses" (*Medical Gazette of Bahia,* 1886: 22). Both journals chose not to think in terms of the individual, but in terms of the "whole," the weakened nation in need of intervention.

The causes of the illnesses the Brazilian physicians were trying to cure ceased to be considered exceptional, because the diseases were so widespread. The medical world went through a phase where "illness expositions" and the exhibition of "monstrosities" were in vogue. These expositions had a dual role: they showcased living evidence of scientists' work and proof of their theses; and they presented a warning against the danger inherent in degeneracy while they gave evidence of future atrocities that could be in store, that should be avoided. For example, at the International Conference of Syphilology, held in 1900, in which the Bahian physician Juliano Moreira participated, the setting was as follows:

> On the upper floor of each of the rooms were displayed the sick with their lesions, and at their side was a summary observation of the physician responsible for the exhibit. . . . At the entrance was a list of the diseases on display. This allowed one to meet the sick persons of most interest to the participant, . . . providing for analysis of interesting causes of degeneracy. (*Medical Gazette of Bahia,* 1901: 344)

Sick and impoverished people were on display, exhibited merely to illustrate theories and demonstrate aberrations.

The same societal trends that led to exhibitions also helped define a new professional type: the "political physician" or, in the words of Mariza Corrêa, "a blend of physician and social scientist" (1983: 2):

> No so, gentlemen! If it pleases one to contemplate the unaffected spectacle of charity embodied in the physician who eases the suffering of individuals, the example of one who is dedicated to the social role of political medicine should please no less. This specialization opens its benefits to all, disproportionately widening the circle of its professional activities, which on the scale of the perfectibility of

> sensitivities aids the society in its transformation from egoism to altruism. The modern physician worthy of his name and status should practice fully within the purview of political medicine. (*Medical Gazette of Bahia,* 1896: 398)

Armed with an awareness of the scope of their activities and evolutionist justifications, the political physicians set out to make new conquests in areas until then reserved for *bacharéis* and "men of law." According to an article in the *Medical Gazette,* the role of these physicians would be to bear the responsibility for a "scientific orientation that would ensure the execution of appropriate laws and give stability and purposefulness to the best plans for the progress and enrichment of the country" (*Medical Gazette of Bahia,* 1899: 138).

The mostly unambiguous dispute that consequently arose between medicine and law was referred to only obliquely in the medical journals. Professor Clementino Fraga said to the graduating doctors in 1914:

> Gentlemen, the immense learnedness in the strength and discipline of your knowledge will effect from afar great changes in humanity. Your profession will multiply toward a perfect, eurythmical social life, whether by extending your tutorial wings in protection and support of communities or through the refinement of races, the formation of nationalities, the world's destiny. Gentlemen, this is medicine! (*Medical Gazette of Bahia,* 1914: 241)

Gentlemen, this was, in broad brushstrokes, the image that medicine yearned for at the turn of the century. Society's tutor, healer of nationalities, our lady of the future and of all destinies.

• • •

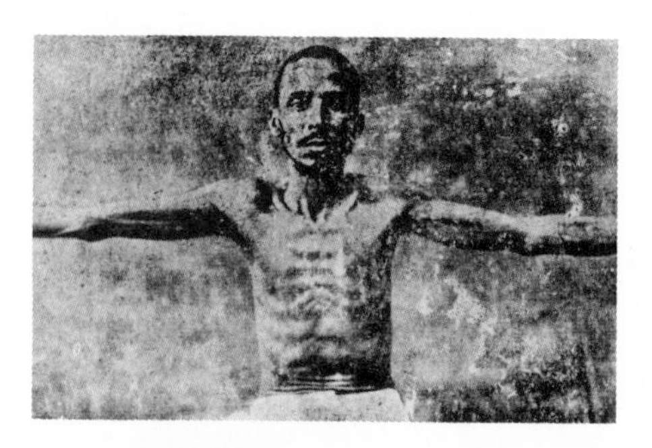

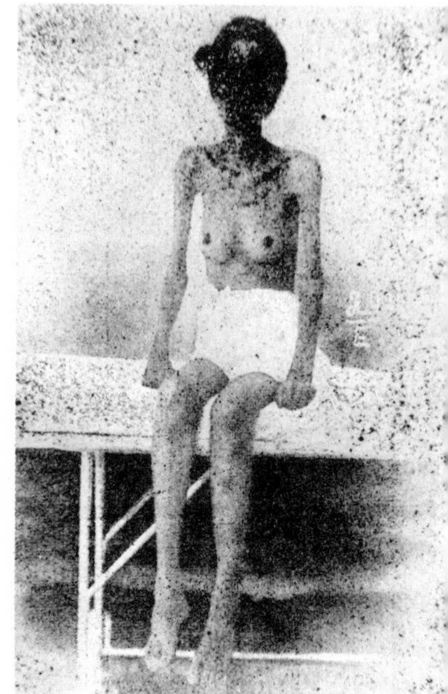

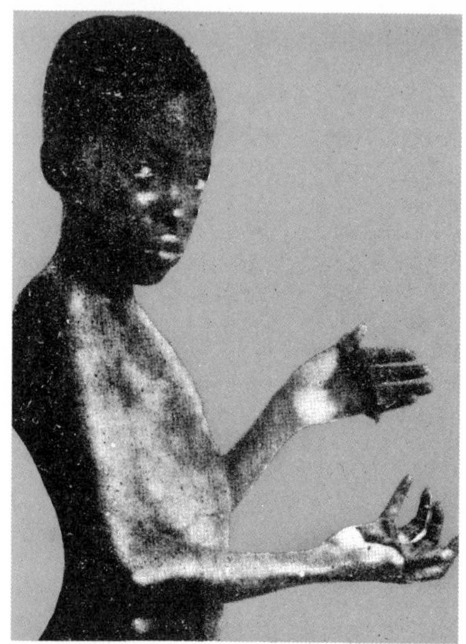

Illness as spectacle (MEDICAL GAZETTE OF BAHIA AND MEDICAL BRAZIL)

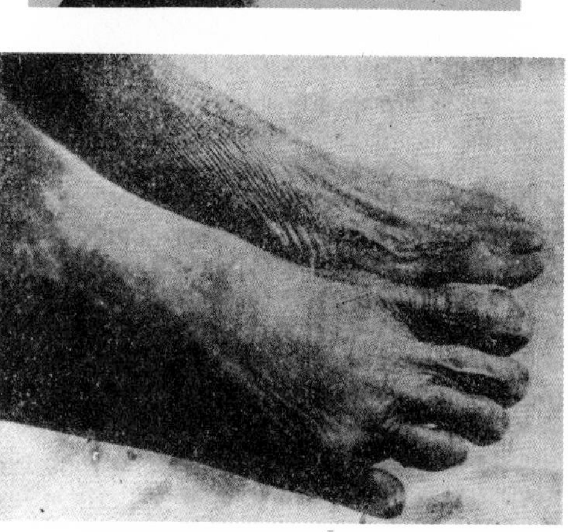

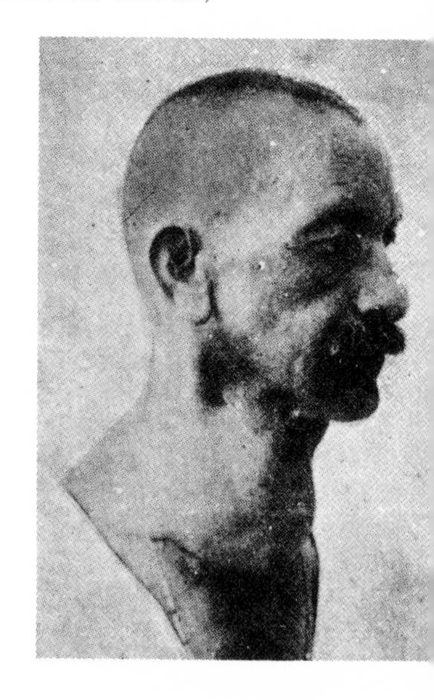

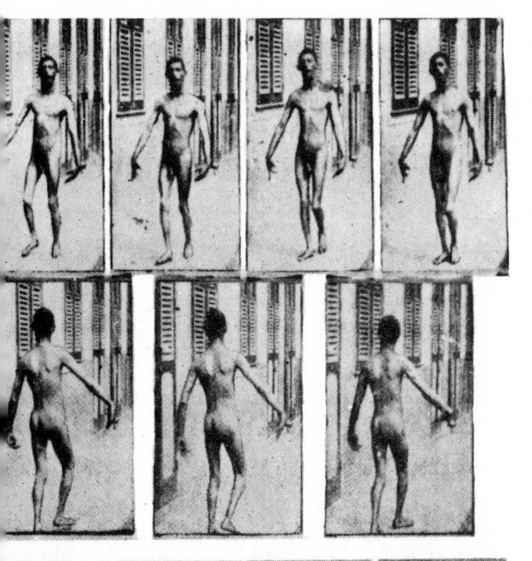

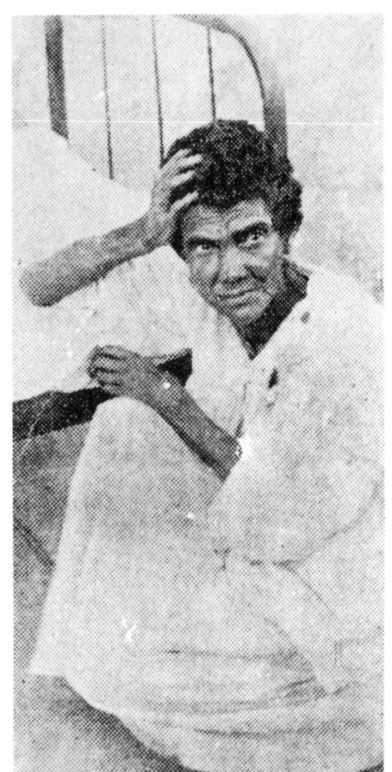

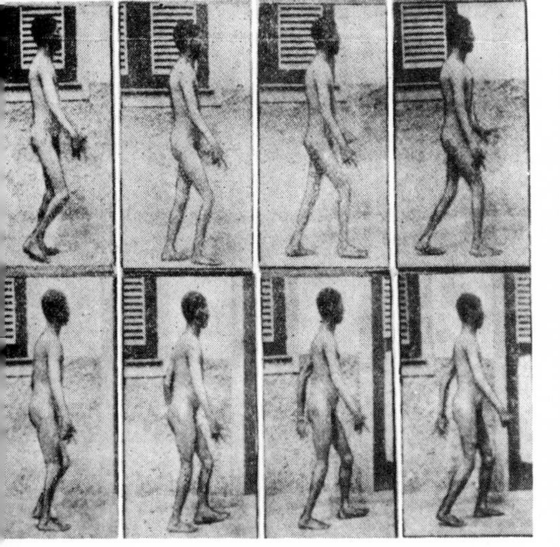

Illness exposition
(MEDICAL GAZETTE OF BAHIA)

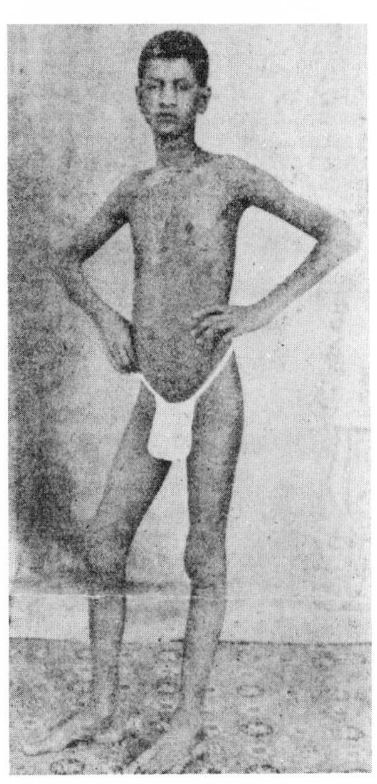

In the following pages we turn to a more detailed look at the content and specifics of the two periodicals under discussion, their thematic changes over sixty years of publication, and specifically the extreme importance that the racial theme assumed in these prominent journals.[13]

MEDICAL GAZETTE OF BAHIA
"Behold a Population That Is Mestizo and Sickly"

In 1865 Dr. Paterson, a well-known physician from the province of Bahia, decided to gather a group of his colleagues every other week in his house, including Professors Januário de Faria, Antônio José Alves, Otto Wucherer, Silva Lima, Pires Caldas, Pacífico Pereira, Maia Bittencourt, Silva Araújo, and Américo Márques. These doctors, who were without immediate academic designs, reported to one another on their clinical cases and shared their professional doubts and convictions in confidence (*Medical Gazette of Bahia,* 1927: 4). Professor Silva Lima said of the era: "there were no statutes, programs, discussion protocols or records. There were no guidelines that established consistency of time, methods or materials" (*Medical Gazette of Bahia,* 1866: 6).

It was precisely during these evening get-togethers that the idea of publishing a Bahian publication emerged. The result was the first Brazilian medical periodical, the *Medical Gazette of Bahia,* which began circulation in July 1866.[14] In its first issue, the founders of the *Medical Gazette* revealed certain apprehensions that were probably behind its creation:

> We can state without fear of contradiction that the medical press has yet to be born. As its establishment has failed several times, one must ask "Why?" Could it be too early for us to inaugurate scientific and literary work? Are we doomed to

> a perpetual inertia that limits us to admiring those who work in the field? . . . Should not all workers in science be obliged to add to the common good to the extent that they are able? (*Medical Gazette of Bahia,* 1866: 2)

The attempt to make an original contribution and to gain greater autonomy and prestige for the profession were some of the objectives that gave meaning to the new publication and urged it into existence. Some fifteen years later the journal was more confident in expressing its goals:

> We propose simply to do the following: to consolidate active constituents of the medical class, so that by uniting and girding itself it might compete for public credit and consideration, to join with the progress of science of more learned countries, to study the issues of particular interest to our country, and to struggle for the unity, dignity, and independence of our profession. (*Medical Gazette of Bahia,* 1881: 3)

It should be noted that nowhere in these opening pages was there mention that the periodical was directly linked to the Bahian school, nor did the editors and writers promise to feature in-house professors. Above all the journal sought to unify medical professionals, and this desire would remain consistent over the years. "Collaboration in the *Medical Gazette,*" they said, "is not the privilege of predetermined persons. All qualified colleagues from this and other provinces are welcome" (*Medical Gazette of Bahia,* 1866: 3).

From that point on, the *Medical Gazette* gained distinction as a monthly publication. The following components were standard: reviews of literature, new medications and medical vocabulary, necrology, previously unpublished essays, and an editorial. Many of the articles were unsigned; editorials and anonymous texts were credited to the publication itself.

If the formal division of the journal remained essentially unchanged from 1866 to 1930, one could not say the same of either the content or the quantity of the essays. The number of articles tended to increase over time, compounding the topics of debate and areas of specialization. Alongside what were then considered the hallowed courses of "internal medicine" (also known as clinical medicine), "surgical medicine," and "natural sciences" (botany, geology, zoology, and biology), new areas of research found space in the publication. Examples include studies on public hygiene, medical law, and neural medicine (or neurology), and essays on the history and internal issues and problems of medicine.

Table 18 shows a breakdown of areas of concentration and interest as reflected in the journal between 1870 and 1930. Certain significant features are apparent in the chart. First, there is the large number of essays on "public hygiene," which include studies not only on epidemiology, but also on sanitation, the promotion of health, demography, and meteorology. The area of "internal medicine" appears in second place and contains within it a broad range of interests, including ophthalmology, gynecology, pediatrics, dentistry, and general practice.

Although there were large numbers of articles on "medicine," for the most part they were little more than short explanatory and introductory notes, which reinforced the notion that physicians wrote little about medicine as such and a lot about their own professional practice. And unlike the other scientific journals that found great importance in publishing biographies, in the *Gazette* such profiles were not only uncommon; they were also only rarely signed.

One might say a good deal more about the data in Table 18, but more general analyses risk flattening the material and glossing over the nuances. An especially useful way of looking at these data is to chart different thematic strengths over time. In the 1870s, for example, the outbreak of the Paraguayan War

Table 18 Thematic Analysis of Articles in the Medical Gazette, *1870–1930*

THEME	NUMBER	PERCENT
Reviews of literature	190	11
Biographies and necrology	84	5
General medicine	217	12
Internal medicine	245	14
Practical medicine	75	4
Surgical medicine	113	7
Medical law	87	5
Public hygiene	617	36
Neural medicine/neurology	61	4
Natural sciences	25	1
Eugenics	28	1
TOTAL	1,742	100

correlates with an increase of essays on "surgical medicine." One can also correlate outbreaks of contagious epidemics and an increase in articles on "public hygiene."

Even without establishing such immediate links between the journal and the social and political context, it is possible to detect an overall trend in the journal. Until the end of the 1870s, essays on "internal medicine" and "surgical medicine" predominated. Into the 1880s and the middle of the 1890s articles on "mental hygiene" were clearly prevalent. Despite the frequency with which it appeared until 1930, from the first years of the century the theme of mental hygiene competed with studies on "medical law" and, in the 1920s, with works on "neural medicine" or "neurology." In addition, beginning in the 1880s the essays increasingly used the racial question as a pivotal argument deriving from an analysis of the social reality.

Public Hygiene, or When "Prevention Is a Cure"

In the first issue of the *Medical Gazette* there is a commentary on "the lovely dream of safeguarding the people's health." On this occasion the writers complained of politicians who "wake up only in the event of danger and only then appeal to their patron saint." The writers drew attention to the "presence of the scourge that ceased, but then returned with renewed strength," and concluded by commending "the nation's destiny to the specialists" (1866: 3).

This article, perhaps better called a pamphlet, directly points to the importance that the subject of public hygiene would assume in the journal. Choosing this subject matter was not coincidental. It was a response to a broader tendency in medicine to view the practice of hygiene as a revolutionary behavior within the community. Those specializing in hygiene adopted the motto: "prevention before the cure," or eradicate the illness before it appears.

It was at this time that the notion of sanitation became linked with the idea of hygiene. Public health officials would assume responsibility for implementing great plans of action within the nation's private and public spaces, while the hygienists would be responsible for research and day-to-day work in the community to fight epidemics and the other most bothersome diseases among the population. The difference between public health officials and hygienists, however, often existed only in theory; in practice, the two did similar work.

Hygiene assumed a fundamentally important role because of the innumerable epidemics that were ravaging Brazil. Since colonial times a number of illnesses had spread throughout the country, and Brazilians viewed these epidemics as a "scourge." Tuberculosis, yellow fever, smallpox, leprosy, plague, measles, typhoid, Chagas' disease, beriberi, malaria, whooping cough, cholera, and scarlet fever were some of the contagious diseases that alarmed medical specialists of the day.

The general response to the national death rate had long been neglect, but in the late nineteenth century Bahian physicians mounted campaigns to eradicate diseases they considered endemic. Dr. Pacífico Pereira, director of the *Medical Gazette,* wrote the following commentary in 1899:

> Hygiene is a nation's first priority. There is no civilized country in which the comprehension and practice of this truth is not ingrained. *Mens sana in corpore sano* [a sound body in a sound mind] is the motto of the individual's mental and physical education. In the same manner, the physical and moral health of a people makes up the energy, the happiness and the primary source of a nation's wealth. . . . Civilization demands sanitation. Patriotism and humanity decree it as an undeferrable need. (*Medical Gazette of Bahia,* 1899: 435–38)

Curing epidemics was not the only thing these physicians considered undeferrable. The nation also had to institute new sanitation measures to prevent further outbreaks. Alongside work done in epidemiology, which conveyed basic notions of diagnosis and treatment of disease, essays began to appear that proposed measures to prevent illness even before it appeared.

This was the beginning of the era of great sanitation projects. The projects addressed needs from homes to churches, from ports to schools. The public officials had a critical eye and missed very little. They prescribed dietary regimens and also made recommendations on matters pertaining to clothing and customs. They advocated discipline in the use of public sanitary facilities, and they pleaded for health education for the youngest of schoolchildren.[15]

Despite its ubiquitousness, the hygiene issue generated little research in Bahia. There were constant references in the journal to Carioca specialists, especially to Oswaldo Cruz and later to Carlos Chagas, and to the publication of articles and analyses written by their colleagues at other institutions. Essays written in

Bahia on the subject of hygiene were limited to commentaries on theories produced elsewhere, or pertinent regional censuses and statistics.[16]

It was only in the middle of the 1880s that Bahian medical research as such began to appear. Some epidemiological studies were published; among them were pieces that concerned the racial question. The authors of these studies did not cease working with their pet themes, but they did establish unforeseen links between disease and race, since they viewed race as a factor in different illnesses. Syphilis, for example, was defined in an article from 1894 as a "degenerative illness, worthy of the attention of those who study racial factors of physical and intellectual development." The piece went on to suggest that the disease was evidence of mestizo degeneracy and concluded that "syphilis had to be studied in the individual as well as in the race" (*Medical Gazette of Bahia,* 1894: 114).

The citations we have seen so far not only reflect thinking on a specific disease; they also reveal a general tendency. These authors used race as a fundamental theme for analyzing disease and public health, and in their considerations and diagnoses of the nation's future. The articles that addressed the topic were numerous: "As raças e seus cheiros" [Races and their odors] (1921); "Raça e civilização" [Race and civilization] (1880); "Raça e degeneração" [Race and degeneracy] (1887); "O cruzamento racial" [Racial blending] (1891); as well as the articles by Raimundo Nina Rodrigues that began to appear in the *Medical Gazette*.[17] The central message about race in all of these articles was always basically the same: races are fundamentally different, and their mixing is reprehensible. The *Medical Gazette*'s writers used social Darwinist models to condemn the blending of races and their consequent degeneracy, and in so doing they provided an original reading of Brazilian national reality by concluding that racial mixing was Brazil's biggest problem.

"O problema negro no Brasil" [The problem of the Negro in Brazil] (Rodrigues, 1933/1988: 1) came to be understood as a scientific issue. In the opening of Nina Rodrigues's book, *Africanos no Brasil* [Africans in Brazil], there is a famous quotation from Silvio Romero in which the legal polemicist from the Recife School of Law states:

> When we see men such as Bleek, who ensconce themselves for dozens and dozens of years in African centers only to study a language and collect a few myths . . . All of this we have at home, with Africa in our cuisine, America in our jungles, and Europe in our salons, we have exploited nothing in these regards! It is a disgrace. . . . The Negro is not only an economic machine; in spite of his ignorance, he is above all an object of science. (Romero, in Rodrigues, 1933/1988: 15)

This quotation also summarizes the views of Nina Rodrigues, who intended that his book be a great inventory of the Negro populations residing in Brazil. His objective in writing the book was to show the differences and hierarchies among the various African Negro groups.[18] He considered these groups as a whole, and in the name of "scientific impartiality" (1933/1988: 4), an impediment to white civilization and even "one of the components of our inferiority as a people" (1933/1988: 7).

The issue was not really whether or not Negroes were biologically and culturally inferior to other races. No one addressed that question. But some writers alleged that there was an inherent inferiority in the organic constitution of the race, a flaw that was irremediable by definition; others believed that the inferiority was transitory and remediable.

The greatest fear was not evoked by the "purebred Negro races such as the Sudanese" (Rodrigues, 1933/1988: 270) or, in other words, those blacks who were not the product of racial blending. Although considered inferior to white groups, the purebred Negro had his or her "potential" evaluated and projected according to evolutionists and determinist models of analysis. The uneasiness centered on the "inexistence of ethnic uniformity" (Rodrigues, 1894/1957) and in the widespread miscegenation prevalent in Brazil. In the words of Nina Rodrigues, one had to take multiple slants on the Negro problem: "one focusing on the past—African Negroes who colonized the country; another on the present—Negroes, Bahians, Creoles, and mestizos; and the last on the future—mestizos and white Creoles" (1933/1988: 10). An issue of the past, present, and future, racial blending concerned Bahian scholars because it was a relatively new concern and because of "the uncertainty of their diagnoses, . . . the difficulties in the scientific evaluation of these communities" (*Medical Gazette of Bahia,* 1901: 212).

The nation thought of Bahia more in racial terms than in economic or cultural terms. So epidemics were not seen merely as epidemics. They seemed to indicate the long road that separated the Brazilian people from "perfectibility." They even signified the "biological debility" thought to predominate in Brazil. Studies published in the *Medical Gazette* demonstrated the association that was made between sickness and racial blending not only via statistics and medical accounts, but also through images and photographs. Often to cruel effect, these images exposed the high incidence of contagious diseases that afflicted the Brazilian mestizo population.

The adherence to racial models of analysis became even more evident in Bahia as the area of medical law developed. This new area of study permitted the most direct use of various social Darwinist theories. Also, and for the first time, they gave the school a leading role on the national medical stage.

Medical Law: "Ignore the Crime, and Focus on the Criminal"

Essays on medical law were constantly seen from the first years of this century. Unlike articles on straight medicine or law (which focused on illness or crime), those on medical law focused on the criminal. The writers abandoned the rigid vocabulary of medicine and adopted a manner of discourse closer to that used by courtroom judges and police officers. Medical law was considered so important that most students in Bahia covered this area in their doctoral theses. From 1839 to 1880, twenty students chose themes involving medical law, but between 1880 and 1915 that number rose to one hundred. The topics under study varied and can be divided into four categories: problems relating to professional autonomy; alcoholism, drunkenness, epilepsy, and mental illness; practical matters of medical law; and the analysis of the criminal profile. The last of these categories was by far the most popular. Following the lead of the Italian school, medical law students steadfastly analyzed the correlation between "criminality and degeneracy." In their capacity as medical experts in the study of the criminal mind, these authors defended the creation of a new medical specialization.

Convinced that the work previously done in this area was arbitrary and unscientific, these specialists sought new theoretical models for analyzing crime and explaining delinquency. They turned first to phrenology and craniology. These disciplines had produced successful models in other Brazilian institutions. In the Bahian school, similar analyses would play a limited role. Specifically, they were used to identify races, to assess mental retardation, and to ponder the fragility of hybrids. "For a people with as heterogeneous a population as Brazil has, craniological identification of races acquires a paramount importance in medical law," wrote Professor Nina Rodrigues in the *Medical Gazette of Bahia* in 1902.

But if phrenology was an appropriate model for identifying races and analyzing their abilities to carry responsibilities, one cannot say the same of its application in the study of the criminal. Craniological studies measured "the evolutionary mental stage" of the delinquent, and with the theories from the "modern school of Italian criminology" one could understand the profile of the criminal, or the traits of his or her habits. The Italian school developed an original use for the data derived from phrenology, but the purpose of the Italian theories was not to examine racial conformation in the light of criminal traits; the use was to identify delinquents.

The Bahian specialists closely followed the teachings of the Italian criminologist Cesare Lombroso and focused primarily on the physical traits of the criminal, giving scant attention to the crimes committed. Professor S. Boccanera Neto's article demonstrates this:

> In general, criminality results from a physical abnormality that arrives suddenly, or proceeds inexorably through degeneration, a deterioration either partially or wholly due to heredity or hybridization. . . . All criminals, when they commit their deed, come from within and in a state of darkness, display customary Lombrosian indications, specific to the moment of the crime. (*Medical Gazette of Bahia,* 1927: 215–16)

Consistent with their adopted principles, the Bahian physicians claimed that they had developed their own methods of treating criminality, which they considered a state of illness different from others only in type: "The criminal is a person with an illness that is more or less curable on both moral and physical levels. Consequently, one must apply to them the great principles of the medical arts: one must confront the range of ills with a variety of remedies" (*Medical Gazette of Bahia,* 1927: 274).

As a professor of medicine and a radical defender of medical law, Nina Rodrigues stood at the forefront of this movement. Going beyond a mere defense of medical law, his work helped give the evolving medical profession a sense of direction. This group of doctors was seeking their own identity, as well as a change in the social image of physicians, because the medical profession until that time had been generally disparaged.

In the 1920s contributors to the Bahian journal occupied a privileged pulpit for disseminating their ideas, and in their pursuit of the topic of medical law, they elevated its prominence in Bahia to an extraordinary level. The articles that examined this specialization were the most contentious, and the most combative editorials defended the issue's freshness and importance: "At this moment in the evolution of our science, in this confident phase of our journey . . . we find the surest foundations to build a new structure that will come to represent *our science, a national science,* freed from foreign tutelage" (*Medical Gazette of Bahia,* 1884).[19]

Through studying medical law with a focus on cases of racial degeneracy, the medical profession was able to demonstrate that conditions in Brazil were unique and required a specifically "Brazilian science." The instances of drunkenness, mental illness, epilepsy, violence, or amorality among people of mixed race bolstered belief in social Darwinist models that condemned racial blending, warning of the inherent "flaws in a mixed heredity." A sinister side to the success of the Bahian specialists was that their studies on "racial debilitation" not only promoted the elevation of this brand of racial typing to a national research specialization but also gained this professional group some notoriety.

As the authors of this new specialization defended their theories they opened up new and formerly unknown areas of endeavor, as well as other areas of controversy. Specifically, another form of dispute emerged between the legal and medical professions. Who was ultimately responsible for the resolution of crimes? Would it be the courtroom judges, who would skillfully apply the law, or would it be the medical experts, who with their science would diagnose the "criminally ill"?

Physicians distrusted the principles of natural rights that informed the drafting of the Brazilian Penal Code, and doctors' critiques of Brazil's legal system proliferated. An editorial in an 1897 issue of the *Medical Gazette* declared:

> The Penal Code is in error; it looks at the crime and not at the criminal. There is no doubt that the nature of the crime

> is of secondary importance. Of supreme interest should be a mental evaluation and classification by means of a physical exam and a medical exam. Science will close the prisons and will substitute physiological correction under the tutelage of physicians who will care for the physical and mental treatment of society's misfits. (*Medical Gazette of Bahia*: 218–19)

Echoing Nina Rodrigues's theses, which typically pointed to the error of punishing races of different levels of evolution by a single standard,[20] the writers as a group upended the notion of human equality recognized under Brazilian law.

> Equality of rights is unacceptable, at least without there simultaneously being equality in evolution. . . . Mankind transcends the individual. Under certain conditions, two distinct men can be considered equals; but they can never be considered such on the basis of their physiology. To make of the individual the foundation and the purpose of society, and to confer upon him a freedom that knows no limits, in the true democratic spirit, is a demagogic excess and an aberration of the principle of the public interest. The French Revolution inscribed on its flag a telling motto that proclaimed the ideas of "liberty, equality, and fraternity," ideas from Voltaire, Rousseau, and Diderot that today are irreconcilable and fundamentally abhorrent. (*Medical Gazette of Bahia,* 1906: 256–57)

By this thinking, free will was becoming "a spiritual assumption" (Corrêa, 1983: 64) made on behalf of a dishonest issue, as if equality were the sole creation of "men of law" and had no scientific basis.

This "illusion of liberty," so-called by Mariza Corrêa, was a common perception in the Bahian school, and it became further entrenched during the 1920s in the journal's "studies on insanity" and "mental medicine." The Bahia journal followed closely in the steps of Nina Rodrigues, whose attention shifted from the physiological to the psychological characteristics of human behavior (Corrêa, 1983: 105). At this point the collective effort of his followers became the defense of "judicial insane asylums."

The "Dangerously Insane" and the Penal Code as Anachronism

Following the same reasoning, studies on insanity returned to the critique of human equality, with the scholars basing their analyses on "the most unbalanced psychological cases." The themes of racial dissimilarity and the degenerative influence of miscegenation remained at the heart of these studies. In addition, the Bahian scholars continued to attack the country's legal code. What was different, however, was the degree to which they refocused their interest on cases of insanity.

> We will not tire of our figurative hammering on the deficiencies and anachronisms embodied by our Penal Code articles on the criminally insane. Note that we're not talking about "crazy" people but about the "insane." . . . The Penal Code is out of date and has not followed the evolution of Criminal Law. . . . At the heart of the question, the sole cause of the illness, the primary catalyst, is the notion of free will, the doctrine that guided our law made obsolete by science. Until this myth is swept clean of our code, our present disorder will continue. (*Medical Gazette of Bahia,* 1913: 499–500)

Using the same arguments developed by Nina Rodrigues in *A assistência medico-legal aos alienados nos estados brasileiros* [Medical-legal aid to the insane in Brazilian states] (1906), in an editorial the *Medical Gazette* supported the struggle for the protection of the insane and for doctors retaining autonomy in diagnosing insanity. By declaring the philosophy of free will "obsolete" and a "myth," the editorial opted for "modernity." The application of science would lend credibility to this choice; whereas it would deny equality and ridicule liberal discourse.

However, advocating a medical law that would be adapted to the development of the races or promoting the idea of establishing judicial insane asylums did not cover up a certain fear that was present in those active in the debate at the periodical. Indeed, as time passed ideas changed.

The journal entered the 1920s disagreeably pessimistic, expressing their conviction that any future project conducted on a national scale would be utterly impossible. Using the polygenist models of social Darwinism, the journal held out little hope for the future of a nation composed of "negligibly developed races such as the Negro and the Indian," not to mention the mestizo, who made up the majority of the population.

There would have been no apparent solution to this situation had it not been for the unexpected reception of European racial theories at the end of the 1920s. At that time scholars began to classify mestizos as "bad" or "good" (and not always degenerate), and the "degeneracy resulting from hybridization" ceased to be thought of as an irreversible phenomenon. Races, on the other hand, were understood as changeable, subject to a continual process of *betterment*. The discourse of *eugenics* gained new adherents, even within the radical ranks of the Bahia School of Medicine.

Eugenics, or "When One Must Care for the Races"

Articles in support of eugenics projects appeared in the Bahia journal for the first time in 1923. In a commemorative edition of the same year, Professor Mário Pontes de Miranda stressed the need for Brazil to struggle "for the somatic regeneration of our Race, the achievement of which our political survival among nations utterly depends" (*Medical Gazette of Bahia,* 1923: 31).

Presenting his program as the only way to combat the pessimism and passivity that had taken root, this scholar proposed an immediate attack on the "somatic misery" that dominated the country (*Medical Gazette of Bahia,* 1923: 32).

The novelty of this article was not in its reaffirmation of Brazil's "pitiable racial situation," however, but in its enthusiasm for the prospect of the nation's "regeneration": "It is a fact that Brazil is ailing, but not entirely. A portion, a large portion, of our people suffers the affliction of sloth, and is overcome by ignorance of the fundamentals of hygiene" (*Medical Gazette of Bahia,* 1923: 36). The central ideal of this essay was the construction of a "eugenic ideal"—the "resurrection of the race" (*Medical Gazette of Bahia,* 1923: 37).

Following this article, many other bizarre eugenicist proposals appeared. An article from 1923 defended the introduction of physical education as a means of achieving human perfection: "*Mens sana in corpore sano*" (*Medical Gazette of Bahia,* 1923: 39). In the same year another text stressed the importance of "matrimonial prophylaxis, an indispensable basis for the public's general health" (*Medical Gazette of Bahia,* 1923: 88). This article did not address itself to encouraging or discouraging a specific kind of marriage; it advised against marriage for those people who harbored vices or transmissible diseases such as tuberculosis, epilepsy, insanity, and alcoholism.

Despite the differences in approach, a common vision seemed to be emerging, a vision of eugenics as a method for "caring for the race" and reversing the process that was leading to the race's complete devolution. The stance on racial mixing, here referred to as "hybridization," was as follows:

> Up to a certain point, one should face hybridization psychologically as a degenerative factor. Among us, it composes elements from various origins. It bears diverse ethnic characteristics and special conditions that under ecological influences ought to bring an inevitable disturbance in the

> organization of unavoidable equilibrium. The extreme hybridization found here . . . retards or encumbers the unification of the types, first by upsetting essential traits, and then by reviving among the people atavistic characteristics of individuals deep in the darkness of the ages. (*Medical Gazette of Bahia,* 1923: 256)

Confronting racial mixing was still uncomfortable, but this new point of view did not lead to paralysis. On the contrary, it attracted a lot of attention because it inspired hope for a "refinement of national races."

The eugenics-inspired solutions that the Bahian physicians boasted in the middle of the 1920s were, however, as radical as their premises were pessimistic. If there was one sector of the population that could be "cured and restored," there was another that was hopelessly ill, and in its name they proposed the most extreme measures:

> For the betterment of the race it could be advantageous to cross clearly mestizo and degenerate persons with normal outsiders when this method gives hope for the regeneration of offspring; but for those profoundly degenerate it would be better to allow them to reproduce among themselves and extinguish their wretched generation through sterility and juvenile mortality as a result of progressive degeneracy. Deriving great advantage from these natural relations, families that possess good qualities would perpetuate themselves free from the germs of the infirmities that would infect them from a fatal mixing with the bastardized. The species would profit. (*Medical Gazette of Bahia,* 1925: 161)

Thinly disguising a profound repugnance for the mixed-blood portion of the population, this article at least defends separating the redeemable mestizos from the unequivocally ill, "the alcoholics, the madmen, the epileptics, and the diseased" (*Medical*

Gazette of Bahia, 1927: 275), for whom the only solution is a Darwinianly predictable disappearance. In the meantime, in articles like this one, racial theories were adopted in a selective and partial manner. Scientists used racial theories to explain natural selection and the elimination of the weak, but they ignored these same ideas when they were looking into the "perfectibility" of the "good mestizos" or the homogenization of the races, subjects incompatible with polygenist models.

Once again, one notes that Brazilian scholars did not simply apply a carbon copy of the foreign models that were available. They applied the ideas selectively in original ways. The practice of eugenics, instead of being used to condemn the country outright for its racial mixing, was used to suggest solutions for at least a portion of the population. Eugenicist projects tended to be authoritarian in nature, just as history would show the era to be, and they gave Bahian physicians license to diagnose the irreversible collapse of the nation with a clean conscience.

A New Era: "The Times Are Bad Only for Those Who Know Not How to Hope"

The arrival of the 1930s brought a change of position. The Bahian medical journal announced the emergence of a "new spirit" (*Medical Gazette of Bahia,* 1928, 1930, and 1931), while its writers berated the era's "reigning paralysis and pessimism" (*Medical Gazette of Bahia,* 1929: 122). Suddenly it was as if one had to believe in the country, and doubts and uncertainties had to be transformed into certainties.

This was also a time when the journal published articles in favor of the creation of a university in Bahia, the thinking being that bringing in a university was "the only way to eliminate minor centers and to promote research with modern methods and greater depth" (*Medical Gazette of Bahia,* 1929: 211).

During this period the journal featured new theories and discoveries, some of which were not so new, dating from many years before. Such was the case with Freud's tenets, which only began to appear in the *Medical Gazette* in 1924 in the "psychiatry and neurology" section.

The transformation was not, however, of such weight that it completely changed the era's themes and jargon. The old theories remained in evidence, although there had been profound changes within their core paradigms. A good example is revealed in the article "A saúde e a raça" [Health and race], published in December 1928. Although this piece included a clear defense of eugenics, its theoretical underpinnings were no longer racial but cultural:

> The health of the race is the health of the Country. Today we place a value on everything, and health is a function of the degree to which a culture values its citizens and is willing to ensure the transmission of that culture's valued qualities to its descendants, in accordance with eugenicist laws. . . . The selection will be made through intelligence and not through physical force. . . . Man will distinguish himself from other animals only if his culture determines his value, and it is because of his culture that nature will select him. We do not believe that his intelligence has advanced. The anthropoid of the human species is a fantasy. *There are no indications to this point that humanity will surpass itself*. . . . White skin is just a skin without pigment. There is no transmission of intellectual characteristics. (*Medical Gazette of Bahia,* 1928: 203–204)

The *Medical Gazette* revealed a certain irony with regard to the models that it had accepted only a short time before. The publication had chosen to transform the present into the past and announced its allegiance to cultural relativism.

The physicians did not, however, surrender the era's vocabulary, which had steeped for so long in the evolutionist mode. It was as if it was necessary to remember just how close the demons were and how hard it was to exorcise them.

The new moment seemed to mark the end of the medical missionary, staunchly committed to "healing the nation." Physicians had eliminated the great epidemics that ravaged the population, and they had instituted medical law and judicial insane asylums during the Estado Novo [New State].* It was time to return to the clinics and to withdraw from projects of greater social involvement.

MEDICAL BRAZIL
"Workers in the Art of Healing"†

Nearly twenty years after the *Medical Gazette of Bahia* began circulation, *Medical Brazil,* a weekly journal associated with the Rio de Janeiro School of Medicine, first appeared in 1887.

Medical Brazil was published every Saturday, and it became known for its extraordinary regularity and stability. Subscriptions and pharmaceutical advertising guaranteed its financial stability; the fact that the journal published continuously for fifty years without ever missing an issue spoke to its production stability; and twenty-five years with the same staff was evidence of its editorial stability.[21]

Commentators were unanimous in attributing the creation and the operation of the journal to Dr. Azevedo Sodré. As owner-director of the journal, Sodré wrote scientific articles, commented on current events, rendered critical judgments, translated essays, and selected news of interest to medical professionals. Until 1895 he did everything. In that year Dr. Bulhões de Carvalho, a professor

* The Estado Novo refers to the administration set up by the authoritarian President Getúlio Vargas in 1937. During this administration Vargas's power was absolute, and he used it to suppress dissent by whatever means necessary. At the same time, legislation was enacted that protected the working class, thus establishing Vargas's place in history as a flawed but beloved part of Brazilian political history.

† The quotation in the subtitle of this section is from *Medical Brazil,* 1903.

in the Department of Surgery, became his associate, and for the next twenty-five years he divided the editorial work with his colleague.[22]

The journal remained closely connected to and dependent on its owner-director. As a professor in the Department of Clinical Medicine and as a medical educator, Sodré gave the journal an often didactic makeup while he sought to present a balanced array of essays. On the other hand, as director of the School of Medicine, Sodré learned not only how to secure finances for the publication, but also how to include the most distinguished names of national medicine in the pages of his journal. Scientists such as Afrânio Peixoto, Nina Rodrigues, Juliano Moreira, Vital Brazil, Emilio Goeldi, Oswaldo Cruz, Oscar Freire, and Franco da Rocha are only a small sampling of the authors who contributed tirelessly to this journal.

Medical Brazil was established at a later date, enjoyed a better location, and had sounder financial resources than the *Medical Gazette of Bahia*. Therefore, from the time of its inception it had the resources to seek an identity separate from its competitor's. Whether because of its volume or its stability, the Carioca journal was able to represent more fully the aspirations and obstacles of Brazilian medicine. *Medical Brazil* appeared on January 15, 1887, with a goal of setting new standards for the profession.

In its first issue, the journal disclosed its philosophical view and diagnosed the same ills that had been treated years before in the *Medical Gazette*. An article in the Carioca publication declared: "But, in the scientific world one measures one's intellectual caliber by the sum total of works one contributes toward the progress of science. And, in this regard, it gives pain to say it, the portion that Brazil has contributed toward the construction of the medical science edifice has been insignificant" (*Medical Brazil,* 1887: 2).

The writer of this piece stated that there were two causes for Brazil's puny contribution: "Let us speak frankly and state that the first cause is a custom peculiar to new nations, and which is still rooted in us, of accepting as dogma everything foreign and discounting everything domestic. The second is the absence of channels for publicity. This makes it difficult to publish scientific works" (*Medical Brazil,* 1887: 2). Ignoring the work of the Bahian journal, *Medical Brazil* stressed how it would be the key to the creation of "an original science."

"Scientific originality" was a recurring theme in both of Brazil's medical schools and was becoming something of an obsession. It became essential to avoid "foreign dogma" and to establish the foundations upon which to build Brazil's own medical institutions, responding to the country's unique needs. In Sodré's words, it was a matter of "a medicine or, rather, a healing art that could not shrink from the overwhelming and transforming influence of the environment and of heritage. Each country has its own pathology." The journal's director, therefore, was pointing out the urgency of building a Brazilian medicine since "everything or nearly everything is yet to be known" (*Medical Brazil,* 1887: 1–2).

The stated principles of *Medical Brazil* were to document and to comment on clinical data as well as on the experiences and research of Brazilian physicians. The journal sought to publicize the most recent experiments being performed in Rio de Janeiro, especially in the promising area of tropical diseases.

By the standards of the time, *Medical Brazil* was unusually prominent from the start. Featuring a series of articles, subdivided into areas of interest, and including numerous contributors and advertisements, *Medical Brazil* was a professional journal, well organized and well produced. Modern and aggressive in its methods, even in its first issues the publication opened with an offer to give all new subscribers "an elegantly bound volume on disorders of the respiratory system."

The advertising in its pages made use of what were then modern techniques, including photographs and drawings of the products for sale. This kind of advertising had rarely been used until then, especially in scientific publications. The Carioca journal

Table 19 Thematic Analysis of Articles in Medical Brazil, *1887–1930*

THEME	NUMBER	PERCENT
Internal medicine	3,349	25
Surgical medicine	1,025	8
Public medicine	5,178	39
Medical law and neurology	617	5
Medicine (internal notes)	1,332	10
Practical medicine	986	6
Obituaries and biographies	379	3
Medical press	381	3
Ophthalmology	128	1
TOTAL	13,375	100

drew on the vigor of its youth as well as on the mature expertise of medical periodicals.

The journal's profile with an overview of its thematic content appears in Table 19. As is clear, the sheer number of essays stands out, evidence of the journal's stability and its continued growth over time. Until 1910 the number of pages it published annually amounted to 400. After that date, the number rose to an average of 550, reaching 800 in 1920 and 1,400 in 1928. These continual changes in the periodical's dimensions were part of an editorial plan that came to value the number of pages over the content of the publication.

A Surgical-Clinical Journal: 1887–1900

Such were the primary characteristics of *Medical Brazil* in its first ten years of life. Above all it was a clinical journal, and it sought specific ways to assist colleagues in the profession.

The percentage of articles on "internal and surgical medicine" was high in the first years, when the publication was establishing itself as an "organ of the medical class" without any particular concern for social status. Texts on gynecology, pediatrics, clinical medicine, orthopedics, surgical case studies, and medical pharmacopoeias made up the bulk of this journal, which seemed to target a select group within the profession.

At that time the dominant view was that medicine should be oriented toward "causes" and concerned with clinical debate and with the daily practice of medicine. The authors of articles in *Medical Brazil* commented on the work of their colleagues, and they disseminated new procedures and therapies. Clinical hospital cases frequently passed from the hospital into the journal and even shifted register from the scientific to the poetic:

> *Oh laryngitis!* Lachesis pathologica!
> *Why do you quash such a lifelong pleasure,*
> *Why do you crush a delight so chaste and pure?*
> *And our medicine, our mother therapeutic,*
> *Is unable to remedy such a disorder,*
> *Not even with antimonial tartar.* (Medical Brazil, *1889)*

On the other hand, if commonplace cases accounted for most of the material, there was no shortage of "freak" cases. References to the physical abnormalities of patients and cases of deformity-producing diseases, with an ample sampling of Negro and mestizo patients, were more frequent in this journal than in the *Medical Gazette*. It was as if alongside the better-known and more curable conditions it was necessary to lay open uncertainty as well, in order to whet the medical appetite. By emphasizing the most extreme and formidable cases, the "abnormal" became a great spectacle.

Texts on general medical practice were frequent during this period. From its inception, *Medical Brazil* was committed to the delivery of information to the profession as well as to reflection on professional dilemmas and problems. A particularly delicate issue was the problem of "charlatanism," or widespread unauthorized medical practice throughout Brazil. As early as 1902, Dr. José Ribeiro Couto addressed this theme: "charlatanism is invading the profession and is reducing our intellectual physicians to a true scientific proletariat" (*Medical Brazil:* 132). Joining the struggle begun by Bahian physicians, *Medical Brazil* roundly condemned other modes of practice. "Quacks and charlatans are spontaneously appearing in our midst and should be fought without mercy. It is imperative that we fight them vigorously. I rest my case" (*Medical Brazil,* 1897: 333). Once the medicine men, unlicensed practitioners, and "herbalists" were identified as a group, they became the archenemies, since by pointing out the "other, the medicine man," the "real" doctors could better recognize "ourselves, the physicians."

Although they were widely dispersed, unoriginal, and represented only 5 percent of the journal's articles, studies in the areas of "medical law" and "insanity" also closely followed the models that appeared in the *Medical Gazette.*

Nina Rodrigues's thoughts were reproduced uncritically and without comment:

> A spiritualistic notion holds that all human races have the same kind of soul. By extension, all races have the same intellectual capacity, varied only by one's cultural education; and all members of inferior races are capable of attaining the lofty intellectual cultural levels of superior races. This is a condemnable assumption in light of modern scientific knowledge. (*Medical Brazil,* 1894: 421)

The tenets of modern criminology, which established a correlation between "delinquency and debility" and between the criminal and certain taints associated with him, were countenanced without discussion in the Carioca publication (*Medical Brazil,*

1898: 192). At that time medical law seemed to be a dominant and unchallenged Bahian specialization.[23]

One might say the same about the journal's studies on mental illness. Updating the evolutionist criteria and models employed by lecturers at the Bahia School of Medicine, the Carioca physicians adopted the conclusions of their colleagues: "An insane individual is not simply a perennial threat to the public tranquillity. He is a danger to existence itself. He is a subnormal being both to himself and among us. A man so perverted should remain under a physician's care" (*Medical Brazil,* 1898: 374). Defending medical autonomy in the treatment of these patients, the Carioca journal sustained the discussion simultaneously developed in Bahia. Faithful to polygenist assumptions, the journal traced parallels between cases of madness and their incidence among "inferior races":

> Of course a white imbecile will be inferior to an intelligent Negro. One does not argue, however, with exceptions. When we refer to a race, we do not individualize types of it. We understand it in terms of its most unambiguous definition. Proceeding in this way, we see that the Negro caste is retarded; the white is progressing and evolving. . . . Dementia appears most frequently among Negroes. One can say that they become demented more frequently, because of their constitution, than do whites. (*Medical Brazil,* 1904: 178)

Despite its acceptance of social Darwinist models, *Medical Brazil* did not seem to disseminate determinist theories as widely as did the *Medical Gazette*. Introduced only in articles on medical law and mental law, these theories did not inspire a great deal of interest at the moment. During the period under study most of the journal's attention focused on clinical medicine and on the propagation of the profession itself.

Public Hygiene: In Furtherance of a "Tropical Medicine," 1900 to 1920

If until the end of the nineteenth century *Medical Brazil* had not found its own niche and an original calling, from that time forward the journal's standing would change. The strength *Medical Brazil* gained in the area of "public hygiene" would alter the journal's profile and would confer on it a vital role in the fight against epidemics, particularly in campaigns for sanitation and in support of "tropical medicine."

The notions of public hygiene, sanitation, and prophylaxis against contagious diseases commingled in the journal in such a way that it is difficult to separate them in a logical manner. In the face of the threatening phenomenon of impending epidemics, the role of "medicine" was, on the one hand, to fight them, and on the other hand, to avoid them. To discover an antidote to an illness that was considered incurable was a task reserved for the new "medical researchers," who accepted the challenge of their century. To halt the spread of the disease and the incidence of new outbreaks was, on the other hand, the function of hygienists and sanitation workers. They worked in the community to educate and to prevent disease. It became the difficult task of the researchers, the hygienists, and the sanitation workers to diagnose and to treat Brazil, that poor, sick country.

Until the first half of the nineteenth century, Brazil enjoyed the reputation of being a healthful country reasonably immune from contagious diseases (Chalhoub, 1993: 1). But thereafter this image suffered a complete reversal. In 1895, for example, in one of the first tables of hygienic demography published by *Medical Brazil,* the incidence of contagious illnesses was terrifying. Holding first place on the mortality index was tuberculosis, the white plague, which was responsible for 15 percent of deaths in Rio de Janeiro. Following, in the order of their frequency of occurrence, were yellow fever, smallpox, malaria, cholera, beriberi, typhoid fever, measles, whooping cough, bubonic plague, leprosy, and scarlet fever; altogether these diseases accounted for 42 percent of the city's deaths (*Medical Brazil,* 1896: 62). These serious outbreaks were not limited to the year 1895. There was no denying the sad fact: the country was in the grip of contagious diseases. (See Table 20.)

Tuberculosis, champion in the death index, frightened the medical analysts with its devastating effects. From 1868 to 1914 the disease caused 111,666 deaths, transforming Rio de Janeiro into the world's leader in tuberculosis cases. In 1916 Rio de Janeiro was still in first place in terms of the number of tuberculosis cases, with 363 infected patients for every 1,000 inhabitants. Following Rio were Paris, 332; Santiago, 326; and Budapest, 316 (*Medical Brazil,* 1916: 65). Articles on the disease stirred up a great deal of fear and apprehension: "Each person living in this city, indeed each person of this region, is suffering, has suffered, or will suffer tuberculosis" (*Medical Brazil,* 1916: 65).

Table 20 Tuberculosis Mortality Index in Relation to Other Transmissible Diseases, Rio de Janeiro (Urban Zone), 1868–1914

ILLNESS	NUMBER OF DEATHS
Tuberculosis	111,666
Yellow fever	46,086
Malaria	41,290
Smallpox	37,415
Typhoid fever	6,559
Influenza	6,522
Beriberi	3,950
Disentery	3,499
Measles	2,979
Diphtheria	1,972
Whooping cough	1,872
Bubonic plague	1,803
Leprosy	472
Scarlet fever	232

Laboratory

Porch added to a private dwelling, as part of the fresh-air cure of tuberculosis

Hospital room

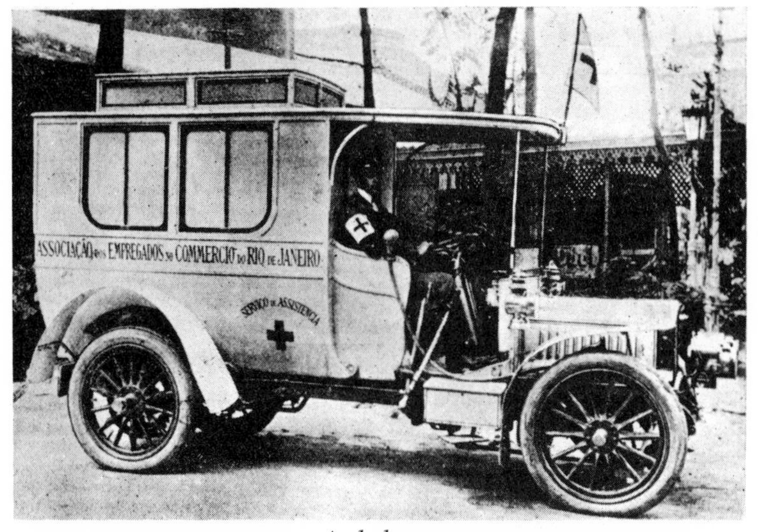

Ambulance

Tuberculosis patients taking fresh air on the rooftop of a clinic in Vanderbilt, New York

Second-story verandah built on a private dwelling

A bed placed partially on a balcony so the patient can receive the benefit of fresh air

The trajectory of other illnesses was no less disconcerting. The first outbreak of smallpox occurred in 1563, and in the 1908 statistics the indices revealed that the mortality rate was trending upward; in that year alone this disease was responsible for 9,046 deaths. A similar trend was apparent for bubonic plague, measles, scarlet fever, and diphtheria, illnesses that accounted for many deaths in the first decade of the twentieth century. (There was a terrible epidemic of bubonic plague in 1899.) Although Brazil had remained nearly free from yellow fever, this disease appeared at the end of 1860, and in 1873 and 1876 the two most deadly outbreaks occurred, claiming 3,659 and 3,476 lives, respectively (Chalhoub, 1993: 19–20).

Yet the prime motivating factor for Brazilian physicians lay not in the gravity of the situation, but in the new possibilities for treatment that were emerging. Encouraged by recent advances in world medicine, as doctors in other countries had become more and more effective in fighting life-threatening illnesses, Carioca physicians took on "tropical diseases" as their primary challenge and objects of study.

The example of yellow fever is a case in point. In 1903 yellow fever was responsible for a large percentage of all deaths in Brazil. By 1906 the disease had been subdued, and in 1908 only 8 deaths were attributed to yellow fever. This kind of turnaround was not an isolated case. The success enjoyed in the fight against yellow fever served to inspire the medical profession and testified to medicine's public service.

With this success as a backdrop, scientific hygienist Oswaldo Cruz (who eliminated yellow fever in Brazil) emerged as a hero,[24] and the Manguinhos Institute for Tropical Diseases became a model of competence for every research facility. After Oswaldo Cruz and some of his followers, such as Carlos Chagas, the "medical researchers" became an influential branch of Brazilian medicine and achieved a standing within the nation that surpassed the barriers of their specialization.[25]

Public Health Programs

With the strengthening of the practice of hygiene came new initiatives. It was not enough to subdue outbreaks of disease. It was necessary to avoid their spread and prevent a weakened and unprepared populace from falling victim to opportunistic infections. Therefore, alongside research on bacteriology and studies on the pathology of tropical diseases, sanitation projects began to gather momentum. As these efforts became disengaged from the strict purview of medicine, public health workers proposed measures involving direct social intervention.

In the first decades of the century *Medical Brazil* included a flood of articles on public hygiene and sanitation. The targets of the public health initiatives were innumerable, including churches, schools, ports, cemeteries, public spaces, and dwellings. Certain types of customary personal behaviors had to be encouraged over others in the interests of promoting hygiene and avoiding "degeneration." The articles condemned types of "sexual perversion" and prescribed appropriate sexual practices. The measures taken with regard to prostitution are revealing: "Since it is impossible to eliminate prostitution, it is necessary to regulate and not abandon the diseased. Not to be able to apply a primary treatment would risk destruction of the organism" (*Medical Brazil,* 1917: 180).

Physicians came to expect absolute passivity from the masses, which they viewed as an immense collection of hospital patients. Physicians planned urban reform, separated the population into the sound and the unsound, and broadly administered medicines. This was the era of the "great inoculations," which were given in the name of the nation's welfare. But there was great resistance to the administration of vaccines:

> Our position is lamentable as long as we cannot resolve the enormous problem of obligatory vaccination. It is an ever

greater impediment to our progress in public health. We do not subscribe to the modern trends that appeal to individual liberty as a reason to deny its execution. The most avid defenders of individual rights must yield to the interests of the community at large. (*Medical Brazil,* 1910: 107)

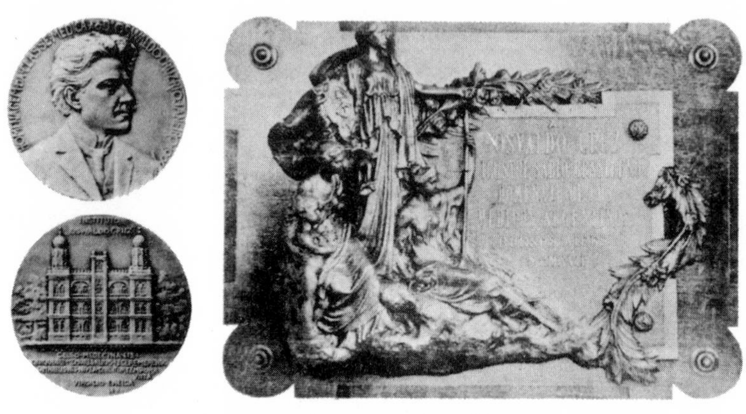

Examples of tributes to Oswaldo Cruz in recognition of his vaccination campaign against yellow fever

In contrast to its exemplary work in eradicating yellow fever, with its inoculation programs Carioca medicine launched an interventionist campaign that denied individual rights in the name of scientific progress, while the discourse surrounding this work was ever more authoritarian. It is not a matter here of questioning the efficacy of the vaccinations or even the reality of epidemics. The issue is the medical profession's construction of a radical discourse that established its basis of legitimacy through medical practice. At that time there were no provisions for public education or for explanations of their programs. Campaigns were abruptly imposed as emergency measures. They were analogous to the treatment of a long-term comatose patient who had neither consciousness nor opinion.

The insurrection known as the "Revolta da Vacina" [Vaccination Revolt] was a response to this logic and context. The fuse that lit the movement was the November 9, 1904, publication of a decree mandating smallpox vaccinations, passed by the president of the republic himself, Rodrigues Alves. Oswaldo Cruz, director of public health and a prime supporter of the campaign, could not conceal the authoritarian nature of his agenda or his belief in his autonomy to issue orders to the Brazilian people. In March 1904 he declared to the *Jornal do Comércio* [Journal of Commerce]: "I need resources and greater independence of action. The government will give me what I need and allow me freedom in my choice of assistants, without any political interference." Despite the propriety of its methods and objectives, the obligatory vaccination program provoked a powerful negative reaction in the streets of Rio de Janeiro. Government police forces promptly subdued the opposition to what the people called the "sanitation dictatorship." Apart from the many vicissitudes and the political maneuvering to which the revolt found itself subject,[26] of most interest for the purposes of this study was the common Brazilian's reaction to the emergence of intrusive and authoritarian medical professionals.

A new kind of medical practice was appearing. Turning away from the individual to treat the community as a whole, the physician-hygienist was groping in matters about which he knew little and in areas that troubled the nation as a whole. Scientists had concluded that disease was the key to the country's failure; the next step was to determine the sources of illness. Beginning in the 1920s *Medical Brazil* began to document the trajectory of epidemics, by which it hoped to predict the nation's destiny. At this point the focus was turning away from bacteriological studies. The terrible epidemic outbreaks had been suppressed, and attention was veering to the population's imperfections and possible safeguards for the future.

It was only after this late date that racial issues became part of *Medical Brazil*'s medical analyses, which by then resembled the primary interests of the Bahian school. Such articles stated that diseases had probably come from Africa, with the slaves, or from Europe and Asia, with the arrival of immigrant laborers (see Chalhoub, 1993). Their conclusion was that the nation's biological infirmity must have come from racial mixing. In light of Brazilian conditions, the matter of hygiene came to be linked to poverty and then to a mestizo and Negro populace.

Eugenics

> If the English are in decline, what can we hope for ourselves?
> —*Medical Brazil,* 1916: 82

In 1918 *Medical Brazil* published "Do conceito de eugenia no habitat brasileiro" [On the concept of eugenics in the Brazilian environment], in which the professor and physician João Henrique informed the medical community of the benefits and uses of eugenics.

> Eugenics is a new science that seeks to explain the causes of the ascent or the decline of races and aims for perfectibility in the human species, not only in the physical domain but also in the intellectual. It proposes several things: to have the healthy intermarry, in an attempt to educate the sexual instinct; to prevent the reproduction of defectives, who transmit deficiencies to their offspring; to give exams for the diagnosis and prevention of syphilis, tuberculosis, and alcoholism, the tripartite cause of decline. These terms imply only an effort to secure a strong and pure race. . . . Our ills derive from our colonization, for which the least we can do is heal what does not belong to us. (*Medical Brazil:* 118–19)

The text was not limited to summarizing the basic notions of eugenics. It also conveyed at least a minimal attempt to adapt these ideas to local conditions, highlighting the relationship between immigration and the introduction of foreign diseases. This theme of the eugenics debate set the physicians who argued theories of contagion against those who advocated theories of infection. Such arguments were examples of the increasingly prevalent idea that disease was linked to certain immigrant races (Chalhoub, 1933).

Until the 1920s the notion that particular races were to blame for disease was rarely encountered. It had been used occasionally as part of a political claim, advanced by scholars from the São Paulo School of Law who sought especially to halt African and Asian immigration to Brazil. But from 1918 on, the justification for curbing the entry of these races more often came from medical and eugenicist sources than from juridical ones. Physicians considered it necessary to instruct politicians in the selection of "good races." "If society has the obligation to protect the weak, it also has the obligation to place the weak in a safe environment so as to be protected in his evolution and to defend himself against the propagation of degeneracy," stated Professor Cypriano Freitas in a commencement address. "This is a matter of the defense of the race, of eugenics, and, consequently, of society itself." Freitas continued with praise for South African examples

> [w]here they admit only those immigrants who display certain economic, social, and racial guarantees . . . The South African Colonisation Society is seeking female domestic help, but it accepts only those who are physically and morally sound, requiring of them a detailed medical examination. This is because most of these women will marry there and will thus establish a healthy and vigorous race of colonizers, and the first condition toward its achievement is to close the doors to the scoria, to the mediocre of body and mind. In a young country such as ours, which needs immigration, we must heal, as they have done in South Africa. . . . We will not correct a people with laws. . . . Only

> the physician, with his knowledge of man, has any influence in the matter. (*Medical Brazil,* 1912: 24–25)

Consistent with the authoritarian models then in place, Carioca physicians introduced a new chapter in the efforts to purify Brazil when they prescribed a eugenics-based immigration policy and took command of the strategic mission.

It is not only the conclusions of such texts that made them so explicitly racist. Behind the attempts to deny entry to certain racial groups lay a theoretical assumption shared by the scholars in question. Proud of their activities in the face of devastating epidemics, they turned their efforts toward "healing races." Since they no longer understood diseases as end products, they concluded that race should be understood along similar lines. They saw Brazilians as a "developing race," whose future success depended on biological refinement. Miguel Pereira, director of the medical school, stated: "We are a new and developing country. . . . Our people are still very far from possessing the specific and definitive imprint of the race that will characterize us in the future" (*Medical Brazil,* 1918: 189).

Concern for the future meant more for these physicians than simply opposing unrestricted immigration, "the ill that comes from beyond." It was necessary to enact measures that aimed at Brazil's internal situation, which had "declined so sharply." The word *eugenics,* distinct from the term *eugenism* used in other Latin American countries, first appeared in Brazil in Alexandre Tepedino's thesis, defended in the Rio de Janeiro School of Medicine in 1914 (Stepan, 1991: 35–36). The solution promised by the new system seemed to mature in the 1920s when the medical profession's approach to curbing disease entailed dividing the population into "the healthy and the sick," or better yet, into "the curable and the incurable," and prescribing separate measures for the two groups.[27]

The first subgroup attracted all the attention. It was necessary to educate its members, to encourage them to marry well, and to teach them to avoid bad habits and misbehavior. The 1920s saw, for example, the publication of a series of articles advocating physical education (*Medical Brazil,* 1912, 1920, 1921, and 1923), believed at that time to be one of the ways to "restore the race" (*Medical Brazil,* 1920: 614). The coverage of this effort was not limited to specialized medical journals. Intellectuals, politicians, and other authorities encouraged the practice of sports as a means of "perfecting the populace." The president of Brazil, Washington Luís, offered his own good example by sponsoring various competitions, among which were the popular "Washington Luís Regattas on the Tietê River" in the city of São Paulo. The recent experience of World War I and the subsequent contact with new biological and social models seemed to demand the creation of a healthy and athletic body, a symbol of what was considered the "physical restoration of our race." It is significant, therefore, that the "Estadinho" [Little State] footrace was initially introduced to further "the cause of the physical restitution of our race" (Sevcenko, 1991: 25).[28] The official origin of the race dates from May 1, 1918, but the first race did not actually take place until July 14 of that year, both of which dates were charged with meaning for the residents of São Paulo.[29] The race took place in the streets of the city of São Paulo and received broad public support (*The State of São Paulo,* 1918).

The eugenicists imagined the nation as a homogeneous and healthful body that ought to pass through an accelerated process of change. One of the more lofty dreams the eugenicists had for the local mestizo population was that these people could be transformed into "pure Greeks," only with different physical and moral characteristics (Stepan, 1991: 135).

Nonetheless, that great mass of "chronically ill," on whom medicine seemed to turn its back, remained. Opinions about the future that lay ahead for this group, what steps if any could be taken to improve the lot of the "sick," were divided. Physicians from the Bahian medical school, who were among the most moderate, predicted a natural disappearance. Other, more radical

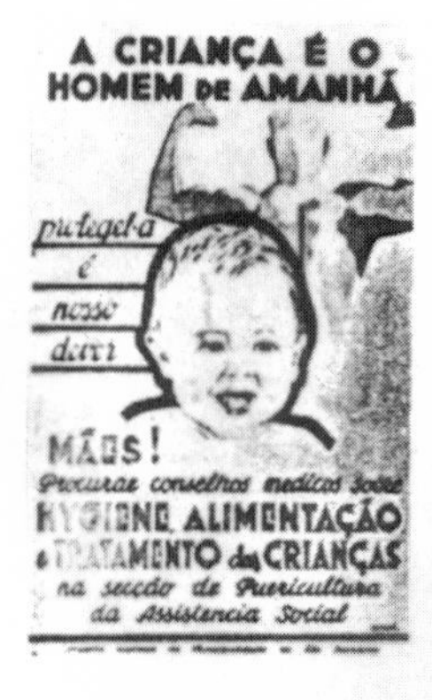

Campanha eugênica da Prefeitura de São Bernardo, SP, 1937

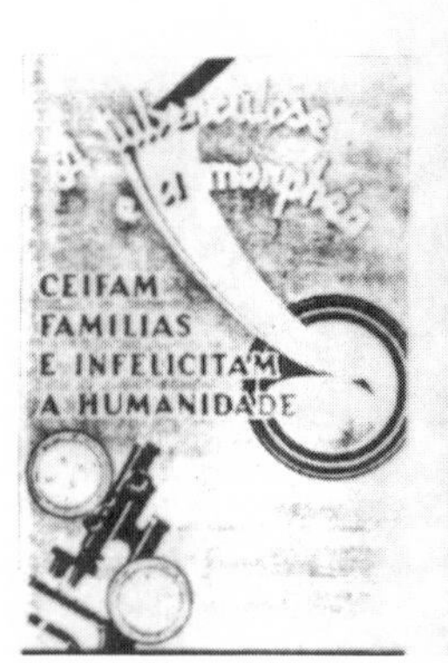

Eugenics campaign posters from 1937,
created by the municipal government of São Bernardo, São Paulo

voices, however, doubtful of the process of natural selection, believed that sterilization would be the only effective course of action. Appealing to the precedent set by a New Jersey state sterilization law, the author of an article in *Medical Brazil* asked: "Why consent to the hereditary perpetuation of imbecility and moral madness, epilepsy, paranoia, and delinquency, if one can sterilize the deficient and degenerate to prevent their procreation while not denying them their sexual pleasure?" In 1921 Dr. Renato Kehl wrote:

> If only it were possible to strike a balance within our population, between, on the one hand, those who produce and turn the great wheels of progress to create well-being, and, on the other hand, the parasites, the indigent and the beggars who wander the streets, the criminals, the amoral, the insane, the offspring of useless people who live by gambling, vice, libertinage, and fraud, and the ill who contribute nothing, who fill the prisons, the hospitals, and the asylums. . . . The number of these parasites is truly frightening. . . . The physicians and eugenicists convinced of this sad reality are seeking the solution to this problem and how to avoid the process of decline . . . it is imperative to stem the proliferation of these diseased, unfit and insane persons. . . . Since the war on epidemics, sociomedical reforms and eugenics have been effervescent. . . . With these examples I have arrived at the following eugenicist conclusion: sterilization will cause the offenders of the human species to disappear, or rather, their proportion will diminish. It will not ensure perfection, as this will only result from a eugenicist process. (*Medical Brazil:* 155–56).

Professor Kehl represented a powerful contingent within the medical school that repudiated the positive vision of racial mixing and viewed the country as demoralized and lacking "robust men" (quoted in Stepan, 1991: 158). For these scientists, familiar with

German eugenicist projects as well as the restrictive policies that the United States had adopted (culminating in the passage of the Immigration Act of 1924), the country's only hope lay in the most radical measures of population control.[30] Although Brazil never implemented projects that proposed the sterilization of certain human groups, other countries did enact eugenicist models. According to Stepan, the first laws of eugenicist sterilization were enacted in the United States in 1919, in the Swiss canton of Vaud in 1928, and in Denmark in 1929. More than eight thousand Danes were sterilized between 1930 and 1940 because of their "physical and sexual abnormalities." As for the United States, Stepan points out that by the end of the 1920s twenty-four states had passed sterilization laws. Between 1907 and the end of World War II, 70,000 persons, mostly poor and frequently black, had been sterilized.

After the victorious cure of epidemics, Kehl believed that it was time to impose strategies of compulsory sterilization. Following Kehl's lead, Carioca medicine broadened the notion of "illness" and started promoting an even more rigid hierarchy consistent with a eugenicist view. By dividing the country into the able and the unable, the perfectible and the degenerate, the eugenicist doctors were muddying the real problem: entrenched socioeconomic divisions. These men understood the nation in terms of race, and through race they explained political successes, economic failures, and established social hierarchies. An eerie portent of the Nazi movement that was about to erupt in Europe, the Brazilian movement also employed science to justify its most violent and authoritarian projects.

By the 1930s *Medical Brazil* focused more on a ceremonial effort to change and modernize medicine and dedicated itself less to theoretical and practical efforts to create new models of social analysis. The journal became even larger, the *z* in the Portuguese title *Brazil Medico* was abolished in 1929,* and the publication became more technical and tended to withdraw from

* Modern Portuguese usage requires that *Brazil* be spelled with an *s*—*Brasil*.

social problems. The studies on clinical medicine were arranged in ever more specialized divisions and grew in the same proportion as the total output.

Neither the medical interpretation of society nor the distinctively arrogant and autarchic attitude about how best to cure the ills of the country, going back to the beginning of the century, had disappeared. Speaking before the First Brazilian Eugenics Congress as late as 1929, Miguel Couto, president of the National Academy of Medicine and professor emeritus of the Carioca school, defended the notion that racial mixing would lead to national decline.[31] In 1933, in the Vargas era, the Carioca scientists, together with their Bahian counterparts, founded in the federal capital the first institute of national identification, under the responsibility of the specialist Leonídio Ribeiro.[32]

One does find both in *Medical Brazil* and in other institutions and publications of the 1920s critiques of racial and determinist models of social analysis, which, according to some physicians, "for a long time had not attracted adherents from among medical professionals" (*Medical Brazil,* 1930: 102). On the other hand, there is still evidence that an interventionist position persisted as a legacy of the scientific models that the profession of medicine and other disciplines had been using since the turn of the century.

The physicians of *Medical Brazil* continued to view themselves as being on a mission of national salvation; they went on exalting in their own calling. Indeed, even into the 1930s, thinking of society as though it were an individual and making the citizenry into one enormous hospital patient remained a great source of inspiration for these physicians.

"IT IS NECESSARY TO CARE FOR THE RACE"

The medical schools arrived at similar conclusions while following diverse paths. It was necessary to care for the race, or, in other words, the nation, and the medical view that was constructed gave physicians the privilege of attending to this task. In the meantime, the constant cooperation between the medical schools in Bahia and Rio de Janeiro and the coincidence in the solutions they found in the 1930s could lead one to a common and mistaken perception about the production of these medical centers: that they cooperated with one another.

To speak in terms of cooperation, one must understand that there were notable differences between the two schools. To summarize briefly, while the study of "medical law and mental medicine" gave the Bahian school renown as a research institution, the Carioca medical school took advantage of its research in epidemiology to establish its professional credentials.

It is more difficult to reflect on the idea of cooperation given the theoretical premises that arose in the 1920s and the beginning of the 1930s. It is a given that both schools had programs that implied imposing a medical vision on society. It is also evident that both of their journals favored the adoption of a program of eugenics within Brazil. but here we encounter some revealing differences. In the 1920s the language of eugenics was common to both schools, but its application was somewhat different and depended on the context.

For Bahian medicine, eugenics signified a way to diminish a monumental sense of pessimism; it was a way to find acceptance for old concepts and theories that were so extreme there was little hope for their application. Eugenics permitted one to prophesy "perfectibility" and to imagine an improvement in the race, which prior to this time had been believed impossible by members of the Bahian school. For the Carioca school, recognizing eugenics made possible the creation of new areas of social intervention. As epidemiologists successfully met their challenges, and as they ceased to be the focus of attention, they found that as eugenicists they could recover their social role.

Thus, in Bahia the eugenicist discourse played out as an adaptation. After all, implied in it was the solution for the Brazilian race. In Rio medical involvement in society became ever more aggressive. The Cariocas had become accustomed to assuming a leadership role in far-reaching programs of public hygiene and campaigns of compulsory vaccination. By implementing eugenicist measures, they may have hoped to find a way to sustain their social involvement and find yet another means to exert their influence. The possibility of foreseeing the country's future generations and of eliminating the transmission of undesirable traits became the issue. Although the movements in Bahia and Rio resembled one another, there was a difference in the particulars. Toward the end of the century, writers for the *Medical Gazette* had shown full confidence in their positions, but by the 1930s they had adopted a more measured and circumscribed level of involvement in public programs. Contributors to *Medical Brazil,* on the other hand, continually sought to widen the scope of their work, the goal of which was nothing less than to determine the nation's destiny.

Finally, one cannot help but consider regional specificities. Since it was a peripheral institution, beset by a precarious financial situation and supported by a clientele with meager economic resources, the Bahian medical school was a mirror of the state that it represented. It lost its combative character in the last years of Empire, and it adjusted to an environment of consolidation that effectively excluded the northern Brazilian institutions from their previous role in decision making.

The situation was completely the reverse in the medical school and in the other medical institutes of Rio de Janeiro. Because of the proximity of these institutes to the nation's centers of financial and political influence, the Carioca clientele had made them wealthy, and because of the successful role they had played in the eradication of epidemics, they enjoyed a glow that surrounded their past and present accomplishments. From this position they launched their most daring and ambitious programs. If it was the Bahians who first proclaimed the sovereignty of medicine, it was the Cariocas who assumed a good part of its leadership. It was the Bahians who first spoke of matrimonial selection, but it was the Cariocas who tried, without success, to institute sterilization for the "diseased sectors." It was the contributors to the *Medical Gazette* who underscored the social function of medicine, but it was the Carioca physicians who most easily rose to positions of prominence in national politics.[33]

Areas of intellectual tension grew ever more evident in the face of the new social medicine. This was a period that saw controversies between physicians and jurists, hygienists and legislators, take root. The question of equality was central. The medical and public health efforts were readily of interest to the law. After the abolition of slavery and the proclamation of the republic, it was the jurists who had to create a code with an egalitarian principle that would unify the country.

It would be difficult to imagine a single victorious discourse. It was time to reflect on how at the beginning they had reconciled such exclusionary visions and how the concept of race had been pivotal in the definition of those avenues. These were the "men of law" and the "men of medicine." Some wielded the law and others the cure. The only thing certain in either case was the desire that each camp had to hold in its hands the reins of the nation's destiny.

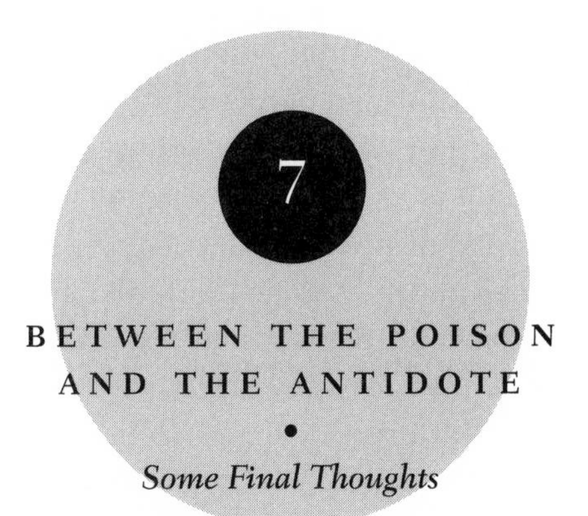

7

BETWEEN THE POISON AND THE ANTIDOTE

Some Final Thoughts

Brazil cares not for us! She is sick and tired of us! Our Brazil is
in another world. This is not Brazil. Brazil does not exist.
And perchance exist Brazilians?
—*Carlos Drummond de Andrade, "National Hymn"*

In 1894, Raimundo Nina Rodrigues pondered: "[I]f a country is too poor to impose itself but not too old to admire itself, it must at least be fascinating." This lucid vision summarized much of the era's perceptions about Brazil. Throughout the nineteenth century, Brazil had played the role of paradise for visiting naturalists, and the country entered the 1890s with this image intact. But it was not the flora, the fauna, and the power of the land but the people, with their unusual racial composition, who gave the nation its truly unique character.

Foreign scientists declared the country's miscegenation to be a recent and previously unknown phenomenon, and at the same time miscegenation became a matter of dispute among the local intellectual elites. This group had read specialized European and North American literature and had elevated the racial question nearly to the level of obsession in their effort to find an original national expression. In the end, Nina Rodrigues declared that "we knew about everyone but ourselves" (1894/1957).

The racial issues studied here employ a language by which one can apprehend observable inequalities, or even a certain national uniqueness. As Eric Hobsbawm has aptly demonstrated (1990), at the moment when racial discourse became linked to nationalistic projects, it seemed opportune to imagine a nation in biological terms, to regulate its reproduction, and to prize a future homogeneity. Meanwhile, despite the "fascinating" and the particular, the verification that this was a "mestizo nation" generated new dilemmas for Brazilian scientists. It suggested that foreign determinist theories were out of phase with Brazil's "internal mestizo reality." This reality revealed the essential rigidity of such theories. If the evolutionist models as a whole led one to believe that progress and civilization were inevitable, they also pointed one toward the conclusion that the mixing of heterogeneous races was always a mistake, one that always led not only to the decline of the individual but also to the decline of the group.

Intellectuals oscillated between determinist models as they reflected upon them, and they found themselves in an uncomfortable place. Their position between the exaltation of "national modernity" and their recognition of the nation's reality was untenable. "It must have been difficult to ignore external criticism and the internalization of the foreign vision that Brazil was an aberration," declared Roberto Ventura (1988: 91). At a moment of national rediscovery, aborigines, Africans, and mestizos came to represent obstacles to the progression of a country on a march toward the splendors of civilization; they posed barriers to the formation of a true national identity (Queiroz, 1989: 32).

The Brazilian fin de siècle played out in this way, with a great deal of disillusion, and the country's "men of science," skeptical of promises of equality, abolition, and the republic, began to wonder ever more about the causes of human differences.

For example, in the ethnographic museums, the wide use of evolutionist arguments permitted a scientific explanation of differences, the classification of species, and the determination of where some Brazilians were underdeveloped. In dialogue with the exterior, Brazilians amassed incisive examples that attested to the specificities of their "exotic country," but their research also helped them to prove the origin of the racial problem.

The delayed arrival of determinist models to the historical institutes led to the acceptance of varied explanations. On the one hand, scholars maintained an optimistic vision, both Catholic and patriotic, which was a traditional model of these institutions. On the other hand, the men of the institutes latched onto a determinist and evolutionist perception of the nation. The result was a monogenist interpretation, but it sought social Darwinist conclusions when it attempted to use race to justify the nation's entrenched social hierarchies.

The Brazilian scientists of the era were a mixture of discoverers and missionaries, who alternated between a sense of admiration and a sense of fear for their nation and proposed reforms and solutions that depended on the scientists' ability to execute them. Viewed through this looking glass, perhaps the debate concentrated primarily in the schools of law and medicine. Two contenders for leadership emerged in the contest for scientific hegemony: the cure and the law; those who worked with the poison and those who worked with the antidote. "Men of law" tied the creation of a unified code to their leadership of the nation. Medical professionals, on the other hand, believed that only they could diagnose and treat the diseases afflicting the country. Whereas medical researchers foresaw the decline, confirmed the ailments, and proposed programs of hygiene and sanitation, legal scholars, or *bacharéis,* believed that the application of law offered a vehicle that transcended racial and social differences.

Understood in these terms, and with the most radical conclusions removed, the racial argument emerged as a workable approach. It appealed to theory to justify the use of programs based on conservative politics and the maintenance of rigid social hierarchies, which by then one could scientifically explain. Thus, as the Brazilian educated elite adopted an evolutionist and racial perspective, they became uniformly aware of their nation's challenges. They also appealed to the evolutionist and racial line of thinking to reconfigure a discussion of human equality and, therefore, of criteria for citizenship.

The same elite that generated a solution for a new, liberal political configuration sought support in determinist and anthropological theories in order to explain social differences in terms of biological and other fundamental barriers. Slavery had ended, the republic had begun, and a racial discourse gathered strength, which was rather belated in light of the liberal model present since 1822. Abolition had promised freedom, and the new constitution had granted citizenship to all. Because of these changes, at that point it seemed imperative to reconsider the country's organization. An article from the *São Paulo Post* from December 21, 1920, stated: "men are not born with absolute equality; equality is presumed before the law, without which there would be no law." Transformed into a utopian ideal by Brazilian scientists, the equality gained through political change was then lost in the name of nature.

More interesting, however, than merely identifying the effect of the racial theory is reflecting on the originality of its diffusion. Speaking of the adoption of racial theories in Brazil implies thinking about a model that incorporated that which it wished to serve and ignored that which did not suit it. In Brazil, evolutionism combined with social Darwinism, as if it were possible to speak about "human evolution," while simultaneously differentiating the races. The effect of this kind of thinking was to deny civilization to blacks and mestizos in Brazil, ignoring the country's long history of miscegenation. The hope was to excise "the gangrenous parts" to guarantee that the nation's future would be "white and Western."

The model was redefined to suit the source that gave it life. Thus new meanings were attached to old ideas: "An event becomes such as it is when interpreted" (Sahlins, 1985: xiv). For example, the notion of "perfectibility" from the eighteenth-century model retained only its name, having lost its original content. No longer did one speak of Rousseau's humanistic concept, understood as a characteristic inherent in every human being, who by his or her nature always bore the potential for self-transcendence. Nineteenth-century writings, especially in Brazil, revealed that few possessed the potential for *perfectibility,* a sign of superiority of some groups in contrast to the inferiority of others, such as the mestizos, who had lost that part of their humanity: "It is sad that we have proven that among us the mestizos are incapable of perfectibility, imprisoned as they are in an advanced state of decline" (*Medical Gazette of Bahia,* 1886: 68). As Gerbi affirmed, "in the midst of historiographical theories, legal arguments, scientific investigations, biological hypotheses, and lay curiosity, we see how complex the life of an idea can be" (1982: 721).

Race provided scientific and comparative data for museums; end-of-the-century historical institutes adopted race as an official discourse; race was a concept that defined in legal terms the nation's uniqueness; and race was a gloomy indicator for the medical profession. One can see how symbols handily redefine themselves for new uses in certain contexts. The Brazilian institutions we have studied here were certainly marked by differences, but during the period in question they took on similar hues.

To understand that the racial theories were adopted as mere copies of foreign models without some alteration from regional input would be inaccurate. One must study the new contextual meanings the theories took on, as well as verify their relationship with the social, political, economic, and intellectual situation at that time in Brazil. It is more useful to think of such theses as "product and production" (Durham, 1977) and to see them as the result of the moment in which they appeared, while at the same time attentively searching for the creation of new values and perceptions. As Roberto Schwarz said, "in Brazil we experiment constantly with false identities, inauthentic ones within the cultural life that we possess, . . . and this appraisal has shaped the nature of our reflections since independence" (1987: 29). This apparent unoriginality has been seen as intellectually deficient, and since the nineteenth century there seems to have been an effort to establish a "subtraction operation," to the extent that the borrowed versions always appeared as inferior to the original (Schwarz, 1987: 33). But it makes no sense to renounce the borrowed in favor of the authentic. The challenge is to think in terms of the originality of the copy and the elasticity of the doctrine when applied in wholly different contexts.

Brazil appropriated several racial theories, and the uses to which they were put varied according to local needs. In the United States, these theories gained acceptance at the same time as the efforts of reformers, so active in the nineteenth century, quieted down (Hofstadter, 1975: 47). Social Darwinism, thought of as a philosophy of inevitability, became a conservative doctrine in the hands of the ruling elites who after the U.S. Civil War wanted to put an end to internal social conflicts.

The English applied a reading of Spencer to Darwinism, which thus acquired liberal connotations and strengthened their laissez-faire economic doctrine. Employed principally by sectors of the mercantile class, the interpretation of social evolutionism in England was mostly political. Little of it referred to social or racial issues (Graham, 1973). In Germany, "The scientific creeds of social Darwinism and eugenics offered general models for constructing an ordered and developing society" (Weindling, 1989: 1).

Finally, in Latin America, according to the historian Thomas Glick, the introduction of Darwinist thought was not only generalized, but its acceptance was linked to certain social sectors: "In societies where the elites are not unified, all ideas, even the scientific ones, are appropriated as weapons. Darwinism is a fine example, since it was easily converted into a symbol of secularism" (1988: 103).

As one can see, understanding the use of racial theories in Brazil is not a matter of seeking an original interpretation. The applications of Darwinism were so numerous that they make up part of the history and logic of racial theories. As Marshall Sahlins wrote, "In their practical projects and social arrangements, informed by the received meanings of persons and things, people submit these cultural categories to empirical risks" (1985: ix), with new meanings appearing through the constant interaction between "convention and action."

Considered in these terms, the racial question extends its scope as it permits one to think of its application to Brazil as *one* of the versions of a single model. In the midst of the turbulent last years of the nineteenth century, the racial theme offered itself as a means of thinking about a national program.

Taking the place of an ideology of national culture, racial science theories fulfilled different roles within Brazil. As a lay discourse, they opposed the Church and religious influence. They also legitimized the voices of the ascendant urban groups that were responsible for taking up new political projects and that saw in these theories signs of "modernity," an index of progress.

But if the racial question was effective to the degree that it isolated Brazilians in how they perceived certain aspects of their society, it impeded or diminished other debates. While a determinist reading strengthened the importance of race to the nation's development, this effect was offset by the weakening of the debate in terms of the diminishment of the meaning of citizenship and individual responsibility. This type of theory understood the subject in terms of his "racio-cultural" group and tended to neutralize individual will in the face of racial coercion.

Such doctrines opposed not only eighteenth-century humanism but also the philosophy of "civic duty," a legacy of the French Revolution, thus excluding the universal principle of equality. But, as Louis Dumont suggested, these two models were not so different. Paradoxically, according to him, as a recent phenomenon racism "puts a new face on an old function" (1966: 320). Reintroduced at the beginning of the nineteenth century as a stratification principle in egalitarian societies, the racial doctrine of inequality may be viewed as a rare bird, a perversion of the humanist Enlightenment, which sought to normalize inequality in societies egalitarian only in theory.

One can see that two contemporaneous debates emerged in Brazil: one that espoused the entrenchment of a liberal judicial model toward the creation of the state; and the other that, while weakening the discussion of citizenship, revived the debate over the notion of equality, based on racial determinist conclusions. Racism and liberalism were formally exclusionary theories in the country at the end of the century, winning distinct arenas of activity.

It is possible to imagine that in Brazil diverse forms of socialization had developed in which egalitarianism from the Enlightenment and the rights of man could exist in a diffuse manner because of the "absence of the notion of citizens' rights" (Montes, 1991). This was a society whose individual, institutional, and governmental privations were extreme, made more so by the dispersion of local powers. Because of this, racial theories seemed "to fit," to the degree that the problem of nationality shifted from a question of acquired culture to a matter of fundamental nature.

Making use of the instruments that they had, Brazil's "men of science" found both liberal and racial discourses uncommonly convivial. If the former played out in legal texts and official pronouncements, the latter appeared frequently in naturalist novels, the natural sciences, and history. The country's "men of medicine" saw in Brazil's racial mixture the country's most potent poison and set out to discover the antidote. Our "men of law," who did not enter that debate only in theory, officially advocated the adoption of a liberal state for the nation. Nevertheless, they became fearful because of an accelerated rate of miscegenation following the Great War. They pondered the justness of "acting on behalf of the whole profile of our populace, composed of so many unequal races, and perhaps little prepared for the exercise of citizenship" (*Academic Journal of the Recife School of Law,* 1919: 156).

In these institutional environments it is often with a sense of guilt, although scientifically legitimized, that the racial argument of social analysis emerged. One cannot say the same of other surroundings, where people employed the scientific determinist model without reservation. In daily speech, public behavior, and daily newspapers it was commonplace to find arguments that translated science into popular terms and confronted race as a question of fundamental importance in the nation's destiny. "Simplifying what scientific theories express so well, it is by means of race that a people, or a nation, determines its destinies" (*The State of São Paulo,* 1901).

In this context there were, however, two distinct models that seemed to enjoy a tacit accord to take charge of two separate arenas of activity: the public versus the private, or the official versus the familiar. But, as historian Sérgio Buarque de Holanda stated, "for detractors steeped in that environment, it was not easy to understand the fundamental distinctions between the two camps" (Holanda, 1936/1979: 105).

A number of Brazilian authors extensively analyzed this confusing relationship between the public and the private spheres. In *Raízes do Brazil* [The roots of Brazil] (1936), Sérgio Buarque de Holanda highlighted the historical implications of a country "where everyone is a baron and there can be no collective accord."[1] Nearly one hundred eighty degrees out of phase with Holanda, jurist and politician Oliveira Vianna pointed to the problem of this confusing and elastic limitation: "people of colonial origins such as ours possess two political constitutions. One is the written document, by which we do not abide . . . that is in our laws and political codes. The other, adapted to our spirit, mentality and structure, is unwritten but is the one by which we do abide" (1918/1952: 422). Anthropologist Roberto Da Matta revisited this theme (1981) when he demonstrated the existence of a dual society in Brazil, where two manners of perceiving the world coexist. This duality is composed of one world of "individuals" subject to legal action, and another of "people" for whom the legal code is merely another platonic and distant formula. Referring to novelist Manuel Antônio de Almeida's *Memórias de um sargento de milícias* [Memories of a militia sergeant], literary critic Antonio Candido comes to similar conclusions in his essay "Dialética da malandragem" [The dialectics of roguery] (1970/1993). He analyzes two reciprocal movements that he calls a "dialectic of order and disorder," which is so characteristic of Brazil. He recognizes greater "flexibility" while at the same time less "integrity and coherence." Almeida's book serves, therefore, as a portrait of that "land of the amoral," which expresses "the vast and universal accommodation that disperses the extremes, throws out the meaning of law and order, and reveals the imprint of the most disparate groups, ideas, and attitudes" (1993: 51).[2]

Approached from various angles, the issue can now be revisited in view of the central argument of this book. One can say that while this "racial vision" emerged from the scientific institutions, it was most evident in personal relations and daily living. It justified social hierarchies based on biological criteria, and this set of behaviors occurred in a movement that began in institutions of higher learning in pursuit of common sense and its inverse. Liberal models governed public spheres, and they consisted of laws and measures of broad scope. "People" discussed race in everyday arguments, in medical clinics, and in the personalities of the era's scientific novels. "Individuals" or, rather, scattered citizens of a great nation who participated in the decision-making process and in external and diplomatic debates, discussed the law.[3] Thus Brazilian laws or official documents never confirmed the conclusions of scholars of the institutes about the uniqueness of the human species, but these ideas did have the effect of informing the debates that led to the execution of those very measures.

Brazil is unique because of its miscegenation, and the racial interpretation of this racial phenomenon has distant and firmly rooted origins. This was the theme of von Martius's winning essay for the Historical and Geographical Institute of Brazil at the beginning of the nineteenth century. Silvio Romero reiterated the ideas in the 1880s, and Brazilian anthropologist Gilberto Freyre extended the thread in the twentieth century,[4] demonstrating the persistence of this interpretation both in the diversity of models and across time. From von Martius's conclusions about hybridization to Romero's Darwinist affirmation, and culminating with Gilberto Freyre's praise for Brazilian racial democracy, the argument that "Brazil defines itself in terms of race" has emerged as a constant.

One notes the original and unexpected uses and applications of philosophical imitation in the unusual directions that this debate has taken. Although they were models of success in the 1870s in Brazil, these racial theories found new adherents beyond this country's borders. In the 1930s, however, the situation nearly reversed itself, and despite cultural theory criticism, certain racial models for social analysis began to gather strength. Examples in Europe and the United States were German Aryanism and North American segregation politics. But it was different in Brazil. Although politicians and scientists addressed these variations of racial theory, Gilberto Freyre's cultural relativist theses, which praised Brazilian racial mixing, lessened their impact. The ideas persisted, nevertheless, above all in truisms and popular perceptions.

If one retrieves the ideas expressed by Sérgio Buarque de Holanda in 1936, perhaps one can say that race forms the basis of the nation even today, as notions of race find their way into some of the "more intimate" and informal aspects of Brazilian life. Such thought has become unacceptable in principle when employed in contexts not defined by personal relationships. Therefore, even if one no longer accepts the scientific interpretation that blamed the decline of a nation on its racial mixing, one can say that "speaking about race" is still a powerful issue in Brazil.

Certainly most of the explanatory paradigms have been abandoned, and with them the scientific acceptance of racial models with their interpretations of a humanity divided into species. By the 1930s the notion advanced by Gilberto Freyre in his *The Masters and the Slaves* that Brazil was a racially and culturally blended country had begun to gather momentum as a kind of unofficial ideology of the state, held above the rifts between race and class and the social conflicts that were breaking out.[5] Preconceptions came under scrutiny, and the legacy of ideas became ever more tenuous. As a case in point, the wonderful example of Jeca Tatu, Monteiro Lobato's well-known character who, while a poor and ignorant mestizo, in certain ways represented the conditions under which the majority of the Brazilian population lived. In 1918, however, in *O problema vital* [The vital problem], Monteiro Lobato seemed to change his stance when, turning his attention toward the racial problem, he portrayed Jeca

Illustration by Belmonte for the book Idéias de Jeca Tatu *[Jeca Tatu's ideas], by Monteiro Lobato* (*REVISTA DO BRASIL* [MAGAZINE OF BRAZIL], 1919)

Tatu not as the result of a hybrid formation but as the aftermath of epidemic diseases. Backed by eugenicists such as Renato Kehl (1923) and intellectuals such as Fernando de Azevedo (1919), Lobato seemed to wrap the figure of Jeca Tatu in new meanings, to confirm the importance of health education and the death of the racial degenerationist argument.[6]

Race has remained, however, a central theme in Brazilian social thought, no longer as a source of discouragement, but perhaps as a source of richness, a symbol of the nation's uniqueness, viewed in a positive light. More than just vestiges of the past, expressions such as "this is a matter of race," "you're worth as much as your race," or "it runs through the race" contribute to a way of thinking that continues today and that has always tended to reflect the nation's image and destiny being a compendium of the races that make up the nation. Once in a while someone will still make a point based on race, whether to reaffirm a certain cultural difference between races, or to affirm the worth of Brazil's racial mixture.

On the other hand, as Nina Rodrigues foresaw at the end of the nineteenth century, the foreign view of Brazil is that of a *fascinating* country. It is fascinating because it is different and because it is composed of a mixed population. It sustains the image established by Freyre of a nation of peaceful racial harmony. This appears in the Disneyesque *Zé Carioca,* the annual Carnival exported by the tourist industry, and the image of the *malandro,* the representation of which has ever less to do with reality.[7] This is the mestizo representation of the country that "morphs" from negative to exotic, from scientific to spectacle. It is not by chance that the postcard Brazil is a multicolored country. If other kinds of apprehension cloud the future of Brazil, a racial representation of the nation persists, a legacy of discussions begun in the last century.

Finding anthropological themes useful to their needs, physicians, jurists, historians, and naturalists seemed to feel responsible for the creation of new identities for the nation, as if all knowledge had to derive from homegrown experience. As anthropologist

Manuela Carneiro da Cunha declared, "Since Nina Rodrigues and especially Gilberto Freyre, anthropologists have become the minstrels of nationality, a phenomenon sui generis in the international panorama" (1986: 7).

Whether in the mestizo image from the end of the nineteenth century, or in the cultural relativism revival of the 1930s, the theme of identity and of the search for a local singularity appears newly outfitted in this country so attracted to the creation of new myths of Brazilianness.

On this broad global map
one land does not appear;
either all of them are bad,
or just one of them, I fear.

—Gregório de Mattos Guerra

NOTES

INTRODUCTION: THE SPECTACLE OF MISCEGENATION

1. The careful eye will notice that many names and titles in this book reflect conventions of accentuation typical of 1870–1930. Thus, and at variance with contemporary usage, names such as Silvio, Oscar, Antonio, and Emilio usually appear without accent marks. Other conventions of spelling and accentuation also reflect the era, such as the use of *ph* where more current usage would choose *f,* such as in the world *geographia*.
2. If we examine the modest goals of this measure we learn something about Brazilian abolitionists' models of freedom. The end of slavery was to come about slowly, deliberately, and by legal means. The Law of the Free Womb is a good example of this position. On the one hand, it established that a slave born after the date that the law went into effect would be "freed," although under the guardianship of his or her former owner, upon turning eighteen. On the other hand, it provided for no change in the status of slaves born prior to the date of its promulgation. One must also emphasize that after the enactment of this law the internal migration of slaves accelerated, and the price of available slaves soared. (For further information see Mattoso, 1982; Conrad, 1978.)
3. The "*Lei dos Sexagenários*" ["Law of the Sexagenarians"], urged by the abolitionist movement and passed on September 28, 1885, reveals the modest aims of these pioneering reformers. This measure gave freedom to slaves

over age sixty, who would otherwise be made to work for another three years. The law had so little effect that even during such a composed era there were strong reactions to it. In a country where slaves survived only an average of fifteen years of enforced labor, a slave who reached sixty was unusual, and to receive freedom at that age was a dubious reward, as freedom would then also mean the loss of security at a vulnerable age.

4. The Ibiacaba plantation, owned by Senator Vergueiro, pioneered the use of incentives to attract European immigrant workers. The story of Thomas Davatz, a Swiss immigrant, who led a workers' revolt on the Vergueiro plantation, is well known. For further information, see Holanda, 1941.
5. According to this philosopher the intellectual output of this era can be summed up as an "unauthorized copy" emended only after the "First World War, when Brazilian thought acquired greater independence" (Cruz Costa, 1956: 417).
6. As Wanderley Guilherme dos Santos affirms, only the social factors were taken into account. It was understood "that all contemplation would clearly and rationally reflect the social structure, and that it was necessary only to imagine any necessary mechanisms" (1978: 27–29).
7. By 1848 Domingos José Gonçalves de Magalhães was defending interpretations of a similar nature in the pages of the *Revista do Instituto Historico e Geographico Brasileiro*: "Our institutions are alien. They have been badly and inopportunely grafted. They are averse to our customs and natural tendencies, and they are incompatible with the vastness of our limitless land and class differences" (142).
8. It is important to remember that during the entire colonial period in Brazil universities and other institutions of higher learning were prohibited, in part to keep the colonists dependent on the Portuguese kingdom. It was not until 1920 that Brazil had its first university, the University of Rio de Janeiro. But, beginning in the early nineteenth century, institutes of higher learning, such as the National Museum, began to serve some of the purposes that the university would fulfill more than a hundred years later. These earlier centers of learning hosted the national debates that are the focus of this book.
9. I will treat these schools, as well as their divergent interpretations of the racial question, in the chapters that follow.
10. Although he does not deal precisely with the same topic, Richard Morse (1988), employing the image of the mirror, also searches for the singularity of Latin American cultures as well as for a historical identity that would not be stillborn.

1. AMONG "MEN OF SCIENCE"

1. According to Fernando Azevedo (1956), until the beginning of the nineteenth century, institutional education in Brazil was far inferior to that of Spanish America.
2. The urgency with which they founded medical schools in Rio and Bahia, for example, reveals the pragmatic character of the king's measures. The goal of the government, founded in 1808, was to care for the "ills" of a population that, swollen by the arrival of the Portuguese court, suffered from contagious diseases and a lack of medical professionals.
3. There is a small factual error in this quotation. The Emilio Goeldi Museum of Pará was reinaugurated in 1893, by which time Goeldi was present.
4. The 1872 census shows a large increase in the urban population. Although the population of Brazil grew at an annual rate of 2.5 percent from 1872 to 1890, the population of cities with more than fifty thousand inhabitants had grown at a rate of 3.7 percent, and those with more than one hundred thousand grew at a rate of 3.1 percent. For more detailed information, see the census of 1872 and Fausto, 1977.
5. The spreading influence of coffee cultivation had reached the region called the Paulista West by the middle of the century. By the 1870s the coffee production of this province had surpassed that of the Paraíba Valley in the Rio de Janeiro region. This economic shift did not result, however, in changes to the political configuration of the Empire. The Republican coup d'état can be partially explained by the imbalance of power between the political and the economic spheres of decision making. See, among others, Holanda, n.d.; Prado Jr., 1945.
6. In the new sociology of Durkheim, certain pivotal dichotomies were fundamental to the comprehension of his work. The "social" opposed the "individual," and "sociology" opposed "psychology." According to sociologist Steven Lukes, "proclaiming sociology an independent science, Durkheim thought it necessary to declare it independent of psychology" (1977: 16). Durkheim affirmed that the same break in continuity that distinguished biology from physics and chemistry existed between psychology and sociology (1893/1978). Consequently, psychology would be "the science of the mind of the individual," pertaining to "states of individual consciousness," as opposed to sociology with its "states of collective conscience" (1895/1978: xv).
7. It is within this context that the Austrian neurologist Sigmund Freud developed the foundations for the new science of psychoanalysis. See, among others, Mezan, 1985; Gay, 1988; Sevcenko, 1991.
8. This theme could be developed quite fully, but what matters here is not the specifics but the breadth and impact of scientific advances, principally when viewed in contrast to their minimal acceptance in Brazil. For greater depth, see Radl, 1988; Ronan, 1987.

9. With a fairly speedy political application, these models would give scientific legitimacy to European domination, primarily on the Asian and African continents (Kuper, 1973). Evolutionist and determinist science toward the end of the nineteenth century had, therefore, gained visibility and acceptance to a degree previously unknown.
10. The great Portuguese novelist Eça de Queirós was not the only one to emphasize the Brazilian emperor's erudition. His friend Pasteur called him a "man of science," Lamartine dubbed him a "philosopher prince," and Victor Hugo referred to him as the "grandson of Marcus Aurelius" (*Journal of the Historical and Geographical Institute of Brazil* 5, no. 75: 131).
11. According to Hardman, "the official reports of the organizing committees instituted by Dom Pedro II provided revealing indicators of the economic, political, and cultural meanings beneath the country's surface appearance" (1988: 67). Until the end of the Empire, Brazil participated in the expositions of 1862 (London), 1867 (Paris), 1873 (Vienna), 1876 (Philadelphia), 1879 (Paris), 1882 (Buenos Aires), and 1884 (Saint Petersburg), as well as having staged other contributions of similar magnitude in 1861, 1866, 1873, and 1875.
12. Nicolau Sevcenko (1991) emphasizes how the theme of modernity was present in the portrait of the era. Alluding to advances in aviation, the introduction of Coca-Cola and the cigarette, the phonograph and motion pictures, urban traffic congestion, and other phenomena, the author outlines the profile of a society that saw itself as modern and civilized.
13. I will analyze in greater detail the characteristics of fin de siècle naturalist literature that enjoyed so much exposure among the academics of the Recife School of Law in Chapter 5, which deals with the law schools.
14. For insight into the impact and intensity of these projects that aimed at instilling notions of hygiene and discipline in urban populations, see Chalhoub, 1986; Dias, 1984; Machado, 1978; Silva, 1984.
15. Chapter 6 of this book will resume the analysis of this theme.
16. Manuela Carneiro da Cunha calls attention to the distinction between the practices of cannibalism and anthropophagy, a fundamental difference that in the sixteenth century would permit the exaltation of the Brazilian native, especially in French literature. "The difference" she says, "is that cannibals eat human flesh to feed themselves. The Tupi, however, are different in that they eat their enemies out of vengeance." (See Cunha, 1990: 99; Cunha and Viveiros de Castro, 1985.) An example of this is the analysis that Montaigne (1533–92) makes of the practice of cannibalism among the Tupinambás. Trying to understand the role of warfare between the peoples of the New World, in "The Cannibals" the philosopher concludes by stating that the Western experience itself is relative: "but returning to the subject, I see nothing barbarous or savage in what they say about those people. Indeed, we all consider barbarous what we do not practice in our own country" (1582/1980: 103).

17. For example, in 1711 the Portuguese Jesuit Antonil was already speaking of a "purgatory colony": "an inferno for Negroes, a purgatory for whites, and a paradise for mulatto women."
18. Couty was one of the first foreign travellers to contemplate the Brazilian racial conformation. He believed that Brazil's escape valve was white immigration.
19. The Empire retained centralized control of the entire country, but regional disharmony and tensions soon began gathering just beneath the surface. The fall of the Empire had the effect of venting pressure and generating the kinds of disputes among the institutes of higher learning that the following chapters will analyze. As I will show, the socioeconomic profiles of the various institutes and their scientists were diverse. Of particular significance was the contrast between the clientele of the Historical and Geographical Institute of Brazil, almost all of whose members were of the agrarian elites, and the Recife intellectuals, a large part of whom belonged to the local urban middle class.
20. It was common for intellectuals to circulate among the institutes. Silvio Romero, for instance, was a member of the Recife Law School, the Historical and Geographical Institute of Brazil, and the Brazilian Academy of Letters; he was also a contributor to several newspapers. Von Ihering, director of the São Paulo Museum, also frequently published his articles in the journals of the Goeldi Museum, the Historical and Geographical Museum of São Paulo, and the São Paulo Law School.
21. He described Machado de Assis as a stammerer and as a representative of a "Brazilian mixed-blood subrace."
22. One must point out that this debate makes sense only when viewed through the lens of Silvio Romero and those intellectuals who called themselves "men of science." For Machado de Assis, that view of a writer's stature did not withstand scrutiny. For more details about this polemic, see Ventura, 1991: 95–107.
23. Joaquim Nabuco (1849–1910) was an influential Brazilian jurist, abolitionist, and defender of ending slavery through legislation.
24. Toward the end of the century scientific racism in Brazil was commonplace. One cannot say, however, that everyone shared these views. There were discordant and influential voices, among whom were Manoel Bonfim, Araripe Júnior, Alberto Torres, and Joaquim Nabuco. Machado de Assis frequently parodied this kind of theory in stories such as "A evolução" [Evolution] and "O alienista" [The psychiatrist].
25. This is the case, for example, of Noiré and Haeckel, disseminators of the doctrines of monogenism. This theory attempted to apply Darwin's theory of evolution to all the phenomena pertaining to the Earth, humanity, plants, and animals. The assumption was that phylogeny recapitulates ontogeny, or that the evolution of the individual closely follows the path of humanity. Monogenist authors had little success in Europe, but in Brazil they saw

their books turned into primers that applied social Darwinist models and introduced their readers to the "inner mysteries of biology, which certainly was the most progressive science of the century" (Haeckel, 1884: 14).

2. RACIAL DOCTRINES IN THE NINETEENTH CENTURY: A HISTORY OF "DIFFERENCES AND DISCRIMINATION"

1. In this chapter I make no effort to treat every racial theory produced throughout the nineteenth century, much less to deal with every scholar who approached the question of human diversity. Instead, I make general references to eighteenth-century thought and explore the doctrines and theories that Brazilian intellectuals of the era cited most frequently.
2. The notion of "perfectibility" carries with it different meanings within different contexts. The tradition of the Enlightenment did not presuppose a linear and cumulative vision of history. Within the precepts of determinist literature of the nineteenth century one notes that the concept of perfectibility is composed of the notion of progress and leads to a fundamentally different perception. Nina Rodrigues, for example, uses the same term in 1894 even though he links it to the Western idea of progress: "Evolution presupposes in the diverse phases of the development of a race, a very different cultural capacity, albeit of growing perfectibility" (*Academic Journal of the Recife School of Law,* 1894: 83). We will have an opportunity to return to the theme when we analyze nineteenth-century evolutionist literature.
3. Claude Lévi-Strauss suggests the possibility of understanding Rousseau as "the first great ethnologist," citing the notion of "compassion" as a key. For more detail, see Lévi-Strauss, 1969.
4. We shall see how Rousseau seemed to personify egalitarianism in the Enlightenment and how this concept stirred debates among nineteenth-century scholars of race.
5. Beginning in 1857, the issue became more complex when Morel drew analogies between this concept and the "racio-cultural" profile of specific groups. According to Morel, once "racial decadence (degeneracy)" began, all hope for mental development was lost not only for the individual but also for the species (Morel, 1857).
6. In the writings of Buffon and De Pauw one can identify the point from which the thesis of American inferiority became entrenched, culminating in the scientific theories of the nineteenth century. With this new logic America no longer represented the model of perfection but rather the most backward and primitive phase of a reinvented evolution.
7. Baron Georges L. C. Cuvier (1769–1832) continued the systematizing begun by Carl von Linné (1701–89). In 1758 Linné (Carolus Linneaus) wrote his *Systema naturae,* perhaps the first great work on the classification

of living species. Present in this study is the notion of species, along with its morphological variants, and the concept of race.

8. Lévi-Strauss, in his book *The Elementary Structures of Kinship,* fully analyzed these cases. He showed how, instead of representing "faithful testimonies of precultural states," these persons were for the most part "cultural monstrosities" (children possessing congenital mental anomalies), and that their "defects" were not the result of their living in "precultural" circumstances.
9. According to Stephen Jay Gould (1981), the debate over the origin of human culture quickened the pulse of the era. Discussion flourished not only about a human chain but also about its missing links, whose transitional indicators had disappeared long ago over the course of humanity's long history.
10. In the eighteenth century the word *evolution* meant something different from what it does today. It was understood that in the first stages humanity was fundamentally diverse and that something converted man internally, little by little, into a civilized being. For Leibniz and other eighteenth-century philosophers, the notion that everything evolves implied a belief that from the very beginning everything is predisposed. This means that from this perspective nothing is reborn. Instead, that which exists becomes perfected. (See Radl, 1988.)
11. It is interesting to consider the rereadings of Rousseau. For the French philosopher the "noble savage" was a model, and "perfectibility" was a concept, neither of which presupposed a single possibility for human development. The interpretations of nineteenth-century ethnological schools reveal a telling evolutionist reading of Rousseau, one that sought links of continuity between "the noble savage" and a civilizing progress.
12. Gould draws attention to the contemporaneity of other theories of the period that also dealt with evolution. The reference in this case is not to Lamarck, who saw evolution not as a function of natural selection but rather as adaptation, but to Alfred Russel Wallace, who was about to publish his new conclusions when Darwin beat him to it (Gould, 1987: 13).
13. According to Gould, Darwin would never intentionally have used the term *evolution,* just the notions of "chance and natural selection." He adds that at various times Darwin would have denied any possible applicability of his theory to other realms of thought (1987: 14). Despite the opinion of this renowned North American scholar, one must remember that in later texts, such as *The Descent of Man,* Darwin explicitly revealed himself as a social evolutionist.
14. Eric J. Hobsbawm (1975: 261) points to the great popularity of these models. In Darwin's era, according to Hobsbawm, Darwin's works sold better than the Christian Bible.
15. The influence of Darwin's book on ethnography was immense. Following the first edition of *On the Origin of Species,* a series of works of the

so-called cultural evolutionist school were published, of which the following titles stand out: *Das Mutterrecht* [The matriarchate] (Bachofen, 1861); *Primitive Marriage* (McLennan, 1865); *The Origin of Civilization and the Primitive Condition of Man: Mental and Social Condition of Savages* (Lubbock, 1870); *Systems of Consanguinity and Affinity* (Morgan, 1870); *Ancient Society or Researches: In the Lines of Human Progress from Savagery through Barbarism to Civilization* (Morgan, 1877); and *Primitive Culture* (Tylor, 1878/1958).

16. It should be noted that on several occasions Darwin declared a belief in monogenism.
17. Much could be said about this school of thought, considered the first school of anthropology, despite its authors' rejection of the title. For the purposes of this chapter, it is sufficient to describe it summarily to introduce the analysis that follows. For an overview of the subject, see Stocking (1982), Leaf (1979), and Kuper (1973).
18. Many authors of the era reconciled analyses of geography with racial philosophies, and thus they produced studies whose primary themes surround the search for social constants. In Brazil, Euclides da Cunha's *Rebellion in the Backlands* [*Os sertões*] is an example of a work that reconciled the models of the two determinist schools. That da Cunha divided the work into "The Land," "The Man," and "The Struggle," and that he included a cast of cited authors, suggests the influence that the European determinist models exerted on him.
19. See Tzvetan Todorov, 1898: 115–16.
20. According to Nancy Stepan (1991: 28), in this era a series of eugenics societies appeared, including the following: German Society for Race Hygiene (1905); Eugenics Education Society in England (1907–8); Eugenics Record Office in the United States (1910); French Eugenics Society in Paris (1912). In addition, several international eugenics congresses were held during this time: London, 1912; New York, 1921 and 1923. Finally, an international federation of eugenics societies was founded in 1921, with Leonard Darwin (Charles's son) as its president (Stepan, 1991: 171).
21. In several countries at the end of the century a debate began over the correlation of "degeneracy and industrialization." For a fuller analysis of how this context reinforced the concept of degeneracy, see Stepan, 1991; Chamberlin, 1985.
22. It is interesting to note how this author overlooks the fact of internal migrations within Central Europe.
23. In his explanation of the hybridization process of corn, Darwin said precisely the opposite. He came to the conclusion that the hybrid product would always be more resistant than the purebred one.
24. Gobineau was the author of the most negative tracts on the "future of the species." He believed that racial blending led to "degeneracy" of the more noble "strains" and, therefore, to a decadent humankind.

25. The more radical social Darwinist theorists, such as Gobineau and Taine, strongly opposed Darwin's theory when they saw that interbreeding would lead to the "elimination of the species." This reading was not common at the time, however, since most of the social Darwinist scholars had not departed from the principles found in the work of Charles Darwin.
26. Gobineau, like a number of other authors who advanced the theory of polygenism, believed that the mestizo inherited only "bad" characteristics from each of the constituent races. In this manner the "degeneracy" proffered by this kind of theory would reveal itself.
27. Hannah Arendt notes that although Gobineau had little impact in Europe at the end of the century, in the 1930s, just before the outbreak of World War II, a revival of interest in his work became apparent.
28. Evolutionism and the social theories of Darwinism reached the height of their popularity from the 1870s to the 1930s. Following that period, the evolutionist paradigm came under severe criticism in practically all of the areas where it had been applied. In anthropology, the North American school of cultural relativism had the strongest reaction to the assumptions of evolutionism. From this critique emerged the foundations of the concept of cultural relativism.
29. These institutes were chosen on the basis of their intellectual production and the relevance of the discussion of race within them. Since the Academies of Letters were little given to the production of research, they were not chosen to represent the intellectual elite. The military schools initiated a moderately isolated debate as compared to the other scientific institutes, but they generally found the study of positivist philosophy their primary interest. Finally, it is necessary to clarify that my intent was not to include all authors and all themes present in the various institutes that are studied in the following chapters, but to understand certain institutes' primary roles in the racial debate that was then beginning to boil.

3. ETHNOGRAPHIC MUSEUMS IN BRAZIL: "CLAMS ARE CLANS, AND MOLLUSKS ARE MEN AS WELL"

1. The chapter's subtitle is a translation of the author's wry poetic observation of some of the chapter's content, expressed in ironic and alliterative Portuguese as "Polvo é povo, molusco também é gente." A literal translation of this line is "Octopus are a people, and mollusks are people too."
2. This is a term used by Stocking (1968) to refer to a group of turn-of-the-century naturalist travellers, primarily European but also American, who turned to distant countries in search of collections that would confirm their preconceived theories.
3. Without wishing to deny the links between the birth of anthropology and imperialist practice, one must also note the importance of these studies for

European governments. Nevertheless, the researchers endured recurring financial problems and other unmet needs, which suggests that their governments bestowed on them a relatively low level of prestige. (See Kuper, 1973: 121–49.)

4. The employment dates of the director-scientists known for the reforms they made in their respective institutions are relevant: João Batista Lacerda (1895–1915); Herman von Ihering (1894–1916); and Emilio Goeldi (1893–1907).
5. From this period date the creation of the Royal Press, the Central Library, the Royal Gardens, and the first schools of higher education meant to train surgeons and engineers.
6. The selection criteria for the position of section and subsection director were (1) Brazilian citizenship; (2) legal age; (3) good moral character; and (4) professional qualifications. Notice that the order was not random and that scientific competence was of lowest priority.
7. The directors of the National Museum were João da Silva Caldeira, Brother Custódio Alves Serrão (1821–47), and Brother Alemão (1866–74).
8. I analyzed *Archives of the National Museum* from its inaugural issue in 1876 through 1926. After 1926 the journal appeared sporadically, and at any rate those issues were published beyond the dates under study here.
9. The members of the board were Ladislau Netto (executive director of the museum and head of the second division of botany); J. J. Pizarro (museum secretary and head of the first division of anthropology and general and applied zoology); and João Batista Lacerda (in that era, associate director of the first division).
10. One finds this same perspective in other writings by Lacerda in volumes 3, 4, 6, and 12.
11. In the middle of the nineteenth century the Botocudos represented the very image of the savage Indian, and the matter of their humanity was a topic of wide discussion. There was a great deal of research conducted at the time about their possible "perfectibility" as well as their "ferocity," which, to these scholars, seemed unique and instinctive. (See Cunha, 1986: 169.)
12. It is useful to point out that Lacerda became renowned as one of the great defenders of the thesis of "whitening" and of the dilution of Indian and African characteristics within Brazilian society. Not only was he the first scientist to give an anthropology course in Brazil; he was also the only Brazilian representative to participate in the International Congress on Race. Besides being the director of the National Museum and the Biology Laboratory, he occupied other notable positions. He was president of the National Academy of Medicine of Rio de Janeiro and a member of the Society of Anthropology of Paris, Berlin, and Lisbon.
13. Herman von Ihering graduated in medicine and natural sciences in Germany. His early studies were linked to physical anthropology. Later von

Ihering turned to zoology, specializing in the study of mollusks. He took up residence in the state of Rio Grande do Sul in 1880, where he studied the flora, the fauna, and the indigenous peoples of the region. During that time he worked as a naturalist for the National Museum. He came to São Paulo in 1893 as a member of the State Geographical Commission.

14. I analyzed the *Journal of the São Paulo Museum* from 1895 to 1929. More detail about the journal contents is available in Schwarcz, quoted in Miceli, 1989.
15. With the change of administration and the arrival of Alfonso d'Escragnolle Taunay in 1916, this specialization was noted. Taunay stated that "until now the publication has been a journal of zoology" (*Journal of the São Paulo Museum,* 1918: 8), in a direct allusion to the preferences of the previous director.
16. Von Ihering's opinions were viewed as scandalous and generated reactions not only from the National Museum but also from other scientific institutions. According to Stauffer (1960), von Ihering's statements produced a heated debate that culminated in the creation of the *Serviço de Proteção ao Índio* [Indian Protection Service]. On this theme also see Lima (1986); Borerlli (1984).
17. John Monteiro (1992) details this episode more thoroughly, revealing how the dispute went far beyond ethnographic issues. It was a clash between the old, idealized image of the historical Tupi and that of the fierce Kaingang at a particular point in the creation of the history of São Paulo.
18. Together with the Baron of Rio Branco, in 1897–99 Emilio Goeldi helped solve the diplomatic issue that surrounded the demarcation of the border between French Guiana and Amapá. In homage to the Swiss naturalist's role in the building of the museum, in 1906 the name of the museum was changed to the Emilio Goeldi Museum of Pará. Goeldi remained head of the museum until March 22, 1907, at which time he returned to Switzerland. He died July 5, 1917.
19. At that moment, for naturalists the Amazonian region played a role similar to what the state of Bahia played for Africanists in the 1930s. See Massi, quoted in Miceli, 1989.
20. For a more detailed treatment of this matter, see Lima, 1986.
21. Von Ihering addressed the communications problems between the São Paulo Museum and the city several times. There were no streetcars, the roads were poorly maintained, and the population of São Paulo did not frequent the museum as much as the director had hoped. Despite the size of the province, museum attendance was considerably below that of the Emilio Goeldi Museum of Pará.
22. In this case Schwarzman refers as much to museums as to other contemporary centers such as the Instituto Agronômico de Campinas [Agricultural Institute of Campinas] and the Instituto Manguinhos [Manguinhos Institute].

23. At that time several institutes were conducting applied research. Examples of this were studies of the "coffee plantation plagues" conducted by the Agricultural Institute of Campinas and the work done on yellow fever at the Manguinhos Institute (Carmo, 1987; Stepan, 1981).
24. These circumstances were particularly evident in the case of the National Museum, where the impact of Dom Pedro was most significant.
25. In his book *Seixos rolados* [Smooth pebbles] (1927), Roquete-Pinto dedicated an entire chapter to the study of "the laws of eugenics," reflecting on their anthropological significance for Brazil.
26. See the *Bulletin of the National Academy of Medicine*, 96.
27. This theme will re-emerge in the chapter on medical schools, which treats in part the activities of medical professionals in the area of eugenics.
28. In 1930 the "Manifesto dos intelectuais brasileiros contra o racismo" [Manifesto of Brazilian intellectuals against racism] appeared. Signed by Roquete-Pinto, Gilberto Freyre, Artur Ramos, and others, the document represented the first public expression by Brazilian scientists opposed to racism. See Stepan, 1991: 169; Ramos, 1935: 177–80.

4. HISTORICAL AND GEOGRAPHICAL INSTITUTES: "GUARDIANS OF THE OFFICIAL STORY"

1. Another version of this chapter can be found in the *Cadernos IDESP* [Notes of the São Paulo Institute of Economic, Social, and Political Research], 1987. While the previous publication focuses on the definition of institutional profile, this chapter seeks to convey the significance of the debates surrounding the racial issue in the Brazilian institutes of history and geography.
2. There were at least twenty different historical and geographical institutes scattered around the country, and their moments of inception are as varied as their locations. Many of them began operations at the end of the nineteenth century or in the first decades of the twentieth century, and some of them were created more recently, for example the Historical and Geographical Institute of Juiz de Fora, which began operation in 1965.
3. A complete list of the twenty-seven founding members of the Brazilian Historical and Geographical Institute can be found in volume 74 of the *Journal of the Historical and Geographical Institute of Brazil* (1911: 282–83).
4. From 1849 to 1889 the emperor presided over and participated in sessions of the Historical and Geographical Institute of Brazil.
5. Le Goff (1976) draws attention to the model of history characteristic of the nineteenth century, a history not only concerned with the enumeration of events, but also engaged in the patriotic exaltation of the nation.
6. For more information, see the regulations of the Brazilian Historical and Geographical Institute or Olegário Herculano's "O Instituto Histórico e

Geográfico Brasileiro," in the *Journal of the Historical and Geographical Institute of Brazil* 60, part 1, 1897.

7. The criteria that the Historical and Geographical Institute of Brazil employed contrasted with those of the other scientific institutes. The Goeldi Museum, for example, revealed among its most prominent regulations notably different policies: "(1) to have studied or had instruction in the natural sciences at a particularly distinguished institution; (2) to have studied deeply within one's specialization; (3) to have proven scientific competence" (*Bulletin of the Emilio Goeldi Museum of Pará,* 1897: 24).
8. Among the less celebrated names the following stand out: Manuel Ferreira de Araújo (1846–51), who dedicated himself to civil service and public education; Canon Caetano Fernandes Pinheiro (1859–76), who was a priest; José Ribeiro de Souza Fontes (1876–80), a chaired professor of medicine; and Duarte Moreira de Azevedo (1880–86), who had degrees in literature and medicine and was the author of several biographies.
9. One notes this same perspective in texts by João Batista Lacerda published in volumes 3, 4, 6, and 12.
10. Joaquim Manuel de Macedo was a physician, but he scarcely practiced his profession. His greatest efforts were as a novelist, playwright, poet, and orator. But it was in his capacity as professor of history at the Colégio Pedro II, as well as institute secretary (1852–56) and active orator (1857–81) of the Historical and Geographical Institute of Brazil that he is relevant to this study. He wrote a historical essay, published in the institute's journal (vol. 25, 1862), titled "Dúvidas sobre alguns pontos da história brasileira" [Doubts about some moments of brazilian history]. Beyond this unique study, his other documents consist of necrological papers and speeches, as well as biographies of his institute colleagues. According to José Honório Rodrigues, Macedo was always a liberal conservative, whether as a historian or as a politician. Like Francisco Adolfo de Varnhagen, whom he claimed as a mentor, Joaquim Manuel de Macedo remained faithful to the monarchy and to the status quo.
11. Having dedicated himself to public service, Max Fleiuss entered the Historical and Geographical Institute of Brazil on August 3, 1900, when he presented his work "Os centenários do Brazil" [Brazilian centennials]. In addition to being responsible for the papers of the "anniversary sections" and innumerable announcements within the institute's journal, Fleiuss undertook the reform of the position of secretary, as well as the recataloging of books, maps, and other library objects.
12. Taunay had a degree in letters from the Colégio Pedro II, a degree in mathematics from the Central School, and in 1864 he graduated in engineering from the Military School. When Brazil went to war with Paraguay, he formed part of the expeditionary force that was to attack upper Paraguay. He remained on active duty, together with the heroic Brazilian commander Caxias, until 1870. After the conflict ended he became a professor in the

Military School and later went into politics. In this capacity he was president of the province of Paraná and senator of Santa Catarina. With the advent of the republic, he retired from public life.

13. After 1864 the journal was printed in two distinct parts. It changed titles several times, appearing first as the *Revista do Instituto Historico e Geographico Brasileiro* [Journal of the Historical and Geographical Institute of Brazil], then as the *Revista Trimensal* [Trimonthly journal], or even as the *Revista do Instituto Historico, Etnographico e Geographico* [Journal of the Brazilian Historical, Ethnographical, and Geographical Institute], to reflect the time when the institute had joined the term *ethnographical* to its name.
14. I will analyze the uninterrupted series of articles from the *Journal of the Historical and Geographical Institute of Brazil* between 1838 and 1938, during which period 109 volumes were published, with increasingly diminished frequency. Until 1864 four volumes appeared annually. After that date the journal became biannual, and then in 1933, annual. During its first century of existence, the institute also published thirty-three special editions that were dedicated to outstanding personalities and episodes from Brazilian history. Written in a laudatory style, these special editions exemplified the patriotic posture of the Historical and Geographical Institute of Brazil. They also revealed what it believed to be the historian's mission, which was "to awaken the love of country, courage, constancy, fidelity, prudence, and, in general, all civic virtues" (*Journal of the Historical and Geographical Institute of Brazil,* 1916: 629).
15. One should note that the same classification system was developed by Poppino (1953: 307–23). My tables summarize the analysis of the three institutions.
16. The naturalist Karl Friedrich Philipp von Martius was born in Erlangen, Bavaria, in 1794 and died in Munich in 1868. A doctor of medicine, he explored Brazil from 1817 to 1820. With his colleague Johan Baptiste von Spix, he undertook expeditions that yielded important studies on Brazilian geography, botany, and zoology, as well as accounts of local indigenous ethnography.
17. Silvio Romero, who began his association with the Historical and Geographical Institute of Brazil in 1890, provided subsequent interpretations, which I will later reveal as parallel to von Martius's model.
18. The Archeological and Geographical Institute of Pernambuco and the São Paulo Historical and Geographical Institute appear in this chapter both for purposes of comparison and to offer a more inclusive institutional profile.
19. See Levine, 1980.
20. See Cabral de Mello, 1984: 15; Eisenberg, 1974.
21. This last characteristic of the Archeological and Geographical Institute of Pernambuco is inconsistent with the pattern of the other institutes studied in this chapter. Whether in Rio de Janeiro or São Paulo, an applicant for an institutional vacancy would present his own writing or work for scrutiny.

22. According to Gilberto Freyre, the bachelor's degree was the equivalent of a "'title of nobility' . . . the stamp of legitimacy awarded by a society willing to bestow its foremost esteem on the products of a ritualistic higher educational system, with the Faculdade at the pinnacle" (quoted in Levine, 1978: 63). We will have an opportunity to return to this theme in the next chapter.
23. In the opinion of Cabral de Mello, Oliveira Lima exaggerated when he attributed the creation of the Archeological and Geographical Institute of Pernambuco solely to a desire to perpetuate the tradition of 1817. According to the author, "the goal was first to preserve the historical tradition of the province in the face of Rio's imperialistic historiography" (Cabral de Mello, 1986: 63).
24. Topics such as "the identification of the house Vieira had lived in while in Coimbra, or the location of his grave, the boundaries of the Arraial Novo and the São Jorge Fort" reveal this tendency.
25. Some intellectuals who left their state, such as Oliveira Lima (1865–1928), who retained only the status of a correspondent member of the institute, ceased working exclusively with these local themes. The activities of Manuel de Oliveira Lima as a diplomat and associate with the Brazilian Academy of Letters are well known in Brazil. In his books he slowly withdrew from issues directly linked to the state of Pernambuco and placed himself at the head of new polemics far from the city of his birth.
26. The solution indicated by the Archeological and Geographical Institute of Pernambuco closely resembles the interpretation adopted by the Recife School of Law. There the acceptance of a "good miscegenation," tempered by a constant influx of white blood, was also grist for debates. See the next chapter for additional information.
27. Articles pertaining to Pernambucan geography and its regional implications were also of concern. Border problems with Bahia, physical characteristics of the region, and the annexation of the island of Fernando de Noronha made up 97 percent of the studies on geography. All of the articles on Brazilian geography, however, accounted for only 17 percent of the journal's total works.
28. While Antônio Pizza and Estevan Leão Bouroul, members of the local museum, made up the new board of directors of the São Paulo Historical and Geographical Institute, Herman von Ihering, director of the São Paulo museum, led a commission of members charged with organizing a public campaign to raise funds for the new institute.
29. This refers to the dispute between the São Paulo Museum and the National Museum, discussed in the previous chapter.
30. See, among others, Morse, 1970; Love, 1980.
31. According to Taunay, "this was the first of all the similar Brazilian associations to enjoy such splendid resources, and so fortunate despite its brief existence" (*Journal of the São Paulo Historical and Geographical Institute,* 1933: 268).

32. This review analyzes 383 articles from the *Journal of the São Paulo Historical and Geographical Institute*. The articles make up twenty-eight volumes, spanning the years 1895–1930, and are organized here by samplings consistent with those selected from the other institutes.
33. It is significant that 28 percent of all the articles found treat themes relating to São Paulo.
34. At the São Paulo Historical and Geographical Institute other themes associated with state geography, such as the railroads, the flora and fauna, and the riverways, were topics of consideration. The influence of engineers and geographers in this regard was considerable. An example of the specialized professionals who engineered a "modernizing" project for the state was Orville A. Derby, who also participated in the Geological Commission and the São Paulo Museum. For more information on the role of these persons, see Silva, 1984.
35. As is clearly seen below, the choice of biographers in the São Paulo institute was not casual. João Monteiro, the celebrated master of law and oratory, wrote the biography of the first president of the São Paulo institute, Cesário Motta. Taunay celebrated the second president of the institute, Manuel A. Duarte. Taunay himself inspired at least five homages, among which stand out those written by Tito Lívio and Luís Teodoro Brito. Plínio Ayrosa wrote the biography of the historian Theodoro Sampaio, while Afonso de Freitas, the journal's most prolific scholar, wrote distinguished biographies of persons such as José Torres de Oliveira, then the president of the institute, and even Ricardo Vampré, master of the São Paulo Academy of Law.
36. The chapter on schools of law will revisit this theme.
37. The motto of the Historical and Geographical Institute of Brazil, "*Pacifica Scientiae Occupatio*," reflects this tone held in common by all the other Brazilian historical institutes.
38. At this moment, for the imperial state the question of territorial unity was fundamental. This was not only because of the Latin American political context, where the Brazilian monarchy was surrounded by numerous republics, but also because of internal revolts based on regional distinctions. See Mattos, 1987.
39. Even with the advent of the republic and the alliances with new political representatives, the ties that bound the Historical and Geographical Institute of Brazil to the Old Regime still held:

    > Unfortunately there is still a faction, although tiny, that imagines the glorious imperial past incompatible with the republic. As if it were possible to eliminate from the pages of Brazilian history that great period of peace, prosperity, harmony and honesty. And the progress of the republic? they ask us. But that very progress had its roots in the old regime, and the first duty of a good patriot is to adore the present and

not disdain the past. Tradition instructs, consoles and inspires." (*Journal of the Historical and Geographical Institute of Brazil,* 1941: 57)

It is also interesting to recall that the Carioca institute was responsible for the idea, which became concrete during the presidency of Getúlio Vargas, of transferring the mortal remains of Dom Pedro II from Portugal to Brazil.

40. Heloísa Maria Bertol Domingues points out how the Dom Pedro II School, the Public Archives, and the Historical and Geographical Institute of Brazil were all created in 1838. All of these institutions supported a strong, centralized government (1986: 44).
41. This image was constructed primarily to underscore the difference between itself and the Carioca institute, whose "death-bed republicanism" was considered dubious.

5. SCHOOLS OF LAW, OR THE NATION'S CHOSEN

1. I do not intend to offer here a full history of these two Brazilian law schools, but rather to trace their profiles in the broadest sense to enable an analysis of how racial theories influenced intellectual life. For a fuller view of the roots of the schools see, among others, Vampré, 1924/1975; Adorno, 1988; Nogueira, 1977; Bevilacqua, 1977; Neto, 1969.
2. Until the beginning of the twentieth century, the great Brazilian landholding families were well known for the orchestration of their offspring's destinies. While the firstborn would lead a life tied to the land and agriculture, the others would pursue careers within the Church or in law. The social profile of the schools' student body was not a casual assemblage either. Particularly during the schools' first fifty years, it was defined by direct links to the elite of agricultural exporters.
3. The previous chapter on historical institutes includes more detailed references about Pernambuco's record of activities.
4. The origins of the students who entered the school in 1828 reveal the institution's importance for the country's northern provinces. Of the forty students accepted, twenty-seven were from Pernambuco, two from Alagoas, three from Ceará, three from Rio Grande do Norte, and two from Bahia. Only one came from Rio de Janeiro, and two were from Portugal.
5. For information on the work prior to this period, see Bevilacqua, 1977; Rabello, 1967.
6. Candido, 1988; Ventura, 1991.
7. In his analysis of Graça Aranha's work, José Paulo Paes (1992) points out that one cannot characterize *Canaan* as a typical naturalistic novel, despite the milieu from which it emerged. It seems correct to say that the book

reflects a broadened view of the uses of literature rather than a rigid adherence to the tenets of literary naturalism.

8. Later in this chapter we will return to the theoretical incentive, championed by the Recife School of Law, that opened the doors to white and European immigration.
9. Recall Silvio Romero's mistaken, derogatory critiques of Machado de Assis, alluded to in Chapter 1.
10. In *Evolucionismo e o Positivismo no Brasil* [Evolutionism and positivism in Brazil] (1895), Silvio Romero highlighted the significance of evolutionist ideas for national concerns, and he attacked what he called "the exteriority of positivist thinking."
11. See Ventura, 1988.
12. See Candido, 1978; Rabello, 1967; Bevilacqua, 1977; Ventura, 1988; Cruz Costa, 1967.
13. It is interesting to consider the power of Romero's interpretation within the Recife School of Law. Although also attached to the school were high-profile persons such as Joaquim Nabuco, who practically ignored discussions of race, their influence was minimal in terms of their effect on the group's identity. Since Nabuco's abolitionism did not appear among the journal's themes, it was as if issues of such immediate national political reality escaped the intellectual curiosity of these persons. On the other hand, after the freedom of the slaves and the work of the abolitionists nearly ended, it was precisely at that time that the Recife scholars helped ignite the nation's racial issue.
14. It is only in the first number that the articles devoted to criminal law amount to 50 percent of the whole.
15. Clovis Bevilacqua was born in Viçosa in 1859 and died in Rio de Janeiro in 1944. He entered the Recife School of Law in 1878, at a time when the influence of Tobias Barreto was enormous. He became a professor of philosophy in the RSL in 1889 and took over the studies of comparative legislation in 1890. He entered the Brazilian Academy of Letters in 1897 and from 1906 to 1934 he worked for the ministry of foreign relations.
16. Works on medical law would appear with greater frequency only in the 1920s, when they assumed the function previously filled by articles on criminal law.
17. Studies in the Italian school of criminology concluded that the physical and anthropological factors exerted more influence than the social.
18. Since a racial discourse did not occupy these scholars, I have taken a more comparative than comprehensive look at the São Paulo School of Law. The analysis and conclusions refer primarily to materials found in its journal and are limited, therefore, to the period extending from 1892 through 1930. A fuller analysis of this school can be found in Adorno, 1988; Dulles, 1984; Morse, 1970; Schwartzman, 1979; Vampré, 1975; and others.
19. For more information on this matter, see Adorno, 1988.

20. The first class of students, who registered in 1828, reveals an obvious regional imbalance: São Paulo, eighteen students; Rio de Janeiro, ten; Minas Gerais, four; Bahia, two (*Journal of the São Paulo School of Law,* 1893).
21. Sevcenko (1983) analyzes the figure of the "missionary intellectual," who at that moment was venturing forth from a more protected environment of intellectual production in order to break into newspapers and other public spheres of debate. Through a close analysis of authors Lima Barreto and Euclides da Cunha, the author carefully follows the correlation of the images of the intellectual and the journalist during the first republic.
22. Despite Rui Barbosa's assertion that "North America and Europe are watching us," it was the Brazilian intellectuals who were looking to them as examples of civilization.
23. Because of the diverse range of articles found in the São Paulo School of Law journal, it was hard to analyze them as a whole. I opted for texts that include the racial issue as a theme in order to outline their characteristics, especially insofar as they contrast with essays in the Recife School of Law journal.
24. "Public Medicine is called to play a role in civilized societies . . . with a view toward creating a healthful society" (*Journal of the São Paulo School of Law,* 1914: 11).
25. It is interesting to compare the journals of the respective institutions. While the *Academic Journal of the Recife School of Law* featured jurists, journalists, men of letters, and politicians, the *Journal of the São Paulo School of Law* showed a preference for high-profile politicians. Of all this journal's biographies, 80 percent fell under this category.
26. It is possible to trace parallels between this position and the one that von Ihering developed in his journal. He also seemed to separate theory from practice. That is, while in the journal only articles of proven scientific importance were published, in the newspapers von Ihering publicized his opinions on more immediate and local realities, such as in the case of the Kaingang Indians.

6. SCHOOLS OF MEDICINE OR HOW TO CURE AN AILING NATION

1. As Mariza Corrêa ably demonstrates, Raimundo Nina Rodrigues's activities had a marked influence on the Bahia School of Medicine. Nina Rodrigues received his diploma from the Bahia School of Medicine in 1888, and in that same year he began lecturing as an adjunct professor. He was transferred to the department of "hygiene and medical law" in 1891, on the occasion of the school's educational reform, and, following the retirement of Professor Virgílio Damázio, he was promoted to distinguished professor, or

catedrático. He was an ardent defender of medical law, and by the 1890s he was the most renowned professional working in this area.

2. The unusual composition of this council, made up of congressional representatives and nurses, clearly reflects the efforts of politicians to assume a degree of control in scientific matters, including the research agenda and other activities of physicians.
3. At that time there was a clear distinction between surgery and clinical practice, also called physic or medical practice. See Giffoni, 1950.
4. One of the first documents about the Bahian school declares that the new center would function "for the welfare of the public's health, in order that there be able and expert professors who, combining medical science with the practical knowledge of surgery, might be useful to those who live in Brazil" (Aragão, 1923: 23).
5. Further details on the early statutes of the Bahian surgical course are available in Santos Filho (1947: 198–99).
6. In 1811 the government commissioned Dr. Vicente Navarro de Andrade, a surgeon who had recently arrived from Europe, to develop a new program of surgical studies. Perhaps because of the many significant changes that it would have made, the proposal was never adopted.
7. Further information on this topic is available in Santos Filho, 1947: 295, and Schwartzman, 1979: 68.
8. This regulation provoked a great deal of discontent, but it remained in effect until Dom Pedro I revoked it. His action gave the two academy presidents the right to grant certifications so that the licensees could practice their specialities.
9. In 1829, for example, only seventeen students enrolled.
10. The new curriculum also foresaw the growth and recognition of the value of hygiene as a subject. At the end of the century hygiene would become one of the primary areas of research, especially in the Rio de Janeiro School of Medicine.
11. Santos Filho lists fifty-five medical periodicals in this period, not counting journals linked with centers of homeopathy (1947: 264).
12. The *Medical Gazette*, a monthly periodical created in 1866, remained active until 1930. Its publication was interrupted from 1870 to 1871, 1874 to 1875, and in 1880. *Medical Brazil*, a weekly journal founded in 1887 and linked to the Rio de Janeiro School of Medicine, has never missed an issue.
13. There is a more inclusive series of analyses of Brazilian medical history. My intention has been simply to contextualize the production of medical scholarship for the period beginning in the 1870s. For more information on the topic, see, among others, Santos Filho, 1947; Freire Costa, 1979; Machado, 1978; Lobo, 1969.
14. This same group of doctors appointed Professor Pacífico Pereira as director of the publication in its second year; he remained in this position for fifty years.

15. For more detail, see Machado, 1978, and Freire Costa, 1979.
16. With the exception of Silva Lima, who did research on an illness called *anhum,* there are few original pieces of Bahian research in this area.
17. Nina Rodrigues published several studies on the theme, some of the most notable titles of which are the following: *As raças humanas e a responsabilidade penal* [Human races and penal responsibility] (1894); "A medicina legal no Brasil" [Medical law in Brazil] (1895); "O problema médico-jurídico" [The medical-juridical problem] (1898); "Liberdade profissional na medicina" [Professional freedom in medicine] (1899); "Manual de autopsia médico-legal" [A medical-legal manual of autopsy] (1901); "Os progressos da medicina legal no Brasil" [Progress in Brazil in the area of medical law] (1902); "Des formes de l'hymen et de leur rôle dans la rupture de cette membrane" [The anatomy of the hymen and its role in the membrane's rupture] (1900). For further information on this author and his work, see Corrêa, 1983.
18. The semblance of a curse surrounded the publication history of *Africans in Brazil*. According to Homero Pires, who was responsible for the 1933 edition, "the book brought misfortune to anyone who touched it" (Rodrigues, 1933/1988: 9). The edition was well along when Nina Rodrigues died in Paris in 1906. Oscar Freire, his most esteemed disciple, also died unexpectedly while working on the book. It was only years later, with the collaboration of Nina Rodrigues's wife, that the materials from *Africans in Brazil* returned to the hands of his faculty colleagues, and the book was first published in 1933 after lengthy study of the materials.
19. This text also introduced another publication of the Bahian school: the *Journal of Courses of the Bahia School of Medicine* (1904). It should be made clear that in Table 18 the percentage of articles on medical law (5 percent) conceals the real importance of the subject. From 1900 to 1915 the theme appeared in the journal with exceptional frequency. During this short period, it published seventy articles on medical law, constituting 42 percent of all articles.
20. The reference here is to the book *As Raças Humanas e a Responsabilidade Penal no Brasil* [Human races and penal responsibility in Brazil], published in 1894, in which Nina Rodrigues advocates a code better adapted to the "mental and evolutionary specifics" of the various races that make up the population of Brazil.
21. Until 1928 the journal had the same owner-director, the same printer, and the same typographer.
22. *Medical Brazil* continued under the control of Azevedo Sodré's family after his death in 1928. Its directorship passed to Drs. Fábio Sodré and Luiz Sodré, both sons of the former owner-director.
23. Until the 1930s most of the articles on medical law show a debt to the studies completed by the Nina Rodrigues School. When Afrânio Peixoto was contracted for a professorship in legal medicine in 1922, the links between

them became even stronger. For further information on this theme, see Corrêa, 1983.

24. At the Fourth Latin American Congress Oswaldo Cruz's colleagues honored him by presenting him with a gold medallion in recognition of his service to the Brazilian community. Cruz was a member of the Brazilian Academy of Letters, and several monuments were erected in his honor. So much renown within scientific circles did not, however, prevent Cruz from becoming very unpopular as a result of his political campaigns.
25. An analysis of the theses defended during this period is revealing. In 1900, of the thirty dissertations approved, twenty dealt with themes pertaining to hygiene.
26. Sectors within the political opposition took advantage of these public reactions to promote their own interests. The revolt saw two distinct political groups emerge: the first consisted of groups influenced by the first military phase of the republican government, generically called Jacobins or radicals; the other consisted of monarchists deposed by the new regime. For further treatment of this subject, see Sevcenko, 1984; Melo Franco, 1973; Fausto, 1977a; Carone, 1971.
27. It is also interesting to point out that the Liga de Higiene Mental [The League of Mental Hygiene], was founded in 1922. Among the scientists who were prominent members and residents of Rio de Janeiro were Juliano Moreira, Miguel Couto, Carlos Chagas, Edgar Roquete-Pinto, and, after 1929, Afrânio Peixoto, and Henrique Rocha.
28. Letícia Vidor Reis (1993) demonstrates how another activity became institutionalized and was transformed into a national sporting practice. This was *capoeira,* a form of ritualized dance and/or mock fight, said to have begun among the colonial slaves, in which two persons engage each other with well-timed and carefully placed sweeping kicks, cartwheels, and any other manner of gymnastic prowess to entertain devotees of both dance and martial arts.
29. May 1 is, of course, Labor Day, and July 14 commemorates the foundation of the city of São Paulo.
30. Renato Kehl founded the *Boletim de Eugenia* [Bulletin of Eugenics] in 1929 and the *Commissão Brasileira de Eugenia* [Brazilian Commission on Eugenics] in 1931. He became known during this time for his public praise of German eugenicist politics, which foresaw the day when nations would have control of their people's reproduction. For more on this topic, see Stepan, 1991: 157–58.
31. As mentioned before, while president of the Congress, Roquete-Pinto, who was also director of the National Museum, played the important role of opposing the medical interpretation. He defended the thesis that the problem with eugenics in Brazil was not a question "of race but of hygiene." See Stepan, 1991: 161.
32. For more information on this topic, see Corrêa, 1983.

33. An analysis of biographies found in *Medical Brazil* reveals that 65 percent of the physicians attained important political positions as representatives, senators, councilmen, and even mayors. In Bahia one finds physicians functioning as politicians, journalists, and writers.

7. BETWEEN THE POISON AND THE ANTIDOTE: SOME FINAL THOUGHTS

1. This was the same author who pointed out that in Brazil there was "a singular adherence to individual values shaped by one's home life." This characteristic would render each person indifferent to the common law if it was ever at variance with his own emotional affinities (Holanda, 1936/1979: 113).
2. Analyzing the most contemporary impasses of the Western urban revolution, Richard Sennett also notes that "confusion has arisen between public life and intimate life; people are working out in terms of personal feelings public matters which properly can be dealt with only through codes of impersonal meaning" (1978: 5).
3. Drawing on Rousseauian philosophy, Richard Morse shows, however, how liberalism also tended to suppress the notion of individuality and uniqueness:

> Rousseau's argument cut athwart the liberal presumption of society as an aggregation of self-made men divided into colliding interest groups. . . . Where general interest is a calculus by experts, "common good" becomes a misnomer, for people no longer share a common life. Shared experience reduces to the capacity for private response to an alien environment. (1989: 160)

4. Gilberto Freyre (1900–1987) is best known for his studies of cultural life in colonial Brazil. For years Brazilians and foreign readers enjoyed the rather romantic notions of his *Casa grande e senzala* (1933) [*The Masters and the Slaves* (1946/1986)]. In fact, his ideas were among those that helped construct the myth of racial democracy in Brazil.
5. Many studies have analyzed the relevance of Freyre's work and his cultural relativist interpretation of the country. Having studied at Columbia University, in New York, he was heavily influenced by Franz Boas and his critique of scientific racism. For more information on this topic see, among others, Skidmore, 1976; Leite, 1983; Freston, 1987.
6. Stepan shows how intellectuals supported Monteiro Lobato's theoretical shift and resumed the debate. Kehl, a physician, declared that Jeca Tatu (a character name that became synonymous with "hillbilly" or "rustic") would become a Jeca Bravo (or "wildman"). On the other hand, Fernando de

Azevedo concluded that Lobato's character, together with the *bandeirantes,* or colonial expeditionaries, would be a symbol of the greatness of the State of São Paulo. On this topic see Stepan, 1991: 157, and Skidmore, 1976.

7. *Zé Carioca* can be translated as "Joe Carioca" or "Joe Rio." He is a caricature of what has affectionately come to represent the fun-loving, rather self-indulgent, clever resident of Rio de Janeiro. The *malandro* is a roguish character who lives by his wits, and through his persistent reappearance in popular culture he has become a recognizable Brazilian stereotype.

GLOSSARY: TRANSLATIONS OF INSTITUTION AND PUBLICATION NAMES

INSTITUTIONS	
ENGLISH TRANSLATION	PORTUGUESE NAME
Archeological and Geographical Institute of Pernambuco	Instituto Archeologico e Geographico Pernambucano
Bahia School of Medicine	Faculdade de Medicina da Bahia
Emilio Goeldi Museum of Pará	Museu Paraense Emilio Goeldi
Historical and Geographical Institute of Brazil	Instituto Historico e Geographico Brasileiro
National Museum or Royal Museum	Museu Nacional or Museu Real
Recife School of Law	Faculdade de Direito do Recife
Rio de Janeiro School of Medicine	Faculdade de Medicina do Rio de Janeiro
São Paulo Historical and Geographical Institute	Instituto Historico e Geographico de São Paulo
São Paulo Museum or Ypiranga Museum	Museu Paulista or Museu do Ypiranga
São Paulo School of Law	Faculdade de Direito de São Paulo

JOURNALS AND NEWSPAPERS	
ENGLISH TRANSLATION	**PORTUGUESE NAME**
Archives of the National Museum	*Archivos do Museu Nacional*
Academic Journal of the Recife School of Law	*Revista Academica da Faculdade de Direito do Recife*
Bulletin of the Emilio Goeldi Museum of Pará	*Boletim do Museu Paraense Emilio Goeldi*
Journal of the Archeological and Geographical Institute of Pernambuco	*Revista do Instituto Archeologico e Geographico Pernambucano*
Journal of the Historical and Geographical Institute of Brazil	*Revista do Instituto Historico e Geographico Brasileiro*
Journal of the São Paulo Historical and Geographical Institute	*Revista do Instituto Historico e Geographico de São Paulo*
Journal of the São Paulo Museum	*Revista do Museu Paulista*
Journal of the São Paulo School of Law	*Revista da Faculdade de Direito de São Paulo*
Medical Brazil	*Brazil Medico*
Medical Gazette of Bahia	*Gazeta Medica da Bahia*
The Province of São Paulo	*A Provincia de São Paulo*
The São Paulo Post	*Correio Paulistano*
The State of São Paulo	*O Estado de São Paulo*

BIBLIOGRAPHY

PERIODICALS

A Provincia de S. Paulo (São Paulo) 1875–1889.
Archivos do Museu Nacional (Rio de Janeiro) 1–23, 1876–1926.
Atas da Faculdade de Direito de Recife (Recife) 1870–1930.
Boletim da Academia Nacional de Medicina (Rio de Janeiro) 94–96, 1928–30.
Boletim do Museu Nacional Paraense de História Natural (Belém) 1–10, 1894–1949.
Boletim do Museu Paraense Emilio Goeldi (Belém) 1–2, 1894.
Brazil Medico (Rio de Janeiro) 6–64, 1892–1930.
Correio Paulistano (São Paulo) 1870–1930.
Gazeta Medica da Bahia (Salvador) 9–60, 1881–1930.
O Estado de S. Paulo (São Paulo) 1890–1930.
Revista Academica da Faculdade de Direito de Recife (Recife) 1–37, 1891–1929.
Revista da Faculdade de Direito de São Paulo (São Paulo) 1–26, 1893–1930.
Revista do Instituto Archeologico e Geographico Pernambucano (Recife) 1–30, 1863–1930.
Revista do Instituto Historico e Geographico Brasileiro (Rio de Janeiro) 1–92, 1839–1930.
Revista do Instituto Historico e Geographico de São Paulo (São Paulo) 1–28, 1895–1930.
Revista do Museu Paulista (São Paulo) 1–16, 1895–1929.

BOOKS AND ARTICLES

Adams, William. *The Modern Voyager and Traveller*. London: Henry Fisher and Son, 1832.

Adorno, Sergio. *Os aprendizes do poder. O bacharelismo liberal na política brasileira*. São Paulo: Brasiliense, 1988.

Agassiz, Louis. *A Journey in Brazil*. Boston: n.p., 1868.

Aimard, Gustave. *Le Brésil nouveau*. Paris: E. Dentú editeur, 1888.

Antonil, André João. *Cultura e opulência do Brasil*. São Paulo: Nacional, 1967.

Aragão, G. M. S. *Medicina na Bahia*. Bahia: Imprensa Oficial, 1923.

Aranha, Graça. *Canãa*. Rio de Janeiro: Livraria Garnier, 1912.

Arendt, Hannah. *The Origins of Totalitarianism*. 1951. Reprint, with added prefaces, New York: Harcourt Brace Jovanovich, 1973.

Aristotle. *Os pensadores*. São Paulo: Abril Cultural, 1978.

Arruda, Maria Arminda do Nascimento. "A temática regional: considerações historiográficas." *Anais do Museu Paulista* 35 (1986).

Assis, Joaquim Maria Machado de. "O alienista." In *Papéis avulsos*. 1882. Reprint, Rio de Janeiro: Livraria Garnier, 1989.

———. "A evolução." In *Relíquias da casa velha*. Rio de Janeiro: Livraria Garnier, 1990.

Azevedo, Fernando. "O segredo da maratona. Anais de eugenia." *Revista do Brasil* (1919).

———. *As ciências sociais no Brasil*. São Paulo: Melhoramentos, 1956.

Bachofen, Johann Jakob. *Das Mutterrecht*. N.p.: 1861.

Barreto, Lima. *Diário íntimo*. São Paulo: Brasiliense, 1956.

Beiguelman, Paula. *A formação do povo no complexo cafeeiro*. São Paulo: Pioneira, 1977.

Bevilacqua, Clovis. *História da Faculdade de Direito do Recife*. 2d ed. Brasília: IHL, 1977.

Boas, Franz. *Anthropology and Modern Life*. New York: Dover Publications, Inc., 1986.

Bonfim, Manoel. *A América Latina: Males de origem*. Rio de Janeiro: Top Books, 1993.

Borelli, Silvia Helena Simões, ed. *Índios do Estado de São Paulo: resistência e transfiguração*. São Paulo: Yankatu, 1984.

Borie, Jean. *Mithologies de l'hérédité au XIXe sièle*. Paris: Éditions Galilée, 1981.

Bosi, Alfredo. *História concisa da literatura brasileira*. São Paulo: Cultrix, 1972.

Bourdieu, Pierre. "Campo intelectual e projecto criador." In *Problemas do estruturalismo,* edited by Jean Pouillon. Rio de Janeiro: Zahar, 1968.

———. *Leçon sur la leçon*. Paris: Les Éditions de Minuit, 1982.

———. *Pierre Bourdieu: sociologia*. São Paulo: Ática, 1983.

Broca, Brito. *A vida literária no Brasil—1900*. Rio de Janeiro: MEC, 1956.

Broca, Paul. *On the Phenomena of Hybridity in the Genus Homo*. London: C. Carter Blake, 1864.

Brookshaw, David. *Raça e cor na literatura brasileira*. Porto Alegre: Mercado Aberto, 1983.

Bruno, Ernani da Silva. *Tradições e reminiscências da cidade de São Paulo*. 2d ed. Rio de Janeiro: José Olympio, 1954.

Buckle, Henry Thomas. *History of Civilization in England*. New York: D. Appleton and Company, 1865.

Buffon, Comte Georges-Louis Leclerc de. *Oeuvres complètes*. Paris: Pouvrat Frères, 1834.

———. *De l'homme*. Paris: Maspero, 1971.

Cabral de Mello, Evaldo. *O Norte agrário e o Império*. Rio de Janeiro: Nova Fronteira, 1984.

———. *Rubro veio, o imaginário da restauração pernambucana*. Rio de Janeiro: Nova Fronteira, 1986.

Candido, Antonio. *Formação da literatura brasileira*. São Paulo: Martins Fontes, 1959.

———. *Silvio Romero: teoria, crítica e história literária*. São Paulo: Edusp, 1978.

———. *O método crítico de Silvio Romero*. São Paulo: Edusp, 1988.

———. *O discurso e a cidade*. 1970. Reprint, São Paulo: Duas Cidades, 1993.

Carmo, Vitú do. *Chão fecundo: 100 anos de história do Instituto Agronômico de Campinas*. São Paulo: Agroceres, 1987.

Carone, Edgard. *A República Velha—evolução política*. São Paulo: Difel, 1971.

Carvalho, Horácio de. *O chromo (estudo de temperamentos)*. Rio de Janeiro: Typographia de Carlos Gaspar da Silva, 1888.

Carvalho, José Murilo de. *A construção da ordem. A elite político-imperial*. Rio de Janeiro: Campus, 1980.

———. *A formação das almas. O imaginário da República no Brasil*. São Paulo: Companhia das Letras, 1990.

Chacon, Vamireh. *Da Escola de Recife ao código civil (Artur Orlando e sua geração)*. Rio de Janeiro: Simões, 1969.

Chalhoub, Sidney. *Trabalho, lar e botequim. O cotidiano dos trabalhadores no Rio de Janeiro da belle époque*. São Paulo: Brasiliense, 1986.

———. "The Politics of Disease Control: Yellow Fever and Race in Nineteenth-Century Rio de Janeiro, Brazil." *Journal of Latin American Studies* (1993).

Chamberlin, Edward, and Sander L. Gilman. *Degeneration: The Dark Side of Progress*. New York: Columbia University Press, 1985.

Clastres, Hélène. "Primitivismo e ciência do homem no século XVIII." *Discurso* 13 (1983) 187–208.

Clavreul, Jean. *A ordem médica. Poder e impotência do discurso médico*. São Paulo: Brasiliense, 1983.

Conrad, Robert. *Os últimos anos da escravatura no Brasil*. 2d ed. Rio de Janeiro: Civilização Brasileira, 1978.

Corrêa, Mariza. "Antropologia e medicina legal." In *Caminhos cruzados*. São Paulo: Brasiliense, 1982.

———. "As ilusões da liberdade. A Escola Nina Rodrigues e a antropologia no Brasil." Ph.D. diss., University of São Paulo, 1983.

Costa, Jurandir Freire. *Ordem médica e norma familiar*. Rio de Janeiro: Graal, 1979.

Cruz Costa, João. *O positivismo na República*. São Paulo: Nacional, 1956.

———. *Contribuição à história das idéias no Brasil*. 2d ed. Rio de Janeiro: Civilização Brasileira, 1967.

Cunha, Euclides da. *Os sertões*. São Paulo: Cultrix, 1973.

Cunha, Manuela Carneiro da. *Negros estrangeiros: Os escravos libertos e sua volta à África*. São Paulo: Brasiliense, 1985.

———. *Antropologia do Brasil: mito, história, etnicidade*. São Paulo: Brasiliense, 1986.

———. *Os direitos do índio: ensaio e documentos*. São Paulo: Brasiliense, 1987.

———. "Imagens de índios do Brasil: o século XVI." *Estudos Avançados* 4/10 (1990).

———. *Soberania e terra indígena. Do descobrimento à República* (forthcoming).

Cunha, Maria Manuela Carneiro da, and Eduardo V. de Castro. "Vingança e temporalidade: os Tupinambá." *Journal de la Société des Américanistes* 51 (1985) 191–208.

Cunha, Oswaldo Rodrigues da, et al. *O Museu Paraense Emilio Goeldi*. São Paulo: Banco Safra, 1966.

Da Matta, Roberto. "Você sabe com quem está falando?" In *Carnaval, malandros e heróis*. 3d ed. Rio de Janeiro: Zahar, 1981.

———. *Introdução a Edmund Leach*. São Paulo: Ática, 1983.

Darnton, Robert. *O beijo de Lamourette*. São Paulo: Companhia das Letras, 1990.

Darwin, Charles. *On the Origin of Species, by Means of Natural Selection, or the Preservation of Favoured Races in the Struggle for Life*. 1859. Reprint, New York: The Heritage Press, 1963.

———. *A origem das espécies*. São Paulo: Hemus, 1968.

Davatz, Thomas. *Memórias de um colono no Brasil*. São Paulo: Edusp, 1980.

Dias, Maria Odila Leite da Silva. *Quotidiano e poder em São Paulo no século XIX*. São Paulo: Brasiliense, 1984.

Domingues, Heloísa Maria Bertol. "Os intelectuais e o poder na construção da memória nacional." *Tempo Brasileiro* 86 (1986).

Domingues, Octavio. *Hereditariedade e eugenia: suas bases, suas teorias, suas aplicações práticas*. Rio de Janeiro: Civilização Brasileira, 1936.

Duchet, Michèle. *Anthropologie et histoire au siècle des Lumières*. Paris: Maspero, 1971.

Dulles, John W. E. *A Faculdade de Direito de São Paulo e a Resistência anti-Vargas*. Rio de Janeiro: Nova Fronteira, 1984.

Dumont, Louis. *Homo hierarchicus. Essai sur le système des castes*. Paris: Gallimard, 1966.

Durham, Eunice. "A dinâmica cultural na sociedade moderna." *Ensaios de Opinião* 4 (1977): 32–35.

Durkheim, Émile. *The Division of Labor in Society*. 1893. Reprint, New York: Free Press of Glencoe, 1964.

———. "Da divisão do trabalho social." In *Os pensadores*. 1893. Reprint, São Paulo: Abril Cultural, 1978.

———. "As formas elementares da vida religiosa." In *Os pensadores*. 1895. Reprint, São Paulo: Abril Cultural, 1978.

———. "Das regras do método sociológico." In *Os pensadores*. 1895. Reprint, São Paulo: Abril Cultural, 1978.

———. *The Rules of Sociological Method*. 1895. Reprint with an introduction by Steven Lukes, translated by W. D. Halls, New York: Free Press, 1982.

Eisenberg, Peter L. *The Sugar Industry in Pernambuco, 1894–1910*. Los Angeles: n.p., 1974.

Faoro, Raimundo. *Os donos do poder*. 4th ed. Porto Alegre: Globo, 1977.

Faria, Castro. "O espectáculo e a excelência." Rio de Janeiro (unpublished manuscript, 1982).

Fausto, Boris. *História geral da civilização brasileira: Brasil Republicano*. São Paulo: Difel, 1977a.

———. *Trabalho urbano e conflito social*. São Paulo: Difel, 1977b.

———. *Controle social e criminalidade em São Paulo*. Campinas: Unicamp, 1982.

Fleiuss, Max. "Recordando esses perfis." *Revista do Instituto Historico e Geographico Brasileiro* (1941).

Foucault, Michel. *As palavras e as coisas*. São Paulo: Martins Fontes, 1966.

———. *The Birth of the Clinic: An Archaeology of Medical Perception*. Translated by A. M. Sheridan Smith. New York: Pantheon Books, 1973.

———. *The Order of Things: An Archeology of the Human Sciences*. New York: Random House, 1973.

———. *O nascimento da clínica*. Rio de Janeiro: Forense, 1977.

Franco, Maria Sylvia de Carvalho. "As idéias estão no lugar." *Cadernos de Debate* 1 (1976).

Freston, Paul. "A carreira de Gilberto Freyre." *Textos IDESP* 3 (1987).

Freyre, Gilberto. *Casa-grande e senzala*. Rio de Janeiro: José Olympio, 1933.

———. *The Masters and the Slaves: A Study in the Development of Brazilian Civilization*. 2d ed. Translated by Samuel Putnam. 1946. Reprint, Berkeley: University of California Press, 1986.

Gagliardi, José Mauro. "O indígena e a República." Ph.D. diss., Pontifícia Universidade Católica, São Paulo, 1985.

Galton, Francis. *Hereditary Genius: An Inquiry into Its Laws and Consequences*. Introduction by C. D. Darlington. Gloucester, Mass.: Peter Smith, 1972.

———. *Herencia y eugenia*. 1869. Reprint, Madrid: Alianza Editorial, 1988.

Gates Jr., Henry Louis. *Race, Writing, and Difference*. Chicago: University of Chicago Press, 1985.

Gay, Peter. *Freud: uma biografia*. São Paulo: Companhia das Letras, 1988.
Gerbi, Antonello. *La disputa del nuevo manda. História de una polémica*. México: Fondo de Cultura Económica, 1982.
Giffoni, Carneiro. *Excertos da história da medicina no Brasil*. N.p., 1950.
Glick, Thomas E. *The Comparative Reception of Darwinism*. Chicago: University of Chicago Press, 1988.
———. *Darwin y el darwinismo en el Uruguay y en la América Latina*. Uruguay: Universidad de la República, 1988.
Gobineau, Arthur de. *Essai sur l'inegalité des races humaines*. 1853. Reprint, Paris: Gallimard-Pléiade, 1983.
Gould, Stephen Jay. *The Mismeasure of Man*. New York: W. W. Norton and Company, 1981.
———. *Darwin e os grandes enigmas da vida*. São Paulo: Martins Fontes, 1987.
Graham, Richard. *Grã-Bretanha e o início da modernização no Brasil (1850–1914)*. São Paulo: Brasiliense, 1973.
———. *The Idea of Race in Latin America, 1870–1940*. Cambridge, England: Cambridge University Press, 1990.
Guimarães, Manoel Luis Salgado. *Nação e civilização nos trópicos*. Rio de Janeiro: Vértice, 1988.
Haeckel, Ernst. *Histoire de la création des êtres organisés d'après les lois naturelles*. Paris: C. Reiwald editeur, 1884.
———. *O monismo. Laço entre a religião e a sciencia*. Porto: Imprensa Moderna de Manoel Lello, 1908.
Hall, Michael. "Reformadores de classe média no Império brasileiro e Sociedade Central de Imigração." *Revista de História* 53 (1976): 148–60.
Hallpike, C. R. *The Principles of Social Evolution*. Oxford: Clarendon Press, 1988.
Halsenbalg, Carlos A. *Discriminação e desigualdades raciais no Brasil*. Rio de Janeiro: Graal, 1979.
Hanke, Lewis. *The First Social Experiments in America. A Study in the Development of Spanish Indian Polity in the Sixteenth Century*. Cambridge, England: Cambridge University Press, 1935.
———. *Bartolomé de Las Casas*. La Habana: La Habana ed., 1949.
Hardman, Francisco Foot. *Trem fantasma: a modernidade na selva*. São Paulo, Companhia das Letras, 1988.
Herculano, Olegario. "O Instituto Histórico e Geográfico Brasileiro." *Revista do Instituto Historico e Geographico Brasileiro* 60, part 1 (1897).
Hobsbawm, E. J. *The Age of Capital: 1848–1875*. New York: Charles Scribner's Sons, 1975.
———. *A era do capital*. Rio de Janeiro: Paz e Terra, 1977.
———. *The Age of Empire, 1875–1914*. London: Weidenfeld and Nicolson, 1987.
———. *A era dos impérios (1875–1914)*. São Paulo: Paz e Terra, 1988.

———. *Nações e nacionalismo desde 1780: programa, mito e realidade*. Rio de Janeiro: Paz e Terra, 1990.

———. *Nations and Nationalism since 1780: Programme, Myth, Reality*. Cambridge: Cambridge University Press, 1990.

Hobsbawm, Eric, and Terence Ranger, eds. *The Invention of Tradition*. New York: Cambridge University Press, 1983.

———. *A invenção das tradições*. São Paulo: Paz e Terra, 1987.

Hofstadter, Richard. *Social Darwinism in American Thought*. Boston: Beacon Press, 1975.

Holanda, Sérgio Buarque de. *Memórias de um colono no Brasil*. São Paulo: Martins Fontes, 1941.

———. "Silvio Romero, o fervor da estética." *Diário Carioca* (1951).

———. *Raízes do Brasil*. 1936. Reprint, Rio de Janeiro: José Olympio, 1979.

———. *Visão do paraíso*. 4th ed. São Paulo: Nacional, 1985.

———. "O Brasil monárquico III." In *História geral da civilização brasileira*. São Paulo: Difel, n.d.

Kehl, Renato. *A cura da fealdade: eugenia e medicina social*. São Paulo: n.p., 1923.

———. *Aparas eugênicas: sexo e civilização (novas diretrizes)*. Rio de Janeiro: Francisco Alves, 1933.

Knight, David. *The Age of Science*. New York: Basil Blackwell, 1986.

Knorr-Cetina, Karin D. *The Manufacture of Knowledge: An Essay on the Constructivist and Contextual Nature of Science*. London: Pergamon Press, 1981.

Kugelmas, Eduardo. "Difícil hegemonia: um estudo sobre São Paulo na Primeira República." Ph.D. diss., University of São Paulo, 1986.

Kuhn, Thomas. *The Structure of Scientific Revolutions*. Chicago: University of Chicago Press, 1962.

Kuper, Adam. *Anthropologists and Anthropology: The British School, 1922–1972*. New York: Pica Press, 1973.

———. *Antropólogos e antropologia*. Rio de Janeiro: Francisco Alves, 1978.

Lacerda, João Batista. *Sur les métis au Brésil*. Paris: Imprimerie Devougue, 1911.

———. *Fatos do Museu Nacional do Rio de Janeiro*. Rio de Janeiro: Imprensa Nacional, 1914.

Las Casas, Frei Bartolomé. *Brevíssima relação da destruição das Índias. O paraíso destruído*. Porto Alegre: L & PM, 1984.

Leaf, Murray. *Man, Mind and Science: A History of Anthropology*. New York: Columbia University Press, 1979.

———. *Uma história da antropolgia*. Rio de Janeiro: Zahar; São Paulo: Edusp, 1981.

Le Bon, Gustave. *Les lois psychologiques de l'évolution des peuples*. Paris: n.p., 1902.

Le Goff, Jacques. *História: novos problemas*. Rio de Janeiro: Francisco Alves, 1976.

———. "Memória e história." In *Enciclopédia Enaudi*. Porto: Imprensa Nacional, 1984.

Leite, Dante Moreira. *O caráter nacional brasileiro*. 1954. 4th ed., São Paulo: Livraria Pioneira, 1983.

Lenharo, Alcir. *Sacralização da política*. 2d ed. Campinas: Unicamp/Papirus, 1986.

Lepenies, Wolf. *Between Literature and Science: The Rise of Sociology*. Translated by R. J. Hollingdale. Cambridge, England: Cambridge University Press, 1988.

Levine, Robert E. "The First Afro-Brazilian Congress: Opportunities for the Study of Race in the Brazilian Northeast." *Race* 15 (1973): 185–93.

———. *Pernambuco in the Brazilian Federation, 1889–1937*. Stanford, Calif.: Stanford University Press, 1978.

———. *Pernambuco na federação brasileira, 1889–1937: a velha usina*. Rio de Janeiro: Paz e Terra, 1980.

Lévi-Strauss, Claude. *Raça e história*. 2d ed. Lisbon: Presença, 1952.

———. *The Elementary Structures of Kinship*. Translated by James Harle Bell, John Richard von Sturmer, and Rodney Needham. Boston: Beacon Press, 1969.

———. *Antropologia estrutural dois*. Rio de Janeiro: Tempo Brasileiro, 1976.

———. *Estruturas elementares do parentesco*. Petrópolis: Vozes, 1976.

———. *O pensamento selvagem*. São Paulo: Nacional, 1976.

Lima, Antônio Carlos. "Aos fetichistas ordem e progresso." Ph.D. diss., Museu Nacional, Rio de Janeiro, 1986.

———. "Os museus de história natural e a construção do indigenismo." *Communicação* 13 (1989).

Lins, Ivan. *História do positivismo no Brasil*. São Paulo: Nacional, 1964.

Lobato, J. B. Monteiro. *O problema vital*. São Paulo: Brasiliense, 1918.

Lobo, Francisco Bruno. *O ensino de medicina no Rio de Janeiro*. Rio de Janeiro: n.p., 1969.

Lombroso, Cesare. *L'uomo delinquente*. Rome: n.p., 1876.

Love, Joseph L. *São Paulo in the Brazilian Federation: 1889–1937*. Stanford, Calif.: Stanford University Press, 1980.

———. *A locomotiva: São Paulo na federação brasileira*. Rio de Janeiro: Paz e Terra, 1982.

Lukes, Steven. *Émile Durkheim: His Life and Work, a Historical and Critical Study*. New York: Harper and Row, Publishers, 1972.

———. "Bases para a interpretação de Durkheim." In *Sociologia para ler os clássicos*, edited by Gabriel Cohn. Rio de Janeiro: Livros Técnicos e Científicos, 1977.

McLennan, John Ferguson. *Primitive Marriage: An Inquiry into the Origin of the Form of Capture in Marriage Ceremonies*. Edited with an introduction by Peter Riviere. Chicago: University of Chicago Press, 1970.

Machado, Roberto. *Danação da norma*. Rio de Janeiro: Graal, 1978.

Martins, Wilson. *História da inteligência brasileira*. Vol. 3. São Paulo: Cultrix/Edusp, 1977.

Massi, Fernanda Peixoto. "Franceses e norte-americanos nas ciências sociais brasileiras (1930–1960)." In *História das ciências sociais no Brasil,* edited by Sergio Miceli. São Paulo: Vértice/IDESP, 1989.

Mattos, Ilmar R. de. *O tempo de Saquarema*. São Paulo: Hucitec, 1987.

Mattoso, Katia de Queirós. *Ser escravo no Brasil*. São Paulo: Brasiliense, 1982.

Mauss, Marcel. "Sociologie." In *Oeuvres*. 1901, Reprint, Paris: Les Éditions de Minuit, 1969.

Mello e Souza, Laura de. *O diabo e a terra de Santa Cruz*. São Paulo: Companhia das Letras, 1986.

Melo Franco, Afonso Arinos de. *Rodrigues Alves: apogeu e declínio do presidencialismo*. Rio de Janeiro: José Olympio, 1973.

Mezan, Renato. *Freud. Pensador de cultura*. São Paulo: Brasiliense, 1985.

Miceli, Sergio. *Poder, sexo e letras na República Velha*. São Paulo: Perspectiva, 1977.

———, ed. *História das ciências sociais no Brasil*. São Paulo: Vértice/IDESP, 1989.

Montaigne, Michel Eyquem de. "Os canibais." In *Os pensadores*. 1582. Reprint, São Paulo: Abril Cultural, 1980. 100–106.

Monteiro, John. "Tupis, Tapuias e a história de São Paulo." *Novos Estudos* (1992).

Montes, Maria Lucia. "1789. Os direitos do homem." São Paulo (unpublished manuscript, 1991).

Morel, August Bénédict. *Traité des dégénérescences physiques, intellectuelles et morales de l'espèce humaine*. Paris: Baillière, 1857.

Morgan, Lewis H. *A sociedade primitiva*. 3d ed. Lisboa: Editorial Presença, 1980.

Morse, Richard M. *Formação histórica de São Paulo: de comunidade a metrópole*. São Paulo: Difel, 1970.

———. *O espelho de Próspero: culturas e idéias nas Américas*. São Paulo: Companhia das Letras, 1988.

———. *New World Soundings: Culture and Ideology in the Americas*. Baltimore: Johns Hopkins University Press, 1989.

Mussolini, Gioconda. *Evolução, raça e cultura*. São Paulo: Nacional, 1974.

Nascimento, José Leonardo. "Euclides da Cunha: un positiviste aux prises avec de millenarisme de Canudos." Paris (unpublished manuscript, 1989).

Néré, Jacques. *História contemporânea*. Rio de Janeiro: Difel, 1975.

Neto, Machado A. L. *História das idéias jurídicas no Brasil*. São Paulo: Grijalbo, 1969.

Nogueira, Almeida. *A Academia de São Paulo: tradições e reminiscências*. São Paulo: Saraiva, 1977.

Nogueira, Marco Aurélio. *As desventuras do liberalismo. Joaquim Nabuco, a monarquia e a República*. Rio de Janeiro: Paz e Terra, 1984.

Ortiz, Renato. *Cultura brasileira e identidade nacional*. São Paulo: Brasiliense, 1985.

Osakabe, Haquira. *Argumentação e discussão política*. São Paulo: Kairós, 1979.

Paes, José Paulo. *Augusto dos Anjos. Os melhores poemas*. São Paulo: Global, 1986.

———. *Canaã e o ideário modernista*. São Paulo: Edusp, 1992.

Paiva, Orlando Marques, ed. *O Museu Paulista e a Universidade de São Paulo*. São Paulo: Banco Safra, 1984.

Peixoto, Afrânio. *A esfinge*. Rio de Janeiro: Francisco Alves, 1911.

Pogliano, Claudio. "Entre forme et fonction." In *La fabrique de la pensée*. Florence: Electa, 1990.

Poliakov, Léon. *Le racisme: mithos et science*. Bruxelles: Édition Complexe, 1981.

Pompéia, Raul. *O Atheneu (chronica de saudades)*. Rio de Janeiro: Francisco Alves, 1889.

Pontes, Heloísa André. "Retratos do Brasil." In *História das ciências sociais no Brasil,* edited by Sergio Miceli. São Paulo: Vértice/IDESP, 1989.

Poppino, Rollie E. "A Century of the *Revista do Instituto Histórico e Geográfico Brasileiro*." *The Hispanic American Historical Review* 33 (1953): 307–23.

Prado Jr., Caio. *História econômica do Brasil*. São Paulo: Brasiliense, 1945.

Queirós, Eça de. *Primo Basílio*. 1878. Reprint, Belo Horizonte: Itatiaia, 1987.

Queiroz, Maria Isaura Pereira de. "Identidade cultural, identidade nacional no Brasil." *Tempo Social* 1 (1989).

Querino, Manuel. *A raça africana*. Salvador: Livraria Progresso, 1955.

Rabello, Sílvio. *Itinerário de Silvio Romero*. Rio de Janeiro: Civilização Brasileira, 1967.

Radl, E. M. *Historia de las teorías biológicas. Desde Lamarck y Cuvier*. Madrid: Alianza Editorial, 1988.

Raeders, Georges. *D. Pedro e os sábios franceses*. Rio de Janeiro: Atlântica, 1944.

———. *O conde Gobineau no Brasil*. 2d ed. Rio de Janeiro: Paz e Terra, 1988.

Ramos, Artur. *Guerra e relação de raça*. Rio de Janeiro: Departamento União Nacional dos Estudos, 1935.

Reis, Letícia Vidor de. "Negros e brancos no jogo da capoeira: a reinvenção da tradição." Ph.D. diss., University of São Paulo, 1993.

Renan, Joseph Ernest. *Oeuvres complètes*. 1872. Reprint, Paris: Calman Levy, 1961.

Ribeiro, Darcy. *Os índios e a civilização*. 3d ed. Petrópolis: Vozes, 1982.

Ribeiro, Julio. *A carne*. Rio de Janeiro: n.p., 1888.

Rodrigues, José Honório. *Teoria da história do Brasil*. São Paulo: Nacional, 1957.

———. *Memória da história do Brasil*. Vol. 1. Brasília: Nacional, 1988.

Rodrigues, Nina. "Os mestiços brasileiros." *Brazil Medico* (1890).

———. "Métissage, dégénérescence et crime." *Archives d'anthropologie criminelle* (1899).

———. *O animismo fetichista dos negros bahianas*. Rio de Janeiro: Civilização Brasileira, 1935.

———. *As raças humanas e a responsabilidade penal no Brasil*. 1894. Bahia: Progresso, 1957.

———. *Os africanos no Brasil*. 1933. 7th ed., São Paulo: Nacional, 1988.

Romero, Silvio. *O naturalismo em literatura*. São Paulo: Lutta, 1882.

———. *O evolucionismo e o positivismo no Brasil*. Rio de Janeiro: Livraria Clássica de Álvares e C., 1895.

———. *Machado de Assis, estudo comparativo de literatura brasileira*. Rio de Janeiro: Laemmert, 1897.

———. *O Brasil social*. Rio de Janeiro: Typographia Jornal do Commercio, 1907.

———. *Provocações e debates*. Rio de Janeiro: Imprensa Moderna, 1910.

———. *Quadro synthetico da evolução dos gêneros na literatura brasileira*. Porto: Chardron de Lelo e Irmãos, 1911.

———. "Explicações indispensáveis." Preface to *Vários escritos,* by Tobias Barreto. Sergipe: Editora do Estado de Sergipe, 1926.

———. *História da literatura brasileira*. 1888. 4th ed., Rio de Janeiro: José Olympio, 1949.

Ronan, Colin A. *História ilustrada da ciência*. Rio de Janeiro: Zahar, 1987.

Roquete-Pinto, Edgar. *Seixos rolados*. Rio de Janeiro: n.p., 1927.

Rousseau, Jean-Jacques. *Discourse on the Origins of Inequality (Second Discourse): Polemics, and Political Economy. The Collected Writings of Rousseau*. Vol. 3. 1775. Reprint, edited by Roger D. Masters and Christopher Kelly, and translated by Judith R. Bush et al., Hanover and London: University Press of New England, 1992.

———. "Discurso sobre a origem e os fundamentos da desigualdade entre os homens." In *Os pensadores* (1978).

Sahlins, Marshal. *Islands of History*. Chicago: University of Chicago Press, 1985.

———. *Ilhas de história*. Rio de Janeiro: Zahar, 1990.

Said, Edward. *Orientalismo*. São Paulo: Companhia das Letras, 1990.

Saint-Hilaire. *Segunda viagem do Rio de Janeiro a Minas Gerais e São Paulo (1822)*. Belo Horizonte: Itatiaia, 1974.

Santos, Afonso Carlos M. dos. "Memória, história, nação: propondo questões." *Tempo Brasileiro* 87 (1986).

Santos, Wanderley Guilherme dos. *A ordem burguesa e o liberalismo político*. São Paulo: Duas Cidades, 1978.

Santos Filho, Lycurgo. *História da medicina no Brasil*. São Paulo: Brasiliense, 1947.

Schorske, Carl E. *Viena fin-de-siècle*. São Paulo: Companhia das Letras, 1988.

Schwarcz, Lilia Moritz. *Retrato em branco e negro. Jornais, escravos e cidadãos em São Paulo no final do século XIX*. São Paulo: Companhia das Letras, 1987.

———. "Os guardiões de nossa história oficial." *Cadernos IDESP* 9 (1989).

———. "O nascimento dos museus brasileiros." In *História das ciências sociais no Brasil,* edited by Sergio Miceli. São Paulo: Vértice/IDESP, 1989.

———. "O romance naturalista: entre a ruptura e a tradução." São Paulo (unpublished manuscript, 1990).

Schwartzman, Simon. *Formação da comunidade científica no Brasil*. São Paulo, Nacional, 1979.

Schwarz, Roberto. *Ao vencedor as batatas*. São Paulo: Duas Cidades, 1977.

———. "Nacional par subtração." *Que horas são?* São Paulo: Companhia das Letras, 1987.

Seiferth, Giralda. "João Batista Lacerda: a antropologia fisica." Rio de Janeiro (unpublished manuscript, 1984).

Sennett, Richard. *The Fall of Public Man: On the Social Psychology of Capitalism*. New York: Vintage Books, 1978.

———. *O declínio do homem público*. São Paulo: Companhia das Letras, 1988.

Sevcenko, Nicolau. *Literatura como missão: tensões sociais e criação na Primeira República*. São Paulo: Brasiliense, 1983.

———. *A revolta da vacina: mentes insanas em corpos rebeldes*. São Paulo: Brasiliense, 1984.

———. "Orfeu extático na metrópole." Ph.D. diss., University of São Paulo, 1991.

Silva, Benedito. *Dicionário de ciências sociais*. Rio de Janeiro: MEC/Fundação Getúlio Vargas, 1986.

Silva, Janice Theodoro da. *São Paulo, 1554–1880. Discurso ideológico e organização espacial*. São Paulo: Moderna, 1984.

Skidmore, Thomas E. *Preto no branco. Raça e nacionalidade no pensamento brasileiro*. Rio de Janeiro: Paz e Terra, 1976.

———. *Black into White: Race and Nationality in Brazilian Thought*. Durham and London: Duke University Press, 1993.

Sodré, Nelson Werneck. *História da literatura brasileira*. 1938. Reprint, São Paulo: Difel, 1982.

Souza, Leonídeo Ribeiro Filho de. *Medicina no Brasil*. Rio de Janeiro: Imprensa Nacional, 1940.

Spencer, Herbert. *Principles of Biology*. London: W. Norgate, 1866.

Starobinski, Jean. *1789: Os emblemas da razão*. São Paulo: Companhia das Letras, 1988.

Stauffer, David Hall. "Origem e fundação do serviço de proteção aos Índios." In *Revista de História*. (São Paulo) 1960.

Stein, Stanley. "Freyre's Brazil Revisited: A Review of *New World in the Tropics*." *Hispanic American Historical Review* 41 (1961).

Stepan, Nancy. *Beginnings of Brazilian Science. Oswaldo Cruz, Medical Research, and Policy, 1890–1920*. New York: Science History Publication, 1981.

———. *The Hour of Eugenics. Race, Gender, and Nation in Latin America*. Ithaca: Cornell University Press, 1991.

Stocking, George W. *Race, Culture, and Evolution: Essays in the History of Anthropology*. Chicago: University of Chicago Press, 1968.

———. *Objects and Others. Essays on Museums and Material Culture*. Madison: University of Wisconsin Press, 1985.

———. *Victorian Anthropology*. New York: The Fare Press, 1987.

———. *Bones, Bodies, Behavior. Essays on Biological Anthropology*. Vol. 5. Madison: University of Wisconsin Press, 1988.

Sussekind, Flora. *O Brasil não é longe daqui*. São Paulo: Companhia das Letras, 1990.

Taine, Hippolyte. *Histoire de la littérature anglaise*. Paris: n.p., 1923.

Taunay, Afonso d'Escragnolle. *História das bandeiras paulistas*. São Paulo: Melhoramentos, n.d.

Tax, Sol. *Panorama da antropologia*. Rio de Janeiro: Fundo de Cultura, 1966.

Tepedino, Alexandre. *Eugenia (esboço)*. Rio de Janeiro: Faculdade de Medicina, 1914.

Todorov, Tzvetan. *A conquista da América: a questão do outro*. São Paulo: Martins Fontes, 1983.

———. *Nous et les autres. La réflexion française sur la diversité humaine*. Paris: Édition du Seuil, 1989.

Torres, João Camilo de Oliveira. *O positivismo no Brasil*. Rio de Janeiro: Vozes, 1943.

Tuchman, Barbara Wertheim. *The Proud Tower: A Portrait of the World before the War, 1890–1914*. New York: Macmillan, 1966.

———. *A terra do orgulho: um retrato do mundo antes da guerra: 1890–1914*. Rio de Janeiro: Paz e Terra, 1990.

Tylor, E. B. *Primitive Culture*. 1878. 6th ed., New York: Harper, 1958.

Vampré, Spencer. *Memórias para a história da Academia de São Paulo*. 1924. Reprint, São Paulo: Saraiva, 1975.

Varnhagen, Francisco Adolfo de. *História geral do Brasil*. São Paulo: Melhoramentos, 1963.

Ventura, Roberto. "Escritores, escravos e mestiços. (Raça e natureza na cultura brasileira)." Ph.D. diss., University of São Paulo, 1988.

———. *Estilo tropical: história cultural e polémicas literárias no Brasil*. São Paulo: Companhia das Letras, 1991.

Vianna, Oliveira. *Populações meridionais do Brasil*. 1918, Reprint, Rio de Janeiro: José Olympio, 1952. (Original edition, 1918.)

Viotti da Costa, Emília. *Da Monarquia a República: momentos decisivos*. São Paulo: Grijalbo, 1977.

von Martius, Karl Friedrich Philipp. "Como escrever a história do Brasil." *Revista do Instituto Historico e Geographico Brasileiro* 6 (1944).

Weindling, Paul. *Health, Race and German Politics between National Unification and Nazism*. Cambridge, England: Cambridge University Press, 1989.

Young, Robert M. *Darwin's Metaphor*. Cambridge, England: Cambridge University Press, 1985.

INDEX

Abreau, Capistrano de, 26
Adams, W., 5
Africans, immigration restrictions on, 229, 231, 232, 287
Afro-Brazilians, 127–29, 157, 206, 300, 320*n12*; herbalism of, 238; medical assumptions about, 275, 277, 286; Romero's views on, 133, 259; and racial blending, 259–60 (*see also* miscegenation); as slaves, *see* slavery; von Martius's views on, 135
Agassiz, Louis, 5, 36, 56, 158
Agostini, Angelo, 32
Agricultural Institute of Campinas, 321*n22*, 322*n23*
Aimard, Gustave, 5, 17
Albuquerque, Maj. Salvador Henrique, 139
Alemão, Brother, 320*n7*
Alencar, Otto, 23
Almeida, Francisco José de, 173
Almeida, Manuel Antônio de, 306
Almeida Couto, José Luiz d', 85
Álvares Cabral, Pedro, 125
Álvaro de Carvalho, Manuel Luís, 241
Alves, Antônio José, 252
Alves Serrão, Brother Custódio, 320*n7*
Amaral, Manuel Maria do, 173
Amaral Gurgel, Leoncio do, 158
anthropology, 33, 55–56, 73, 318*n17*, 319*nn1, 28*, 320*n12*; criminal, 51, 189, 191–208, 222–23; cultural, 60–61, 66; and historical and geographical institutes, 126–30, 143–44, 156–58; and museums, 79–81, 89; physical, 66
anthropometry, 51, 192
Antonil (Portuguese Jesuit), 315*n17*
Aranha, Graça, 182, 327*n7*
Arantes, Altino, 153
Araújo, Silva, 252
Araújo Vianna, Cândido José de, Marques of Sapucahy, 119
Archeological and Geographical Institute of Pernambuco, 112, 136–48, 160, 164, 166, 176, 324*nn18, 21*, 325*nn23, 26*; journal of, 136, 137, 139–47, 160, 166

Arendt, Hannah, 55, 68, 319*n27*
Aryanism, German, 307
Asians, immigration restrictions on, 229, 230–32, 287
Autran, Pedro, 173
Ayrosa, Plínio, 152, 326*n35*
Azevedo, Fernando de, 23–24, 74, 309, 313*n1*, 333–34*n6*
Azevedo Sodré, A. A. de, 41, 271–73, 331*n22*

bacharel degree, 169–71, 178, 221, 240; *bacharéis* (legal scholars), 249, 299
Bahia School of Medicine, 19, 157, 234–38, 241–69, 273, 276, 277, 286, 289, 293–95, 313*n2*, 329*n1*, 330*n4*, 331*n19*; journal of, 246–49, 252–58, 260–73, 277, 295, 296
bandeirantes (colonial expeditionary forces), 150–51, 159–60, 164, 334*n6*
barbeiros (surgical barbers), 239
Barreto, Tobias, 38, 40, 177, 178, 180, 328*n15*, 329*n21*
beriberi, 256, 278
Bevilacqua, Clovis, 173, 188, 191, 218, 328*n15*
Bezzi, Tommaso Gaudenzio, 85
Bible, the, 50, 144, 156
Bittencourt, Maia, 252
Boas, Franz, 108, 333*n5*
Boccanera Neto, S., 262
Bom Retiro, Viscount of, 77, 119
Bonfim, Manoel, 315*n24*
Bonifácio, José, 125
Bopp, Franz, 59
Botocudo Indians, 79, 82–84, 105, 320*n11*
Bouroul, Estevan Leão, 325*n28*
Bragança, House of, 115, 121, 225*n*
branqueamento, *see* racial whitening
Brazil, Vital, 272
Brazilian Academy of Letters, 122, 315*n20*, 325*n25*, 328*n15*, 332*n24*
British Museum, 73
Brito, Luís Teodoro, 326*n35*
Broca, Paul, 56, 60, 77, 81, 158
Broccos, M., 3–4
Buarque de Holanda, Sérgio, 42, 138, 156, 158, 305, 307
bubonic plague, 256, 278, 282
Buckle, Henry Thomas, 36, 59, 61–62, 134, 178, 228
Buffon, Georges Louis Leclerc, Comte de, 44, 47, 48, 158, 316*n6*

caboclos (Brazilian "racial type"), 206
Cabral de Mello, Evaldo, 147, 148, 325*n23*
Caldas, Pires, 252
Câmara, Phaelante, 178
Campello, Netto, 210
Candido, Antonio, 42, 103, 116, 126, 129, 183, 306
Carneiro de Cunha, Manuela, 35–36, 310, 314*n16*
Carneiro Lessa, Pedro A., 134
Carnival, 309
Carvalho, Bulhões de, 271–72
Carvalho, Horácio de, 33–34, 181, 182
Chagas, Carlos, 257, 282,332*n27*
Chagas, Father, 172–73
Chagas' disease, 235, 256
Charcot, Jean-Martin, 182
cholera, 245, 256, 278
Clavreul, Jean, 245
Coelho de Almeida, Thomas, 77
Coimbra, University of, 172, 237, 238, 240, 242
Comte, Auguste, 11*n*, 31
Constant, Benjamin, 186, 217
Cook, Capt. James, 73
Corrêa, Mariza, 25, 234, 248–49, 264, 329*n1*
Correia Picanço, José, 240
Couto, Miguel, 108, 293, 332*n27*
Couty, Louis, 36, 315*n18*
craniology, 53, 56, 63, 261; *see also* phrenology
criminology, 51, 189, 191–208, 222–23; medicine and, 260–66
Cruz, Oswaldo, 24, 41, 257, 272, 282, 284, 285, 332*n24*
Cruz Costa, João, 13, 43, 312*n5*
cultural relativism, 20, 108, 319*n28*

Cunha, Euclides da, 40, 116, 132–34, 318*n18*, 329*n21*
Cunha Barboza, Januário da, 114, 115, 120
Cuvier, Baron Georges L.C., 49, 316*n7*

Damázio, Virgílio, 329*n1*
Darwin, Charles, 31, 33, 34, 57–59, 65, 77, 178, 182, 184, 187, 317*nn13–15*, 318*nn16, 23*
Darwin, Leonard, 318*n20*
Darwinism, 44, 59, 60, 67, 302, 307; *see also* social Darwinism
Davatz, Thomas, 312*n4*
degeneracy, 48, 64, 68, 318*n21, 24*, 319*n26*
De Pauw, Cornelius, 44, 47, 48, 316*n6*
Derby, Orville A., 86, 106, 326*n34*
determinism, 299; geographical, 61–62, 205; racial, *see* social Darwinism
Dias, Gonçalves, 116, 129, 131
diphtheria, 282
Domingues, Heloísa Maria Bertol, 327*n40*
Drummond de Andrade, Carlos, 297
Duarte de Azevedo, Manuel Antônio, 152, 326*n35*
Ducke, Adolph, 93
Dumont, Louis, 303
Durkheim, Emile, 28, 29, 313*n6*
Dutch West Indies Company, 141*n*

Emilio Goeldi Museum of Pará, 18, 71, 74, 87, 88, 92–101, 107, 108, 313*n3*, 315*n20*, 321*nn18, 21*, 323*n7*
endireitas (bonesetters), 239
Enlightenment, 46, 47, 49, 55, 66, 73, 112, 185, 220, 304, 316*nn2, 4*
epidemics, 255–57, 260, 285, 292, 295, 309
Equatorial Confederation (1824), 148
Estado Novo (1937), 271
ethnography, 38, 80, 317*n15*; museums of, 27 (*see also specific institutions*)
ethnology, 55–56, 126; social, 60, 66
eugenics, 17, 62–65, 236, 267–70, 286–95, 302, 309, 318*n20*, 322*n27*, 332*n30*
evolutionism, 11, 20, 34, 38, 42, 44, 39, 57–60, 300, 317*n11*, 319*n28*; cultural, 64, 318*n15*; ethnographic museums and, 74, 89, 91, 298; historical institutes and, 158; humanism versus, 45; imperialism and, 29; law schools influenced by, 170, 188–89, 212; modernity and, 31; monogenism and, 58, 70; Romero's views on, 184, 328*n10*; social, 61, 66, 91, 103, 128, 302

Fabre, J. H., 212–13
Faoro, Raimundo, 225
Faria, Januário de, 252
Fernandes Pinheiro, Canon Caetano, 323*n8*
Fernandes Pinheiro, José Feliciano, Viscount of São Leopoldo, 114, 118–19, 126
Ferreira de Araújo, Manuel, 323*n8*
Ferreira Penna, Domingos Soares, 77, 92–93
Ferri, Enrico, 187, 191, 195, 222, 228
First Brazilian Eugenics Congress (1929), 108, 293
First Universal Races Congress (1911), 105
Fleiuss, Max, 121, 323*n11*
Foucault, Michel, 48, 102, 237
Fraga, Clementino, 249
Frazer, James Gregor, 60
"free schooling," 176
Freire, Oscar, 272, 331*n18*
Freitas, Afonso de, 152, 326*n35*
Freitas, Cypriano, 287–88
French National Archives, 72
French Revolution, 46, 48, 49, 72, 264, 303
Freud, Sigmund, 270, 313*n7*
Freyre, Gilberto, 307–10, 322*n28*, 325*n22*, 333*nn4, 5*

Gall, Franz Joseph, 56
Galton, Francis, 62–64
Gama, Lopes, 173
Garófalo (criminologist), 191, 194, 195, 228
genetics, 108
geographical determinism, 61–62, 205, 318*n18*
Gerbi, Antonello, 301
Germanism, 17, 43, 178
Glick, Thomas, 302
Gobineau, Count Arthur de, 5, 36, 60, 65, 66, 68–69, 178, 208, 318*n24*, 319*nn25–27*
Goeldi, Emilio, 23, 93–99, 107, 272, 313*n3*, 320*n4*, 321*n18*
Gonçalves de Magalhães, Domingos José, 115, 129, 131, 312*n7*
Gould, Stephen Jay, 317*nn9, 12, 13*

Haeckel, Ernst, 178, 182, 184, 187, 212, 228, 315*n25*
Hagman, Gottfried, 93
Hardman, Francisco Foot, 314*n11*
Harvard University, 73
Henrique, João, 286
herbalism, 238
Herculano, Olegario, 119
Hippocrates, 55
Historical and Geographical Institute of Brazil, 111–36, 139, 144, 149, 152, 153, 161–63, 165, 306, 315*nn19, 20*, 322*n4*, 323*nn7, 10, 11*, 324*nn14, 17*, 326*nn37, 39*, 327*n40*; journal of, 111, 114, 115, 121, 123–35, 162–63
Historical Institute of Minias Gerais and Bahia, 121
Hobsbawm, Eric J., 27, 161, 298, 317*n14*
Hofstadter, Richard, 58
House of Representatives, Brazilian, 229
Hubert, Jacques, 93, 107
Hugo, Victor, 314*n10*
humanism, 44–46, 301, 304
hygiene, *see* public hygiene

Ihering, Hermann von, 23, 41, 72, 84, 86–89, 91–92, 98, 105, 110, 157, 315*n20*, 320*nn4, 13*, 321*nn16, 21*, 325*n28*
immigrants: diseases endemic among, 245; restrictions on, 229–32, 287
Indians, 121, 127–29, 133, 157, 206, 320*n12*, 238; *see also specific tribes*
Ingenieros, José, 36
insanity, 265–66
Institute of Biology (São Paulo), 108
Instituto de Pesquisas da Amazônia, 108
International Conference of Syphilology (1900), 248
International Congress on Race, 320*n12*
Italian immigrants, 245

Jesuits, 21, 36, 127, 315*n17*
João VI (king of Portugal), 6, 21–22, 75, 113, 115, 132, 240–41
journals: ethnographic, 76–81, 84, 86–91, 94–99, 103–7; historical and geographical, 92, 111, 114, 115, 121, 123–37, 139–48, 150–63, 166; law, 168, 170, 172–74, 178–79, 181, 183, 186–91, 194, 195, 200, 208–14, 217–26, 228, 232; medical, 246–58, 260–79, 283–86, 288–89, 291–93, 295, 296

Kaingang Indians, 91–92, 157, 321*n17*
Katzer, Friedrich, 93
Kehl, Renato, 108, 291, 292, 309, 332*n30*, 333*n6*
Knight, David, 27

Lacerda, João Batista, 3, 24, 41, 76, 79, 81, 84, 105–7, 320*nn4, 9, 12*
Lamarck, Jean-Baptiste de Monet de, 317*n12*
Lamartine, Alphonse-Marie-Louis de Prat de, 314*n10*
League of Mental Hygiene, 332*n27*
Leal, Antônio Henrique, 244
Leão, Laurindo, 179, 195, 200, 210

Le Bon, Gustave, 60, 66, 67, 178, 187
Le Goff, Jacques, 72, 322*n5*
Leibniz, Gottfried Wilhelm, 317*n10*
Lei dos Sexagenários (Law of the Sexagenarians), 311*n3*
Lei do ventre livre (Law of the free womb), 7, 25, 311*n2*
Leite Chermont, Justo, 93
Lepenies, Wolf, 27
Le Play, Frédéric, 133, 178
leprosy, 256, 278
Lessa, Pedro, 126, 218, 222
Levine, Robert, 138, 146–47
Lévi-Strauss, Claude, 316*n3*, 317*n8*
liberal political model, 170, 224–27
Lima, Oliveira, 126, 325*nn23, 25*
Lima, Silva, 252, 332*n16*
Linné, Carl von (Carolus Linneaus), 316*n7*
Lívio, Tito, 326*n35*
Livramento, Baron of, 139
Lixto, K., 39
Lobato, Monteiro, 308, 333*n6*
Lombroso, Cesare, 51, 53, 187, 191, 194, 195, 228, 262
Lonse, Ernst, 94
Louvre, 72
Love, Joseph, 159
Luís, Washington, 289
Luís e Silva (criminologist), 208
Lukes, Steven, 313*n6*

Macedo, Joaquim Manuel de, 121, 122, 126, 323*n10*
Machado de Assis, Joaquim Maria, 27, 37–38, 315*nn21, 22, 24*
Machado Oliveira, Col. José de, 127
Machado Portello, Joaquim Pires, 136
Magalhães, Couto, 152
Magnus, H., 59
malaria, 256, 278
Manguinhos Institute for Tropical Diseases, 24, 282, 321*n22*, 322*n23*
Márques, Américo, 252
Martius, Karl Friedrich Philipp von, 128–29, 135, 165, 182, 306, 307, 324*nn16, 17*
Matta, Roberto da, 102–3, 305
Mattos Guerra, Gregório, 310
Mauá, Viscount of, 125
Mauss, Marcel, 28
measles, 256, 278, 282
medical law, 235–236, 260–66; *see also* Recife School of Law; São Paulo School of Law
medical practice: in colonial Brazil, 238–40; history of, 237–38; law and, 260–66; medical press and, 245–79; public hygiene and, 222–23, 256–60, 278–79; *see also* Bahia School of Medicine; Rio de Janeiro School of Medicine
Mello, Baron Homem de, 126
Mello e Souza, Laura, 47
Mendel, Gregor Johann, 108
mestizos, 200, 201, 206, 298, 300, 301, 308, 319*n26*; eugenics and, 289; immigration restrictions on, 231; medical assumptions about, 275, 286; as medical practitioners, 238, 244; Romero's views on, 133, 185
Miranda, Alípio, 79
miscegenation, 16, 144–45, 260, 300, 304
Moniz Barettos, Domingos Alves, 127
monogenism, 33*n*, 50, 56–58, 67, 70, 144, 145, 158, 299, 315*n25*, 318*n16*
Montaigne, Michel Eyquem de, 314*n16*
Monteiro, João, 326*n35*
Monteiro, John, 321*n17*
Monteiro Barros, Lucas António, 85, 229
Montenegro, Jonas, 92
Moraes Barros, Prudente José de, 152, 153, 163
Moreira, Juliano, 248, 272, 332*n27*
Moreira de Azevedo, Duarte, 323*n8*
Moreira Leite, Dante, 13
Morel, August Bénédict, 316*n5*
Morgan, Lewis H., 60
Morse, Richard, 312*n10*, 333*n3*
Morton, Samuel George, 56, 65, 81, 158
Motta Júnior, Cesário, 152, 326*n35*

Muniz Tavares, Francisco, 139, 140
Murilo de Carvalho, José, 105

Nabuco, Joaquim, 38, 137, 315*nn23, 24*, 328*n13*
National Academy of Medicine, 293
National Guard, 8, 170
National Historical Museum (Rio de Janeiro), 18, 24
National Industrial Auxiliary Association, 113
National Museum (Rio de Janeiro), 71, 74–84, 93, 97–98, 100, 101, 108, 114, 182, 312*n8*, 320*nn7, 12*, 321*nn13, 16*, 322*n24*, 325*n29*, 332*n31*; journal of, 76–81, 84, 87–88, 103, 106, 107
National Museum of Ethnology (Leiden, Netherlands), 73
National School of Medicine (Rio de Janeiro), 19
natural selection, 59–60
naturalism, 31–33, 180–84
Navarro de Andrade, Vicente, 330*n6*
Nazism, 292
Negroes, *see* Afro-Brazilians
Nestor, Odilon, 213–14
Netto, Ladislau, 76, 77, 79, 182, 320*n9*
neurology, 29
Nimuendaju, Curt, 94
Nina Rodrigues, Raimundo, 24, 41, 234, 258–62, 264, 265, 272, 276, 297, 309, 310, 316*n2*, 329*n1*, 331*nn17, 18, 20*
"noble savage," 46
Nogueira, Almeida, 216, 220
Nogueira, Marco Aurélio, 231–32
Northeastern Brazilian Railroad, 91
novels, naturalist, 31–33, 181–83

Old Republic (1889–1930), 20
Oliveira Lima, Manoel de, 40
Oliveira Vianna, Francisco José, 40, 305

Paes, José Paulo, 327*n7*
Pará Museum, *see* Emilio Goeldi Museum of Pará
Paraguayan War, 8, 25, 247, 254, 323*n12*
Paranaguá, Marques of, 119
Paris, University of, 172
Partido Republicano Paulista (São Paulo Republican Party), 9
Pasteur, Louis, 314*n10*
Paula, Francisco de, 173
Paulista Museum, 23–24
Peabody Museum of Archaeology and Ethnology (Harvard University), 73
Pedro I, Dom (emperor of Brazil), 6, 22–23, 85, 125, 330*n8*
Pedro II, Dom (emperor of Brazil), 6–7, 24, 25, 30–31, 42, 85, 107, 121, 124, 125, 140, 322*n24*, 327*n39*
Peixoto, Afrânio, 39, 182, 272, 331*n23*, 332*n27*
Peixoto, Floriano, 229
Penal Code, Brazilian, 263–66
Pereira, Miguel, 41, 288
Pereira, Pacífico, 252, 257, 330*n14*
"perfectibility," concept of, 45, 316*n2*
Pernambuco Institute of Archeology, 121
Pernambuco Revolt (1817), 140, 146, 148, 164
phrenology, 17, 51–55, 81, 202, 207, 261–62
Pimenta, Joaquim, 181, 200, 210
Pires, Homero, 331*n18*
Pizarro, J. J., 320*n9*
Pizza, Antônio Toledo, 152, 325*n28*
plague, *see* bubonic plague
Planck, Max, 29
Pogliano, Claudio, 51
polygenism, 33, 49–51, 55–59, 65, 66, 68, 145, 158, 319*n26*
Pombal, Marques of, 125
Pompéia, Raul, 182
Pontes de Miranda, Mário, 266
Poppino, Rollie E., 324*n15*
positivism, 11, 31, 42, 44, 184
Prado Museum, 72
Praieira Revolt (1848–49), 148
Proto-Medicato council, 238
public hygiene, 255–60, 278–79, 282–86
"purification eugenics," 236

quantum mechanics, 29
Quatrefage, Armand de, 77
Queirós, Eça de, 314*n10*

Rabello, Silvio, 185
racial determinism, *see* social Darwinism
racial whitening (*branqueamento*), 3–4, 160, 320*n12*
Ramos, Artur, 322*n28*
Ratzel, Friedrich, 61
Ratzius, André, 51
Recife School of Law, 17, 19, 20, 24, 38, 133, 138, 157, 165, 168, 170–83, 186–91, 200, 208–14, 218, 222, 224, 227–33, 259, 315*nn19, 20*, 325*n26*, 328*nn13, 15*, 329*nn23, 25*, journal of, 168, 170, 172–74, 178–79, 181, 183, 186–91, 194, 195, 200, 208–14, 218, 228, 232
Renan, Joseph Ernest, 66–67
Ribeiro, Júlio, 181, 182
Ribeiro, Leonídio, 293
Ribeiro Couto, José, 276
Rio Branco, Baron of, 152
Rio de Janeiro, Legislative Assembly of, 230
Rio de Janeiro, University of, 312*n8*
Rio de Janeiro Geographic Society, 121
Rio de Janeiro School of Medicine, 235–36, 240–45, 271–79, 283–86, 288, 293–96, 313*n2*, 330*nn11, 12*; journal of, 246, 247, 271–79, 283–89, 291–93, 295
Rocha, Franco da, 272
Rocha, Henrique, 332*n27*
Rodrigues, Barbosa, 24
Rodrigues, Coelho, 177
Rodrigues, José Honório, 120–21, 160, 323*n25*
Rodrigues Alves, Francisco de Paula, 285
Roman Catholic Church, 9, 26, 50, 127–28, 136, 138, 152, 154, 158, 172, 175, 177, 221, 299, 303, 327*n2*
romanticism, 26; literary, 181
Romero, Silvio, 3, 23, 26, 27, 37–38, 41, 116, 133, 165, 177–78, 180, 183–86, 191, 200, 259, 307, 315*nn20, 22*, 324*n17*, 328*nn10, 13*
Roquete-Pinto, Edgar, 40, 108, 322*nn25, 28*, 332*nn27, n31*
Rosa, Tito, 191
Rousseau, Jean-Jacques, 44–47, 57, 84, 104, 156, 301, 316*nn3, 4*, 317*n11*, 333*n3*
Royal Academy of Madrid, 121
Rui Barbosa, Counsellor, 152, 216–17, 220, 329*n22*

Sahlins, Marshall, 303
Saint Petersburg Ethnographic Museum of Sciences, 73
Sampaio, Theodoro, 326*n35*
Santos, Wanderley Guilherme dos, 312*n6*
São Bento Monastery (Olinda), 172–75, 179, 215
São Francisco, Convent of, 215–16
São Paulo, University of, 108
São Paulo Academy of Letters, 153
São Paulo Historical and Geographical Institute, 112, 148–60, 163–64, 166, 217, 315*n20*, 325*n18*, 325*n28*, 326*nn34, 35*; journal of, 148, 150–59, 166
São Paulo Museum, 18, 71, 74, 84–92, 100–1, 106, 108, 149, 157, 217, 315*n20*, 321*n21*, 325*nn28, 29*, 326*n34*; journal of, 86–91, 97, 104–6
São Paulo School of Law, 17, 19, 24, 134, 149, 152, 170–71, 214–33, 287, 315*n20*, 326*n25*, 328*n18*, 329*nn23, 25*; journal of, 217–26, 228, 232
scarlet fever, 256, 278, 282
Scheacke, S., 106
Schonnann, Joseph, 93–94
Schwartzman, Simão, 101, 107, 321*n22*
Schwarz, Roberto, 301–2
scientifism, 30–34

segregation, North American, 307
Sennett, Richard, 333*n2*
Sertório, Joaquim, 85
Sevcenko, Nicolau, 314*n12*, 329*n21*
Silva Caldeira, João da, 320*n7*
Silva Paranhos Júnior, José Maria da, Baron of Rio Branco, 119, 125, 321*n18*
Silva Paula, Inocêncio da, 173
Skidmore, Thomas E., 13–14
slavery, 9, 26, 27, 85, 128, 150*n*, 231, 286; abolition of, 7, 25, 145, 229, 247, 300, 311*nn2, 3*
smallpox, 245, 256, 278, 282 vaccinations against, 285
Snethlage, Emília, 107
social Darwinism, 16, 61–69, 258, 277, 299, 300, 316*n25*, 319*nn25*, 28; elites and, 34, 39, 42, 302; ethnographic museums and, 74, 91, 92; eugenics and, 269; historical institutes and, 158, 165; imperialism and, 29; law schools and, 24, 170, 211, 228, 230; medical law and, 260, 263, 266; Romero's rejection of, 185
Society of Medicine, 242
sociology, 28, 29, 313*n6*
Sodré, Lauro, 93
Souza Arruda, Braz de, 232
Souza Fontes, José Ribeiro de, 323*n8*
Souza Gomes, Miranda de, 143
Souza Mello, Ladislau de, 92
Spencer, Herbert, 31, 33, 59, 133, 178, 184, 302
Spix, Johan Baptiste von, 324*n16*
Stauffer, David Hall, 321*n16*
Stepan, Nancy, 292, 318*n20*
sterilization, eugenicist, 292
Stocking, George W., 319*n1*
syphilis, 258

Taine, Hippolyte-Adolphe, 66–68, 319*n25*
Taunay, Alfonso d'Escragnolle, 106, 122, 131, 151, 321*n15*, 323*n12*, 325*n31*, 326*n35*
Tavares, Octávio, 181
Tax, Sol, 56
tenentistas (1920s), 227*n*
Tepedino, Alexandre, 288
Toledo Rendon, José Arouche de, 216
Topinard, Paul, 56, 179
Torres, Alberto, 315*n24*
Torres Homem, Francisco de Sales, 242
Torres de Oliveira, José, 326*n35*
tuberculosis, 256, 278, 279–81
Tupi Indians, 84, 157, 314*n16*, 321*n17*
Turlaine, L. R., 77
Tylor, E. B., 60
typhoid fever, 256, 278

U.S. Immigration Act (1924), 292

Vaccination Revolt, 34, 285
Valois de Castro, José, 152
Vampré, Ricardo, 326*n35*
Vargas, Getúlio, 271*n*, 293, 327*n39*
Varnhagen, Francisco Adolfo de, Viscount of Porto Alegre, 116, 120–22, 126, 129, 131, 140, 323*n10*
Vasconcelos, Luiz de, 238
Ventura, Roberto, 298
Vergueiro, Senator, 312*n4*
Veríssimo de Mattos, José, 93
Viana, Barboza, 143
Vidor Reis, Letícia , 332*n28*
Vries, Hugo Marie de, 29

Wallace, Alfred Russel, 317*n12*
Weber, Max, 29
Werneck Sodré, Nelson, 12
whitening, *see* racial whitening (*branqueamento*)
whooping cough, 256, 278
workers' movement (1920s), 227*n*
World War I, 289
Wucherer, Otto, 252

yellow fever, 235, 245, 256, 278, 282
Ypiranga Museum, *see* São Paulo Museum